SOFTWARE PROJECT MANAGEMENT

A Unified Framework

WALKER ROYCE

The Addison-Wesley Object Technology Series

Grady Booch, Ivar Jacobson, and James Rumbaugh, Series Editors

For more information check out the series web site [http://www.awl.com /cseng/otseries/] as well as the pages on each book [http://www.awl.com/cseng/I-S-B-N/] (I-S-B-N represents the actual ISBN, including dashes).

David Bellin and Susan Suchman Simone, *The CRC Card Book*
ISBN 0-201-89535-8

Grady Booch, *Object Solutions: Managing the Object-Oriented Project*
ISBN 0-8053-0594-7

Grady Booch, *Object-Oriented Analysis and Design with Applications, Second Edition*
ISBN 0-8053-5340-2

Grady Booch, James Rumbaugh, and Ivar Jacobson, *The Unified Modeling Language User Guide*
ISBN 0-201-57168-4

Don Box, *Essential COM*
ISBN 0-201-63446-5

Don Box, Keith Brown, Tim Ewald, and Chris Sells, *Effective COM: 50 Ways to Improve Your COM and MTS-based Applications*
ISBN 0-201-37968-6

Alistair Cockburn, *Surviving Object-Oriented Projects: A Manager's Guide*
ISBN 0-201-49834-0

Dave Collins, *Designing Object-Oriented User Interfaces*
ISBN 0-8053-5350-X

Bruce Powel Douglass, *Real-Time UML: Developing Efficient Objects for Embedded Systems*
ISBN 0-201-32579-9

Desmond F. D'Souza and Alan Cameron Wills, *Objects, Components, and Frameworks with UML: The Catalysis Approach*
ISBN 0-201-31012-0

Martin Fowler, *Analysis Patterns: Reusable Object Models*
ISBN 0-201-89542-0

Martin Fowler with Kendall Scott, *UML Distilled: Applying the Standard Object Modeling Language*
ISBN 0-201-32563-2

Peter Heinckiens, *Building Scalable Database Applications: Object-Oriented Design, Architectures, and Implementations*
ISBN 0-201-31013-9

Ivar Jacobson, Grady Booch, and James Rumbaugh, *The Unified Software Development Process*
ISBN 0-201-57169-2

Ivar Jacobson, Magnus Christerson, Patrik Jonsson, and Gunnar Overgaard, *Object-Oriented Software Engineering: A Use Case Driven Approach*
ISBN 0-201-54435-0

Ivar Jacobson, Maria Ericsson, and Agneta Jacobson, *The Object Advantage: Business Process Reengineering with Object Technology*
ISBN 0-201-42289-1

Ivar Jacobson, Martin Griss, and Patrik Jonsson, *Software Reuse: Architecture, Process and Organization for Business Success*
ISBN 0-201-92476-5

David Jordan, *C++ Object Databases: Programming with the ODMG Standard*
ISBN 0-201-63488-0

Philippe Kruchten, *The Rational Unified Process: An Introduction*
ISBN 0-201-60459-0

Wilf LaLonde, *Discovering Smalltalk*
ISBN 0-8053-2720-7

Lockheed Martin Advanced Concepts Center and Rational Software Corporation, *Succeeding with the Booch and OMT Methods: A Practical Approach*
ISBN 0-8053-2279-5

Thomas Mowbray and William Ruh, *Inside CORBA: Distributed Object Standards and Applications*
ISBN 0-201-89540-4

Ira Pohl, *Object-Oriented Programming Using C++, Second Edition*
ISBN 0-201-89550-1

Rob Pooley and Perdita Stevens, *Using UML: Software Engineering with Objects and Components*
ISBN 0-201-36067-5

Terry Quatrani, *Visual Modeling with Rational Rose and UML*
ISBN 0-201-31016-3

Walker Royce, *Software Project Management: A Unified Framework*
ISBN 0-201-30958-0

James Rumbaugh, Ivar Jacobson, and Grady Booch, *The Unified Modeling Language Reference Manual*
ISBN 0-201-30998-X

Geri Schneider and Jason P. Winters, *Applying Use Cases: A Practical Guide*
ISBN 0-201-30981-5

Yen-Ping Shan and Ralph H. Earle, *Enterprise Computing with Objects: From Client/Server Environments to the Internet*
ISBN 0-201-32566-7

David N. Smith, *IBM Smalltalk: The Language*
ISBN 0-8053-0908-X

Daniel Tkach, Walter Fang, and Andrew So, *Visual Modeling Technique: Object Technology Using Visual Programming*
ISBN 0-8053-2574-3

Daniel Tkach and Richard Puttick, *Object Technology in Application Development, Second Edition*
ISBN 0-201-49833-2

Jos Warmer and Anneke Kleppe, *The Object Constraint Language: Precise Modeling with UML*
ISBN 0-201-37940-6

SOFTWARE
PROJECT
MANAGEMENT

A Unified
Framework

WALKER ROYCE

RATIONAL SOFTWARE CORPORATION

ADDISON–WESLEY

An Imprint of Addison Wesley Longman, Inc.

Reading, Massachusetts   Harlow, England   Menlo Park, California
Berkeley, California   Don Mills, Ontario   Sydney
Bonn   Amsterdam   Tokyo   Mexico City

The publisher offers discounts on this book when ordered in quantity for special sales. For more information, please contact:

AWL Direct Sales
Addison Wesley Longman, Inc.
One Jacob Way
Reading, Massachusetts 01867
(781) 944-3700

Library of Congress Cataloging-in-Publication Data

Royce, Walker, 1955–
    Software project management : a unified framework / Walker Royce.
        p. cm.—(The Addison-Wesley object technology series)
    Includes bibliographical references and index.
    ISBN 0-201-30958-0
    1. Computer software—Development—Management.   I. Title.
II. Series.
QA76.76.D47R69 1998
005.1'2—dc21   98–20071
                                              CIP

Special permission to paraphrase and use the *Maturity Questionnaire, CMU/SEI-94-SR-007* © 1998 by Carnegie Mellon University, in the book *Software Project Management: A Unified Framework* is granted by the Software Engineering Institute.

Capability Maturity Model is a service mark of Carnegie Mellon University, CMM[SM] registered in the U.S. Patent and Trademark Office.

Text printed on recycled and acid-free paper.
3 4 5 6 7 8 MA 02 01 00 99
3rd Printing March 1999

This work is dedicated to my father, Winston Royce, whose vision and practicality were always in balance.

—Walker

Contents

List of Figures

List of Tables

Foreword

This book blazes the way toward the next generation of software management practice. Many organizations still cling to the waterfall model because, even with its shortfalls, it provides the most fully elaborated management guidelines on how to proceed in a given software situation.

It has been difficult to find a fully articulated alternative management approach for dealing with such issues as commercial component integration, software reuse, risk management, and evolutionary/incremental/spiral software processes. This book provides a new experience-tested framework and set of guidelines on how to proceed.

Walker Royce developed and tested this software management approach during his inception-to-delivery participation in the large, successful CCPDS-R project performed by TRW for the U.S. Air Force. He then refined and generalized it across a wide spectrum of government, aerospace, and commercial software development experiences at Rational.

Chapters 1 through 4 of the book motivate the approach by showing how it gives you management control of the key software economics leverage points with respect to traditional software management. These are (1) reducing the amount of software you need to build, (2) reducing rework via improved processes and teamwork, and (3) reducing the labor-intensiveness of the remaining work via automation.

Chapters 5 through 10 present the specifics of a new organization of the software life cycle, which also forms the management basis for Rational's Unified process. It combines the flexibility of the spiral model with the discipline of risk management and a set of major life-cycle phases and milestones. These milestones are focused on major management commitments to life-cycle courses of action.

As with our Anchor Point approach at USC, the life-cycle objectives milestone involves a management commitment to engage in a software architecting effort based on a business case analysis (or not to engage, in which case the project is mercifully killed). The life-cycle architecture milestone involves a management commitment to proceed into full-scale development based on establishing and demonstrating a sound architecture and resolving all major risk items. The initial operational capability milestone involves a management commitment to proceed to beta testing the product with outside users, or its equivalent.

In these chapters, Royce provides a set of views showing how these milestones differ from conventional document-oriented or code-oriented milestones. Instead, the key product artifact sets (requirements, design, implementation, deployment) concurrently evolve and coalesce in a manner consistent with the project's objectives and its strategies for controlling risk.

In Chapters 10 through 14, Royce addresses how to ensure that the software project's management artifacts are also concurrently evolving and coalescing. These include the project's plans and associated cost and schedule estimates, the project's organization and team-building activities, and the project's metrics, instrumentation, and control processes. Chapter 14 is particularly noteworthy. It not only emphasizes that the management solutions are situation-dependent, it also provides guidelines for tailoring them to the project's scale, team culture, process maturity, architectural risk, and domain experience.

In Chapters 15 through 17, Royce looks forward to where the best software developers are going with their practices: toward product line management, round-trip engineering, and smaller teams with managers as performers and quality assurance as everyone's job. Appendixes relate his software management approach to the current state of the practice, to the COCOMO and COCOMO II family of cost models, and to the SEI Capability Maturity Model. Appendix D provides a convincing case study of how the approach was successfully used on the large, technically challenging CCPDS-R project.

Royce has a refreshing candor about some of the fads, follies, and excesses in the software field. This comes out particularly in several "pragmatic" sections that address such topics as software cost estimation, inspections, artifacts, planning, and metrics. Not everyone will agree with all of his assessments, particularly on inspections, but they are incisive and thought-provoking.

I feel extremely fortunate to have been able to work with both Walker Royce and his equally insightful father, Winston Royce; to have learned from their experiences; and to have interacted with them as they evolved their path-breaking ideas.

Barry Boehm
Director, USC Center for Software Engineering
April 1998

Preface

The software industry moves unrelentingly toward new methods for managing the ever-increasing complexity of software projects. In the past, we have seen evolutions, revolutions, and recurring themes of success and failure. While software technologies, processes, and methods have advanced rapidly, software engineering remains a people-intensive process. Consequently, techniques for managing people, technology, resources, and risks have profound leverage.

This book captures a software management perspective that emphasizes a balanced view of these elements:

- Theory and practice

- Technology and people

- Customer value and provider profitability

- Strategies and tactics

Throughout, you should observe a recurring management theme of paramount importance: *balance.* It is especially important to achieve balance among the objectives of the various stakeholders, who communicate with one another in a variety of languages and notations. Herein is the motivation for the part opener art, an abstract portrayal of the Rosetta stone. The three fundamental representation languages inherent in software engineering are requirements (the language of the problem space), design (the transformation languages of software engineers), and realizations (the language of the solution space executable on computers). Just as the Rosetta stone enabled the translation of Egyptian hieroglyphics, software management techniques enable the translation of a problem statement into a solution that satisfies all stakeholders.

There is no cookbook for software management. There are no recipes for obvious good practices. I have tried to approach the issues with as much science, realism, and experience as possible, but management is largely a matter of judgment, (un)common sense, and situation-dependent decision making. That's why managers are paid big bucks.

Some chapters include sections with a pragmatic and often hard-hitting treatment of a particular topic. To differentiate this real-world guidance from the general process models, techniques, and disciplines, headings of these sections include the word *pragmatic.* By pragmatic I mean having no illusions and facing reality squarely, which is exactly the intent of these sections. They contain strong opinions and provocative positions, and will strike nerves in readers who are entrenched in some obsolete or overhyped practices, tools, or techniques.

I have attempted to differentiate among proven techniques, new approaches, and obsolete techniques using appropriate substantiation. In most cases, I support my positions with simple economic arguments and common sense, along with anecdotal experience from field applications. Much of the material synthesizes lessons learned (state-of-the-practice) managing successful software projects over the past 10 years. On the other hand, some of the material represents substantially new (state-of-the-art), hypothesized approaches that do not have clear substantiation in practice.

I have struggled with whether to position this book as management *education* or management *training*. The distinction may seem nitpicky, but it is important. An example I heard 15 years ago illustrates the difference. Suppose your 14-year-old daughter came home from school one day and asked, "Mom and Dad, may I take the sex education course offered at school?" Your reaction would likely be different if she asked, "May I take the sex training course offered at school?" (This meant less to me then than it does now that my three daughters are teenagers!)

Training has an aspect of applied knowledge that makes the knowledge more or less immediately useful. Education, on the other hand, is focused more on teaching the principles, experience base, and spirit of the subject, with the application of such knowledge left to the student. I have tried to focus this book as a vehicle for software management education. (I am not sure there is such a thing as management training other than on-the-job experience.) I will not pretend that my advice is directly applicable on every project. Although I have tried to substantiate as many of the position statements as possible, some of them are left unsubstantiated as pure hypotheses. I hope my conjecture and advice will stimulate further debate and progress.

My intended audience runs the gamut of practicing software professionals. Primary target readers are decision makers: those people who authorize investment and expenditure of software-related budgets. This group includes organization managers, project managers, software acquisition officials, and their staffs. For this audience, I am trying to provide directly applicable guidance for use in today's tactical decision making and tomorrow's strategic investments. Another important audience is software practitioners who negotiate and execute software project plans and deliver on organizational and project objectives.

Style

Because I am writing for a wide audience, I do not delve into technical perspectives or technical artifacts, many of which are better discussed in other books. Instead, I provide fairly deep discussions of the economics, management artifacts, work breakdown strategies, organization strategies, and metrics necessary to plan and execute a successful software project.

Illustrations are included to make these complex topics more understandable. The precision and accuracy of the figures and tables merit some comment. While most of the numerical data accurately describe some concept, trend, expectation, or relationship, the presentation formats are purposely imprecise. In the context of software management, the difference between precision and accuracy is not as trivial as it may seem, for two reasons:

1. Software management is full of gray areas, situation dependencies, and ambiguous trade-offs. It is difficult, if not impossible, to provide an accurate depiction of many concepts *and* to retain precision of the presentation across a broad range of domains.

2. Understanding the difference between precision and accuracy is a fundamental skill of good software managers, who must accurately forecast estimates, risks, and the effects of change. Unjustified precision—in requirements or plans—has proven to be a substantial, yet subtle, recurring obstacle to success.

In many of my numeric presentations, the absolute values are unimportant and quite variable across different domains and project circumstances. The relative values constitute the gist of most of the figures and tables.

I occasionally provide anecdotal evidence and actual field experience to put the management approaches into a tangible context and provide relatively accurate and precise benchmarks of performance under game conditions. Several appendixes clarify how the techniques presented herein can be applied in real-world contexts. My flagship case study is a thoroughly documented, successful, large-scale project that provides a concrete example of how well many of these management approaches can work. It also provides a framework for rationalizing some of the improved processes and techniques.

Organization

The book is laid out in five parts, each with multiple chapters:

- **Part I, Software Management Renaissance.** Describes the current state of software management practice and software economics, and introduces the state transitions necessary for improved software return on investment.

- **Part II, A Software Management Process Framework.** Describes the process primitives and a framework for modern software management, including the life-cycle phases, artifacts, workflows, and checkpoints.

- **Part III, Software Management Disciplines.** Summarizes some of the critical techniques associated with planning, controlling, and automating a modern software process.

- **Part IV, Looking Forward.** Hypothesizes the project performance expectations for modern projects and next-generation software economics, and discusses the culture shifts necessary for success.

- **Part V, Case Studies and Backup Material.** Five appendixes provide substantial foundations for some of the recommendations, guidance, and opinions presented elsewhere.

Acknowledgments

Although my perspective of iterative development has been influenced by many sources, I have drawn on relatively few published works in writing this book. Providing a more detailed survey of related publications might have helped some readers and satisfied some authors, but most of the correlation with my views would be coincidental.

The foundation of my material comes basically from three sources, on which I have drawn extensively:

1. TRW's *Ada Process Model Guidebook* [Royce, Walker, 1989]. I wrote this guidebook to capture the process description implemented successfully on a large-scale TRW project so that it could be used throughout TRW.

2. Rational Software Corporation's software management seminar [Royce, Walker, 1997]. I wrote this two-day seminar on software best practices to describe Rational's software management approach. The peer reviewers for this material included Don Andres (TRW), Barry Boehm (University of Southern California), Larry Druffel (Software Engineering Institute), Lloyd Mosemann (U.S. Air Force), and Winston Royce (TRW), in addition to numerous field practitioners and executives within Rational. The seminar was delivered dozens of times in the mid-1990s to a broad range of audiences, including government groups, defense contractors, and commercial organizations.

3. Rational's Unified process. The acquisition of Objectory by Rational resulted in a large internal investment to merge the techniques of the Objectory process (focused on use-case-driven techniques) and the existing Rational process (focused on management techniques and object-oriented modeling). This investment is on-going, as Rational continues to broaden the process description and prescription across more of the life-cycle activities, tools, and methods, resulting in the Unified process.

Several other sources had a significant effect on the management process presented in this book. Their influence is the result of long-term relationships that encapsulate years of interaction, exchange of ideas, and extensive firsthand communication.

- My association with Barry Boehm over the past 15 years has been a rich source of software engineering knowledge.

- Don Andres's extraordinary leadership and project management expertise set him apart from the many project managers I have worked for and with, and I have learned much from him.

- Dave Bernstein, Robert Bond, Mike Devlin, Kevin Haar, Paul Levy, John Lovitt, and Joe Marasco, senior managers at Rational, have evolved a nimble company with a clear vision of software engineering as a business.

- Philippe Kruchten's work on software architecture and process frameworks, as well as his own field experience, has helped gel many of my perspectives and presentations.

- Grady Booch, Ivar Jacobson, and Jim Rumbaugh, Rational's three senior methodologists, have done the software engineering community a great service in defining the Unified Modeling Language.

- Hundreds of dedicated software professionals in the Rational field organization have been responsible for delivering value to software projects and transitioning software engineering theory into practice.

The most important influence on this work was my father, Winston Royce, who set my context, validated my positions, critiqued my presentation, and strengthened my resolve to take a provocative stand and stimulate progress.

Several people invested their own time reviewing early versions of my manuscript and contributing to the concepts, presentation, and quality contained herein. My special thanks go to Ali Ali, Don Andres, Peter Biche, Barry Boehm, Grady Booch, Doug Ishigaki, Ivar Jacobson, Capers Jones, Hartmut Kocher, Philippe Kruchten, Eric Larsen, Joe Marasco, Lloyd Mosemann, Roger Oberg, Rich Reitman, Jim Rumbaugh, and John Smith.

Finally, the overall presentation quality, consistency, and understandability of this material are substantially the work of Karen Ailor. Her critique, sense of organization, attention to detail, and aggressive nitpicking contributed greatly to the overall substance captured in this book.

PART I

SOFTWARE
MANAGEMENT
RENAISSANCE

The software industry is experiencing a renaissance. Many ingrained software engineering principles are going by the wayside, obsolesced by new technology or replaced by better techniques or advanced levels of automation.

No matter what the discipline, it is important that the practitioner understand the current state before attempting to transition to a new one. Before considering a software management framework for the future, it is necessary to understand where the industry is today and how it got here.

In the past 10 years, I have participated in the software process improvement efforts of several Fortune 500 companies. Typical goals of these efforts are to achieve a 2X, 3X, or 10X increase in productivity, quality, time to market, or some combination of all three, where X corresponds to how well the company does now. The funny thing is that many of these organizations have no idea what X is, in objective terms.

The chapters in Part I introduce the state of the practice in the software industry and define the X associated with the conventional software management process.

Conventional Software Management

The best thing about software is its flexibility: It can be programmed to do almost anything. The worst thing about software is also its flexibility: The "almost anything" characteristic has made it difficult to plan, monitor, and control software development. This unpredictability is the basis of what has been referred to for the past 30 years as the "software crisis."

Key Points

▲ Conventional software management practices are mostly sound in theory, but practice is still tied to archaic technology and techniques.

▲ Conventional software economics provides a benchmark of performance for conventional software management principles.

In the mid-1990s, at least three important analyses of the state of the software engineering industry were performed. The results were presented in *Patterns of Software Systems Failure and Success* [Jones, 1996], in "Chaos" [Standish Group, 1995], and in *Report of the Defense Science Board Task Force on Acquiring Defense Software Commercially* [Defense Science Board, 1994]. Appendix A highlights some of the relevant results.

All three analyses reached the same general conclusion: The success rate for software projects is very low. Although the analyses had some differing perspectives, their primary messages were complementary and consistent. They can be summarized as follows:

1. Software development is still highly unpredictable. Only about 10% of software projects are delivered successfully within initial budget and schedule estimates.

2. Management discipline is more of a discriminator in success or failure than are technology advances.

3. The level of software scrap and rework is indicative of an immature process.

The three analyses provide a good introduction to the magnitude of the software problem and the current norms for conventional software management performance. There is much room for improvement.

The remainder of this chapter summarizes the software management process framework that most conventional software projects have used. While this framework, known as the waterfall model, has many derivatives, it is the baseline process for most of the software project experience amassed to date. And while it is dangerous to generalize, it is important to lay out a good context for the process improvement techniques discussed throughout this book.

1.1 THE WATERFALL MODEL

Most software engineering texts present the waterfall model as the source of the "conventional" software process. I regard it more as a benchmark of that process. This section examines and critiques the waterfall model theory, then looks at how most of the industry has practiced the conventional software process. In reality, although the industry has ignored much of the theory, it has still managed to evolve many good practices (and some not-so-good practices), especially when they are used with modern technologies.

1.1.1 IN THEORY

In 1970, my father, Winston Royce, presented a paper titled "Managing the Development of Large Scale Software Systems" at IEEE WESCON [Royce, Winston, 1970]. This paper, based on lessons he had learned managing large software projects, remains the most quoted source of the waterfall model. It provides an insightful and concise summary of conventional software management philosophy circa 1970, and most of its 30-year-old advice has stood the test of time in the face of immense technology turnover.

The paper made three primary points. (Quotations and paraphrased statements are presented in *italics.*)

1. *There are two essential steps common to the development of computer programs: analysis and coding.*

2. *In order to manage and control all of the intellectual freedom associated with software development, one must introduce several other "overhead" steps, including system requirements definition, software requirements definition, program design, and testing. These steps supplement the analysis and coding steps. Figure 1-1 illustrates the resulting project profile and the basic steps in developing a large-scale program.*

Waterfall Model Part 1 : The two basic steps to building a program

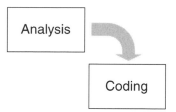

Analysis and coding both involve creative work that directly contributes to the usefulness of the end product.

Waterfall Model Part 2 : The large-scale system approach

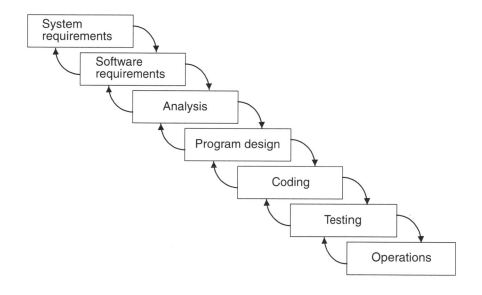

Waterfall Model Part 3 : Five necessary improvements for this approach to work

1. Complete program design before analysis and coding begin.
2. Maintain current and complete documentation.
3. Do the job twice, if possible.
4. Plan, control, and monitor testing.
5. Involve the customer.

FIGURE 1-1. *The waterfall model*

3. *The basic framework described in the waterfall model is risky and invites failure. The testing phase that occurs at the end of the development cycle is the first event for which timing, storage, input/output transfers, etc., are experienced as distinguished from analyzed. The resulting design changes are likely to be so disruptive that the software requirements upon which the design is based are likely violated. Either the requirements must be modified or a substantial design change is warranted.*

Item 1, which is seemingly trivial, will be expanded later into one of my overall management themes: the separation of the engineering stage from the production stage.

Seven of the article's nine pages are devoted to describing five improvements to the basic waterfall process that would eliminate most of the development risks alluded to in item 3. These five improvements are presented next. (Quotations and paraphrased statements are presented in *italics*, followed by my comments, in the context of today's technology and terminology.)

1. ***Program design comes first.*** *The first step toward a fix is to insert a preliminary program design phase between the software requirements generation phase and the analysis phase. By this technique, the program designer assures that the software will not fail because of storage, timing, and data flux. As analysis proceeds in the succeeding phase, the program designer must impose on the analyst the storage, timing, and operational constraints in such a way that he senses the consequences. If the total resources to be applied are insufficient or if the embryonic operational design is wrong, it will be recognized at this early stage and the iteration with requirements and preliminary design can be redone before final design, coding, and test commences. How is this program design procedure implemented? The following steps are required:*

   Begin the design process with program designers, not analysts or programmers.

   Design, define, and allocate the data processing modes even at the risk of being wrong. Allocate processing functions, design the database, allocate execution time, define interfaces and processing modes with the operating system, describe input and output processing, and define preliminary operating procedures.

   Write an overview document that is understandable, informative, and current so that every worker on the project can gain an elemental understanding of the system.

▲ The essence of the process framework I present in later chapters is architecture-first development. Although a few terms may be changed (for example, *architecture* is used instead of *program design*), the essence of a modern process is congruent with the explanation given here. As described later, the architecture comes first and is designed and developed in parallel with planning and requirements definition as part of the engineering stage of a project.

2. *Document the design. The amount of documentation required on most software programs is quite a lot, certainly much more than most program-mers, analysts, or program designers are willing to do if left to their own devices. Why do we need so much documentation? (1) Each designer must communicate with interfacing designers, managers, and possibly custom-ers. (2) During early phases, the documentation **is** the design. (3) The real monetary value of documentation is to support later modifications by a separate test team, a separate maintenance team, and operations personnel who are not software literate.*

▲ If we ignore the technological inadequacies of the time frame in which the paper was written, the essence of this "document the design" message is still valid. Under-standable representations of the artifacts, accessible by all stakeholders and teams, are essential. However, major advances in notations, languages, browsers, tools, and methods have rendered the need for many of the documents obsolete. In later chapters, I argue at length that to focus on documentation is wrong and counter-productive. This is because today's technologies support rigorous and self-docu-menting notations for requirements, designs, and implementations.

3. *Do it twice. If a computer program is being developed for the first time, arrange matters so that the version finally delivered to the customer for operational deployment is actually the second version insofar as critical design/operations are concerned. Note that this is simply the entire process done in miniature, to a time scale that is relatively small with respect to the overall effort. In the first version, the team must have a special broad com-petence where they can quickly sense trouble spots in the design, model them, model alternatives, forget the straightforward aspects of the design that aren't worth studying at this early point, and, finally, arrive at an error-free program.*

▲ This is a concise and simplistic description of architecture-first development, in which an architecture team is responsible for the initial engineering. Generalizing this practice, as I do later, results in a "do it N times" approach that is a principle of modern-day iterative development.

Without this first pass, the project manager is at the mercy of human judgment. With this first-pass "simulation," he can at least perform experimental test of some key hypotheses and scope down what remains for human judgment, which in the area of computer program design (as in the estimation of takeoff gross weight, costs to complete, or the daily double) is invariably and seriously optimistic.

▲ This is a great description of the spirit of iterative development and its inherent advantages for risk management.

4. ***Plan, control, and monitor testing.*** *Without question, the biggest user of project resources—manpower, computer time, and/or management judgment—is the test phase. This is the phase of greatest risk in terms of cost and schedule. It occurs at the latest point in the schedule, when backup alternatives are least available, if at all. The previous three recommendations were all aimed at uncovering and solving problems before entering the test phase. However, even after doing these things, there is still a test phase and there are still important things to be done, including: (1) employ a team of test specialists who were not responsible for the original design; (2) employ visual inspections to spot the obvious errors like dropped minus signs, missing factors of two, jumps to wrong addresses (do not use the computer to detect this kind of thing, it is too expensive); (3) test every logic path; (4) employ the final checkout on the target computer.*

▲ Here we have some good advice and some obsolete advice. Items 1 and 4, still good advice, are discussed at length in later chapters. Item 2 is still a popular quality assurance fad (use software inspections), but its purpose as presented here is mostly obsolete. Although it may have been a good, cost-effective practice using 1970 technology, it is not today. Computers, compilers, analyzers, and other tools are far more efficient mechanisms for catching obvious errors. As for item 3, testing every logic path was difficult enough in 1970, without the added complexity of distribution, reusable components, and several other complicating factors. It is certainly not feasible with most of today's systems. This is especially true with distributed computing, in which, with time as an additional dimension, there are an infinite number of logic paths. In a modern process, testing is a life-cycle activity that, when executed properly, requires fewer total resources and uncovers issues far earlier in the life cycle, when backup alternatives can still be used.

5. ***Involve the customer.*** *For some reason, what a software design is going to do is subject to wide interpretation, even after previous agreement. It is important to involve the customer in a formal way so that he has committed*

himself at earlier points before final delivery. There are three points follow-
ing requirements definition where the insight, judgment, and commitment
of the customer can bolster the development effort. These include a "prelim-
inary software review" following the preliminary program design step, a
sequence of "critical software design reviews" during program design, and a
"final software acceptance review" following testing.

▲ This insight has been pursued for many years and, where practiced, has produced
positive results. Involving the customer with early demonstrations and planned
alpha/beta releases is a proven, valuable technique.

I have always been overwhelmed by the insight presented in this paper. While
most of the industry has spent considerable energy bashing the waterfall model
approach, I find only minor flaws in the theory even when it is applied in the context
of today's technology. The criticism should have been targeted at the *practice* of the
approach, which incorporated various unsound and unworkable elements. I suspect
that most critics never really understood this theory; they just understood the default
practice.

Throughout this book, I refer to the past and current practice of the waterfall
model approach, discussed next, as the "conventional" software management
approach or process. I argue that it is no longer a good framework for modern software engineering practices and technologies, and I use it as the reality benchmark to
rationalize an improved process that eliminates some of its fundamental flaws.

1.1.2   In Practice

Despite the advice of many software experts and the theory behind the waterfall
model, some software projects still practice the conventional software management
approach. However, because its use is declining and was far more prevalent in the
past, I refer to it in the past tense throughout.

It is useful to summarize the characteristics of the conventional process as it has
typically been applied, which is not necessarily as it was intended. Projects destined
for trouble frequently exhibit the following symptoms:

- Protracted integration and late design breakage
- Late risk resolution
- Requirements-driven functional decomposition
- Adversarial stakeholder relationships
- Focus on documents and review meetings

Protracted Integration and Late Design Breakage

For a typical development project that used a waterfall model management process, Figure 1-2 illustrates development progress versus time. Progress is defined as percent coded, that is, demonstrable in its target form. (The software was compilable and executable; it was not necessarily complete, compliant, nor up to specifications.) The following sequence was common:

- Early success via paper designs and thorough (often *too* thorough) briefings
- Commitment to code late in the life cycle
- Integration nightmares due to unforeseen implementation issues and interface ambiguities
- Heavy budget and schedule pressure to get the system working
- Late shoe-horning of nonoptimal fixes, with no time for redesign
- A very fragile, unmaintainable product delivered late

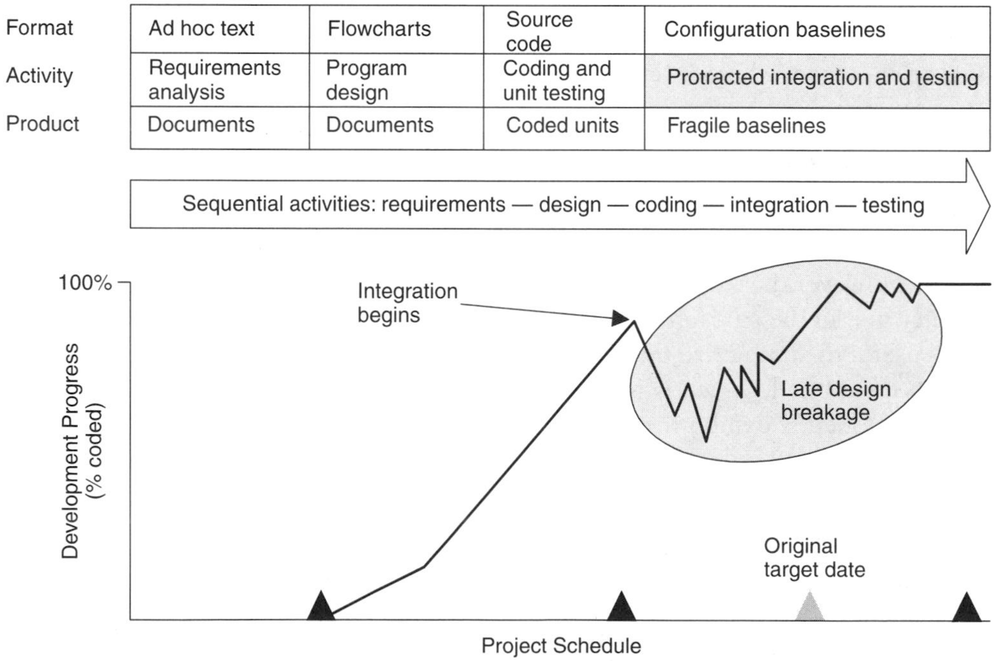
Format
Activity
Product
Ad hoc text
Flowcharts
Source code
Configuration baselines
Requirements analysis
Program design
Coding and unit testing
Protracted integration and testing
Documents
Documents
Coded units
Fragile baselines
Sequential activities: requirements — design — coding — integration — testing
100%
Development Progress (% coded)
Integration begins
Late design breakage
Original target date
Project Schedule

FIGURE 1-2. *Progress profile of a conventional software project*

TABLE **1-1.** *Expenditures by activity for a*
                conventional software project

ACTIVITY	COST
Management	5%
Requirements	5%
Design	10%
Code and unit testing	30%
Integration and test	40%
Deployment	5%
Environment	5%
Total	100%

Given the immature languages and technologies used in the conventional approach, there was substantial emphasis on perfecting the "software design" before committing it to the target programming language, where it was difficult to understand or change. This practice resulted in the use of multiple formats (requirements in English, preliminary design in flowcharts, detailed design in program design languages, and implementations in the target language, such as FORTRAN, COBOL, or C) and error-prone, labor-intensive translations between formats.

Conventional techniques that imposed a waterfall model on the design process inevitably resulted in late integration and performance showstoppers. In the conventional model, the entire system was designed on paper, then implemented all at once, then integrated. Only at the end of this process was it possible to perform system testing to verify that the fundamental architecture (interfaces and structure) was sound. One of the recurring themes of projects following the conventional process was that testing activities consumed 40% or more of life-cycle resources. Table 1-1 provides a typical profile of cost expenditures across the spectrum of software activities.

Late Risk Resolution

A serious issue associated with the waterfall life cycle was the lack of early risk resolution. This was not so much a result of the waterfall life cycle as it was of the focus on early paper artifacts, in which the real design, implementation, and integration risks were still relatively intangible. Figure 1-3 illustrates a typical risk profile for conventional waterfall model projects. It includes four distinct periods of risk exposure, where risk is defined as the probability of missing a cost, schedule, feature, or quality goal. Early in the life cycle, as the requirements were being specified, the actual risk

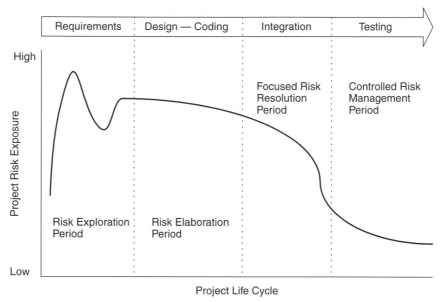

FIGURE 1-3.   *Risk profile of a conventional software project across its life cycle*

exposure was highly unpredictable. After a design concept was available to balance the understanding of the requirements, even if it was just on paper, the risk exposure stabilized. However, it usually stabilized at a relatively high level because there were too few tangible facts for a software manager to achieve an objective assessment. As the system was coded, some of the individual component risks got resolved. Then integration began, and the real system-level qualities and risks started becoming tangible. It was usually during this period that many of the real design issues were resolved and engineering trade-offs were made. However, resolving these issues late in the life cycle, when there was great inertia inhibiting changes to the mass of artifacts, was very expensive. Consequently, projects tended to have a protracted integration phase (as illustrated in Figure 1-2) as major redesign initiatives were implemented. This process tended to resolve the important risks, but not without sacrificing the quality of the end product, especially its maintainability. I use the term *redesign* loosely. Most of this effort would be described better as shoe-horning late fixes and patches into the existing implementation so that the overall resolution effort was minimized. These sorts of changes did not conserve the overall design integrity and its corresponding maintainability.

Requirements-Driven Functional Decomposition

Traditionally, the software development process has been requirements-driven: An attempt is made to provide a precise requirements definition and then to implement exactly those requirements. This approach depends on specifying requirements completely and unambiguously before other development activities begin. It naïvely treats all requirements as equally important, and depends on those requirements remaining constant over the software development life cycle. These conditions rarely occur in the real world. Specification of requirements is a difficult and important part of the software development process. As discussed in Appendix A, virtually every major software program suffers from severe difficulties in requirements specification. Moreover, the equal treatment of all requirements drains away substantial numbers of engineering hours from the driving requirements and wastes those efforts on paperwork associated with traceability, testability, logistics support, and so on—paperwork that is inevitably discarded later as the driving requirements and subsequent design understanding evolve.

As an example, consider a large-scale project such as CCPDS-R, presented as a case study in Appendix D, where the software requirements included 2,000 *shall*s. (A *shall* is a discrete requirement such as "the system shall tolerate all single-point hardware failures with no loss of critical capabilities.") Dealing adequately with the design drivers in such systems (typically only 20 to 50 of the shalls) is difficult when the contractual standards require that all 2,000 shalls be defined first and dealt with at every major milestone. The level of engineering effort that can be expended on the important design issues is significantly diluted by carrying around the excess baggage of more than 1,950 shalls and dealing with traceability, testability, documentation, and so on.

Another property of the conventional approach is that the requirements were typically specified in a functional manner. Built into the classic waterfall process was the fundamental assumption that the software itself was decomposed into functions; requirements were then allocated to the resulting components. This decomposition was often very different from a decomposition based on object-oriented design and the use of existing components. The functional decomposition also became anchored in contracts, subcontracts, and work breakdown structures, often precluding a more architecture-driven approach. Figure 1-4 illustrates the result of requirements-driven approaches: a software structure that is organized around the requirements specification structure.

Adversarial Stakeholder Relationships

The conventional process tended to result in adversarial stakeholder relationships, in large part because of the difficulties of requirements specification and the exchange of information solely through paper documents that captured engineering information in ad hoc formats. The lack of rigorous notation resulted mostly in subjective reviews and opinionated exchanges of information.

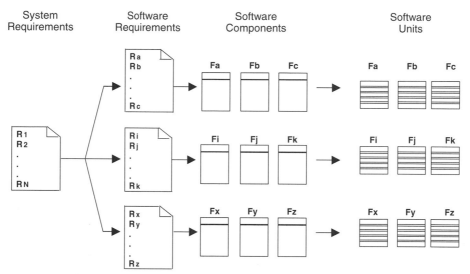

FIGURE 1-4. *Suboptimal software component organization resulting from a requirements-driven approach*

The following sequence of events was typical for most contractual software efforts:

1. The contractor prepared a draft contract-deliverable document that captured an intermediate artifact and delivered it to the customer for approval.

2. The customer was expected to provide comments (typically within 15 to 30 days).

3. The contractor incorporated these comments and submitted (typically within 15 to 30 days) a final version for approval.

This one-shot review process encouraged high levels of sensitivity on the part of customers and contractors. The overhead of such a paper exchange review process was intolerable. This approach also resulted in customer-contractor relationships degenerating into mutual distrust, making it difficult to achieve a balance among requirements, schedule, and cost.

Focus on Documents and Review Meetings

The conventional process focused on producing various documents that attempted to describe the software product, with insufficient focus on producing tangible increments of the products themselves. Major milestones were usually implemented as cer-

TABLE 1-2. *Results of conventional software project design reviews*

APPARENT RESULTS	REAL RESULTS
Big briefing to a diverse audience	Only a small percentage of the audience understands the software.
	Briefings and documents expose few of the important assets and risks of complex software systems.
A design that appears to be compliant	There is no tangible evidence of compliance.
	Compliance with ambiguous requirements is of little value.
Coverage of requirements (typically hundreds)	Few (tens) are design drivers.
	Dealing with all requirements dilutes the focus on the critical drivers.
A design considered "innocent until proven guilty"	The design is always guilty.
	Design flaws are exposed later in the life cycle.

emonious meetings defined solely in terms of specific documents. Contractors were driven to produce literally tons of paper to meet milestones and demonstrate progress to stakeholders, rather than spend their energy on tasks that would reduce risk and produce quality software. Typically, presenters and the audience reviewed the simple things that they understood rather than the complex and important issues. Most design reviews therefore resulted in low engineering value and high cost in terms of the effort and schedule involved in their preparation and conduct. They presented merely a facade of progress. Table 1-2 summarizes the results of a typical design review.

Diagnosing the five symptoms of projects headed for trouble (just discussed) can be difficult, especially in early phases of the life cycle when problems with the conventional approach would have been most easily cured. Consequently, modern software projects must use mechanisms that assess project health in early life-cycle phases and that continue with objective, periodic checkups.

1.2   CONVENTIONAL SOFTWARE MANAGEMENT PERFORMANCE

Barry Boehm's one-page "Industrial Software Metrics Top 10 List" [Boehm, 1987] is a good, objective characterization of the state of software development. (There is very little evidence of significant changes in the past decade.) Although many of the metrics are gross generalizations, they accurately describe some of the fundamental economic relationships that resulted from the conventional software process practiced over the past 30 years.

In the following paragraphs, quotations from Boehm's top 10 list are presented in *italics*, followed by my comments.

1. *Finding and fixing a software problem after delivery costs 100 times more than finding and fixing the problem in early design phases.*

   ▲ This metric dominates the rationale for virtually every dimension of process improvement discussed in this or any other book. It is not unique to software development. When one of the big automobile companies implements a recall for a post-delivery defect, the cost of repair can be many orders of magnitude greater than the cost of fixing the defect during the engineering or production stage.

2. *You can compress software development schedules 25% of nominal, but no more.*

   ▲ One reason for this is that an N% reduction in schedule would require an M% increase in personnel resources (assuming that other parameters remain fixed). Any increase in the number of people requires more management overhead. In general, the limit of flexibility in this overhead, along with scheduling concurrent activities, conserving sequential activities, and other resource constraints, is about 25%. Optimally, a 100-staff-month effort may be achievable in 10 months by 10 people. Could the job be done in one month with 100 people? Two months with 50 people? How about 5 months with 20 people? Clearly, these alternatives are unrealistic. The 25% compression metric says that the limit in this case is 7.5 months (and would require additional staff-months, perhaps as many as 20). Any further schedule compression is doomed to fail. On the other hand, an optimal schedule could be extended almost arbitrarily and, depending on the people, could be performed in a much longer time with many fewer staff resources. For example, if you have the luxury of a 25-month schedule, you may need only 75 staff-months and three people.

3. *For every $1 you spend on development, you will spend $2 on maintenance.*

   ▲ Boehm calls this the "iron law of software development." Whether you build a long-lived product that undergoes commercial version upgrades twice a year or build a one-of-a-kind custom software system, twice as much money will probably be spent over the maintenance life cycle than was spent in the development life cycle. It is hard to tell at first whether this relationship is good or bad. In the commercial product domain, the primary driver of this relationship is the product's success in the marketplace. Successful software products (such as Oracle, Microsoft applications, Rational Rose, and the UNIX operating system) are very long lived and can result in much higher ratios of maintenance cost to development cost. Managers of one-of-a-kind software projects, on the other hand, rarely plan to expend this much on software maintenance. In either case, anyone working in the software industry over the past 10 to 20 years knows that most of the software in operation is considered to be difficult to maintain.

4. *Software development and maintenance costs are primarily a function of the number of source lines of code.*

▲ This metric is primarily the result of the predominance of custom software development, lack of commercial componentry, and lack of reuse inherent in the era of the conventional process.

5. *Variations among people account for the biggest differences in software productivity.*

▲ This is a key piece of conventional wisdom: Hire good people. This metric is a subject of both overhype and underhype. When you don't know objectively why you succeeded or failed, the obvious scapegoat is the quality of the people. This judgment is subjective and difficult to challenge.

6. *The overall ratio of software to hardware costs is still growing. In 1955 it was 15:85; in 1985, 85:15.*

▲ The fact that software represents 85% of the cost of most systems is not so much a statement about software productivity (which is, arguably, not as good as we want) as it is about the level of functionality being allocated to software in system solutions. The need for software, its breadth of applications, and its complexity continue to grow almost without limits.

7. *Only about 15% of software development effort is devoted to programming.*

▲ This is an important indicator of the need for balance. Many activities besides coding are necessary for software project success. Requirements management, design, testing, planning, project control, change management, and toolsmithing are equally important considerations that consume roughly 85% of the resources.

8. *Software systems and products typically cost 3 times as much per SLOC as individual software programs. Software-system products (i.e., system of systems) cost 9 times as much.*

▲ This exponential relationship is the essence of what is called *diseconomy of scale*. Unlike other commodities, the more software you build, the more expensive it is per source line.

9. *Walkthroughs catch 60% of the errors.*

▲ This may be true. However, given metric 1, walkthroughs are not catching the errors that matter and certainly are not catching them early enough in the life cycle. All defects are not created equal. In general, walkthroughs and other forms of human inspection are good at catching surface problems and style issues. If you are using ad hoc design notations, human review may be your primary quality assurance mechanism, but it is not good at uncovering second-, third-, and Nth-order issues such as resource contention, performance bottlenecks, control conflicts, and so on. Furthermore, few humans are good at reviewing even first-order semantic issues in a code segment. How many programmers get their code to compile the first time?

10. *80% of the contribution comes from 20% of the contributors.*

▲ This is a motherhood statement that is true across almost any engineering discipline (or any professional discipline, for that matter). I have expanded this metric into a more specific interpretation for software. The following fundamental postulates underlie the rationale for a modern software management process framework:

80% of the engineering is consumed by 20% of the requirements.

80% of the software cost is consumed by 20% of the components.

80% of the errors are caused by 20% of the components.

80% of software scrap and rework is caused by 20% of the errors.

80% of the resources are consumed by 20% of the components.

80% of the engineering is accomplished by 20% of the tools.

80% of the progress is made by 20% of the people.

These relationships provide some good benchmarks for evaluating process improvements and technology improvements. They represent rough rules of thumb that objectively characterize the performance of the conventional software management process and conventional technologies. In later chapters, I return to many of these measures to rationalize a new approach, defend an old approach, and quantify process or technology improvements.

Evolution of Software Economics

Software engineering is dominated by intellectual activities that are focused on solving problems of immense complexity with numerous unknowns in competing perspectives. The early software approaches of the 1960s and 1970s can best be described as craftsmanship, with each project using a custom process and custom tools. In the 1980s and 1990s, the software industry matured and transitioned to more of an engineering discipline. However, most software projects in this era were still primarily research-intensive, dominated by human creativity and diseconomies of scale. The next generation of software processes, specifically the techniques presented in this book, is driving toward a more production-intensive approach dominated by automation and economies of scale.

Key Points

▲ Economic results of conventional software projects reflect an industry dominated by custom development, ad hoc processes, and diseconomies of scale.

▲ Today's cost models are based primarily on empirical project databases with very few modern iterative development success stories.

▲ Good software cost estimates are difficult to attain. Decision makers must deal with highly imprecise estimates.

▲ A modern process framework attacks the primary sources of the inherent diseconomy of scale in the conventional software process.

2.1   SOFTWARE ECONOMICS

Most software cost models can be abstracted into a function of five basic parameters: size, process, personnel, environment, and required quality.

1. The *size* of the end product (in human-generated components), which is typically quantified in terms of the number of source instructions or the number of function points required to develop the required functionality

2. The *process* used to produce the end product, in particular the ability of the process to avoid non-value-adding activities (rework, bureaucratic delays, communications overhead)

3. The capabilities of software engineering *personnel,* and particularly their experience with the computer science issues and the applications domain issues of the project

4. The *environment,* which is made up of the tools and techniques available to support efficient software development and to automate the process

5. The required *quality* of the product, including its features, performance, reliability, and adaptability

The relationships among these parameters and the estimated cost can be written as follows:

$$\text{Effort} = (\text{Personnel})(\text{Environment})(\text{Quality})(\text{Size}^{\text{Process}})$$

Several parametric models have been developed to estimate software costs; all of them can be generally abstracted into this form. One important aspect of software economics (as represented within today's software cost models) is that the relationship between effort and size exhibits a diseconomy of scale. The diseconomy of scale of software development is a result of the process exponent being greater than 1.0. Contrary to most manufacturing processes, the more software you build, the more expensive it is per unit item.

For example, for a given application, a 10,000-line software solution will cost less per line than a 100,000-line software solution. How much less? Assume that a 100,000-line system requires 900 staff-months for development, or about 111 lines per staff-month, or 1.37 hours per line. If this same system were only 10,000 lines, and all other parameters were held constant, this project would be estimated at 62 staff-months, or about 175 lines per staff-month, or 0.87 hour per line. (Figure B-1 in Appendix B provides a more detailed description of this example using the COCOMO cost estimation model.) The per-line cost for the smaller application is much less than for the larger application. The reason is primarily the complexity of managing interpersonal communications as the number of team members (and corresponding objectives, win conditions, technical biases) scales up. This diseconomy of scale is characteristic of any research project in which the product is a one-of-a-kind instance of intellectual property.

Figure 2-1 shows three generations of basic technology advancement in tools, components, and processes. The required levels of quality and personnel are assumed to be constant. The ordinate of the graph refers to software unit costs (pick your favorite: per SLOC, per function point, per component) realized by an organization.

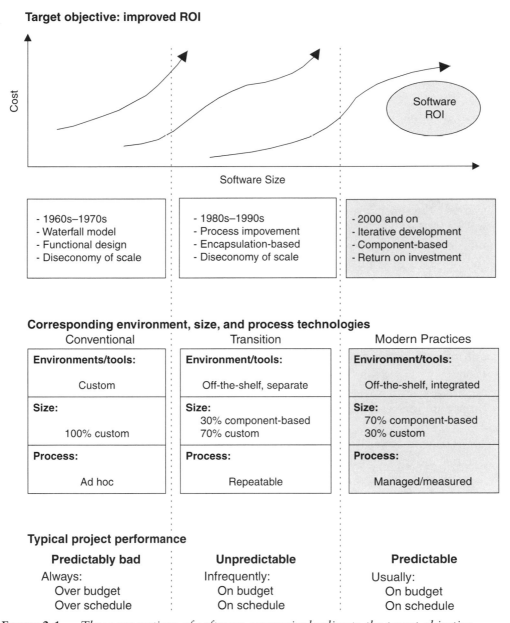

Target objective: improved ROI

FIGURE 2-1.   *Three generations of software economics leading to the target objective*

The abscissa represents the life cycle of the software business engaged in by the organization. The three generations of software development are defined as follows:

1. *Conventional:* 1960s and 1970s, craftsmanship. Organizations used custom tools, custom processes, and virtually all custom components built in primitive languages. Project performance was highly predictable in that cost, schedule, and quality objectives were almost always underachieved.

2. *Transition:* 1980s and 1990s, software engineering. Organizations used more-repeatable processes and off-the-shelf tools, and mostly (>70%) custom components built in higher level languages. Some of the components (<30%) were available as commercial products, including the operating system, database management system, networking, and graphical user interface. During the 1980s, some organizations began achieving economies of scale, but with the growth in applications complexity (primarily in the move to distributed systems), the existing languages, techniques, and technologies were just not enough to substain the desired business performance.

3. *Modern practices:* 2000 and later, software production. This book's philosophy is rooted in the use of managed and measured processes, integrated automation environments, and mostly (70%) off-the-shelf components. Perhaps as few as 30% of the components need to be custom built. With advances in software technology and integrated production environments, these component-based systems can be produced very rapidly.

Technologies for environment automation, size reduction, and process improvement are not independent of one another. In each new era, the key is complementary growth in all technologies. For example, the process advances could not be used successfully without new component technologies and increased tool automation.

The transition to modern practices and the promise of improved software economics are by no means guaranteed. We must be realistic in comparing the promises of a well-executed, next-generation process using modern technologies against the ugly realities of history. It is a sure bet that many organizations attempting to carry out modern projects with modern techniques and technologies will end up with the same old snafu.

Organizations are achieving better economies of scale in successive technology eras—with very large projects (systems of systems), long-lived products, and lines of business comprising multiple similar projects. Figure 2-2 provides an overview of how a return on investment (ROI) profile can be achieved in subsequent efforts across life cycles of various domains.

Achieving ROI across a line of business

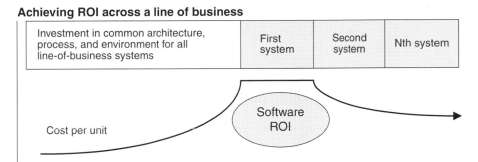

Line-of-Business Life Cycle: Successive Systems

Achieving ROI across a project with multiple iterations

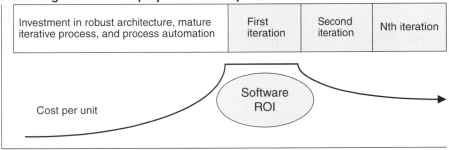

Project Life Cycle: Successive Iterations

Achieving ROI across a life cycle of product releases

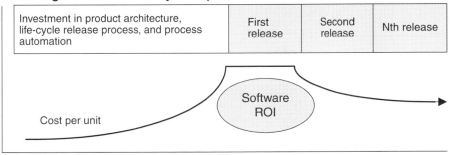

Product Life Cycle: Successive Releases

FIGURE 2-2. *Return on investment in different domains*

2.2 PRAGMATIC SOFTWARE COST ESTIMATION

One critical problem in software cost estimation is a lack of well-documented case studies of projects that used an iterative development approach. Although cost model vendors claim that their tools are suitable for estimating iterative development projects, few are based on empirical project databases with modern iterative development success stories. Furthermore, because the software industry has inconsistently defined metrics or atomic units of measure, the data from actual projects are highly suspect in terms of consistency and comparability. It is hard enough to collect a homogeneous set of project data within one organization; it is extremely difficult to homogenize data across different organizations with different processes, languages, domains, and so on. For example, the fundamental unit of size (a source line of code or a function point) can be, and is, counted differently across the industry. It is surprising that modern language standards (such as Ada 95 and Java) don't make a simple definition of a source line reportable by the compiler. The exact definition of a function point or a SLOC is not very important, just as the exact length of a foot or a meter is equally arbitrary. It is simply important that everyone uses the same definition.

There have been many long-standing debates among developers and vendors of software cost estimation models and tools. Three topics of these debates are of particular interest here:

1. Which cost estimation model to use

2. Whether to measure software size in source lines of code or function points

3. What constitutes a good estimate

About 50 vendors of software cost estimation tools, data, and services compete within the software industry. There are several popular cost estimation models (such as COCOMO, CHECKPOINT, ESTIMACS, KnowledgePlan, Price-S, ProQMS, SEER, SLIM, SOFTCOST, and SPQR/20), as well as numerous organization-specific models. Because my firsthand experience with these models has been centered on COCOMO and its successors, Ada COCOMO and COCOMO II, it is the basis of many of my software economics arguments and perspectives. COCOMO is also one of the most open and well-documented cost estimation models. The evolution of COCOMO into its current version, COCOMO II, is summarized in Appendix B. While portions of the appendix are not directly applicable to today's techniques and technologies, it provides an interesting historical perspective on the evolution of the issues and priorities of software economics over the past 20 years.

The measurement of software size has been the subject of much rhetoric. There are basically two objective points of view: source lines of code and function points. Both perspectives have proven to be more valuable than a third, which is the subjective or ad hoc point of view practiced by many immature organizations that use no systematic measurement of size.

Many software experts have argued that SLOC is a lousy measure of size. However, when a code segment is described as a 1,000-source-line program, most people feel comfortable with its general "mass." If the description were 20 function points, 6 classes, 5 use cases, 4 object points, 6 files, 2 subsystems, 1 component, or 6,000 bytes, most people, including software experts, would ask further questions to gain an understanding of the subject code. (Many of them would ask how many SLOC.) So SLOC is one measure that still has some value.

I was a SLOC zealot a decade ago because SLOC worked well in applications that were predominantly custom-built and because SLOC measurement was easy to automate and instrument. Today, language advances and the use of components, automatic source code generation, and object orientation have made SLOC a much more ambiguous measure. As an acute example, the case study in Appendix D describes the carefully crafted approaches for counting SLOC to accommodate reuse, custom development, and code generation tools on a large software project.

The use of function points has a large following, including Capers Jones, who cites the hazards associated with using SLOC metrics for object-oriented programs [Jones, 1994]. The International Function Point User's Group, formed in 1984, is the dominant software measurement association in the industry. The primary advantage of using function points is that this method is independent of technology and is therefore a much better primitive unit for comparisons among projects and organizations. The main disadvantage is that the primitive definitions are abstract and measurements are not easily derived directly from the evolving artifacts.

Although both measures of size have their drawbacks, I think an organization can make either one work. The use of *some* measure is better than none at all. Anyone doing cross-project or cross-organization comparisons should be using function points as the measure of size. Function points are also probably a more accurate estimator in the early phases of a project life cycle. In later phases, however, SLOC becomes a more useful and precise measurement basis of various metrics perspectives. Chapter 16 presents my hypothesis of a next-generation cost model that could minimize or even obsolesce the need to measure SLOC.

The general accuracy of conventional cost models (such as COCOMO) has been described as "within 20% of actuals, 70% of the time." This level of unpredictability in the conventional software development process should be truly frightening to every investor, especially in light of the fact that few projects miss their estimate by doing better than expected. This is an interesting phenomenon to be considered when scheduling labor-intensive efforts. Unless specific incentives are provided for beating the overall schedule, projects rarely do better than planned. Why? Teams and individuals perform subplanning to meet their objectives. If the time objective is lenient, they either expend energy elsewhere (in further training, helping others, or goofing off), or they continue to add quality beyond what is necessary. They almost never propose to accelerate the schedule. If they did, their suggestion would most likely meet with

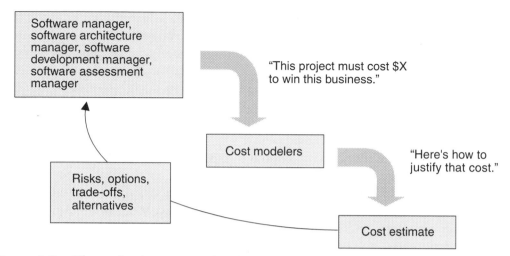

FIGURE 2-3. *The predominant cost estimation process*

resistance from other stakeholders who are expecting to synchronize. So plans need to be as ambitious as can possibly be achieved.

Most real-world use of cost models is bottom-up (substantiating a target cost) rather than top-down (estimating the "should" cost). Figure 2-3 illustrates the predominant practice: The software project manager defines the target cost of the software, then manipulates the parameters and sizing until the target cost can be justified. The rationale for the target cost may be to win a proposal, to solicit customer funding, to attain internal corporate funding, or to achieve some other goal.

The process described in Figure 2-3 is not all bad. In fact, it is absolutely necessary to analyze the cost risks and understand the sensitivities and trade-offs objectively. It forces the software project manager to examine the risks associated with achieving the target costs and to discuss this information with other stakeholders. The result is usually various perturbations in the plans, designs, process, or scope being proposed. This process provides a good vehicle for a basis of estimate and an overall cost analysis.

A practical lesson learned from the field is that independent cost estimates (those done by people who are independent of the development team) are usually inaccurate. The only way to produce a credible estimate is for a competent team—the software project manager and the software architecture, development, and test managers—to iterate through several estimates and sensitivity analyses. This team must then take ownership of that cost estimate for the project to succeed.

What constitutes a good software cost estimate? This tough question is discussed in detail in Chapter 10. In summary, a good estimate has the following attributes:

- It is conceived and supported by the project manager, architecture team, development team, and test team accountable for performing the work.

- It is accepted by all stakeholders as ambitious but realizable.

- It is based on a well-defined software cost model with a credible basis.

- It is based on a database of relevant project experience that includes similar processes, similar technologies, similar environments, similar quality requirements, and similar people.

- It is defined in enough detail so that its key risk areas are understood and the probability of success is objectively assessed.

Extrapolating from a good estimate, an *ideal* estimate would be derived from a mature cost model with an experience base that reflects multiple similar projects done by the same team with the same mature processes and tools. Although this situation rarely exists when a project team embarks on a new project, good estimates can be achieved in a straightforward manner in later life-cycle phases of a mature project using a mature process.

Improving Software Economics

Improvements in the economics of software development have been not only difficult to achieve but also difficult to measure and substantiate. In software textbooks, trade journals, and product literature, the treatment of this topic is plagued by inconsistent jargon, inconsistent units of measure, disagreement among experts, and unending hyperbole. If we examine any one aspect of improving software economics, we end up with fairly narrow conclusions and an observation of limited value.

Key Points

▲ Modern software technology is enabling systems to be built with fewer human-generated source lines.

▲ Modern software processes are iterative.

▲ Modern software development and maintenance environments are the delivery mechanism for process automation.

Similarly, if an organization focuses too much on improving only one aspect of its software development process, it will not realize any significant economic improvement even though it improves this one aspect spectacularly.

The key to substantial improvement is a balanced attack across several interrelated dimensions. I have structured the presentation of the important dimensions around the five basic parameters of the software cost model presented in Chapter 2.

1. Reducing the *size* or complexity of what needs to be developed

2. Improving the development *process*

3. Using more-skilled *personnel* and better teams (not necessarily the same thing)

4. Using better *environments* (tools to automate the process)

5. Trading off or backing off on *quality* thresholds

These parameters are given in priority order for most software domains. Table 3-1 lists some of the technology developments, process improvement efforts, and management approaches targeted at improving the economics of software development and integration.

Most software experts would also stress the significant dependencies among these trends. For example, tools enable size reduction and process improvements, size-reduction approaches lead to process changes, and process improvements drive tool requirements. Consider the domain of user interface software. Two decades ago, teams developing a user interface would spend extensive time analyzing operations, human factors, screen layout, and screen dynamics. All this would be done on paper because it was extremely expensive to commit designs, even informal prototypes, to executable code. Therefore, the process emphasized a fairly heavyweight set of early paper artifacts and user concurrence so that these "requirements" could be frozen and the high construction costs could be minimized.

TABLE 3-1. *Important trends in improving software economics*

COST MODEL PARAMETERS	TRENDS
Size Abstraction and component-based development technologies	Higher order languages (C++, Ada 95, Java, Visual Basic, etc.)
	Object-oriented (analysis, design, programming)
	Reuse
	Commercial components
Process Methods and techniques	Iterative development
	Process maturity models
	Architecture-first development
	Acquisition reform
Personnel People factors	Training and personnel skill development
	Teamwork
	Win-win cultures
Environment Automation technologies and tools	Integrated tools (visual modeling, compiler, editor, debugger, change management, etc.)
	Open systems
	Hardware platform performance
	Automation of coding, documents, testing, analyses
Quality Performance, reliability, accuracy	Hardware platform performance
	Demonstration-based assessment
	Statistical quality control

Graphical user interface (GUI) technology is a good example of tools enabling a new and different process. As GUI technology matured, the conventional user interface process became obsolete. GUI builder tools permitted engineering teams to construct an executable user interface faster and at less cost. The paper descriptions were now unnecessary; in fact, they were an obstacle to the efficiency of the process. Operations analysis and human factors analysis were still important, but these activities could now be done in a realistic target environment using existing primitives and building blocks. Engineering and feedback cycles that used to take months could now be done in days or weeks. The old process was geared toward ensuring that the user interface was completely analyzed and designed, because the project could afford only one construction cycle. The new process was geared toward taking the user interface through a few realistic versions, incorporating user feedback all along the way, and achieving a stable understanding of the requirements and the design issues in balance with one another.

It could be argued that the process advances (such as the need for iteration and experimentation in defining user interfaces) drove the development of the tools, or that the technology advances drove the process change. Reality is probably a mixture of both. The point is that the five basic parameters of the cost estimation equation are not mutually exclusive, nor are they independent of one another. They are interrelated.

Another important factor that has influenced software technology improvements across the board is the ever-increasing advances in hardware performance. The availability of more cycles, more memory, and more bandwidth has eliminated many sources of software implementation complexity. Simpler, brute-force solutions are now possible, and hardware improvements are probably the enabling advance behind most software technology improvements of substance.

3.1   REDUCING SOFTWARE PRODUCT SIZE

The most significant way to improve affordability and return on investment (ROI) is usually to produce a product that achieves the design goals with the minimum amount of human-generated source material. *Component-based development* is introduced here as the general term for reducing the "source" language size necessary to achieve a software solution. Reuse, object-oriented technology, automatic code production, and higher order programming languages are all focused on achieving a given system with fewer lines of human-specified source directives (statements). This size reduction is the primary motivation behind improvements in higher order languages (such as C++, Ada 95, Java, Visual Basic, and fourth-generation languages), automatic code generators (CASE tools, visual modeling tools, GUI builders), reuse of commercial components (operating systems, windowing environments, database management systems, middleware, networks), and object-oriented technologies (Unified Modeling Language, visual modeling tools, architecture frameworks).

One caveat is warranted when discussing a reduction in product size. On the surface, this recommendation stems from a simple observation: Code that isn't there doesn't need to be developed and can't break. But this is not entirely the case. The reduction is defined in terms of human-generated source material. In general, when size-reducing technologies are used, they reduce the number of human-generated source lines. However, all of them tend to increase the amount of computer-processable executable code. So the first part of the observation is true, but the second part is not necessarily true. The bottom line, as experienced by many project teams, is that mature and reliable size reduction technologies are extremely powerful at producing economic benefits. Immature size reduction technologies may reduce the development size but require so much more investment in achieving the necessary levels of quality and performance that they have a negative impact on overall project performance.

3.1.1 LANGUAGES

Universal function points (UFPs) are useful estimators for language-independent, early life-cycle estimates. The basic units of function points are external user inputs, external outputs, internal logical data groups, external data interfaces, and external inquiries. SLOC metrics are useful estimators for software after a candidate solution is formulated and an implementation language is known. Substantial data have been documented relating SLOC to function points [Jones, 1995]. Some of these results are shown in Table 3-2.

The data in the table illustrate why people are interested in modern languages such as C++, Ada 95, Java, and Visual Basic: The level of expressibility is very attractive. However, care must be taken in applying these data because of numerous possible

TABLE 3-2.   *Language expressiveness of some of today's popular languages*

LANGUAGE	SLOC PER UFP
Assembly	320
C	128
FORTRAN 77	105
COBOL 85	91
Ada 83	71
C++	56
Ada 95	55
Java	55
Visual Basic	35

misuses. While I believe that the data accurately represent an important relationship, the numbers are far too precise. (They are undoubtedly the precise average of several imprecise numbers.) Each language has a domain of usage. Visual Basic is very expressive and powerful in building simple interactive applications, but it would not be a wise choice for a real-time, embedded, avionics program. Similarly, Ada 95 might be the best language for a catastrophic cost-of-failure system that controls a nuclear power plant, but it would not be the best choice for a highly parallel, scientific, number-crunching program running on a supercomputer. Software industry data such as these, which span application domains, corporations, and technology generations, must be interpreted and used with great care.

Two interesting observations within the data concern the differences and relationships between Ada 83 and Ada 95, and between C and C++. The interest of the Department of Defense (DOD) in developing Ada 83 was due in part to the increase it would provide in expressiveness. (Other reasons included reliability, support for real-time programming, maintainability, and improved ROI through language standardization.) A significant economic motivation was the ability to develop a program in substantially fewer lines of code than were required in the traditional language alternatives of FORTRAN, COBOL, C, and assembly. Embodied in the Ada language are numerous software engineering technology advances, including language-enforced configuration control, separation of interface and implementation, architectural control primitives, encapsulation, concurrency support, and many others. Ada 95 represented a well-planned language upgrade to accommodate new technology and incorporate lessons learned in field applications. The difference in expressibility between Ada 83 and Ada 95 is mainly due to the features added to support object-oriented programming. Thus, a first-order estimation of the value of object-oriented programming is that it allows programs to be written in 30% fewer source lines.

The difference between C and C++ is even more profound. C++ incorporated several (although not all) of the advances within Ada as well as advanced support for object-oriented programming. However, C++ was also developed to support C as a subset. This requirement has its pros and cons. On one hand, the C compatibility made it very easy for C programmers to transition to C++. On the downside, one noticeable trend in the industry is a significant population of programmers using a C++ compiler but programming with a C mindset, therefore failing to achieve the expressibility of object-oriented C++. The evolution of Java has eliminated many of the problems in the C++ language (particularly the native support for C, which encourages several dangerous programming practices) while conserving the object-oriented features and adding further support for portability and distribution.

Universal function points can be used to indicate the relative program sizes required to implement a given functionality. For example, to achieve a given application with a fixed number of function points, one of the following program sizes would be required:

1,000,000 lines of assembly language

400,000 lines of C

220,000 lines of Ada 83

175,000 lines of Ada 95 or C++

The values indicate the relative expressiveness provided by various languages. Commercial components and automatic code generators (such as CASE tools and GUI builders) can further reduce the size of human-generated source code, which in turn reduces the size of the team and the time needed for development. Extending this example, adding a commercial database management system (DBMS), commercial GUI builder, and commercial middleware could reduce the effective size of development to the following final size:

75,000 lines of Ada 95 or C++ plus integration of several commercial components

Because the difference between large and small projects has a greater than linear impact on the life-cycle cost, the use of the highest level language and appropriate commercial components has a large potential impact on cost. Furthermore, simpler is generally better: Reducing size usually increases understandability, changeability, and reliability. One typical negative side effect is that the higher level abstraction technologies tend to degrade performance, increasing consumption of resources such as processor cycles, memory, and communications bandwidth. Most of these drawbacks have been overcome by hardware performance improvements and optimizations. These improvements are far less effective in embedded platforms.

3.1.2   OBJECT-ORIENTED METHODS AND VISUAL MODELING

There has been a widespread movement in the 1990s toward object-oriented technology. I spend very little time on this topic because object-oriented technology is not germane to most of the software management topics discussed here, and books on object-oriented technology abound. Some studies have concluded that object-oriented programming languages appear to benefit both software productivity and software quality [Jones, 1994], but an economic benefit has yet to be demonstrated because of the steep cost of training in object-oriented design methods such as the Unified Modeling Language (UML).

By providing more-formalized notations for capturing and visualizing software abstractions, the fundamental impact of object-oriented technology is in reducing the overall size of what needs to be developed. Booch has described three other reasons that certain object-oriented projects succeed [Booch, 1996]. These are interesting examples of the interrelationships among the dimensions of improving software economics. (Quotations are presented in *italics*.)

1. *An object-oriented model of the problem and its solution encourages a common vocabulary between the end users of a system and its developers, thus creating a shared understanding of the problem being solved.*

   ▲ Here is an example of how object-oriented technology permits corresponding improvements in teamwork and interpersonal communications.

2. *The use of continuous integration creates opportunities to recognize risk early and make incremental corrections without destabilizing the entire development effort.*

   ▲ This aspect of object-oriented technology enables an architecture-first process, in which integration is an early and continuous life-cycle activity.

3. *An object-oriented architecture provides a clear separation of concerns among disparate elements of a system, creating firewalls that prevent a change in one part of the system from rending the fabric of the entire architecture.*

   ▲ This feature of object-oriented technology is crucial to the supporting languages and environments available to implement object-oriented architectures.

Booch also summarized five characteristics of a successful object-oriented project.

1. *A ruthless focus on the development of a system that provides a well-understood collection of essential minimal characteristics*

2. *The existence of a culture that is centered on results, encourages communication, and yet is not afraid to fail*

3. *The effective use of object-oriented modeling*

4. *The existence of a strong architectural vision*

5. *The application of a well-managed iterative and incremental development life cycle*

These characteristics have little to do with object orientation. However, object-oriented methods, notations, and visual modeling provide strong technology support for the process framework.

3.1.3   REUSE

Reusing existing components and building reusable components have been natural software engineering activities since the earliest improvements in programming languages. Software design methods have always dealt implicitly with reuse in order to minimize development costs while achieving all the other required attributes of performance, feature set, and quality. Reuse achieves undeserved importance within the software engineering community only because we don't do it as well as we should. In all other engineering and manufacturing disciplines, reuse is more or less an underlying assumption, not some necessary technological breakthrough. I try to treat reuse as a mundane part of achieving a return on investment. Common architectures, common processes, precedent experience, and common environments are all instances of reuse.

One of the biggest obstacles to reuse has been fragmentation of languages, operating systems, notations, machine architectures, tools, and even "standards." As a counterexample, the level of reuse made possible by Microsoft's success on the PC platform has been immense.

In general, things get reused for economic reasons. Therefore, the key metric in identifying whether a component (or a class of components, or a commercial product) is truly reusable is to see whether some organization is making money on it. Without this economic motive, reusable components are rare. Beware of "open" reuse libraries sponsored by nonprofit organizations. They lack economic motivation, trustworthiness, and accountability for quality, support, improvement, and usability. Most truly reusable components of value are transitioned to commercial products supported by organizations with the following characteristics:

- They have an economic motivation for continued support.
- They take ownership of improving product quality, adding new features, and transitioning to new technologies.
- They have a sufficiently broad customer base to be profitable.

The cost of developing a reusable component is not trivial. Figure 3-1 examines the economic trade-offs. The steep initial curve illustrates the economic obstacle to developing reusable components. It is difficult to develop a convincing business case for development unless the objective is to support reuse across many projects. Positive business cases rarely occur in software development organizations that are not focused on selling commercial components as their main line of business. Most organizations cannot compete economically with established commercial organizations whose investments are broadly amortized across the user base. To succeed in the marketplace for commercial components, an organization needs three enduring elements: a development group, a support infrastructure, and a product-oriented sales and mar-

Many-project solution: Operating with high value per unit investment, typical of commercial products

5 project solution: 125% more cost and 150% more time

2 project solution: 50% more cost and 100% more time

1 project solution: $N and M months

Number of Projects Using Reusable Components

Development Cost and Schedule Resources

FIGURE 3-1. *Cost and schedule investments necessary to achieve reusable components*

keting infrastructure. Another consideration is that the complexity and cost of developing reusable components are often naïvely underestimated.

Although the value of reuse can be immense, I have never been a fan of identifying reuse as a separate "technology." Reuse is an important discipline that has an impact on the efficiency of all workflows and the quality of most artifacts. I think of it as a synonym for return on investment, which should be a consideration in almost every activity and decision. There have been very few success stories in software component reuse except for commercial products such as operating systems, database management systems, middleware, networking, GUI builders, and office applications. On the other hand, every software success story has probably exploited some key avenues of reuse (without calling it that) to achieve results efficiently.

3.1.4 COMMERCIAL COMPONENTS

A common approach being pursued today in many domains is to maximize integration of commercial components and off-the-shelf products. While the use of commercial components is certainly desirable as a means of reducing custom development, it has not proven to be straightforward in practice. Table 3-3 identifies some of the advantages and disadvantages of using commercial components. (These trade-offs are particularly acute in mission-critical domains.) Because the trade-offs frequently have global effects on quality, cost, and supportability, the selection of commercial components over development of custom components has significant impact on a project's overall architecture. The paramount message here (discussed further in Chapter 7) is that these decisions must be made early in the life cycle as part of the architectural design.

TABLE 3-3. *Advantages and disadvantages of commercial components versus custom software*

APPROACH	ADVANTAGES	DISADVANTAGES
Commercial components	Predictable license costs	Frequent upgrades
	Broadly used, mature technology	Up-front license fees
	Available now	Recurring maintenance fees
	Dedicated support organization	Dependency on vendor
	Hardware/software independence	Run-time efficiency sacrifices
	Rich in functionality	Functionality constraints
		Integration not always trivial
		No control over upgrades and maintenance
		Unnecessary features that consume extra resources
		Often inadequate reliability and stability
		Multiple-vendor incompatibilities
Custom development	Complete change freedom	Expensive, unpredictable development
	Smaller, often simpler implementations	Unpredictable availability date
		Undefined maintenance model
	Often better performance	Often immature and fragile
	Control of development and enhancement	Single-platform dependency
		Drain on expert resources

3.2   IMPROVING SOFTWARE PROCESSES

Process is an overloaded term. For software-oriented organizations, there are many processes and subprocesses. I use three distinct process perspectives.

- *Metaprocess:* an organization's policies, procedures, and practices for pursuing a software-intensive line of business. The focus of this process is on organizational economics, long-term strategies, and a software ROI.

- *Macroprocess:* a project's policies, procedures, and practices for producing a complete software product within certain cost, schedule, and quality constraints. The focus of the macroprocess is on creating an adequate instance of the metaprocess for a specific set of constraints.

- *Microprocess:* a project team's policies, procedures, and practices for achieving an artifact of the software process. The focus of the microprocess is on achieving an intermediate product baseline with adequate quality and adequate functionality as economically and rapidly as practical.

TABLE 3-4. *Three levels of process and their attributes*

ATTRIBUTES	METAPROCESS	MACROPROCESS	MICROPROCESS
Subject	Line of business	Project	Iteration
Objectives	Line-of-business profitability Competitiveness	Project profitability Risk management Project budget, schedule, quality	Resource management Risk resolution Milestone budget, schedule, quality
Audience	Acquisition authorities, customers Organizational management	Software project managers Software engineers	Subproject managers Software engineers
Metrics	Project predictability Revenue, market share	On budget, on schedule Major milestone success Project scrap and rework	On budget, on schedule Major milestone progress Release/iteration scrap and rework
Concerns	Bureaucracy vs. standardization	Quality vs. financial performance	Content vs. schedule
Time scales	6 to 12 months	1 to many years	1 to 6 months

Although these three levels of process overlap somewhat, they have different objectives, audiences, metrics, concerns, and time scales, as shown in Table 3-4. The macroprocess is the project-level process that affects the cost estimation model discussed in this chapter.

To achieve success, most software projects require an incredibly complex web of sequential and parallel steps. As the scale of a project increases, more overhead steps must be included just to manage the complexity of this web. All project processes consist of productive activities and overhead activities. Productive activities result in tangible progress toward the end product. For software efforts, these activities include prototyping, modeling, coding, debugging, and user documentation. Overhead activities that have an intangible impact on the end product are required in plan preparation, documentation, progress monitoring, risk assessment, financial assessment, configuration control, quality assessment, integration, testing, late scrap and rework, management, personnel training, business administration, and other tasks. Overhead activities include many value-added efforts, but, in general, the less effort devoted to these activities, the more effort that can be expended in productive activities. The objective of process improvement is to maximize the allocation of resources to productive activities and minimize the impact of overhead activities on resources such as personnel, computers, and schedule.

Some people may be offended by my categorization of late scrap and rework and personnel training as overhead activities that need to be minimized. I have modified scrap and rework with *late* to differentiate it from the sort of scrap and rework that is a natural by-product of prototyping efforts. Early scrap and rework is a productive necessity for most projects to resolve the innumerable unknowns in the solution space, but it is clearly undesirable in the later phases of the life cycle. With a good process, it is clearly unnecessary.

People will argue that personnel training cannot be a bad thing, but it is for a project. Training is an organizational responsibility, not a project responsibility. Any project manager who bears the burden of training people in processes, technologies, or tools is far worse off than a project manager who has a fully trained work force. Staffing every project with a fully trained work force may not be possible, but employing trained people is always better than employing untrained people, other things being equal. In this sense, training is not considered a value-added activity.

The quality of the software process strongly affects the required effort and therefore the schedule for producing the software product. In practice, the difference between a good process and a bad one will affect overall cost estimates by 50% to 100%, and the reduction in effort will improve the overall schedule. Furthermore, a better process can have an even greater effect in reducing the time it will take for the team to achieve the product vision with the required quality. Why is this true?

Schedule improvement has at least three dimensions.

1. We could take an N-step process and improve the efficiency of each step.

2. We could take an N-step process and eliminate some steps so that it is now only an M-step process.

3. We could take an N-step process and use more concurrency in the activities being performed or the resources being applied.

Many organizational time-to-market improvement strategies emphasize the first dimension. However, the focus of most process improvements described in this book is on achieving the second and third dimensions, where there is greater potential. In particular, the primary focus of process improvement should be on achieving an adequate solution in the minimum number of iterations and eliminating as much downstream scrap and rework as possible.

Every instance of rework introduces a sequential set of tasks that must be redone. For example, suppose that a team completes the sequential steps of analysis, design, coding, and testing of a feature, then uncovers a design flaw in testing. Now a sequence of redesign, recode, and retest is required. These task sequences are the primary obstacle to schedule compression. Notwithstanding technological breakthroughs that

3.3 IMPROVING TEAM EFFECTIVENESS   **43**

can eliminate complete process steps, the primary impact of process improvement should be the reduction of scrap and rework in late life-cycle phases.

In a perfect software engineering world with an immaculate problem description, an obvious solution space, a development team of experienced geniuses, adequate resources, and stakeholders with common goals, we could execute a software development process in one iteration with almost no scrap and rework. Because we work in an imperfect world, however, we need to manage engineering activities so that scrap and rework profiles do not have an impact on the win conditions of any stakeholder. This should be the underlying premise for most process improvements.

3.3   IMPROVING TEAM EFFECTIVENESS

It has long been understood that differences in personnel account for the greatest swings in productivity. The original COCOMO model, for example, suggests that the combined effects of personnel skill and experience can have an impact on productivity of as much as a factor of four. This is the difference between an unskilled team of amateurs and a veteran team of experts. In practice, it is risky to assess a given team as being off-scale in either direction. For a large team of, say, 50 people or more, you almost always end up with nominal people and experience. It is impossible to staff a nontrivial project with personnel who all have optimal experience, are fully trained in the tools and technologies, and possess IQs greater than 130. If you did pull this off, the team would likely be dysfunctional. So the old "Just hire good people" approach needs to be applied carefully. A better way to state this is "Just formulate a good team."

Balance and coverage are two of the most important aspects of excellent teams. Whenever a team is out of balance, it is vulnerable. To use a sports analogy, a football team has a need for diverse skills, very much like a software development team. There has rarely been a great football team that didn't have great coverage: offense, defense, and special teams, coaching and personnel, first stringers and reserve players, passing and running. Great teams need coverage across key positions with strong individual players. But a team loaded with superstars, all striving to set individual records and competing to be the team leader, can be embarrassed by a balanced team of solid players with a few leaders focused on the team result of winning the game.

Teamwork is much more important than the sum of the individuals. With software teams, a project manager needs to configure a balance of solid talent with highly skilled people in the leverage positions. Some maxims of team management include the following:

- A well-managed project can succeed with a nominal engineering team.

- A mismanaged project will almost never succeed, even with an expert team of engineers.

- A well-architected system can be built by a nominal team of software builders.

- A poorly architected system will flounder even with an expert team of builders.

In examining how to staff a software project, Boehm offered the following five staffing principles [Boehm, 1981]. (Quotations are presented in *italics*.)

1. *The principle of top talent: Use better and fewer people.*

   ▲ This tenet is fundamental, but it can be applied only so far. There is a "natural" team size for most jobs, and being grossly over or under this size is bad for team dynamics because it results in too little or too much pressure on individuals to perform.

2. *The principle of job matching: Fit the tasks to the skills and motivation of the people available.*

   ▲ This principle seems obvious. On a football team you use a good leader as your coach, a good passer as the quarterback, a superfast runner as a wide receiver, and a 300-pound bruiser as a lineman. With software engineers, it is more difficult to discriminate the mostly intangible personnel skills and optimal task allocations. Personal agendas also complicate assignments. In football, the 300-pound lineman would never think about being promoted to quarterback; the skill sets are too obviously different. On software teams, however, it is common for talented programmers to seek promotions to architects and managers. I think the skill sets are equally different, because most superstar programmers are innately unqualified to be architects and managers, and vice versa. Yet individuals and even their organizations often view such promotions as desirable. There are countless cases of great software engineers being promoted prematurely into positions for which they were unskilled and unqualified. This makes a B player out of an A player, taking an A player out of a moderate- to high-leverage position and putting a B player in a higher leverage position. It's a double whammy.

3. *The principle of career progression: An organization does best in the long run by helping its people to self-actualize.*

   ▲ Good performers usually self-actualize in any environment. Organizations can help and hinder employee self-actualization, but organizational energy will benefit average and below-average performers the most. Organizational training programs are typically strategic undertakings with educational value. Project training programs are purely tactical, intended to be useful and applied the day after training ends.

4. *The principle of team balance: Select people who will complement and harmonize with one another.*

▲ Although this principle sounds a little drippy, its spirit is the paramount factor in good teamwork. Software team balance has many dimensions, and when a team is unbalanced in any one of them, a project becomes seriously at risk. These dimensions include:

Raw skills: intelligence, objectivity, creativity, organization, analytical thinking

Psychological makeup: leaders and followers, risk takers and conservatives, visionaries and nitpickers, cynics and optimists

Objectives: financial, feature set, quality, timeliness

5. *The principle of phaseout: Keeping a misfit on the team doesn't benefit anyone.*

▲ This is really a subprinciple of the other four. A misfit gives you a reason to find a better person or to live with fewer people. A misfit demotivates other team members, will not self-actualize, and disrupts the team balance in some dimension. Misfits are obvious, and it is almost never right to procrastinate weeding them out.

Software development is a team sport. Managers must nurture a culture of teamwork and results rather than individual accomplishment. Of the five principles, team balance and job matching should be the primary objectives. The top talent and phaseout principles are secondary objectives because they must be applied within the context of team balance. Finally, although career progression needs to be addressed as an employment practice, individuals or organizations that stress it over the success of the team will not last long in the marketplace.

Software project managers need many leadership qualities in order to enhance team effectiveness. Although these qualities are intangible and outside the scope of this book, I would be remiss if I didn't mention them. The following are some crucial attributes of successful software project managers that deserve much more attention:

1. Hiring skills. Few decisions are as important as hiring decisions. Placing the right person in the right job seems obvious but is surprisingly hard to achieve.

2. Customer-interface skill. Avoiding adversarial relationships among stakeholders is a prerequisite for success.

3. Decision-making skill. The jillion books written about management have failed to provide a clear definition of this attribute. We all know a good leader when we run into one, and decision-making skill seems obvious despite its intangible definition.

4. Team-building skill. Teamwork requires that a manager establish trust, motivate progress, exploit eccentric prima donnas, transition average people into top performers, eliminate misfits, and consolidate diverse opinions into a team direction.

5. Selling skill. Successful project managers must sell all stakeholders (including themselves) on decisions and priorities, sell candidates on job positions, sell changes to the status quo in the face of resistance, and sell achievements against objectives. In practice, selling requires continuous negotiation, compromise, and empathy.

3.4   IMPROVING AUTOMATION THROUGH SOFTWARE ENVIRONMENTS

The tools and environment used in the software process generally have a linear effect on the productivity of the process. Planning tools, requirements management tools, visual modeling tools, compilers, editors, debuggers, quality assurance analysis tools, test tools, and user interfaces provide crucial automation support for evolving the software engineering artifacts. Above all, configuration management environments provide the foundation for executing and instrumenting the process. At first order, the isolated impact of tools and automation generally allows improvements of 20% to 40% in effort. However, tools and environments must be viewed as the primary delivery vehicle for process automation and improvement, so their impact can be much higher.

Section 3.2 focused on process improvements that reduce scrap and rework, thereby eliminating steps and minimizing the number of iterations in the process. The other form of process improvement is to increase the efficiency of certain steps. This is one of the primary contributions of the environment: to automate manual tasks that are inefficient or error-prone. The transition to a mature software process introduces new challenges and opportunities for management control of concurrent activities and for tangible progress and quality assessment. Project experience has shown that a highly integrated environment is necessary both to facilitate and to enforce management control of the process. An environment that provides semantic integration (in which the environment understands the detailed meaning of the development artifacts) and process automation can improve productivity, improve software quality, and accelerate the adoption of modern techniques. An environment that supports incremental compilation, automated system builds, and integrated regression testing can provide rapid turnaround for iterative development and allow development teams to iterate more freely.

An important emphasis of a modern approach is to define the development and maintenance environment as a first-class artifact of the process. A robust, integrated development environment must support the automation of the development process. This environment should include requirements management, document automation, host/target programming tools, automated regression testing, continuous and integrated change management, and feature/defect tracking. A common thread in successful software projects is that they hire good people and provide them with good tools to accomplish their jobs. Automation of the design process provides payback in quality, the ability to estimate costs and schedules, and overall productivity using a smaller team. Integrated toolsets play an increasingly important role in incremental/iterative development by allowing the designers to traverse quickly among development artifacts and keep them up-to-date.

Round-trip engineering is a term used to describe the key capability of environments that support iterative development. As we have moved into maintaining different information repositories for the engineering artifacts, we need automation support to ensure efficient and error-free transition of data from one artifact to another. *Forward engineering* is the automation of one engineering artifact from another, more abstract representation. For example, compilers and linkers have provided automated transition of source code into executable code. *Reverse engineering* is the generation or modification of a more abstract representation from an existing artifact (for example, creating a visual design model from a source code representation).

Round-trip engineering describes the environment support needed to change an artifact freely and have other artifacts automatically changed so that consistency is maintained among the entire set of requirements, design, implementation, and deployment artifacts. This concept is developed more fully in Chapter 12.

As architectures started using heterogeneous components, platforms, and languages, the complexity of building, controlling, and maintaining large-scale webs of components introduced new needs for configuration control and automation of build management. However, today's environments do not come close to supporting automation to the extent possible. For example, automated test case construction from use case and scenario descriptions has not yet evolved to support anything beyond the most trivial cases, such as unit test scenarios.

One word of caution is necessary in describing the economic improvements associated with tools and environments. It is common for tool vendors to make relatively accurate individual assessments of life-cycle activities to support claims about the potential economic impact of their tools. For example, it is easy to find statements such as the following from companies in a particular tool niche:

- Requirements analysis and evolution activities consume 40% of life-cycle costs.

- Software design activities have an impact on more than 50% of the resources.

- Coding and unit testing activities consume about 50% of software development effort and schedule.

- Test activities can consume as much as 50% of a project's resources.

- Configuration control and change management are critical activities that can consume as much as 25% of resources on a large-scale project.

- Documentation activities can consume more than 30% of project engineering resources.

- Project management, business administration, and progress assessment can consume as much as 30% of project budgets.

Taken individually, none of these claims is really wrong; they are just too simplistic. (Given these claims, no wonder it takes 275% of budget and schedule resources to complete most projects!) When taken together, the claims can be very misleading. Beware of this type of conclusion:

> *This testing tool will improve your testing productivity by 20%. Because test activities consume 50% of the life cycle, there will be a 10% net productivity gain to the entire project. With a $1 million budget, you can afford to spend $100,000 on test tools.*

The interrelationships of all the software development activities and tools are far too complex for such simple assertions to be reasonable. In my experience, the combined effect of all tools tends to be less than about 40%, and most of this benefit is not realized without some corresponding change in process. It is unlikely that any individual tool will improve a project's productivity by more than 5%. In general, you are better off normalizing most vendor claims to the virtual 275% total than the 100% total you must deal with in the real world.

3.5 ACHIEVING REQUIRED QUALITY

Many of what are accepted today as software best practices are derived from the development process and technologies summarized in this chapter. These practices have impact in addition to improving cost efficiency. Many of them also permit improvements in quality for the same cost. Table 3-5 summarizes some dimensions of quality improvement.

TABLE 3-5.   *General quality improvements with a modern process*

QUALITY DRIVER	CONVENTIONAL PROCESS	MODERN ITERATIVE PROCESSES
Requirements misunderstanding	Discovered late	Resolved early
Development risk	Unknown until late	Understood and resolved early
Commercial components	Mostly unavailable	Still a quality driver, but trade-offs must be resolved early in the life cycle
Change management	Late in the life cycle, chaotic and malignant	Early in the life cycle, straight-forward and benign
Design errors	Discovered late	Resolved early
Automation	Mostly error-prone manual procedures	Mostly automated, error-free evolution of artifacts
Resource adequacy	Unpredictable	Predictable
Schedules	Overconstrained	Tunable to quality, performance, and technology
Target performance	Paper-based analysis or separate simulation	Executing prototypes, early per-formance feedback, quantitative understanding
Software process rigor	Document-based	Managed, measured, and tool-supported

Key practices that improve overall software quality include the following:

- Focusing on driving requirements and critical use cases early in the life cycle, focusing on requirements completeness and traceability late in the life cycle, and focusing throughout the life cycle on a balance between requirements evolution, design evolution, and plan evolution

- Using metrics and indicators to measure the progress and quality of an architecture as it evolves from a high-level prototype into a fully compliant product

- Providing integrated life-cycle environments that support early and contin-uous configuration control, change management, rigorous design methods, document automation, and regression test automation

- Using visual modeling and higher level languages that support architectural control, abstraction, reliable programming, reuse, and self-documentation

- Early and continuous insight into performance issues through demonstration-based evaluations

Improved insight into run-time performance issues is even more important as projects incorporate mixtures of commercial components and custom-developed components. Conventional development processes stressed early sizing and timing estimates of computer program resource utilization. However, the typical chronology of events in performance assessment was as follows:

- Project inception. The proposed design was asserted to be low risk with adequate performance margin.

- Initial design review. Optimistic assessments of adequate design margin were based mostly on paper analysis or rough simulation of the critical threads. In most cases, the actual application algorithms and database sizes were fairly well understood. However, the infrastructure—including the operating system overhead, the database management overhead, and the interprocess and network communications overhead—and all the secondary threads were typically misunderstood.

- Mid-life-cycle design review. The assessments started whittling away at the margin, as early benchmarks and initial tests began exposing the optimism inherent in earlier estimates.

- Integration and test. Serious performance problems were uncovered, necessitating fundamental changes in the architecture. The underlying infrastructure was usually the scapegoat, but the real culprit was immature use of the infrastructure, immature architectural solutions, or poorly understood early design trade-offs.

This sequence occurred because early performance insight was based solely on naïve engineering judgment of innumerable criteria. In most large-scale distributed systems composed of many interacting components, a demonstration-based approach can provide significantly more-accurate assessments of performance issues. These early demonstrations may be on host or target platforms or partial network configurations. In any case, they can be planned and managed to provide a fruitful engineering exercise. Early performance issues are typical. They may even be healthy, because they tend to expose architectural flaws or weaknesses in commercial components early in the life cycle when the right trade-offs can be made.

3.6   PEER INSPECTIONS: A PRAGMATIC VIEW

Peer inspections are frequently overhyped as the key aspect of a quality system. In my experience, peer reviews are valuable as secondary mechanisms, but they are rarely significant contributors to quality compared with the following primary quality mechanisms and indicators, which should be emphasized in the management process:

- Transitioning engineering information from one artifact set to another, thereby assessing the consistency, feasibility, understandability, and technology constraints inherent in the engineering artifacts

- Major milestone demonstrations that force the artifacts to be assessed against tangible criteria in the context of relevant use cases

- Environment tools (compilers, debuggers, analyzers, automated test suites) that ensure representation rigor, consistency, completeness, and change control

- Life-cycle testing for detailed insight into critical trade-offs, acceptance criteria, and requirements compliance

- Change management metrics for objective insight into multiple-perspective change trends and convergence or divergence from quality and progress goals

Although I believe that inspections are overemphasized, in certain cases they provide a significant return. One value of inspections is in the professional development of a team. It is generally useful to have the products of junior team members reviewed by senior mentors. Putting the products of amateurs into the hands of experts and vice versa is a good mechanism for accelerating the acquisition of knowledge and skill in new personnel. Gross blunders can be caught and feedback can be appropriately channeled, so that bad practices are not perpetuated. This is one of the best ways for junior software engineers to learn.

Inspections are also a good vehicle for holding authors accountable for quality products. All authors of software and documentation should have their products scrutinized as a natural by-product of the process. Therefore, the coverage of inspections should be across all authors rather than across all components. Junior authors need to have a random component inspected periodically, and they can learn by inspecting the products of senior authors. Varying levels of informal inspection are performed continuously when developers are reading or integrating software with another author's software, and during testing by independent test teams. However, this "inspection" is much more tangibly focused on integrated and executable aspects of the overall system.

Finally, a critical component deserves to be inspected by several people, preferably those who have a stake in its quality, performance, or feature set. An inspection focused on resolving an existing issue can be an effective way to determine cause or arrive at a resolution once the cause is understood.

Notwithstanding these benefits of inspections, many organizations overemphasize meetings and formal inspections, and require coverage across all engineering products. This approach can be extremely counterproductive. Only 20% of the technical artifacts (such as use cases, design models, source code, and test cases) deserve such detailed scrutiny when compared with other, more useful quality assurance activities. A process whose primary quality assurance emphasis is on inspections will not be cost-effective. Several published studies emphasize the importance and high ROI of inspections. I suspect that many of these studies have been written by career quality assurance professionals who exaggerate the need for their discipline. I am frequently a lone voice on this topic, but here is my rationale.

Significant or substantial design errors or architecture issues are rarely obvious from a superficial review unless the inspection is narrowly focused on a particular issue. And most inspections *are* superficial. Today's systems are highly complex, with innumerable components, concurrent execution, distributed resources, and other equally demanding dimensions of complexity. It would take human intellects similar to those of world-class chess players to comprehend the dynamic interactions within some simple software systems under some simple use cases. Consequently, random human inspections tend to degenerate into comments on style and first-order semantic issues. They rarely result in the discovery of real performance bottlenecks, serious control issues (such as deadlocks, races, or resource contention), or architectural weaknesses (such as flaws in scalability, reliability, or interoperability). In all but trivial cases, architectural issues are exposed only through more rigorous engineering activities such as the following:

- Analysis, prototyping, or experimentation

- Constructing design models

- Committing the current state of the design model to an executable implementation

- Demonstrating the current implementation strengths and weaknesses in the context of critical subsets of the use cases and scenarios

- Incorporating lessons learned back into the models, use cases, implementations, and plans

Achieving architectural quality is inherent in an iterative process that evolves the artifact sets together in balance. The checkpoints along the way are numerous, including human review and inspections focused on critical issues. But these inspections are not the primary checkpoints. Early life-cycle artifacts are certainly more dependent on subjective human review than later ones are. Focusing a large percentage of a project's resources on human inspections is bad practice and only perpetuates the existence of low-value-added box checkers who have little impact on project success. Look at any successful software effort and ask the key designers, testers, or developers about the discriminators of their success. It is unlikely that any of them will cite meetings, inspections, or documents.

Quality assurance is everyone's responsibility and should be integral to almost all process activities instead of a separate discipline performed by quality assurance specialists. Evaluating and assessing the quality of the evolving engineering baselines should be the job of an engineering team that is independent of the architecture and development team. Their life-cycle assessment of the evolving artifacts would typically include change management, trend analysis, and testing, as well as inspection.

The Old Way and the New

Over the past two decades there has been a significant re-engineering of the software development process. Many of the conventional management and technical practices have been replaced by new approaches that combine recurring themes of successful project experience with advances in software engineering technology. This transition was motivated by the insatiable demand for more software features produced more rapidly under more competitive pressure to reduce cost. In the commercial software industry, the combination of competitive pressures, profitability, diversity of customers, and rapidly changing technology caused many organizations to initiate new management approaches. In the defense and aerospace industries, many systems required a new management paradigm to respond to budget pressures, the dynamic and diverse threat environment, the long operational lifetime of systems, and the predominance of large-scale, complex applications.

> **Key Points**
>
> ▲ Conventional software engineering has numerous well-established principles. Many are still valid; others are obsolete.
>
> ▲ A modern software management process will incorporate many conventional principles but will also transition to some substantially new approaches.

4.1   THE PRINCIPLES OF CONVENTIONAL SOFTWARE ENGINEERING

There are many descriptions of engineering software "the old way." After years of software development experience, the software industry has learned many lessons and formulated many principles. This section describes one view of today's software engineering principles as a benchmark for introducing the primary themes discussed throughout the remainder of the book. The benchmark I have chosen is a brief article titled "Fifteen Principles of Software Engineering" [Davis, 1994]. The article was subsequently expanded into a book [Davis, 1995] that enumerates 201 principles. Despite its title, the article describes the top 30 principles, and it is as good a summary as any of the conventional wisdom within the software industry. While I endorse much of this wisdom, I believe some of it is obsolete. Davis's top 30 principles are quoted next, in *italics*. For each principle, I comment on whether the perspective provided later in this book would endorse or change it. I make several assertions here that are left unsubstantiated until later chapters.

1. *Make quality #1. Quality must be quantified and mechanisms put into place to motivate its achievement.*

    ▲ Defining quality commensurate with the project at hand is important but is not easily done at the outset of a project. Consequently, a modern process framework strives to understand the trade-offs among features, quality, cost, and schedule as early in the life cycle as possible. Until this understanding is achieved, it is not possible to specify or manage the achievement of quality.

2. *High-quality software is possible. Techniques that have been demonstrated to increase quality include involving the customer, prototyping, simplifying design, conducting inspections, and hiring the best people.*

    ▲ This principle is mostly redundant with the others.

3. *Give products to customers early. No matter how hard you try to learn users' needs during the requirements phase, the most effective way to determine real needs is to give users a product and let them play with it.*

    ▲ This is a key tenet of a modern process framework, and there must be several mechanisms to involve the customer throughout the life cycle. Depending on the domain, these mechanisms may include demonstrable prototypes, demonstration-based milestones, and alpha/beta releases.

4. *Determine the problem before writing the requirements. When faced with what they believe is a problem, most engineers rush to offer a solution. Before you try to solve a problem, be sure to explore all the alternatives and don't be blinded by the obvious solution.*

    ▲ This principle is a clear indication of the issues involved with the conventional requirements specification process. The parameters of the problem become more tangible as a solution evolves. A modern process framework evolves the problem and the solution together until the problem is well enough understood to commit to full production.

5. *Evaluate design alternatives. After the requirements are agreed upon, you must examine a variety of architectures and algorithms. You certainly do*

not want to use an "architecture" simply because it was used in the requirements specification.

▲ This principle seems anchored in the waterfall mentality in two ways: (1) The requirements precede the architecture rather than evolving together. (2) The architecture is incorporated in the requirements specification. While a modern process clearly promotes the analysis of design alternatives, these activities are done concurrently with requirements specification, and the notations and artifacts for requirements and architecture are explicitly decoupled.

6. *Use an appropriate process model. Each project must select a process that makes the most sense for that project on the basis of corporate culture, willingness to take risks, application area, volatility of requirements, and the extent to which requirements are well understood.*

   ▲ It's true that no individual process is universal. I use the term *process framework* to represent a flexible class of processes rather than a single rigid instance. Chapter 14 discusses configuration and tailoring of the process to the various needs of a project.

7. *Use different languages for different phases. Our industry's eternal thirst for simple solutions to complex problems has driven many to declare that the best development method is one that uses the same notation throughout the life cycle. Why should software engineers use Ada for requirements, design, and code unless Ada were optimal for all these phases?*

   ▲ This is an important principle. Chapter 6 describes an appropriate organization and recommended languages/notations for the primitive artifacts of the process.

8. *Minimize intellectual distance. To minimize intellectual distance, the software's structure should be as close as possible to the real-world structure.*

   ▲ This principle has been the primary motivation for the development of object-oriented techniques, component-based development, and visual modeling.

9. *Put techniques before tools. An undisciplined software engineer with a tool becomes a dangerous, undisciplined software engineer.*

   ▲ Although this principle is valid, it misses two important points: (1) A disciplined software engineer with good tools will outproduce disciplined software experts with no tools. (2) One of the best ways to promote, standardize, and deliver good techniques is through automation.

10. *Get it right before you make it faster. It is far easier to make a working program run faster than it is to make a fast program work. Don't worry about optimization during initial coding.*

▲ This is an insightful statement. It has been misstated by several software experts more or less as follows: "Early performance problems in a software system are a sure sign of downstream risk." Every successful, nontrivial software project I know of had performance issues arise early in the life cycle. I would argue that almost all immature architectures (especially large-scale ones) have performance issues in their first executable iterations. Having something executing (working) early is a prerequisite to understanding the complex performance trade-offs. It is just too difficult to get this insight through analysis.

11. *Inspect code. Inspecting the detailed design and code is a much better way to find errors than testing.*

▲ The value of this principle is overhyped for all but the simplest software systems. Today's hardware resources, programming languages, and automated environments enable automated analyses and testing to be done efficiently throughout the life cycle. Continuous and automated life-cycle testing is a necessity in any modern iterative development. General, undirected inspections (as opposed to inspections focused on known issues) rarely uncover architectural issues or global design trade-offs. This is not to say that all inspections are ineffective. When used judiciously and focused on a known issue, inspections are extremely effective at resolving problems. But this principle should not be in the top 15, especially considering that the industry's default practice is to overinspect.

12. *Good management is more important than good technology. The best technology will not compensate for poor management, and a good manager can produce great results even with meager resources. Good management motivates people to do their best, but there are no universal "right" styles of management.*

▲ My belief in this principle caused me to write this book. My only argument here is that the term *meager resources* is ambiguous. A great, well-managed team can do great things with a meager budget and schedule. Good management and a team meager in quality, on the other hand, are mutually exclusive, because a good manager will attract, configure, and retain a quality team.

13. *People are the key to success. Highly skilled people with appropriate experience, talent, and training are key. The right people with insufficient tools, languages, and process will succeed. The wrong people with appropriate tools, languages, and process will probably fail.*

▲ This principle is too low on the list.

14. *Follow with care. Just because everybody is doing something does not make it right for you. It may be right, but you must carefully assess its*

applicability to your environment. Object orientation, measurement, reuse, process improvement, CASE, prototyping—all these might increase quality, decrease cost, and increase user satisfaction. The potential of such techniques is often oversold, and benefits are by no means guaranteed or universal.

▲ This is sage advice, especially in a rapidly growing industry in which technology fads are difficult to distinguish from technology improvements. Trading off features, costs, and schedules does not always favor the most modern technologies.

15. *Take responsibility. When a bridge collapses we ask, "What did the engineers do wrong?" Even when software fails, we rarely ask this. The fact is that in any engineering discipline, the best methods can be used to produce awful designs, and the most antiquated methods to produce elegant designs.*

▲ This is a great corollary to item 14. It takes more than good methods, tools, and components to succeed. It also takes good people, good management, and a learning culture that is focused on forward progress even when confronted with numerous and inevitable intermediate setbacks.

16. *Understand the customer's priorities. It is possible the customer would tolerate 90% of the functionality delivered late if they could have 10% of it on time.*

▲ Understanding the customer's priorities is important, but only in balance with other stakeholder priorities. "The customer is always right" is a mentality that has probably resulted in more squandering of money than any other misconception. Particularly in the government contracting domain, but more generally whenever a customer contracts with a system integrator, the customer is frequently wrong.

17. *The more they see, the more they need. The more functionality (or performance) you provide a user, the more functionality (or performance) the user wants.*

▲ This principle is true, but it suggests that you would never want to show a user anything. It should read, "The more users see, the better they understand." Not all stakeholders are 100% driven by greed. They know that they have limited resources and that developers have constraints. Demonstrating intermediate results is a high-visibility activity that is necessary to synchronize stakeholder expectations. The ramification of this principle on a modern process is that the software project manager needs to have objective data with which to argue the inevitable change requests and maintain a balance of affordability, features, and risk.

18. ***Plan to throw one away.*** *One of the most important critical success factors is whether or not a product is entirely new. Such brand-new applications, architectures, interfaces, or algorithms rarely work the first time.*

▲ You should not *plan* to throw one away. Rather, you should plan to evolve a product from an immature prototype to a mature baseline. If you have to throw it away, OK, but don't plan on it from the outset. This may have been sage advice for the 100% custom, leading-edge software development projects of the past. In today's software systems, however, much of the componentry exists (at least the operating system, DBMS, GUI, network, and middleware), and much of what is built in the first pass can be conserved.

19. ***Design for change.*** *The architectures, components, and specification techniques you use must accommodate change.*

▲ This is a very simple statement that has proven to be exceedingly complex to realize. Basically, it says that we must predict the future and construct a framework that can accommodate change that is not yet well defined. Nevertheless, I endorse this principle wholeheartedly because it is critical to success. It is difficult to predict the future accurately, but attempting to predict the sorts of changes that are likely to occur in a system's life cycle is a useful exercise in risk management and a recurring theme of successful software projects.

20. ***Design without documentation is not design.*** *I have often heard software engineers say, "I have finished the design. All that is left is the documentation."*

▲ This principle is also anchored in the document-driven approach of the past, in which the documentation was separate from the software itself. With visual modeling and higher order programming languages, it is usually counterproductive to maintain separate documents for the purpose of describing the software design. High-level architecture documents can be extremely helpful if they are written crisply and concisely, but the primary artifacts used by the engineering team are the design notations, source code, and test baselines. I would modify this principle as follows, to better exploit today's technological advances: "Software artifacts should be mostly self-documenting." This principle is discussed at length in Chapter 6.

21. ***Use tools, but be realistic.*** *Software tools make their users more efficient.*

▲ This principle trivializes a crucial aspect of modern software engineering: the importance of the development environment. A mature process must be well established, automated, and instrumented. Iterative development projects require extensive automation. It is unwise to underinvest in the capital environment.

22. *Avoid tricks. Many programmers love to create programs with tricks—constructs that perform a function correctly, but in an obscure way. Show the world how smart you are by avoiding tricky code.*

   ▲ I find it hard to believe that this is one of the top 30 principles. It is difficult to draw the line between a "trick" and an innovative solution. I know exactly what Davis is getting at, but I would not want to enact a principle that has any connotation of stifling innovation. Obfuscated coding techniques should be avoided unless there are compelling reasons to use them. Unfortunately, such compelling reasons are common in nontrivial projects.

23. *Encapsulate. Information-hiding is a simple, proven concept that results in software that is easier to test and much easier to maintain.*

   ▲ Component-based design, object-oriented design, and modern design and programming notations have advanced this principle into mainstream practice. Encapsulation is as fundamental a technique to a software engineer as mathematics is to a physicist. It should be the sole subject of a semester course in universities that teach software engineering.

24. *Use coupling and cohesion. Coupling and cohesion are the best ways to measure software's inherent maintainability and adaptability.*

   ▲ This vital principle is difficult to apply. Coupling and cohesion are abstract descriptions of components for which I know of no well-established, objective definitions. Coupling and cohesion are therefore difficult to measure. Modern metrics for addressing maintainability and adaptability are centered on measuring the amount of software scrap and rework. Cohesive components with minimal coupling are more easily adapted with less scrap and rework. We can reason about the disease (too much coupling and too little cohesion) only by observing and measuring the symptoms (scrap and rework).

25. *Use the McCabe complexity measure. Although there are many metrics available to report the inherent complexity of software, none is as intuitive and easy to use as Tom McCabe's.*

   ▲ Complexity metrics are important for identifying some of the critical components that need special attention. In my experience, however, the really complex stuff is obvious, and it is rare to see these complexity measures used in field applications to manage a project or make decisions. These metrics are interesting from an academic perspective (metaproject research and strategic decision making) and can be useful in project management (if automated), but they do not belong in the top principles.

26. *Don't test your own software. Software developers should never be the primary testers of their own software.*

▲ This principle is often debated. On one hand, an independent test team offers an objective perspective. On the other hand, software developers need to take ownership of the quality of their products. In Chapter 11, I endorse both perspectives: Developers should test their own software, and so should a separate team.

27. *Analyze causes for errors. It is far more cost-effective to reduce the effect of an error by preventing it than it is to find and fix it. One way to do this is to analyze the causes of errors as they are detected.*

▲ On the surface, this is a good principle, especially in the construction phase, when errors are likely to repeat. But analyses of errors in complex software systems have found one of the critical sources to be overanalysis and overdesign on paper in the early stages of a project. To some degree, these activities were "error prevention" efforts. They resulted in a lower return on investment than would have been realized from committing to prototyping and construction activities, which would have made the errors more obvious and tangible. Therefore, I would restate this as two principles: (1) Don't be afraid to make errors in the engineering stage. (2) Analyze the cause for errors in the production stage.

28. *Realize that software's entropy increases. Any software system that undergoes continuous change will grow in complexity and will become more and more disorganized.*

▲ This is another remnant of conventional software architectures. Almost all software systems undergo continuous change, and the sign of a poor architecture is that its entropy increases in a way that is difficult to manage. Entropy tends to increase dangerously when interfaces are changed for tactical reasons. The integrity of an architecture is primarily strategic and inherent in its interfaces, and it must be controlled with intense scrutiny. Modern change management tools force a project to respect and enforce interface integrity. A quality architecture is one in which entropy increases minimally and change can be accommodated with stable, predictable results. An ideal architecture would permit change without any increase in entropy.

29. *People and time are not interchangeable. Measuring a project solely by person-months makes little sense.*

▲ This principle is timeless.

30. *Expect excellence. Your employees will do much better if you have high expectations for them.*

▲ This principle applies to all disciplines, not just software management.

I have used some provocative words in my comments. My purpose was neither to endorse nor to refute specifically Davis's principles, but rather to expose my biases and provoke thought. While I see tremendous merit in about half of the principles, the other half either need a change in priority or have been obsolesced by new technology.

4.2   THE PRINCIPLES OF MODERN SOFTWARE MANAGEMENT

Although the current software management principles described in Section 4.1 evolved from and improved on conventional techniques, they still do not emphasize the modern principles on which this book is based. Building on Davis's format, here are my top 10 principles of modern software management. (The first five, which are the main themes of my definition of an iterative process, are summarized in Figure 4-1.) The principles are in priority order, and the **bold-faced italicized** words are used throughout the book as shorthand for these expanded definitions.

1. Base the process on an ***architecture-first approach.*** This requires that a demonstrable balance be achieved among the driving requirements, the architecturally significant design decisions, and the life-cycle plans before the resources are committed for full-scale development.

2. Establish an ***iterative life-cycle process*** that confronts risk early. With today's sophisticated software systems, it is not possible to define the entire problem, design the entire solution, build the software, then test the end product in sequence. Instead, an iterative process that refines the problem understanding, an effective solution, and an effective plan over several iterations encourages a balanced treatment of all stakeholder objectives. Major risks must be addressed early to increase predictability and avoid expensive downstream scrap and rework.

3. Transition design methods to emphasize ***component-based development.*** Moving from a line-of-code mentality to a component-based mentality is necessary to reduce the amount of human-generated source code and custom development. A component is a cohesive set of preexisting lines of code, either in source or executable format, with a defined interface and behavior.

4. Establish a ***change management environment.*** The dynamics of iterative development, including concurrent workflows by different teams working on shared artifacts, necessitates objectively controlled baselines.

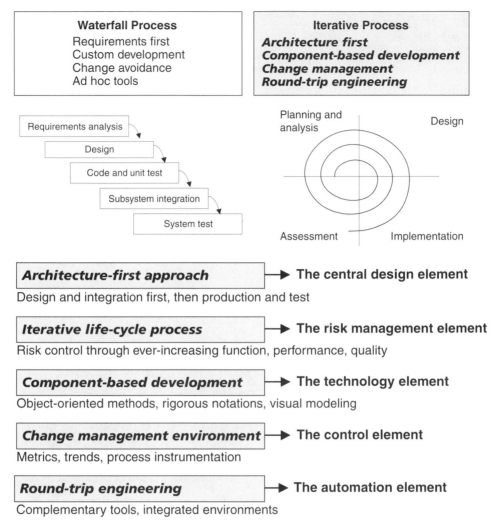

FIGURE 4-1. *The top five principles of a modern process*

5. **Enhance change freedom through tools that support *round-trip engineering*.** Round-trip engineering is the environment support necessary to automate and synchronize engineering information in different formats (such as requirements specifications, design models, source code, executable code, test cases). Without substantial automation of this bookkeeping, change management, documentation, and testing, it is difficult to reduce iteration cycles to manageable time frames in which change is encouraged rather than avoided. Change freedom is a necessity in an iterative process, and establishing an integrated environment is crucial.

6. **Capture design artifacts in rigorous, *model-based notation.*** A model-based approach (such as UML) supports the evolution of semantically rich graphical and textual design notations. Visual modeling with rigorous notations and a formal machine-processable language provides for far more objective measures than the traditional approach of human review and inspection of ad hoc design representations in paper documents.

7. **Instrument the process for *objective quality control* and progress assessment.** Life-cycle assessment of the progress and the quality of all intermediate products must be integrated into the process. The best assessment mechanisms are well-defined measures derived directly from the evolving engineering artifacts and integrated into all activities and teams.

8. **Use a *demonstration-based approach* to assess intermediate artifacts.** Transitioning the current state-of-the-product artifacts (whether the artifact is an early prototype, a baseline architecture, or a beta capability) into an executable demonstration of relevant scenarios stimulates earlier convergence on integration, a more tangible understanding of design trade-offs, and earlier elimination of architectural defects.

9. **Plan intermediate releases in groups of usage scenarios with *evolving levels of detail.*** It is essential that the software management process drive toward early and continuous demonstrations within the operational context of the system, namely its use cases. The evolution of project increments and generations must be commensurate with the current level of understanding of the requirements and architecture. Cohesive usage scenarios are then the primary mechanism for organizing requirements, defining iteration content, assessing implementations, and organizing acceptance testing.

10. **Establish a *configurable process* that is economically scalable.** No single process is suitable for all software developments. A pragmatic process framework must be configurable to a broad spectrum of applications. The process must ensure that there is economy of scale and return on investment by exploiting a common process spirit, extensive process automation, and common architecture patterns and components.

My top 10 principles have no scientific basis. They do, however, capture a balanced view of the recurring themes presented throughout this book. Table 4-1 maps what I consider to be the top 10 risks of the conventional process to the key attributes and principles of a modern process. Although the table contains gross generalities, at a high level it provides an introduction to the principles of a modern process.

TABLE 4-1. *Modern process approaches for solving conventional problems*

CONVENTIONAL PROCESS: TOP 10 RISKS	IMPACT	MODERN PROCESS: INHERENT RISK RESOLUTION FEATURES
1. Late breakage and excessive scrap/rework	Quality, cost, schedule	Architecture-first approach
		Iterative development
		Automated change management
		Risk-confronting process
2. Attrition of key personnel	Quality, cost, schedule	Successful, early iterations
		Trustworthy management and planning
3. Inadequate development resources	Cost, schedule	Environments as first-class artifacts of the process
		Industrial-strength, integrated environments
		Model-based engineering artifacts
		Round-trip engineering
4. Adversarial stakeholders	Cost, schedule	Demonstration-based review
		Use-case-oriented requirements/testing
5. Necessary technology insertion	Cost, schedule	Architecture-first approach
		Component-based development
6. Requirements creep	Cost, schedule	Iterative development
		Use case modeling
		Demonstration-based review
7. Analysis paralysis	Schedule	Demonstration-based review
		Use-case-oriented requirements/testing
8. Inadequate performance	Quality	Demonstration-based performance assessment
		Early architecture performance feedback
9. Overemphasis on artifacts	Schedule	Demonstration-based assessment
		Objective quality control
10. Inadequate function	Quality	Iterative development
		Early prototypes, incremental releases

4.3 TRANSITIONING TO AN ITERATIVE PROCESS

Modern software development processes have moved away from the conventional waterfall model, in which each stage of the development process is dependent on completion of the previous stage. Although there are variations, modern approaches generally require that an initial version of the system be rapidly constructed early in the development process, with an emphasis on addressing the high-risk areas, stabilizing the basic architecture, and refining the driving requirements (with extensive user input where possible). Development then proceeds as a series of iterations, building on the core architecture until the desired levels of functionality, performance, and robustness are achieved. (These iterations have been called spirals, increments, generations, or releases.) An iterative process emphasizes the whole system rather than the individual parts. Risk is reduced early in the life cycle through continuous integration and refinement of requirements, architecture, and plans. The downstream surprises that have plagued conventional software projects are avoided.

The economic benefits inherent in transitioning from the conventional waterfall model to an iterative development process are significant but difficult to quantify. As one benchmark of the expected economic impact of process improvement, consider the process exponent parameters of the COCOMO II model. (Appendix B provides more detail on the COCOMO model.) This exponent can range from 1.01 (virtually no diseconomy of scale) to 1.26 (significant diseconomy of scale). The parameters that govern the value of the process exponent are application precedentedness, process flexibility, architecture risk resolution, team cohesion, and software process maturity.

The following paragraphs map the process exponent parameters of COCOMO II to my top 10 principles of a modern process.

- **Application precedentedness.** Domain experience is a critical factor in understanding how to plan and execute a software development project. For unprecedented systems, one of the key goals is to confront risks and establish early precedents, even if they are incomplete or experimental. This is one of the primary reasons that the software industry has moved to an ***iterative life-cycle process.*** Early iterations in the life cycle establish precedents from which the product, the process, and the plans can be elaborated in ***evolving levels of detail.***

- **Process flexibility.** Development of modern software is characterized by such a broad solution space and so many interrelated concerns that there is a paramount need for continuous incorporation of changes. These changes may be inherent in the problem understanding, the solution space, or the plans. Project artifacts must be supported by an efficient ***change management*** environment commensurate with project needs. Both a rigid process and a chaotically changing process are destined for failure except with the most trivial projects. A ***configurable process*** that allows a common framework to be adapted across a range of projects is necessary to achieve a software return on investment.

- **Architecture risk resolution.** *Architecture-first* development is a crucial theme underlying a successful iterative development process. A project team develops and stabilizes an architecture before developing all the components that make up the entire suite of applications components. An *architecture-first* and *component-based development approach* forces the infrastructure, common mechanisms, and control mechanisms to be elaborated early in the life cycle and drives all component make/buy decisions into the architecture process. This approach initiates integration activity early in the life cycle as the verification activity of the design process and products. It also forces the development environment for life-cycle software engineering to be configured and exercised early in the life cycle, thereby ensuring early attention to testability and a foundation for *demonstration-based* assessment.

- **Team cohesion.** Successful teams are cohesive, and cohesive teams are successful. I am not sure which is the cause and which is the effect, but successful teams and cohesive teams share common objectives and priorities. Cohesive teams avoid sources of project turbulence and entropy that may result from difficulties in synchronizing project stakeholder expectations. While there are many reasons for such turbulence, one of the primary reasons is miscommunication, particularly in exchanging information solely through paper documents that present engineering information subjectively. Advances in technology (such as programming languages, UML, and visual modeling) have enabled more rigorous and understandable notations for communicating software engineering information, particularly in the requirements and design artifacts that previously were ad hoc and based completely on paper exchange. These *model-based* formats have also enabled the *round-trip engineering* support needed to establish change freedom sufficient for evolving design representations.

- **Software process maturity.** The Software Engineering Institute's Capability Maturity Model (CMM) is a well-accepted benchmark for software process assessment. Just as domain experience is crucial for avoiding the application risks and exploiting the available domain assets and lessons learned, software process maturity is crucial for avoiding software development risks and exploiting the organization's software assets and lessons learned. (The pros and cons of the CMM are discussed at length in Appendix E.) One of my key themes is that truly mature processes are enabled through an integrated environment that provides the appropriate level of automation to instrument the process for *objective quality control.*

A SOFTWARE MANAGEMENT PROCESS FRAMEWORK

Standardizing on a common process is a courageous undertaking for a software organization, and there is a wide spectrum of implementations. The process framework recommended in this book comprises only a handful of specific standards: life-cycle phases, life-cycle artifacts, life-cycle workflows, and life-cycle checkpoints. These elements are key discriminators in making the transition from the conventional approach to an iterative, line-of-business approach. I have seen organizations attempt to do less (too little, or no, standardization) and more (too much standardization), with little success in improving software return on investment. Process standardization requires a balanced approach.

The chapters in Part II describe the framework of a modern, iterative software management process: the life-cycle phases, the artifacts, the workflows, and the checkpoints. Architecture first is a key theme integrated throughout these chapters, and a chapter on architecture is sandwiched in with the others. Although this book is not intended to be about architecture, the management perspective of architecture and of the architecture's emphasis is vital to the success of the whole approach.

Life-Cycle Phases

The most discriminating characteristic of a successful software development process is the well-defined separation between "research and development" activities and "production" activities. When software projects do not succeed, the primary reason is usually a failure to crisply define and execute these two stages, with proper balance and appropriate emphasis. This is true for conventional as well as iterative processes. Most unsuccessful projects exhibit one of the following characteristics:

> **Key Points**
>
> ▲ The engineering stage of the life cycle evolves the plans, the requirements, and the architecture together, resolving the development risks. This stage concludes with an executable architecture baseline.
>
> ▲ The production stage of the life cycle constructs usable versions of capability within the context of the baseline plans, requirements, and architecture developed in the engineering stage.

- An overemphasis on research and development. Too many analyses or paper studies are performed, or the construction of engineering baselines is procrastinated. This emphasis is typical of and promoted in the conventional software process.

- An overemphasis on production. Rush-to-judgment designs, premature work by overeager coders, and continuous hacking are typical.

Successful modern projects—and even successful projects developed under the conventional process—tend to have a very well-defined project milestone when there is a noticeable transition from a research attitude to a production attitude. Earlier phases focus on achieving functionality. Later phases revolve around achieving a product that can be shipped to a customer, with explicit attention to robustness, performance, fit, and finish. This life-cycle balance, which is somewhat subtle and still too intangible, is one of the underpinnings of successful software project management.

A modern software development process must be defined to support the following:

- Evolution of the plans, requirements, and architecture, together with well-defined synchronization points
- Risk management and objective measures of progress and quality
- Evolution of system capabilities through demonstrations of increasing functionality

5.1   ENGINEERING AND PRODUCTION STAGES

The economic foundations presented in previous chapters provide a simple framework for deriving a life-cycle description. To achieve economies of scale and higher returns on investment, we must move toward a software manufacturing process driven by technological improvements in process automation and component-based development. At first order are the following two stages of the life cycle:

1. The engineering stage, driven by less predictable but smaller teams doing design and synthesis activities
2. The production stage, driven by more predictable but larger teams doing construction, test, and deployment activities

Table 5-1 summarizes the differences in emphasis between these two stages.

TABLE 5-1.   *The two stages of the life cycle: engineering and production*

LIFE-CYCLE ASPECT	ENGINEERING STAGE EMPHASIS	PRODUCTION STAGE EMPHASIS
Risk reduction	Schedule, technical feasibility	Cost
Products	Architecture baseline	Product release baselines
Activities	Analysis, design, planning	Implementation, testing
Assessment	Demonstration, inspection, analysis	Testing
Economics	Resolving diseconomies of scale	Exploiting economies of scale
Management	Planning	Operations

The transition between engineering and production is a crucial event for the various stakeholders. The production plan has been agreed upon, and there is a good enough understanding of the problem and the solution that all stakeholders can make a firm commitment to go ahead with production. Depending on the specifics of a project—and particularly the key discriminants described later in this chapter—the time and resources dedicated to these two stages can be highly variable.

Attributing only two stages to a life cycle is a little too coarse, too simplistic, for most applications. Consequently, the engineering stage is decomposed into two distinct phases, inception and elaboration, and the production stage into construction and transition. These four phases of the life-cycle process are loosely mapped to the conceptual framework of the spiral model [Boehm, 1988], as shown in Figure 5-1, and are named to depict the state of the project. In the figure, the size of the spiral corresponds to the inertia of the project with respect to the breadth and depth of the artifacts that have been developed. This inertia manifests itself in maintaining artifact consistency, regression testing, documentation, quality analyses, and configuration control. Increased inertia may have little, or at least very straightforward, impact on changing any given discrete component or activity. However, the reaction time for accommodating major architectural changes, major requirements changes, major planning shifts, or major organizational perturbations clearly increases in subsequent phases.

In most conventional life cycles, the phases are named after the primary activity within each phase: requirements analysis, design, coding, unit test, integration test, and system test. Conventional software development efforts emphasized a mostly sequential process, in which one activity was required to be complete before the next was begun.

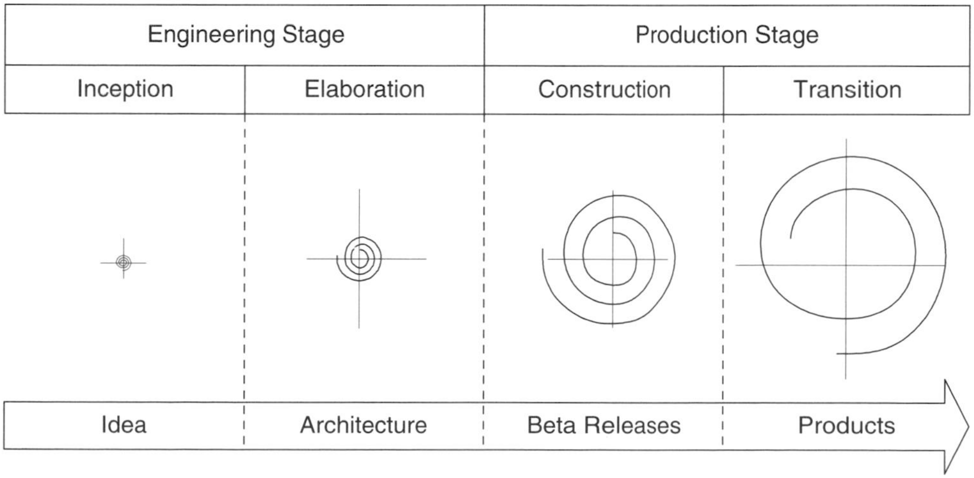

Engineering Stage		Production Stage	
Inception	Elaboration	Construction	Transition

Idea	Architecture	Beta Releases	Products

FIGURE 5-1. *The phases of the life-cycle process*

With an iterative process, each phase includes all the activities, in varying proportions. The activity levels during the four phases are discussed in Chapter 8. The primary objectives, essential activities, and general evaluation criteria for each phase are discussed here.

5.2 INCEPTION PHASE

The overriding goal of the inception phase is to achieve concurrence among stakeholders on the life-cycle objectives for the project.

PRIMARY OBJECTIVES

- Establishing the project's software scope and boundary conditions, including an operational concept, acceptance criteria, and a clear understanding of what is and is not intended to be in the product

- Discriminating the critical use cases of the system and the primary scenarios of operation that will drive the major design trade-offs

- Demonstrating at least one candidate architecture against some of the primary scenarios

- Estimating the cost and schedule for the entire project (including detailed estimates for the elaboration phase)

- Estimating potential risks (sources of unpredictability)

ESSENTIAL ACTIVITIES

- Formulating the scope of the project. This activity involves capturing the requirements and operational concept in an information repository that describes the user's view of the requirements. The information repository should be sufficient to define the problem space and derive the acceptance criteria for the end product.

- Synthesizing the architecture. Design trade-offs, problem space ambiguities, and available solution-space assets (technologies and existing components) are evaluated. An information repository is created that is sufficient to demonstrate the feasibility of at least one candidate architecture and an initial baseline of make/buy decisions so that the cost, schedule, and resource estimates can be derived.

- Planning and preparing a business case. Alternatives for risk management, staffing, iteration plans, and cost/schedule/profitability trade-offs are evaluated. The infrastructure (tools, processes, automation support) sufficient to support the life-cycle development task is determined.

PRIMARY EVALUATION CRITERIA

- Do all stakeholders concur on the scope definition and cost and schedule estimates?

- Are requirements understood, as evidenced by the fidelity of the critical use cases?

- Are the cost and schedule estimates, priorities, risks, and development processes credible?

- Do the depth and breadth of an architecture prototype demonstrate the preceding criteria? (The primary value of prototyping a candidate architecture is to provide a vehicle for understanding the scope and assessing the credibility of the development group in solving the particular technical problem.)

- Are actual resource expenditures versus planned expenditures acceptable?

5.3 ELABORATION PHASE

It is easy to argue that the elaboration phase is the most critical of the four phases. At the end of this phase, the "engineering" is considered complete and the project faces its reckoning: The decision is made whether or not to commit to the production phases. For most projects, this decision corresponds to the transition from a nimble operation with low cost risk to an operation with higher cost risk and substantial inertia. While the process must always accommodate changes, the elaboration phase activities must ensure that the architecture, requirements, and plans are stable enough, and the risks sufficiently mitigated, that the cost and schedule for the completion of the development can be predicted within an acceptable range. Conceptually, this level of fidelity would correspond to that necessary for an organization to commit to a fixed-price construction phase.

During the elaboration phase, an executable architecture prototype is built in one or more iterations, depending on the scope, size, risk, and novelty of the project. This effort addresses at least the critical use cases identified in the inception phase, which typically expose the top technical risks of the project. Although an evolutionary prototype of production-quality components is always a goal, it does not exclude the development of one or more exploratory, throw-away prototypes to mitigate specific risks such as design/requirements trade-offs, component feasibility analyses, or demonstrations to investors.

PRIMARY OBJECTIVES

- Baselining the architecture as rapidly as practical (establishing a configuration-managed snapshot in which all changes are rationalized, tracked, and maintained)

- Baselining the vision

- Baselining a high-fidelity plan for the construction phase

- Demonstrating that the baseline architecture will support the vision at a reasonable cost in a reasonable time

ESSENTIAL ACTIVITIES

- Elaborating the vision. This activity involves establishing a high-fidelity understanding of the critical use cases that drive architectural or planning decisions.

- Elaborating the process and infrastructure. The construction process, the tools and process automation support, and the intermediate milestones and their respective evaluation criteria are established.

- Elaborating the architecture and selecting components. Potential components are evaluated and make/buy decisions are sufficiently understood so that construction phase cost and schedule can be determined with confidence. The selected architectural components are integrated and assessed against the primary scenarios. Lessons learned from these activities may well result in a redesign of the architecture as alternative designs are considered or the requirements are reconsidered.

PRIMARY EVALUATION CRITERIA

- Is the vision stable?

- Is the architecture stable?

- Does the executable demonstration show that the major risk elements have been addressed and credibly resolved?

- Is the construction phase plan of sufficient fidelity, and is it backed up with a credible basis of estimate?

- Do all stakeholders agree that the current vision can be met if the current plan is executed to develop the complete system in the context of the current architecture?

- Are actual resource expenditures versus planned expenditures acceptable?

5.4   CONSTRUCTION PHASE

During the construction phase, all remaining components and application features are integrated into the application, and all features are thoroughly tested. Newly developed software is integrated where required. The construction phase represents a production process, in which emphasis is placed on managing resources and controlling operations to optimize costs, schedules, and quality. In this sense, the management mindset undergoes a transition from the development of intellectual property during inception and elaboration activities to the development of deployable products during construction and transition activities.

Many projects are large enough that parallel construction increments can be spawned. These parallel activities can significantly accelerate the availability of deployable releases; they can also increase the complexity of resource management and synchronization of workflows and teams. A robust architecture is highly correlated with an understandable plan. In other words, one of the critical qualities of any architecture is its ease of construction. This is one reason that the balanced development of the architecture and the plan is stressed during the elaboration phase.

PRIMARY OBJECTIVES

- Minimizing development costs by optimizing resources and avoiding unnecessary scrap and rework

- Achieving adequate quality as rapidly as practical

- Achieving useful versions (alpha, beta, and other test releases) as rapidly as practical

ESSENTIAL ACTIVITIES

- Resource management, control, and process optimization

- Complete component development and testing against evaluation criteria

- Assessment of product releases against acceptance criteria of the vision

PRIMARY EVALUATION CRITERIA

- Is this product baseline mature enough to be deployed in the user community? (Existing defects are not obstacles to achieving the purpose of the next release.)

- Is this product baseline stable enough to be deployed in the user community? (Pending changes are not obstacles to achieving the purpose of the next release.)

- Are the stakeholders ready for transition to the user community?

- Are actual resource expenditures versus planned expenditures acceptable?

5.5   TRANSITION PHASE

The transition phase is entered when a baseline is mature enough to be deployed in the end-user domain. This typically requires that a usable subset of the system has been achieved with acceptable quality levels and user documentation so that transition to the user will provide positive results. This phase could include any of the following activities:

1. Beta testing to validate the new system against user expectations

2. Beta testing and parallel operation relative to a legacy system it is replacing

3. Conversion of operational databases

4. Training of users and maintainers

The transition phase concludes when the deployment baseline has achieved the complete vision. For some projects, this life-cycle end point may coincide with the life-cycle starting point for the next version of the product. For others, it may coincide with a complete delivery of the information sets to a third party responsible for operation, maintenance, and enhancement.

The transition phase focuses on the activities required to place the software into the hands of the users. Typically, this phase includes several iterations, including beta releases, general availability releases, and bug-fix and enhancement releases. Considerable effort is expended in developing user-oriented documentation, training users, supporting users in their initial product use, and reacting to user feedback. (At this point in the life cycle, user feedback should be confined mostly to product tuning, configuring, installing, and usability issues.)

PRIMARY OBJECTIVES

- Achieving user self-supportability

- Achieving stakeholder concurrence that deployment baselines are complete and consistent with the evaluation criteria of the vision

- Achieving final product baselines as rapidly and cost-effectively as practical

ESSENTIAL ACTIVITIES

- Synchronization and integration of concurrent construction increments into consistent deployment baselines

- Deployment-specific engineering (cutover, commercial packaging and production, sales rollout kit development, field personnel training)
- Assessment of deployment baselines against the complete vision and acceptance criteria in the requirements set

EVALUATION CRITERIA

- Is the user satisfied?
- Are actual resource expenditures versus planned expenditures acceptable?

Each of the four phases consists of one or more iterations in which some technical capability is produced in demonstrable form and assessed against a set of criteria. An iteration (discussed in Chapter 8) represents a sequence of activities for which there is a well-defined intermediate event (a milestone, discussed in Chapter 9); the scope and results of the iteration are captured via discrete artifacts (discussed in Chapter 6). Whereas major milestones at the end of each phase use formal (stakeholder-approved) versions of evaluation criteria and release descriptions, minor milestones use informal (internally controlled) versions of these artifacts. Each phase corresponds to the completion of a sufficient number of iterations to achieve a given overall project state. The transition from one phase to the next maps more to a significant business decision than to the completion of a specific software development activity. These intermediate phase transitions are the primary anchor points of the software process, when technical and management perspectives are brought into synchronization and agreement among all stakeholders is achieved with respect to the current understanding of the requirements, design, and plan to complete.

Artifacts of the Process

Conventional software projects focused on the sequential development of software artifacts: build the requirements, construct a design model traceable to the requirements, build an implementation traceable to the design model, and compile and test the implementation for deployment. This process can work for small-scale, purely custom developments in which the design representation, implementation representation, and deployment representation are closely aligned. For example, a single program that is intended to run on a single computer of a single type and is composed entirely of special-purpose custom components can be constructed with straightforward traceability among all the representations.

> **Key Points**
>
> ▲ The artifacts of the process are organized into five sets: management, requirements, design, implementation, and deployment.
>
> ▲ The management artifacts capture the information necessary to synchronize stakeholder expectations.
>
> ▲ The requirements, design, implementation, and deployment artifacts are captured in rigorous notations that support automated analysis and browsing.

However, this approach doesn't work very well for most of today's software systems, in which the system complexity (in many dimensions) results in such numerous risks and subtle traceability relationships that you cannot efficiently use a simplistic sequential transformation. Most modern systems are composed of numerous components (some custom, some reused, some commercial products) intended to execute in a heterogeneous network of distributed platforms. They require a very different sequence of artifact evolution and a very different approach to traceability.

Over the past 20 years, the software industry has matured and has transitioned the management process to be iterative. Rather than being built sequentially, the artifacts are evolved together, and the constraints, the different levels of abstractions, and the degrees of freedom are balanced among competing alternatives. Recurring themes from successful projects demonstrate that the software artifacts evolve together with balanced levels of detail. Artifacts do not evolve in a one-way, linear progression from requirements to design to implementation to deployment. Choices about implementation and deployment affect the way in which the requirements are stated and the way in which the design proceeds. Information and decisions can flow in various ways among artifacts. The purpose of a good development process is to remove inappropriate, premature constraints on the design and to accommodate the real engineering constraints.

And what is the impact of iterative development on evolving artifacts? The primary difference from the conventional approach is that within each life-cycle phase, the workflow activities do not progress in a simple linear way, nor does artifact building proceed monotonically from one artifact to another. Instead, the focus of activities sweeps across artifacts repeatedly, incrementally enriching the entire system description and the process with the lessons learned in preserving balance across the breadth and depth of information.

6.1   THE ARTIFACT SETS

To make the development of a complete software system manageable, distinct collections of information are organized into artifact sets. Each set comprises related artifacts that are persistent and in a uniform representation format (such as English text, C++, Visual Basic, Java, a standard document template, a standard spreadsheet template, or a UML model). While a *set* represents a complete aspect of the system, an *artifact* represents cohesive information that typically is developed and reviewed as a single entity. In any given organization, project, or system, some of these artifacts— and even some sets—may be trivial or unnecessary. In general, however, some information needs to be captured in each set to satisfy all stakeholders.

Life-cycle software artifacts are organized into five distinct sets that are roughly partitioned by the underlying language of the set: management (ad hoc textual formats), requirements (organized text and models of the problem space), design (models of the solution space), implementation (human-readable programming language and associated source files), and deployment (machine-processable languages and associated files).

The emergence of rigorous and more powerful engineering notations for requirements and design artifacts that support architecture-first development was a major technology advance. In particular, the Unified Modeling Language has evolved into a suitable representation format, namely visual models with a well-specified syntax and semantics for requirements and design artifacts. Visual modeling using UML is a primitive notation for early life-cycle artifacts. The artifact sets are shown in Figure 6-1; their purposes and notations are described next.

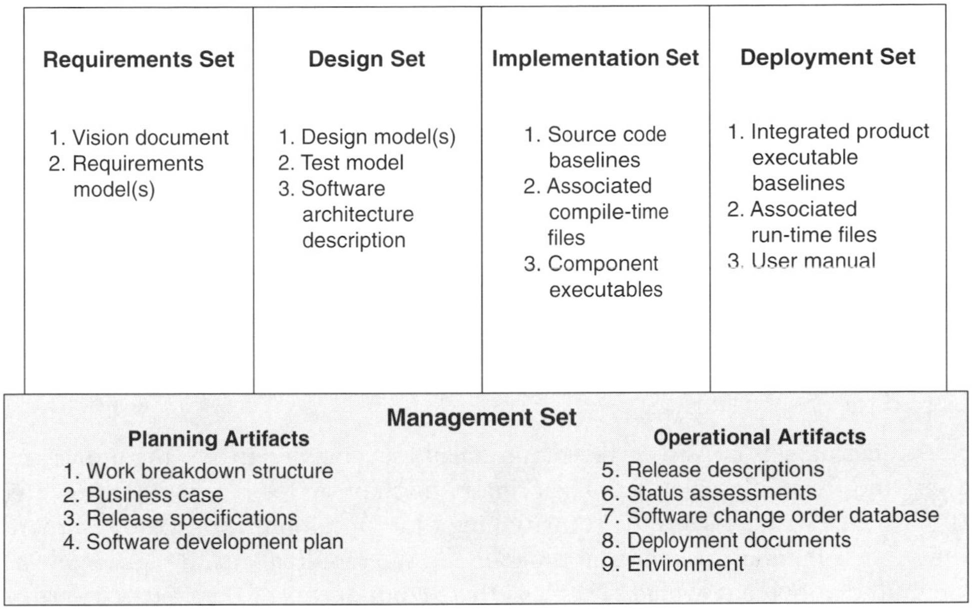

Requirements Set	Design Set	Implementation Set	Deployment Set
1. Vision document 2. Requirements model(s)	1. Design model(s) 2. Test model 3. Software architecture description	1. Source code baselines 2. Associated compile-time files 3. Component executables	1. Integrated product executable baselines 2. Associated run-time files 3. User manual

Management Set

Planning Artifacts	Operational Artifacts
1. Work breakdown structure 2. Business case 3. Release specifications 4. Software development plan	5. Release descriptions 6. Status assessments 7. Software change order database 8. Deployment documents 9. Environment

FIGURE 6-1. *Overview of the artifact sets*

6.1.1   THE MANAGEMENT SET

The management set captures the artifacts associated with process planning and execution. These artifacts use ad hoc notations, including text, graphics, or whatever representation is required to capture the "contracts" among project personnel (project management, architects, developers, testers, marketers, administrators), among stakeholders (funding authority, user, software project manager, organization manager, regulatory agency), and between project personnel and stakeholders. Specific artifacts included in this set are the work breakdown structure (activity breakdown and financial tracking mechanism), the business case (cost, schedule, profit expectations), the release specifications (scope, plan, objectives for release baselines), the software development plan (project process instance), the release descriptions (results of release baselines), the status assessments (periodic snapshots of project progress), the software change orders (descriptions of discrete baseline changes), the deployment documents (cutover plan, training course, sales rollout kit), and the environment (hardware and software tools, process automation, documentation, training collateral necessary to support the execution of the process described in the software development plan and the production of the engineering artifacts).

Management set artifacts are evaluated, assessed, and measured through a combination of the following:

- Relevant stakeholder review

- Analysis of changes between the current version of the artifact and previous versions (management trends and project performance changes in terms of cost, schedule, and quality)

- Major milestone demonstrations of the balance among all artifacts and, in particular, the accuracy of the business case and vision artifacts

6.1.2   THE ENGINEERING SETS

The engineering sets consist of the requirements set, the design set, the implementation set, and the deployment set. The primary mechanism for evaluating the evolving quality of each artifact set is the transitioning of information from set to set, thereby maintaining a balance of understanding among the requirements, design, implementation, and deployment artifacts. Each of these components of the system description evolves over time.

Requirements Set

Structured text is used for the vision statement, which documents the project scope that supports the contract between the funding authority and the project team. Ad hoc formats may also be used for supplementary specifications (such as regulatory requirements) and user mockups or other prototypes that capture requirements. UML notation is used for engineering representations of requirements models (use case models, domain models). The requirements set is the primary engineering context for evaluating the other three engineering artifact sets and is the basis for test cases.

Requirements artifacts are evaluated, assessed, and measured through a combination of the following:

- Analysis of consistency with the release specifications of the management set

- Analysis of consistency between the vision and the requirements models

- Mapping against the design, implementation, and deployment sets to evaluate the consistency and completeness and the semantic balance between information in the different sets

- Analysis of changes between the current version of requirements artifacts and previous versions (scrap, rework, and defect elimination trends)

- Subjective review of other dimensions of quality

Design Set

UML notation is used to engineer the design models for the solution. The design set contains varying levels of abstraction that represent the components of the solution space (their identities, attributes, static relationships, dynamic interactions). The design models include enough structural and behavioral information to ascertain a bill of materials (quantity and specification of primitive parts and materials, labor, and other direct costs). Design model information can be straightforwardly and, in many cases, automatically translated into a subset of the implementation and deployment set artifacts. Specific design set artifacts include the design model, the test model, and the software architecture description (an extract of information from the design model that is pertinent to describing an architecture).

The design set is evaluated, assessed, and measured through a combination of the following:

- Analysis of the internal consistency and quality of the design model

- Analysis of consistency with the requirements models

- Translation into implementation and deployment sets and notations (for example, traceability, source code generation, compilation, linking) to evaluate the consistency and completeness and the semantic balance between information in the sets

- Analysis of changes between the current version of the design model and previous versions (scrap, rework, and defect elimination trends)

- Subjective review of other dimensions of quality

Because the level of automated analysis available on design models is currently limited, human analysis must be relied on. This situation should change over the next few years with the maturity of design model analysis tools that support metrics collection, complexity analysis, style analysis, heuristic analysis, and consistency analysis.

Implementation Set

The implementation set includes source code (programming language notations) that represents the tangible implementations of components (their form, interface, and dependency relationships) and any executables necessary for stand-alone testing of components. These executables are the primitive parts needed to construct the end product, including custom components, application programming interfaces (APIs) of commercial components, and APIs or reusable or legacy components in a programming language source (such as Ada 95, C++, Visual Basic, Java, or Assembly). Implementation set artifacts can also be translated (compiled and linked) into a subset of the deployment set (end-target executables). Specific artifacts include self-documenting product source code baselines and associated files (compilation scripts, configuration management infrastructure, data files), self-documenting test source code baselines and associated files (input test data files, test result files), stand-alone component executables, and component test driver executables.

Implementation sets are human-readable formats that are evaluated, assessed, and measured through a combination of the following:

- Analysis of consistency with the design models

- Translation into deployment set notations (for example, compilation and linking) to evaluate the consistency and completeness among artifact sets

- Assessment of component source or executable files against relevant evaluation criteria through inspection, analysis, demonstration, or testing

- Execution of stand-alone component test cases that automatically compare expected results with actual results

- Analysis of changes between the current version of the implementation set and previous versions (scrap, rework, and defect elimination trends)

- Subjective review of other dimensions of quality

Deployment Set

The deployment set includes user deliverables and machine language notations, executable software, and the build scripts, installation scripts, and executable target-specific data necessary to use the product in its target environment. These machine language notations represent the product components in the target form intended for distribution to users. Deployment set information can be installed, executed against scenarios of use (tested), and dynamically reconfigured to support the features required in the end product. Specific artifacts include executable baselines and associated run-time files, and the user manual.

Deployment sets are evaluated, assessed, and measured through a combination of the following:

- Testing against the usage scenarios and quality attributes defined in the requirements set to evaluate the consistency and completeness and the semantic balance between information in the two sets

- Testing the partitioning, replication, and allocation strategies in mapping components of the implementation set to physical resources of the deployment system (platform type, number, network topology)

- Testing against the defined usage scenarios in the user manual such as installation, user-oriented dynamic reconfiguration, mainstream usage, and anomaly management

- Analysis of changes between the current version of the deployment set and previous versions (defect elimination trends, performance changes)

- Subjective review of other dimensions of quality

The rationale for selecting the management, requirements, design, implementation, and deployment sets was not scientific. The goal was to optimize presentation of the process activities, artifacts, and objectives. Some of the rationale that resulted in this conceptual framework is described next. Although there are several minor exceptions to these generalizations, they are useful in understanding the overall artifact sets.

Each artifact set uses different notation(s) to capture the relevant artifacts. Management set notations (ad hoc text, graphics, use case notation) capture the plans, process, objectives, and acceptance criteria. Requirements notations (structured text and UML models) capture the engineering context and the operational concept. Design notations (in UML) capture the engineering blueprints (architectural design, component design). Implementation notations (software languages) capture the building blocks of the solution in human-readable formats. Deployment notations (executables and data files) capture the solution in machine-readable formats.

Each artifact set is the predominant development focus of one phase of the life cycle; the other sets take on check and balance roles. As illustrated in Figure 6-2, each

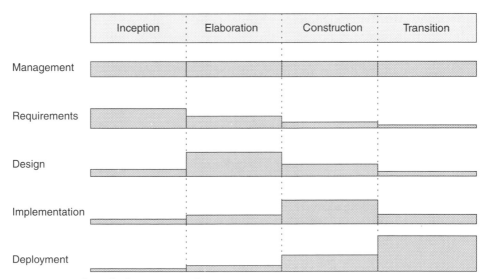

FIGURE 6-2. *Life-cycle focus on artifact sets*

phase has a predominant focus: Requirements are the focus of the inception phase; design, the elaboration phase; implementation, the construction phase; and deployment, the transition phase. The management artifacts also evolve, but at a fairly constant level across the life cycle.

Most of today's software development tools map closely to one of the five artifact sets.

1. Management: scheduling, workflow, defect tracking, change management, documentation, spreadsheet, resource management, and presentation tools

2. Requirements: requirements management tools

3. Design: visual modeling tools

4. Implementation: compiler/debugger tools, code analysis tools, test coverage analysis tools, and test management tools

5. Deployment: test coverage and test automation tools, network management tools, commercial components (operating systems, GUIs, DBMSs, networks, middleware), and installation tools

Allocation of responsibilities among project teams is straightforward and aligns with the process workflows presented in Chapter 8.

Implementation Set versus Deployment Set

The separation of the implementation set (source code) from the deployment set (executable code) is important because there are very different concerns with each set. The structure of the information delivered to the user (and typically the test organization) is very different from the structure of the source code information. Engineering decisions that have an impact on the quality of the deployment set but are relatively incomprehensible in the design and implementation sets include the following:

- Dynamically reconfigurable parameters (buffer sizes, color palettes, number of servers, number of simultaneous clients, data files, run-time parameters)

- Effects of compiler/link optimizations (such as space optimization versus speed optimization)

- Performance under certain allocation strategies (centralized versus distributed, primary and shadow threads, dynamic load balancing, hot backup versus checkpoint/rollback)

- Virtual machine constraints (file descriptors, garbage collection, heap size, maximum record size, disk file rotations)

- Process-level concurrency issues (deadlock and race conditions)
- Platform-specific differences in performance or behavior

Much of this configuration information is important engineering source data that should be captured either in the implementation set (if it is embedded within source code) or in the deployment set (if it is embedded within data files, configuration files, installation scripts, or other target-specific components). In dynamically reconfigurable systems or portable components, it is usually better to separate the source code implementation concerns from the target environment concerns (for reasons of performance, dynamic adaptability, or source code change management). With this approach, the implementation can be decoupled from the actual platform type and from the number and topology of the underlying computing infrastructure, which includes operating systems, middleware, networks, and DBMSs.

As an example, consider the software architecture of a one million SLOC missile warning system (a project described in detail in the case study, Appendix D) with extreme requirements for fault tolerance and data processing performance. On this project, significantly different configurations of executables could be built from the same source sets.

- A version that includes only the primary thread of processing on a development host to do a subset of scenario tests
- A version that includes primary and backup processing threads on a development host, which could then exercise some of the logical reconfiguration scenarios
- Functionally equivalent versions of the two preceding configurations that could execute on the target processors to assess the required throughput and response time of the critical-thread scenarios on the candidate target configuration
- A version that could execute a primary thread of servers on one target processor, a shadow thread of servers on a separate backup target processor, a test/exercise thread on either target, and a suite of thread-independent user interface clients on user workstations. The latter, which could support a broad range of dynamic reconfigurations, was essentially the final target configuration.

Deployment of commercial products to customers can also span a broad range of test and deployment configurations. For example, middleware products provide high-performance, reliable object request brokers that are delivered on several platform implementations, including workstation operating systems, bare embedded processors, large mainframe operating systems, and several real-time operating systems. The product configurations support various compilers and languages as well as various implementations of network software. The heterogeneity of all the various target configurations results in the need for a highly sophisticated source code structure and a huge suite of different deployment artifacts.

6.1.3 ARTIFACT EVOLUTION OVER THE LIFE CYCLE

Each state of development represents a certain amount of precision in the final system description. Early in the life cycle, precision is low and the representation is generally high. Eventually, the precision of representation is high and everything is specified in full detail. At any point in the life cycle, the five sets will be in different states of completeness. However, they should be at compatible levels of detail and reasonably traceable to one another. Performing detailed traceability and consistency analyses early in the life cycle (when precision is low and changes are frequent) usually has a low return on investment. As development proceeds, the architecture stabilizes, and maintaining traceability linkage among artifact sets is worth the effort.

Each phase of development focuses on a particular artifact set. At the end of each phase, the overall system state will have progressed on all sets, as illustrated in Figure 6-3.

The inception phase focuses mainly on critical requirements, usually with a secondary focus on an initial deployment view, little focus on implementation except perhaps choice of language and commercial components, and possibly some high-level focus on the design architecture but not on design detail.

During the elaboration phase, there is much greater depth in requirements, much more breadth in the design set, and further work on implementation and deployment issues such as performance trade-offs under primary scenarios and make/buy analyses. Elaboration phase activities include the generation of an executable

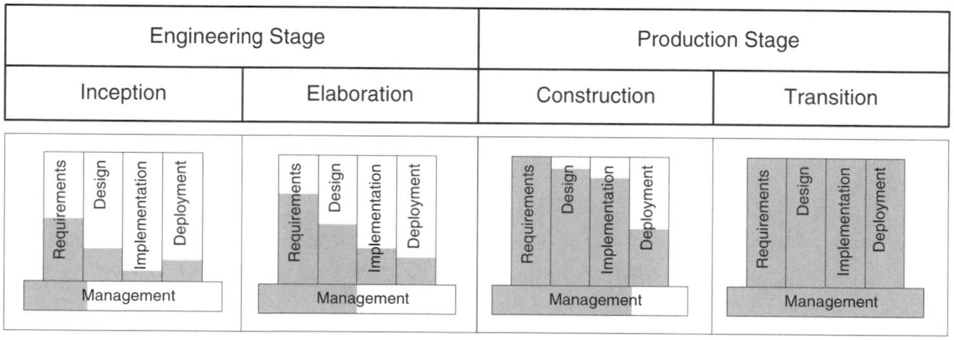

FIGURE 6-3. *Life-cycle evolution of the artifact sets*

prototype. This prototype involves subsets of development in all four sets and specifically assesses whether the interfaces and collaborations among components are consistent and complete within the context of the system's primary requirements and scenarios. Although there is generally a broad understanding of component interfaces, there is usually not much depth in implementation for custom components. (However, commercial or other existing components may be fully elaborated.) A portion of all four sets must be evolved to some level of completion before an architecture baseline can be established. This evolution requires sufficient assessment of the design set, implementation set, and deployment set artifacts against the critical use cases of the requirements set to suggest that the project can proceed predictably with well-understood risks.

The main focus of the construction phase is design and implementation. The main focus early in this phase should be the depth of the design artifacts. Later in construction, the emphasis is on realizing the design in source code and individually tested components. This phase should drive the requirements, design, and implementation sets almost to completion. Substantial work is also done on the deployment set, at least to test one or a few instances of the programmed system through a mechanism such as an alpha or beta release.

The main focus of the transition phase is on achieving consistency and completeness of the deployment set in the context of the other sets. Residual defects are resolved, and feedback from alpha, beta, and system testing is incorporated.

As development proceeds, each of the parts evolves in more detail. When the system is complete, all four sets are fully elaborated and consistent with one another. In contrast to the conventional practice, you do not specify the requirements, then do the design, and so forth. Instead, you evolve the entire system; decisions about the deployment may affect requirements, not just the other way around. The key emphasis here is to break the conventional mold, in which the default interpretation is that one set precedes another. Instead, one state of the entire system evolves into a more elaborate state of the system, usually involving evolution in each of the parts. During the transition phase, traceability between the requirements set and the deployment set is extremely important. The evolving requirements set captures a mature and precise representation of the stakeholders' acceptance criteria, and the deployment set represents the actual end-user product. Therefore, during the transition phase, completeness and consistency between these two sets are important. Traceability among the other sets is necessary only to the extent that it aids the engineering or management activities.

6.1.4 TEST ARTIFACTS

Conventional software testing followed the same document-driven approach that was applied to software development. Development teams built requirements documents, top-level design documents, and detailed design documents before constructing any source files or executables. Similarly, test teams built system test plan documents, system test procedure documents, integration test plan documents, unit test plan documents, and unit test procedure documents before building any test drivers, stubs, or instrumentation. This document-driven approach caused the same problems for the test activities that it did for the development activities.

One of the truly discriminating tenets of a modern process is to use exactly the same sets, notations, and artifacts for the products of test activities as are used for product development. In essence, we are simply identifying the test infrastructure necessary to execute the test process as a required subset of the end product. By doing this, we have forced several engineering disciplines into the process.

- The test artifacts must be developed concurrently with the product from inception through deployment. Thus, testing is a full-life-cycle activity, not a late life-cycle activity.

- The test artifacts are communicated, engineered, and developed within the same artifact sets as the developed product.

- The test artifacts are implemented in programmable and repeatable formats (as software programs).

- The test artifacts are documented in the same way that the product is documented.

- Developers of the test artifacts use the same tools, techniques, and training as the software engineers developing the product.

These disciplines allow for significant levels of homogenization across project workflows, which are described in Chapter 8. Everyone works within the notations and techniques of the four sets used for engineering artifacts, rather than with separate sequences of design and test documents. Interpersonal communications, stakeholder reviews, and engineering analyses can be performed with fewer distinct formats, fewer ad hoc notations, less ambiguity, and higher efficiency.

Testing is only one aspect of the assessment workflow. Other aspects include inspection, analysis, and demonstration. Testing refers to the explicit evaluation through execution of deployment set components under a controlled scenario with an expected and objective outcome. The success of a test can be determined by comparing the expected outcome to the actual outcome with well-defined mathematical precision. Tests are exactly the forms of assessment that are automated.

Although the test artifact subsets are highly project-specific, the following example clarifies the relationship between test artifacts and the other artifact sets. Consider a project to perform seismic data processing for the purpose of oil exploration. This system has three fundamental subsystems: (1) a sensor subsystem that captures raw seismic data in real time and delivers these data to (2) a technical operations subsystem that converts raw data into an organized database and manages queries to this database from (3) a display subsystem that allows workstation operators to examine seismic data in human-readable form. Such a system would result in the following test artifacts:

- Management set. The release specifications and release descriptions capture the objectives, evaluation criteria, and results of an intermediate milestone. These artifacts are the test plans and test results negotiated among internal project teams. The software change orders capture test results (defects, testability changes, requirements ambiguities, enhancements) and the closure criteria associated with making a discrete change to a baseline.

- Requirements set. The system-level use cases capture the operational concept for the system and the acceptance test case descriptions, including the expected behavior of the system and its quality attributes. The entire requirements set is a test artifact because it is the basis of all assessment activities across the life cycle.

- Design set. A test model for nondeliverable components needed to test the product baselines is captured in the design set. These components include such design set artifacts as a seismic event simulation for creating realistic sensor data; a "virtual operator" that can support unattended, after-hours test cases; specific instrumentation suites for early demonstration of resource usage; transaction rates or response times; and use case test drivers and component stand-alone test drivers.

- Implementation set. Self-documenting source code representations for test components and test drivers provide the equivalent of test procedures and test scripts. These source files may also include human-readable data files representing certain statically defined data sets that are explicit test source files. Output files from test drivers provide the equivalent of test reports.

- Deployment set. Executable versions of test components, test drivers, and data files are provided.

For any release, all the test artifacts and product artifacts are maintained using the same baseline version identifier. They are created, changed, and obsolesced as a consistent unit. Because test artifacts are captured using the same notations, methods, and tools, the approach to testing is consistent with design and development. This approach forces the evolving test artifacts to be maintained so that regression testing can be automated easily.

6.2   MANAGEMENT ARTIFACTS

The management set includes several artifacts that capture intermediate results and ancillary information necessary to document the product/process legacy, maintain the product, improve the product, and improve the process. These artifacts are summarized next and discussed in detail in subsequent chapters, where the management workflows and activities are elaborated. Although the following descriptions use the word *document* to describe certain artifacts, this is only meant to imply that the data *could* be committed to a paper document. In many cases, the data may be processed, reviewed, and exchanged via electronic means only.

Work Breakdown Structure

A work breakdown structure (WBS) is the vehicle for budgeting and collecting costs. To monitor and control a project's financial performance, the software project manager must have insight into project costs and how they are expended. The structure of cost accountability is a serious project planning constraint. Lessons learned in numerous less-than-successful projects have shown that if the WBS is structured improperly, it can drive the evolving design and product structure in the wrong direction. A project manager should not lay out lower levels of a WBS (thereby defining specific boundaries of accountability) until a commensurate level of stability in the product structure is achieved. A functional breakdown in the WBS will result in a functional decomposition in the software. The concept of an evolutionary WBS is developed further in Chapter 10.

Business Case

The business case artifact provides all the information necessary to determine whether the project is worth investing in. It details the expected revenue, expected cost, technical and management plans, and backup data necessary to demonstrate the risks and realism of the plans. In large contractual procurements, the business case may be implemented in a full-scale proposal with multiple volumes of information. In a small-scale endeavor for a commercial product, it may be implemented in a brief plan with an attached spreadsheet. The main purpose is to transform the vision into economic terms so that an organization can make an accurate ROI assessment. The financial forecasts are evolutionary, updated with more accurate forecasts as the life cycle progresses. Figure 6-4 provides a default outline for a business case.

Release Specifications

The scope, plan, and objective evaluation criteria for each baseline release are derived from the vision statement as well as many other sources (make/buy analyses, risk management concerns, architectural considerations, shots in the dark, implementa-

```
 I.   Context (domain, market, scope)
 II.  Technical approach
      A.  Feature set achievement plan
      B.  Quality achievement plan
      C.  Engineering trade-offs and technical risks
 III. Management approach
      A.  Schedule and schedule risk assessment
      B.  Objective measures of success
 IV.  Evolutionary appendixes
      A.  Financial forecast
          1.  Cost estimate
          2.  Revenue estimate
          3.  Bases of estimates
```

FIGURE 6-4. *Typical business case outline*

tion constraints, quality thresholds). These artifacts are intended to evolve along with the process, achieving greater fidelity as the life cycle progresses and requirements understanding matures. Figure 6-5 provides a default outline for a release specification.

There are two important forms of requirements. The first is the vision statement (or user need), which captures the contract between the development group and the buyer. This information should be evolving, but varying slowly, across the life cycle. It should be represented in a form that is understandable to the buyer (an ad hoc format that may include text, mockups, use cases, spreadsheets, or other formats). A use case model in the vision statement context serves to capture the operational concept in terms the user/buyer will understand.

Evaluation criteria, the second form of requirements contained in release specifications, are transient snapshots of objectives for a given intermediate life-cycle milestone. Evaluation criteria in release specifications are defined as management artifacts rather than as part of the requirements set. They are derived from the vision statement as well as many other sources (make/buy analyses, risk management concerns, architectural considerations, shots in the dark, implementation constraints, quality

```
 I.   Iteration content
 II.  Measurable objectives
      A.  Evaluation criteria
      B.  Followthrough approach
 III. Demonstration plan
      A.  Schedule of activities
      B.  Team responsibilities
 IV.  Operational scenarios (use cases demonstrated)
      A.  Demonstration procedures
      B.  Traceability to vision and business case
```

FIGURE 6-5. *Typical release specification outline*

thresholds). These management-oriented requirements may be represented by use cases, use case realizations, annotations on use cases, or structured text representations.

The system requirements (user/buyer concerns) are captured in the vision statement. Lower levels of requirements are driven by the process (organized by iteration rather than by lower level component) in the form of evaluation criteria (typically captured by a set of use cases and other textually represented objectives). Thus, the lower level requirements can evolve as summarized in the following conceptual example for a relatively large project:

1. Inception iterations. Typically, 10 to 20 evaluation criteria capture the driving issues associated with the critical use cases that have an impact on architecture alternatives and the overall business case.

2. Elaboration iterations. These evaluation criteria (perhaps 50 or so), when demonstrated against the candidate architecture, verify that the critical use cases and critical requirements of the vision statement can be met with low risk.

3. Construction iterations. These evaluation criteria (perhaps hundreds) associated with a meaningful set of use cases, when passed, constitute useful subsets of the product that can be transitioned to formal test or to alpha or beta releases.

4. Transition iterations. This complete set of use cases and associated evaluation criteria (perhaps thousands) constitutes the acceptance test criteria associated with deploying a version into operation.

This process is naturally evolutionary and is loosely coupled to the actual design and architecture that evolves. In the end, 100% traceability becomes important, but intermediate activities and milestones are far less concerned with consistency and completeness than they were when the conventional approach to software development was used. Each iteration's evaluation criteria are discarded once the milestone is completed; they are transient artifacts. A better version is created at each stage, so there is much conservation of content and lessons learned in each successive set of evaluation criteria. Release specification artifacts and their inherent evaluation criteria are more concerned early on with ensuring that the highest risk issues are resolved.

Software Development Plan

The software development plan (SDP) elaborates the process framework into a fully detailed plan. It is the defining document for the project's process. It must comply with the contract (if any), comply with organization standards (if any), evolve along with the design and requirements, and be used consistently across all subordinate organizations doing software development. Two indications of a useful SDP are peri-

I. **Context (scope, objectives)**
II. **Software development process**
    A. Project primitives
        1. Life-cycle phases
        2. Artifacts
        3. Workflows
        4. Checkpoints
    B. Major milestone scope and content
    C. Process improvement procedures
III. **Software engineering environment**
    A. Process automation (hardware and software resource configuration)
    B. Resource allocation procedures (sharing across organizations, security access)
IV. **Software change management**
    A. Configuration control board plan and procedures
    B. Software change order definitions and procedures
    C. Configuration baseline definitions and procedures
V. **Software assessment**
    A. Metrics collection and reporting procedures
    B. Risk management procedures (risk identification, tracking, and resolution)
    C. Status assessment plan
    D. Acceptance test plan
VI. **Standards and procedures**
    A. Standards and procedures for technical artifacts
VII. **Evolutionary appendixes**
    A. Minor milestone scope and content
    B. Human resources (organization, staffing plan, training plan)

FIGURE 6-6. *Typical software development plan outline*

odic updating (it is not stagnant shelfware) and understanding and acceptance by managers and practitioners alike. Figure 6-6 provides a default outline for a software development plan.

Release Descriptions

Release description documents describe the results of each release, including performance against each of the evaluation criteria in the corresponding release specification. Release baselines should be accompanied by a release description document that describes the evaluation criteria for that configuration baseline and provides substantiation (through demonstration, testing, inspection, or analysis) that each criterion has been addressed in an acceptable manner. This document should also include a metrics summary that quantifies its quality in absolute and relative terms (compared to the previous versions, if any). The results of a post-mortem review of any release would be documented here, including outstanding issues, recommendations for process and product improvement, trade-offs in addressing evaluation criteria, follow-up actions, and similar information. Figure 6-7 provides a default outline for a release description.

I.   **Context**
   A.   Release baseline content
   B.   Release metrics
II. **Release notes**
   A.   Release-specific constraints or limitations
III. **Assessment results**
   A.   Substantiation of passed evaluation criteria
   B.   Follow-up plans for failed evaluation criteria
   C.   Recommendations for next release
IV. **Outstanding issues**
   A.   Action items
   B.   Post-mortem summary of lessons learned

FIGURE 6-7. *Typical release description outline*

Status Assessments

Status assessments provide periodic snapshots of project health and status, including the software project manager's risk assessment, quality indicators, and management indicators. Although the period may vary, the forcing function needs to persist. The paramount objective of a good management process is to ensure that the expectations of all stakeholders (contractor, customer, user, subcontractor) are synchronized and consistent. The periodic status assessment documents provide the critical mechanism for managing everyone's expectations throughout the life cycle; for addressing, communicating, and resolving management issues, technical issues, and project risks; and for capturing project history. They are the periodic heartbeat for management attention. Section 9.3 discusses status assessments in more detail.

Typical status assessments should include a review of resources, personnel staffing, financial data (cost and revenue), top 10 risks, technical progress (metrics snapshots), major milestone plans and results, total project or product scope, action items, and follow-through. Continuous open communications with objective data derived directly from on-going activities and evolving product configurations are mandatory in any project.

Software Change Order Database

Managing change is one of the fundamental primitives of an iterative development process. With greater change freedom, a project can iterate more productively. This flexibility increases the content, quality, and number of iterations that a project can achieve within a given schedule. Change freedom has been achieved in practice through automation, and today's iterative development environments carry the burden of change management. Organizational processes that depend on manual change management techniques have encountered major inefficiencies. Consequently, the change management data have been elevated to a first-class management artifact that is described as a database to instill the concept of a need for automation. Once software is placed in a controlled baseline, all changes must be formally tracked and managed. By automating data entry and maintaining change records on-line, most of the change management bureaucracy and metrics collection and reporting activities can be automated. Software change orders are discussed in detail in Chapter 12.

Deployment

A deployment document can take many forms. Depending on the project, it could include several document subsets for transitioning the product into operational status. In big contractual efforts in which the system is delivered to a separate maintenance organization, deployment artifacts may include computer system operations manuals, software installation manuals, plans and procedures for cutover (from a legacy system), site surveys, and so forth. For commercial software products, deployment artifacts may include marketing plans, sales rollout kits, and training courses.

Environment

An important emphasis of a modern approach is to define the development and maintenance environment as a first-class artifact of the process. A robust, integrated development environment must support automation of the development process. This environment should include requirements management, visual modeling, document automation, host and target programming tools, automated regression testing, integrated change management, and defect tracking. A common theme from successful software projects is that they hire good people and provide them with good tools to accomplish their jobs. Automation of the software development process provides payback in quality, the ability to estimate costs and schedules, and overall productivity using a smaller team. By allowing the designers to traverse quickly among development artifacts and easily keep the artifacts up-to-date, integrated toolsets play an increasingly important role in incremental and iterative development.

Management Artifact Sequences

In each phase of the life cycle, new artifacts are produced and previously developed artifacts are updated to incorporate lessons learned and to capture further depth and breadth of the solution. Some artifacts are updated at each major milestone, others at each minor milestone. Figure 6-8 identifies a typical sequence of artifacts across the life-cycle phases.

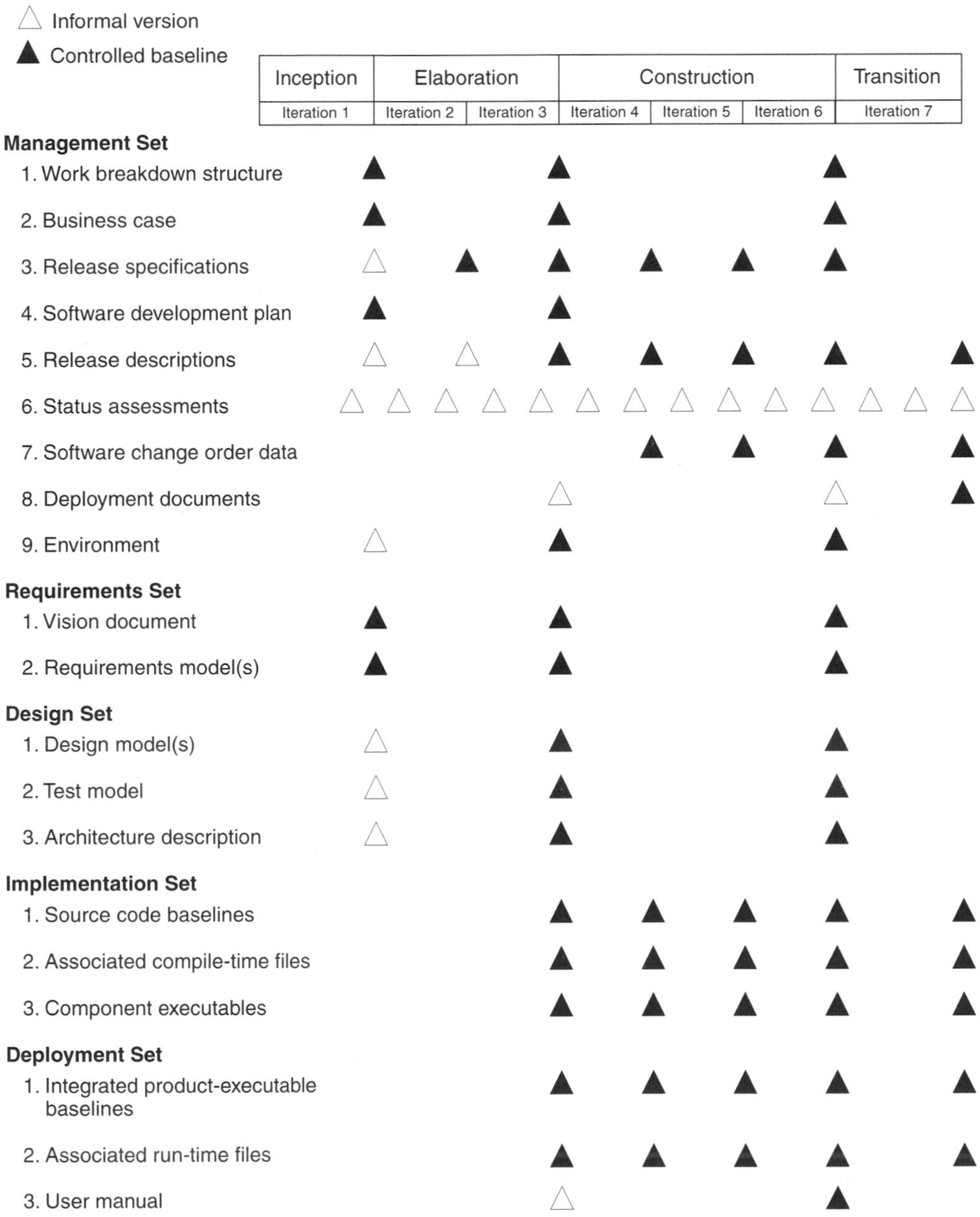

△ Informal version
▲ Controlled baseline

	Inception	Elaboration		Construction			Transition
	Iteration 1	Iteration 2	Iteration 3	Iteration 4	Iteration 5	Iteration 6	Iteration 7
Management Set							
1. Work breakdown structure	▲		▲			▲	
2. Business case	▲		▲			▲	
3. Release specifications	△	▲	▲	▲	▲	▲	
4. Software development plan	▲		▲				
5. Release descriptions	△	△	▲	▲	▲	▲	▲
6. Status assessments	△	△	△	△	△	△	△
7. Software change order data				▲	▲	▲	▲
8. Deployment documents			△			△	▲
9. Environment	△		▲			▲	
Requirements Set							
1. Vision document	▲		▲			▲	
2. Requirements model(s)	▲		▲			▲	
Design Set							
1. Design model(s)	△		▲			▲	
2. Test model	△		▲			▲	
3. Architecture description	△		▲			▲	
Implementation Set							
1. Source code baselines			▲	▲	▲	▲	▲
2. Associated compile-time files			▲	▲	▲	▲	▲
3. Component executables			▲	▲	▲	▲	▲
Deployment Set							
1. Integrated product-executable baselines			▲	▲	▲	▲	▲
2. Associated run-time files			▲	▲	▲	▲	▲
3. User manual			△			▲	

FIGURE 6-8. *Artifact sequences across a typical life cycle*

6.3   ENGINEERING ARTIFACTS

Most of the engineering artifacts are captured in rigorous engineering notations such as UML, programming languages, or executable machine codes. Because this book is written from a management perspective, it does not dwell on these artifacts. However, three engineering artifacts are explicitly intended for more general review, and they deserve further elaboration.

Vision Document

The vision document provides a complete vision for the software system under development and supports the contract between the funding authority and the development organization. Whether the project is a huge military-standard development (whose vision could be a 300-page system specification) or a small, internally funded commercial product (whose vision might be a two-page white paper), every project needs a source for capturing the expectations among stakeholders. A project vision is meant to be changeable as understanding evolves of the requirements, architecture, plans, and technology. A good vision document should change slowly. Figure 6-9 provides a default outline for a vision document.

The vision document is written from the user's perspective, focusing on the essential features of the system and acceptable levels of quality. The vision document should contain at least two appendixes. The first appendix should describe the operational concept using use cases (a visual model and a separate artifact). The second appendix should describe the change risks inherent in the vision statement, to guide defensive design efforts.

The vision statement should include a description of what will be included as well as those features considered but not included. It should also specify operational capacities (volumes, response times, accuracies), user profiles, and interoperational interfaces with entities outside the system boundary, where applicable. The vision should not be defined only for the initial operating level; its likely evolution path

---

> **I.   Feature set description**
>   A.   Precedence and priority
> **II.   Quality attributes and ranges**
> **III. Required constraints**
>   A.   External interfaces
> **IV.   Evolutionary appendixes**
>   A.   Use cases
>   1.   Primary scenarios
>   2.   Acceptance criteria and tolerances
>   B.   Desired freedoms (potential change scenarios)

FIGURE 6-9.   *Typical vision document outline*

should be addressed so that there is a context for assessing design adaptability. The operational concept involves specifying the use cases and scenarios for nominal and off-nominal usage. The use case representation provides a dynamic context for understanding and refining the scope, for assessing the integrity of a design model, and for developing acceptance test procedures. The vision document provides the contractual basis for the requirements visible to the stakeholders.

Architecture Description

The architecture description provides an organized view of the software architecture under development. It is extracted largely from the design model and includes views of the design, implementation, and deployment sets sufficient to understand how the operational concept of the requirements set will be achieved. The breadth of the architecture description will vary from project to project depending on many factors. The architecture can be described using a subset of the design model or as an abstraction of the design model with supplementary material, or a combination of both. As examples of these two forms of descriptions, consider the architecture of this book:

- A subset form could be satisfied by the table of contents. This description of the architecture of the book is directly derivable from the book itself.

- An abstraction form could be satisfied by a "Cliffs Notes" treatment. (Cliffs Notes are condensed versions of classic books used as study guides by some college students.) This format is an abstraction that is developed separately and includes supplementary material that is not directly derivable from the evolving product.

The approach described in Section 7.2 allows an architecture description to be tailored to the specific needs of a project. Figure 6-10 provides a default outline for an architecture description.

Software User Manual

The software user manual provides the user with the reference documentation necessary to support the delivered software. Although content is highly variable across application domains, the user manual should include installation procedures, usage procedures and guidance, operational constraints, and a user interface description, at a minimum. For software products with a user interface, this manual should be developed early in the life cycle because it is a necessary mechanism for communicating and stabilizing an important subset of requirements. The user manual should be written by members of the test team, who are more likely to understand the user's perspective than the development team. If the test team is responsible for the manual, it can be generated in parallel with development and can be evolved early as a tangible and rel-

```
  I.   Architecture overview
       A.  Objectives
       B.  Constraints
       C.  Freedoms
 II.   Architecture views
       A.  Design view
       B.  Process view
       C.  Component view
       D.  Deployment view
III.   Architectural interactions
       A.  Operational concept under primary scenarios
       B.  Operational concept under secondary scenarios
       C.  Operational concept under anomalous conditions
 IV.   Architecture performance
  V.   Rationale, trade-offs, and other substantiation
```

FIGURE 6-10. *Typical architecture description outline*

evant perspective of evaluation criteria. It also provides a necessary basis for test plans and test cases, and for construction of automated test suites.

6.4 PRAGMATIC ARTIFACTS

Conventional document-driven approaches squandered incredible amounts of engineering time on developing, polishing, formatting, reviewing, updating, and distributing documents. Why? There are several reasons that documents became so important to the process. First, there were no rigorous engineering methods or languages for requirements specification or design. Consequently, paper documents with ad hoc text and graphical representations were the default format. Second, conventional languages of implementation and deployment were extremely cryptic and highly unstructured. To present the details of software structure and behavior to other interested reviewers (testers, maintainers, managers), a more human-readable format was needed. Probably most important, software progress needed to be "credibly" assessed. Documents represented a tangible but misleading mechanism for demonstrating progress.

In some domains, document-driven approaches have degenerated over the past 30 years into major obstacles to process improvement. The quality of the documents became more important than the quality of the engineering information they represented. And evaluating quality through human review of abstract descriptions is a highly subjective process. Much effort was expended assessing single-dimensional surface issues, with very little attention devoted to the multidimensional issues that drive architecture qualities, such as performance and adaptability.

Document production cycles, review cycles, and update cycles also injected very visible and formal snapshots of progress into the schedule, thereby introducing more schedule dependencies and synchronization points. For example, the following scenario was not uncommon on large defense projects: Spend a month preparing a design document, deliver the document to the customer for review, wait a month to receive comments back, then spend a month responding to comments and incorporating changes. With many, many multiple-month document review cycles to be managed, scheduled, and synchronized, it is not surprising that many such projects ended up with five-year development life cycles. Lengthy and highly detailed documents, which were generally perceived to demonstrate more progress, resulted in premature engineering details and increased scrap and rework later in the life cycle.

A more effective approach is to redirect this documentation effort to improving the rigor and understandability of the information source and allowing on-line review of the native information source by using smart browsing and navigation tools. Such an approach can eliminate a huge, unproductive source of scrap and rework in the process and allow for continuous review by everyone who is directly concerned with the evolving on-line artifacts.

This philosophy raises the following cultural issues:

- **People want to review information but don't understand the language of the artifact.** Many interested reviewers of a particular artifact will resist having to learn the engineering language in which the artifact is written. It is not uncommon to find people (such as veteran software managers, veteran quality assurance specialists, or an auditing authority from a regulatory agency) who react as follows: "I'm not going to learn UML, but I want to review the design of this software, so give me a separate description such as some flowcharts and text that I can understand." Would we respond to a similar request by someone reviewing the engineering blueprints of a building? No. We would require that the reviewer be knowledgeable in the engineering notation. We should stop patronizing audiences who resist treating software as an engineering discipline. These interested parties typically add cost and time to the process without adding value.

- **People want to review the information but don't have access to the tools.** It is not very common for the development organization to be fully tooled; it is extremely rare that the other stakeholders have any capability to review the engineering artifacts on-line. Consequently, organizations are forced to exchange paper documents. Standardized formats (such as UML, spreadsheets, Visual Basic, C++, and Ada 95), visualization tools, and the Web are rapidly making it economically feasible for all stakeholders to exchange information electronically. The approach to artifacts is one area in which the optimal software development process can be polluted if the philosophy of the process is not accepted by the other stakeholders.

- **Human-readable engineering artifacts should use rigorous notations that are complete, consistent, and used in a self-documenting manner.** Properly spelled English words should be used for all identifiers and descriptions. Acronyms and abbreviations should be used only where they are well-accepted jargon in the context of the component's usage. No matter what languages or tools are used, there is no reason to abbreviate and encrypt modeling or programming language source identifiers. Saving keystrokes through abbreviation may simplify the artifact author's job, but it introduces errors throughout the rest of the life cycle. Disallowing this practice will pay off in both productivity and quality. Software is written only once, but it is read many times. Therefore, readability should be emphasized and the use of proper English words should be required in all engineering artifacts. This practice enables understandable representations, browseable formats (paperless review), more-rigorous notations, and reduced error rates.

- **Useful documentation is self-defining: It is documentation that gets used.** Above all, building self-documenting engineering artifacts gives the development organization the "right" to work solely in the engineering notations and avoid separate documents to describe all the details of a model, component, or test procedure. If you find that information, and particularly a document, is getting produced but not used, eliminate it in favor of whatever is getting used to accomplish the intended purpose. Strive to improve its self-documenting nature.

- **Paper is tangible; electronic artifacts are too easy to change.** One reason some stakeholders prefer paper documents is that once they are delivered, they are tangible, static, and persistent. On-line and Web-based artifacts can be changed easily and are viewed with more skepticism because of their inherent volatility. Although electronic artifacts will and should be met with healthy skepticism by many stakeholders, it is simply a matter of time before the whole world operates this way. The advantages are substantial and far-reaching across many domains. Rest assured that tools and environments will evolve to support change management, audit trails, electronic signatures, and other advances in groupware so that electronic interchange replaces paper.

It is extremely important that the information inherent in the artifact be emphasized, not the paper on which it is written. Short documents are usually more useful than long ones. Software is the primary product; documentation is merely support material.

Model-Based Software Architectures

Software architecture is the central design problem of a complex software system, in the same way that architecture is the central design problem of a complex skyscraper. However, a software architecture has several additional dimensions of complexity. In contrast to the architecture of a large building, the critical performance attributes and features of a complex software system cannot be described through stable laws of physics. They are not governed by any well-accepted form of mathematics. Thus, software architects have no irrefutable first principles. There are many heuristics and fuzzy guidelines, but the fundamental measures of goodness are highly situation-dependent. Lacking established theory, software architects must rely on some form of experimentation in formulating software architectures. This is one of the main reasons for transitioning to an iterative process, in which early activities emphasize and promote architecture evolution through prototyping and demonstration.

> **Key Points**
> ▲ An architecture is the software system design.
> ▲ The ultimate goal of the engineering stage is to converge on a stable architecture baseline.
> ▲ An architecture baseline is not a paper document; it is a collection of information across all the engineering sets.
> ▲ Architectures are described by extracting the essential information from the design models.

Previous chapters have made many assertions about architecture without defining the term. No definition of software architecture is accepted throughout the industry. This chapter condenses some perspectives on architecture to build a context in which the management perspective of an architecture-first process can be understood.

Because early software systems were far less powerful than present-day systems, architectures were much simpler and required only informal representations. In a single-computer, single-program system, the mapping among design objects, implementation objects, and deployment objects was generally trivial. In today's complex software systems, we have evolved to multiple, distinct models and views to exploit the advantages of modern technologies such as commercial components, object-oriented methods, open systems, distributed systems, host and target environments, and modern languages. A *model* is a relatively independent abstraction of a system. A *view* is a subset of a model that abstracts a specific, relevant perspective.

7.1 ARCHITECTURE: A MANAGEMENT PERSPECTIVE

The most critical technical product of a software project is its architecture: the infrastructure, control, and data interfaces that permit software components to cooperate as a system and software designers to cooperate efficiently as a team. Establishing accurate and precise communications among teams of people is a timeless problem in any organization. When the communications media include multiple languages and intergroup literacy varies, the communications problem can become extremely complex and even unsolvable. If a software development team is to be successful, the interproject communications, as captured in the software architecture, must be both accurate and precise.

From a management perspective, there are three different aspects of an architecture.

1. An *architecture* (the intangible design concept) is the design of a software system, as opposed to the design of a component. This includes all engineering necessary to specify a complete bill of materials. Significant make/buy decisions are resolved, and all custom components are elaborated so that individual component costs and construction/assembly costs can be determined with confidence.

2. An *architecture baseline* (the tangible artifacts) is a slice of information across the engineering artifact sets sufficient to satisfy all stakeholders that the vision (function and quality) can be achieved within the parameters of the business case (cost, profit, time, technology, people).

3. An *architecture description* (a human-readable representation of an architecture, which is one of the components of an architecture baseline) is an organized subset of information extracted from the design set model(s). It includes the additional ad hoc notation (text and graphics) necessary to clarify the information in the models. The architecture description communicates how the intangible concept is realized in the tangible artifacts.

These definitions are necessarily abstract, because architecture takes on different forms across different system domains. In particular, the number of views and the level of detail in each view can vary widely. The architecture of a resume, for example, has a much simpler form than the architecture of a major motion picture, even though both products may represent different forms of biographies. The architecture of a glider has a much simpler form than the architecture of a jumbo jet, even though both products are aircraft. Similarly, the architecture of the software for an air traffic control system is very different from the software architecture of a small development tool.

The importance of software architecture and its close linkage with modern software development processes can be summarized as follows:

- Achieving a stable software architecture represents a significant project milestone at which the critical make/buy decisions should have been resolved. This life-cycle event represents a transition from the engineering stage of a project, characterized by discovery and resolution of numerous unknowns, to the production stage, characterized by management to a predictable development plan.

- Architecture representations provide a basis for balancing the trade-offs between the problem space (requirements and constraints) and the solution space (the operational product).

- The architecture and process encapsulate many of the important (high-pay-off or high-risk) communications among individuals, teams, organizations, and stakeholders.

- Poor architectures and immature processes are often given as reasons for project failures.

- A mature process, an understanding of the primary requirements, and a demonstrable architecture are important prerequisites for predictable planning.

- Architecture development and process definition are the intellectual steps that map the problem to a solution without violating the constraints; they require human innovation and cannot be automated.

7.2   ARCHITECTURE: A TECHNICAL PERSPECTIVE

Although software architecture has been discussed at length over the past decade, convergence on definitions, terminology, and principles has been lacking. The following discussion draws generally on the foundations of architecture developed at Rational Software Corporation and particularly on Philippe Kruchten's concepts of software architecture [Kruchten, 1995].

Software architecture encompasses the structure of software systems (the selection of elements and the composition of elements into progressively larger subsystems), their behavior (collaborations among elements), and the patterns that guide these elements, their collaborations, and their composition. The context of software architecture structure, behavior, and patterns must include functionality, performance, resilience, comprehensibility, economic trade-offs, technology constraints, and aesthetic concerns.

An architecture framework is defined in terms of views that are abstractions of the UML models in the design set. The design model includes the full breadth and depth of information. An architecture view is an abstraction of the design model; it contains only the architecturally significant information. Most real-world systems require four views: design, process, component, and deployment. The purposes of these views are as follows:

- Design: describes architecturally significant structures and functions of the design model

- Process: describes concurrency and control thread relationships among the design, component, and deployment views

- Component: describes the structure of the implementation set

- Deployment: describes the structure of the deployment set

The design view is probably necessary in every system; the other three views can be added to deal with the complexity of the system at hand. For example, any distributed system would need a process view and a deployment view. Most large systems, as well as systems that comprise a mixture of custom and commercial components, would also require a separate component view.

Figure 7-1 summarizes the artifacts of the design set, including the architecture views and architecture description. The architecture description is usually captured electronically but is always maintained so that it is printable as a single cohesive document. The engineering models and architectural views are defined as collections of UML diagrams.

The requirements model addresses the behavior of the system as seen by its end users, analysts, and testers. This view is modeled statically using use case and class diagrams, and dynamically using sequence, collaboration, state chart, and activity diagrams.

- The *use case view* describes how the system's critical (architecturally significant) use cases are realized by elements of the design model. It is modeled statically using use case diagrams, and dynamically using any of the UML behavioral diagrams.

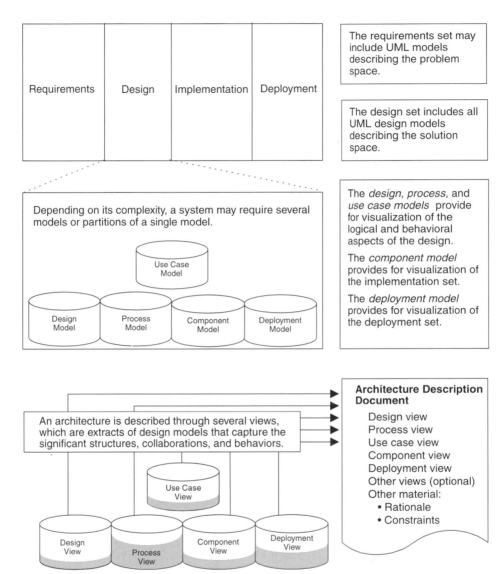

FIGURE 7-1. *Architecture, an organized and abstracted view into the design models*

The design model addresses the architecture of the system and the design of the components within the architecture, including the functional structure, concurrency structure, implementation structure, and execution structure of the solution space, as seen by its developers. Static descriptions are provided with structural diagrams (class, object, component, deployment diagrams). Dynamic descriptions are provided with any of the UML behavioral diagrams (collaboration, sequence, state chart, activity diagrams).

- The *design view* describes the architecturally significant elements of the design model. This view, an abstraction of the design model, addresses the basic structure and functionality of the solution. It is modeled statically using class and object diagrams, and dynamically using any of the UML behavioral diagrams.

- The *process view* addresses the run-time collaboration issues involved in executing the architecture on a distributed deployment model, including the logical software network topology (allocation to processes and threads of control), interprocess communication, and state management. This view is modeled statically using deployment diagrams, and dynamically using any of the UML behavioral diagrams.

- The *component view* describes the architecturally significant elements of the implementation set. This view, an abstraction of the design model, addresses the software source code realization of the system from the perspective of the project's integrators and developers, especially with regard to releases and configuration management. It is modeled statically using component diagrams, and dynamically using any of the UML behavioral diagrams.

- The *deployment view* addresses the executable realization of the system, including the allocation of logical processes in the distribution view (the logical software topology) to physical resources of the deployment network (the physical system topology). It is modeled statically using deployment diagrams, and dynamically using any of the UML behavioral diagrams.

Architecture descriptions take on different forms and styles in different organizations and domains. At any given time, an architecture requires a subset of artifacts in each engineering set. The actual level of content in each set is situation-dependent, and there are few good heuristics for describing objectively what is architecturally significant and what is not.

Generally, an architecture baseline should include the following:

- Requirements: critical use cases, system-level quality objectives, and priority relationships among features and qualities

- Design: names, attributes, structures, behaviors, groupings, and relationships of significant classes and components

- Implementation: source component inventory and bill of materials (number, name, purpose, cost) of all primitive components

- Deployment: executable components sufficient to demonstrate the critical use cases and the risk associated with achieving the system qualities

Although the technical details of architecture description are not central to software management, the underlying spirit of architecture-first development is crucial to success. Drawing this line (what's in the architecture and what's not) is the challenge of project management, for it is the ultimate question of balance that significantly influences project success.

An architecture baseline is defined as a balanced subset of information across all sets, whereas an architecture description is completely encapsulated within the design set. This distinction is a subtle but important difference between conventional approaches and modern iterative development processes. Conventional approaches would equate an architecture baseline with an architecture description (realized as a document with no rigorous design notation), without any representation in the other engineering artifact sets to validate the integrity of the description. In iterative development, an architecture baseline is a partial realization of the architecture description that is sufficient to provide tangible evidence that the architecture is valid in the context of the requirements and plans.

The architecture description will take a wide range of forms, from a simple, direct subset of UML diagrams to a complex set of models with a variety of distinct views that capture and compartmentalize the concerns of a sophisticated system. The former may be applicable for a small, highly skilled team building a development tool, the latter for a highly distributed, large-scale, catastrophic-cost-of-failure command and control system.

The artifact sets evolve through a project life cycle from the engineering stage (when the focus is on the requirements and design artifacts) to the production stage (when the focus shifts to the implementation and deployment artifacts). The transition point from the engineering stage to the production stage constitutes a state in which the project has achieved a stable architecture baseline. From a management perspective, this state is achieved when relevant stakeholders agree that the vision (as supported by the requirements set and the architecture, represented in the design set, and partially realized in the implementation and deployment sets) can be achieved with a highly predictable cost and schedule (as supported in the management set). Substantiation of this state typically requires not only briefings and documents, but also executable prototypes that demonstrate evolving capabilities. These demonstrations provide far more tangible feedback on the maturity of the solution. The more standard components are used, the simpler this state is to achieve. The more custom components are used, the harder it is to achieve and the harder it is to estimate construction costs.

Workflows of the Process

Most process descriptions use sequences of activities as their primary representation format. Sequentially oriented process descriptions are simple to understand, represent, plan, and conduct. From an individual's point of view, all activities are inherently sequential. However, simplistic activity sequences are not realistic on software projects that are team efforts. Such efforts may include many teams, making progress on many artifacts that must be synchronized, cross-checked, homogenized, merged, and integrated. The distributed nature of the software process and its subordinate workflows is the primary source of management complexity.

Key Points

▲ The activities of the process are organized into seven major workflows: management, environment, requirements, design, implementation, assessment, and deployment.

▲ These activities are performed concurrently, with varying levels of effort and emphasis as a project progresses through the life cycle.

▲ The management workflow is concerned primarily with three disciplines: planning, project control, and organization.

One of the more subtle flaws in the conventional software process was in presenting the life-cycle macroprocess as a sequential thread of activities, from requirements analysis to design to code to test to delivery. In an abstract way, successful projects did implement this progression, but the boundaries between the phases were fuzzy and were accepted as such by nonadversarial stakeholders. Unsuccessful projects, on the other hand, typically got mired in striving for crisp boundaries between phases. For example, a typical project team might have pursued 100% frozen requirements baselines before transitioning to design, or might have tried to write a fully detailed design documentation before transitioning to coding. As a result, excessive effort would have been expended in minutia while progress on the important engineering decisions slowed or even stopped.

A modern process avoids naming the life-cycle phases after the predominant activities. The phase names—inception, elaboration, construction, and transition—specify the state of the project rather than a sequence of activities as in the waterfall model. The intent is to recognize explicitly the continuum of activities in all phases and avoid the inference that there is a sequential progression from requirements to design to code to test to delivery.

8.1 SOFTWARE PROCESS WORKFLOWS

Previous chapters introduced a life-cycle macroprocess and the fundamental sets of artifacts. The macroprocess comprises discrete phases and iterations, but not discrete activities. A continuum of activities occurs in each phase and iteration. The next-level process description is the microprocesses, or workflows, that produce the artifacts. The term *workflow* is used to mean a thread of cohesive and mostly sequential activities. Workflows are mapped to product artifacts as described in Chapter 6 and to project teams as described in Chapter 11. There are seven top-level workflows:

1. Management workflow: controlling the process and ensuring win conditions for all stakeholders

2. Environment workflow: automating the process and evolving the maintenance environment

3. Requirements workflow: analyzing the problem space and evolving the requirements artifacts

4. Design workflow: modeling the solution and evolving the architecture and design artifacts

5. Implementation workflow: programming the components and evolving the implementation and deployment artifacts

6. Assessment workflow: assessing the trends in process and product quality

7. Deployment workflow: transitioning the end products to the user

Figure 8-1 illustrates the relative levels of effort expected across the phases in each of the top-level workflows. It represents one of the key signatures of a modern process framework and provides a viewpoint from which to discuss several of the key principles introduced in Chapter 4.

1. ***Architecture-first approach.*** Extensive requirements analysis, design, implementation, and assessment activities are performed before the construction phase, when full-scale implementation is the focus. This early life-cycle focus on implementing and testing the architecture must precede full-scale

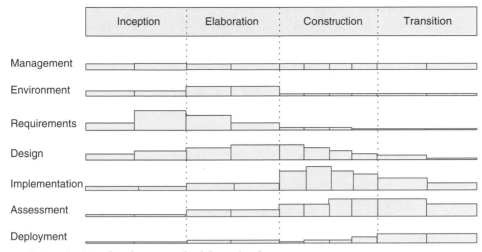

FIGURE 8-1. *Activity levels across the life-cycle phases*

development and testing of all the components and must precede the downstream focus on completeness and quality of the entire breadth of the product features.

2. ***Iterative life-cycle process.*** In Figure 8-1, each phase portrays at least two iterations of each workflow. This default is intended to be descriptive, not prescriptive. Some projects may require only one iteration in a phase; others may require several iterations. The point is that the activities and artifacts of any given workflow may require more than one pass to achieve adequate results.

3. ***Round-trip engineering.*** Raising the environment activities to a first-class workflow is critical. The environment is the tangible embodiment of the project's process, methods, and notations for producing the artifacts.

4. ***Demonstration-based approach.*** Implementation and assessment activities are initiated early in the life cycle, reflecting the emphasis on constructing executable subsets of the evolving architecture.

Some key themes of the conventional process are not carried over in the workflows of the modern process. Their absence is equally important. Documentation is omitted because most documentation should be merely a secondary by-product of the other activities. Quality assurance is omitted because it is worked into all activities, not separated into a distinct workflow that operates independently from engineering or management.

Table 8-1 shows the allocation of artifacts and the emphasis of each workflow in each of the life-cycle phases of inception, elaboration, construction, and transition.

TABLE 8-1. *The artifacts and life-cycle emphases associated with each workflow*

WORKFLOW	ARTIFACTS	LIFE-CYCLE PHASE EMPHASIS
Management	Business case Software development plan Status assessments Vision Work breakdown structure	Inception: Prepare business case and vision Elaboration: Plan development Construction: Monitor and control development Transition: Monitor and control deployment
Environment	Environment Software change order database	Inception: Define development environment and change management infrastructure Elaboration: Install development environment and establish change management database Construction: Maintain development environment and software change order database Transition: Transition maintenance environment and software change order database
Requirements	Requirements set Release specifications Vision	Inception: Define operational concept Elaboration: Define architecture objectives Construction: Define iteration objectives Transition: Refine release objectives
Design	Design set Architecture description	Inception: Formulate architecture concept Elaboration: Achieve architecture baseline Construction: Design components Transition: Refine architecture and components
Implementation	Implementation set Deployment set	Inception: Support architecture prototypes Elaboration: Produce architecture baseline Construction: Produce complete componentry Transition: Maintain components
Assessment	Release specifications Release descriptions User manual Deployment set	Inception: Assess plans, vision, prototypes Elaboration: Assess architecture Construction: Assess interim releases Transition: Assess product releases
Deployment	Deployment set	Inception: Analyze user community Elaboration: Define user manual Construction: Prepare transition materials Transition: Transition product to user

The engineering workflows of requirements, design, implementation, and assessment are more fully covered in other books about the Unified Modeling Language. Activities in the management workflow and the environment workflow are the main focus in Part III. Deployment is discussed minimally because it is usually project-specific.

8.2 ITERATION WORKFLOWS

An iteration consists of a loosely sequential set of activities in various proportions, depending on where the iteration is located in the development cycle. Each iteration is defined in terms of a set of allocated usage scenarios. The components needed to implement all selected scenarios are developed and integrated with the results of previous iterations. An individual iteration's workflow, illustrated in Figure 8-2, generally includes the following sequence:

- Management: iteration planning to determine the content of the release and develop the detailed plan for the iteration; assignment of work packages, or tasks, to the development team

- Environment: evolving the software change order database to reflect all new baselines and changes to existing baselines for all product, test, and environment components

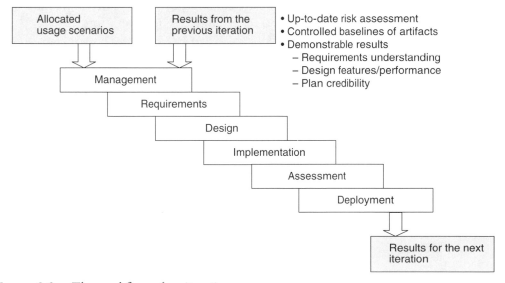

FIGURE 8-2. *The workflow of an iteration*

- Requirements: analyzing the baseline plan, the baseline architecture, and the baseline requirements set artifacts to fully elaborate the use cases to be demonstrated at the end of this iteration and their evaluation criteria; updating any requirements set artifacts to reflect changes necessitated by results of this iteration's engineering activities

- Design: evolving the baseline architecture and the baseline design set artifacts to elaborate fully the design model and test model components necessary to demonstrate against the evaluation criteria allocated to this iteration; updating design set artifacts to reflect changes necessitated by the results of this iteration's engineering activities

- Implementation: developing or acquiring any new components, and enhancing or modifying any existing components, to demonstrate the evaluation criteria allocated to this iteration; integrating and testing all new and modified components with existing baselines (previous versions)

- Assessment: evaluating the results of the iteration, including compliance with the allocated evaluation criteria and the quality of the current baselines; identifying any rework required and determining whether it should be performed before deployment of this release or allocated to the next release; assessing results to improve the basis of the subsequent iteration's plan

- Deployment: transitioning the release either to an external organization (such as a user, independent verification and validation contractor, or regulatory agency) or to internal closure by conducting a post-mortem so that lessons learned can be captured and reflected in the next iteration

As with any sequence of a software development workflow, many of the activities occur concurrently. For example, requirements analysis is not done all in one continuous lump; it intermingles with management, design, implementation, and so forth.

Iterations in the inception and elaboration phases focus on management, requirements, and design activities. Iterations in the construction phase focus on design, implementation, and assessment. Iterations in the transition phase focus on assessment and deployment. Figure 8-3 shows the emphasis on different activities across the life cycle.

These descriptions are pretty simplistic. In practice, the various sequences and overlaps among iterations become more complex. The terms *iteration* and *increment* deal with some of the pragmatic considerations. An iteration represents the state of the overall architecture and the complete deliverable system. An increment represents the current work in progress that will be combined with the preceding iteration to form the next iteration. Figure 8-4, an example of a simple development life cycle, illustrates the difference between iterations and increments. This example also illustrates a typical build sequence from the perspective of an abstract layered architecture.

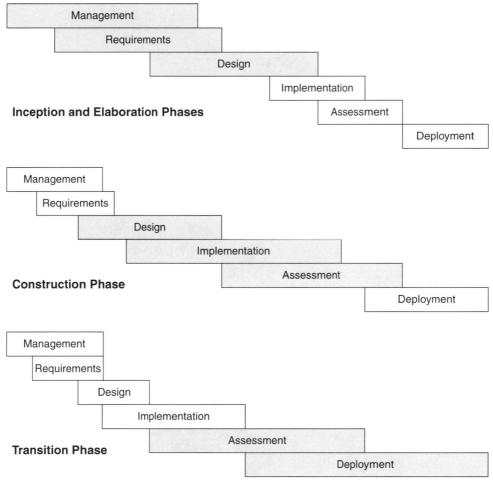

FIGURE 8-3. *Iteration emphasis across the life cycle*

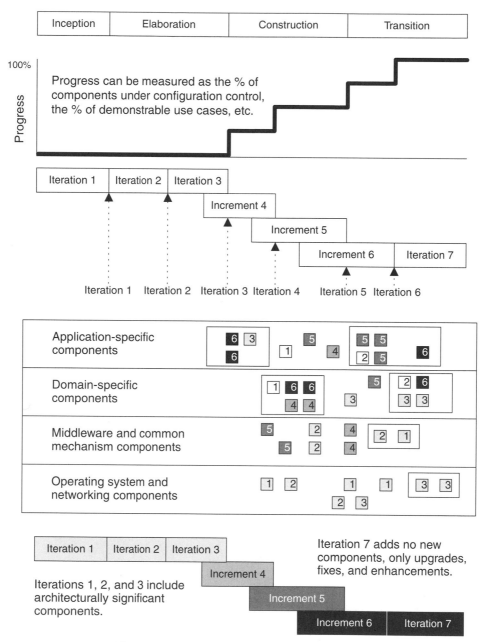

FIGURE 8-4. *A typical build sequence associated with a layered architecture*

Checkpoints
of the Process

It is always important to have visible milestones in the life cycle where various stakeholders meet, face to face, to discuss progress
and plans. The purpose of these events is not
only to demonstrate how well a project is performing but also to achieve the following:

Key Points

▲ Three sequences of project checkpoints are used to synchronize stakeholder expectations throughout the life
cycle: major milestones, minor milestones, and status assessments.

▲ The most important major milestone
is usually the event that transitions the
project from the elaboration phase into
the construction phase.

▲ The format and content of minor
milestones are highly dependent on the
project and the organizational culture.

▲ Periodic status assessments are crucial
for focusing continuous attention on
the evolving health of the project and
its dynamic priorities.

- Synchronize stakeholder expectations
  and achieve concurrence on three evolving perspectives: the requirements, the
  design, and the plan

- Synchronize related artifacts into a consistent and balanced state

- Identify the important risks, issues, and
  out-of-tolerance conditions

- Perform a global assessment for the whole life cycle, not just the current situation of an individual perspective or intermediate product

Milestones must have well-defined expectations and provide tangible results. This
does not preclude the renegotiation of the milestone's objectives once the project has
gained further understanding of the trade-offs among the requirements, the design,
and the plan.

Three types of joint management reviews are conducted throughout the process:

1. *Major milestones.* These systemwide events are held at the end of each development phase. They provide visibility to systemwide issues, synchronize the management and engineering perspectives, and verify that the aims of the phase have been achieved.

2. *Minor milestones.* These iteration-focused events are conducted to review the content of an iteration in detail and to authorize continued work.

3. *Status assessments.* These periodic events provide management with frequent and regular insight into the progress being made.

Each of the four phases—inception, elaboration, construction, and transition—consists of one or more iterations and concludes with a major milestone when a planned technical capability is produced in demonstrable form. An iteration represents a cycle of activities for which there is a well-defined intermediate result—a minor milestone—captured with two artifacts: a release specification (the evaluation criteria and plan) and a release description (the results). Major milestones at the end of each phase use formal, stakeholder-approved evaluation criteria and release descriptions; minor milestones use informal, development-team-controlled versions of these artifacts.

The level of ceremony and the number of milestones will vary depending on several parameters, such as scale, number of stakeholders, business context, technical risk, and sensitivity of cost and schedule perturbations. Most projects should establish all four major milestones. Only in exceptional cases would you add other major milestones or operate with fewer. (For a nationally important project under broad scrutiny, you might add more; for a scientific experiment with an organic user, you might have fewer.) For simpler projects, very few or no minor milestones may be necessary to manage intermediate results, and the number of status assessments may be infrequent (for example, quarterly). Figure 9-1 illustrates a typical sequence of project checkpoints for a relatively large project.

9.1 MAJOR MILESTONES

The descriptions in this section closely follow the life-cycle anchor points approach described in "Anchoring the Software Process" [Boehm, 1996]. The four major milestones occur at the transition points between life-cycle phases. They can be used in many different process models, including the conventional waterfall model. In an iterative model, the major milestones are used to achieve concurrence among all

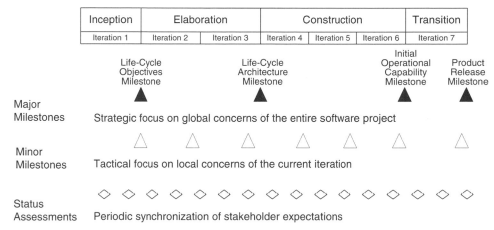

FIGURE 9-1. *A typical sequence of life-cycle checkpoints*

stakeholders on the current state of the project. Different stakeholders have very different concerns:

- Customers: schedule and budget estimates, feasibility, risk assessment, requirements understanding, progress, product line compatibility

- Users: consistency with requirements and usage scenarios, potential for accommodating growth, quality attributes

- Architects and systems engineers: product line compatibility, requirements changes, trade-off analyses, completeness and consistency, balance among risk, quality, and usability

- Developers: sufficiency of requirements detail and usage scenario descriptions, frameworks for component selection or development, resolution of development risk, product line compatibility, sufficiency of the development environment

- Maintainers: sufficiency of product and documentation artifacts, understandability, interoperability with existing systems, sufficiency of maintenance environment

- Others: possibly many other perspectives by stakeholders such as regulatory agencies, independent verification and validation contractors, venture capital investors, subcontractors, associate contractors, and sales and marketing teams

The milestones described in this section may be conducted as one continuous meeting of all concerned parties or incrementally through mostly on-line review of the various artifacts. There are considerable differences in the levels of ceremony for these

TABLE 9-1. *The general status of plans, requirements, and products across the major milestones*

MILESTONES	PLANS	UNDERSTANDING OF PROBLEM SPACE (REQUIREMENTS)	SOLUTION SPACE PROGRESS (SOFTWARE PRODUCT)
Life-cycle objectives milestone	Definition of stakeholder responsibilities Low-fidelity life-cycle plan High-fidelity elaboration phase plan	Baseline vision, including growth vectors, quality attributes, and priorities Use case model	Demonstration of at least one feasible architecture Make/buy/reuse trade-offs Initial design model
Life-cycle architecture milestone	High-fidelity construction phase plan (bill of materials, labor allocation) Low-fidelity transition phase plan	Stable vision and use case model Evaluation criteria for construction releases, initial operational capability Draft user manual	Stable design set Make/buy/reuse decisions Critical component prototypes
Initial operational capability milestone	High-fidelity transition phase plan	Acceptance criteria for product release Releasable user manual	Stable implementation set Critical features and core capabilities Objective insight into product qualities
Product release milestone	Next-generation product plan	Final user manual	Stable deployment set Full features Compliant quality

events, depending on several factors discussed in Chapter 14. The essence of each major milestone is to ensure that the requirements understanding, the life-cycle plans, and the product's form, function, and quality are evolving in balanced levels of detail and to ensure consistency among the various artifacts. Table 9-1 summarizes the balance of information across the major milestones.

Life-Cycle Objectives Milestone

The life-cycle objectives milestone occurs at the end of the inception phase. The goal is to present to all stakeholders a recommendation on how to proceed with development, including a plan, estimated cost and schedule, and expected benefits and cost savings. The vision statement and the critical issues relative to requirements and the operational concept are addressed. A draft architecture document and a prototype architecture demonstration provide evidence of the completeness of the vision and the software development plan. A successfully completed life-cycle objectives milestone will result in authorization from all stakeholders to proceed with the elaboration phase.

Life-Cycle Architecture Milestone

The life-cycle architecture milestone occurs at the end of the elaboration phase. The primary goal is to demonstrate an executable architecture to all stakeholders. A more detailed plan for the construction phase is presented for approval. Critical issues relative to requirements and the operational concept are addressed. This review will also produce consensus on a baseline architecture, baseline vision, baseline software development plan, and evaluation criteria for the initial operational capability milestone. The baseline architecture consists of both a human-readable representation (the architecture document) and a configuration-controlled set of software components captured in the engineering artifacts. A successfully completed life-cycle architecture milestone will result in authorization from the stakeholders to proceed with the construction phase.

Because the most important major milestone is usually the event that transitions the project from the elaboration phase into the construction phase, the general content of a typical milestone is elaborated here in more detail. From a management and contractual standpoint, this major milestone corresponds to achieving a software development state in which the research and development stage is concluding and the production stage is being initiated. A software development project ready for this transition exhibits the following characteristics:

- The critical use cases have been defined, agreed upon by stakeholders, and codified into a set of scenarios for evaluating the evolving architecture.

- A stable architecture has been baselined (subjected to configuration management) in the source language format. Stability here means that the important qualities of the architecture (performance, robustness, scalability, adaptability) have been demonstrated against the critical use cases sufficient to resolve all major requirements and design and planning risks. (Although the risks may not be resolved, the path to resolution has been defined.)

- The risk profile is well understood. Although all risks do not need to be fully resolved, there should be a common understanding among stakeholders of outstanding risks that could have serious consequences, and mitigation plans should be fully elaborated.

- The development plan for the construction and transition phases is defined with enough fidelity that construction iterations can proceed with predictable results. Predictable here means that the development organization will commit to fixed-price increments that can be transitioned to the user in less than one year.

The content of this milestone will vary across project domains. It should include at least the following:

- A presentation and overview of the current project state
- A configuration-controlled set of engineering information, available electronically or in hard copy
- An executable demonstration of capability

The technical data listed in Figure 9-2 should have been reviewed by the time of the life-cycle architecture milestone. Figure 9-3 provides default agendas for this milestone.

Initial Operational Capability Milestone

The initial operational capability milestone occurs late in the construction phase. The goals are to assess the readiness of the software to begin the transition into customer/user sites and to authorize the start of acceptance testing. Issues are addressed concerning

---

I.   **Requirements**
    A.   Use case model
    B.   Vision document (text, use cases)
    C.   Evaluation criteria for elaboration (text, scenarios)
II. **Architecture**
    A.   Design view (object models)
    B.   Process view (if necessary, run-time layout, executable code structure)
    C.   Component view (subsystem layout, make/buy/reuse component identification)
    D.   Deployment view (target run-time layout, target executable code structure)
    E.   Use case view (test case structure, test result expectation)
        1.   Draft user manual
III. **Source and executable libraries**
    A.   Product components
    B.   Test components
    C.   Environment and tool components

FIGURE 9-2. *Engineering artifacts available at the life-cycle architecture milestone*

Presentation Agenda
  I.   **Scope and objectives**
       A.   Demonstration overview
  II. **Requirements assessment**
       A.   Project vision and use cases
       B.   Primary scenarios and evaluation criteria
  III. **Architecture assessment**
       A.   Progress
            1.   Baseline architecture metrics (progress to date and baseline for measuring future architectural stability, scrap, and rework)
            2.   Development metrics baseline estimate (for assessing future progress)
            3.   Test metrics baseline estimate (for assessing future progress of the test team)
       B.   Quality
            1.   Architectural features (demonstration capability summary vs. evaluation criteria)
            2.   Performance (demonstration capability summary vs. evaluation criteria)
            3.   Exposed architectural risks and resolution plans
            4.   Affordability and make/buy/reuse trade-offs
  IV. **Construction phase plan assessment**
       A.   Iteration content and use case allocation
       B.   Next iteration(s) detailed plan and evaluation criteria
       C.   Elaboration phase cost/schedule performance
       D.   Construction phase resource plan and basis of estimate
       E.   Risk assessment

Demonstration Agenda
  I.   **Evaluation criteria**
  II. **Architecture subset summary**
  III. **Demonstration environment summary**
  IV. **Scripted demonstration scenarios**
  V.   **Evaluation criteria results and follow-up items**

FIGURE 9-3. *Default agendas for the life-cycle architecture milestone*

installation instructions, software version descriptions, user and operator manuals, and the ability of the development organization to support user sites. Software quality metrics are reviewed to determine whether quality is sufficient for transition. The readiness of the test environment and the test software for acceptance testing is assessed. Acceptance testing can be done incrementally across multiple iterations or can be completed entirely during the transition phase. The initiation of the transition phase is not necessarily the completion of the construction phase. These phases typically overlap until an initial product is delivered to the user for self-sufficient operation.

Product Release Milestone

The product release milestone occurs at the end of the transition phase. The goal is to assess the completion of the software and its transition to the support organization, if any. The results of acceptance testing are reviewed, and all open issues are addressed. These issues could include installation instructions, software version descriptions, user and operator manuals, software support manuals, and the installation of the development environment at the support sites. Software quality metrics are reviewed to determine whether quality is sufficient for transition to the support organization.

9.2   MINOR MILESTONES

The number of iteration-specific, informal milestones needed depends on the content and length of the iteration. For most iterations, which have a one-month to six-month duration, only two minor milestones are needed: the iteration readiness review and the iteration assessment review. For longer iterations, more intermediate review points may be necessary. For example, on projects with very formal test procedures that must be witnessed by other stakeholders, a test readiness review may be held at which the test plans are reviewed and approved. Large-scale, unprecedented projects may also use intermediate design walkthroughs as forcing functions for progress assessment and dissemination throughout the project.

All iterations are not created equal. An iteration can take on very different forms and priorities, depending on where the project is in the life cycle. Early iterations focus on analysis and design, with substantial elements of discovery, experimentation, and risk assessment. Later iterations focus much more on completeness, consistency, usability, and change management. The milestones of an iteration and its associated evaluation criteria need to focus the engineering activities on the project priorities as defined in the overall software development plan, business case, and vision.

- **Iteration Readiness Review.** This informal milestone is conducted at the start of each iteration to review the detailed iteration plan and the evaluation criteria that have been allocated to this iteration.

- **Iteration Assessment Review.** This informal milestone is conducted at the end of each iteration to assess the degree to which the iteration achieved its objectives and satisfied its evaluation criteria, to review iteration results, to review qualification test results (if part of the iteration), to determine the amount of rework to be done, and to review the impact of the iteration results on the plan for subsequent iterations.

The format and content of these minor milestones tend to be highly dependent on the project and the organizational culture. Figure 9-4 identifies the various minor milestones to be considered when a project is being planned.

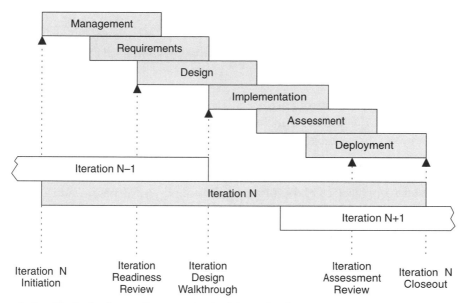

FIGURE 9-4. *Typical minor milestones in the life cycle of an iteration*

9.3 PERIODIC STATUS ASSESSMENTS

Managing risks requires continuous attention to all the interacting activities of a software development effort. Periodic status assessments are management reviews conducted at regular intervals (monthly, quarterly) to address progress and quality indicators, ensure continuous attention to project dynamics, and maintain open communications among all stakeholders. The paramount objective of these assessments is to ensure that the expectations of all stakeholders (contractor, customer, user, subcontractor) are synchronized and consistent.

Periodic status assessments serve as project snapshots. While the period may vary, the recurring event forces the project history to be captured and documented. Status assessments provide the following:

- A mechanism for openly addressing, communicating, and resolving management issues, technical issues, and project risks

- Objective data derived directly from on-going activities and evolving product configurations

- A mechanism for disseminating process, progress, quality trends, practices, and experience information to and from all stakeholders in an open forum

Recurring themes from unsuccessful projects include status assessments that are (1) high-overhead activities, because the work associated with generating the status is separate from the everyday work, and (2) frequently canceled, because of higher priority issues that require resolution. Recurring themes from successful projects include status assessments that are (1) low-overhead activities, because the material already exists as everyday management data, and (2) rarely canceled, because they are considered too important.

Periodic status assessments are crucial for focusing continuous attention on the evolving health of the project and its dynamic priorities. They force the software project manager to collect and review the data periodically, force outside peer review, and encourage dissemination of best practices to and from other stakeholders. By standardizing the format and the metrics that are reviewed, an organization can also enable project-to-project comparisons and dissemination of best practices far more efficiently.

The default content of periodic status assessments should include the topics identified in Table 9-2. The only content the software project manager should have to generate from scratch for each review is an assessment of the top 10 risks. Even this will be predominantly an update of the previous assessment. A good rule of thumb is that the status assessment charts should be easily produced by the project manager with one day's notice. This minimal effort is possible if the data exist within an automated environment. The topic *technical progress*, shown in the table, is discussed in Chapter 13.

TABLE 9-2. *Default content of status assessment reviews*

TOPIC	CONTENT
Personnel	Staffing plan vs. actuals
	Attritions, additions
Financial trends	Expenditure plan vs. actuals for the previous, current, and next major milestones
	Revenue forecasts
Top 10 risks	Issues and criticality resolution plans
	Quantification (cost, time, quality) of exposure
Technical progress	Configuration baseline schedules for major milestones
	Software management metrics and indicators
	Current change trends
	Test and quality assessments
Major milestone plans and results	Plan, schedule, and risks for the next major milestone
	Pass/fail results for all acceptance criteria
Total product scope	Total size, growth, and acceptance criteria perturbations

SOFTWARE MANAGEMENT DISCIPLINES

Software management efforts span a broad range of domains. The chapters in Part III discuss the major disciplines necessary for an effective management workflow: planning, organization, automation, and project control. These disciplines of software project management are not easy to define in generic terms. Therefore, another important discipline is tailoring the process framework to the specific management needs of a given project.

Planning is the crux of management. The challenge is to develop a plan that best balances the available resources to provide optimal win conditions for all stakeholders. The project organization discipline concerns itself with the management of people—organizing them into teams and allocating responsibilities for efficient operations. Automating the development process with an electronic repository for the artifacts provides a foundation for objective instrumentation. Project control activities act as the "senses" of the project. They are used to assess the health of the plan, the quality of the artifacts, and the need for changes to any of the management set artifacts that define the expectations among stakeholders.

CHAPTER 10

Iterative Process Planning

Like software development, project planning requires an iterative process. Like software, a plan is an intangible piece of intellectual property to which all the same concepts must be applied. Plans have an engineering stage, during which the plan is developed, and a production stage, when the plan is executed. Plans must evolve as the understanding evolves of the problem space and the solution space. Planning errors are just like product errors: The sooner in the life cycle they are resolved, the less impact they have on project success.

> **Key Points**
>
> ▲ Projects can underplan and they can overplan. Once again, balance is paramount in the level of planning detail and the buy-in among stakeholders.
>
> ▲ The work breakdown structure is the "architecture" of the project plan. It must encapsulate change and evolve with the appropriate level of detail throughout the life cycle.
>
> ▲ Cost and schedule budgets should be estimated using macroanalysis techniques (top-down project level) and microanalysis techniques (bottom-up task level) to achieve predictable results.

Comprehensive project plans are highly dependent on numerous parameters, any one of which can have a significant impact on the direction of a project. Nevertheless, generic planning advice is sought by every software project manager as a skeleton from which to begin. This chapter is not a plan, a cookbook for a plan, nor a recipe for a plan. It is simply a rough model of a few dimensions, perhaps a starting point for a plan.

10.1 WORK BREAKDOWN STRUCTURES

A good work breakdown structure and its synchronization with the process framework are critical factors in software project success. Although the concept and practice of using a WBS are well established, this topic is largely avoided in the published literature. This is primarily because the development of a work breakdown structure is dependent on the project management style, organizational culture, customer preference, financial constraints, and several other hard-to-define, project-specific parameters. *Software Engineering Economics* [Boehm, 1981] contains background material on software-oriented work breakdown structures.

A WBS is simply a hierarchy of elements that decomposes the project plan into the discrete work tasks. A WBS provides the following information structure:

- A delineation of all significant work

- A clear task decomposition for assignment of responsibilities

- A framework for scheduling, budgeting, and expenditure tracking

Many parameters can drive the decomposition of work into discrete tasks: product subsystems, components, functions, organizational units, life-cycle phases, even geographies. Most systems have a first-level decomposition by subsystem. Subsystems are then decomposed into their components, one of which is typically the software. This section focuses on software WBS elements, whether the software is the whole project or simply one component of a larger system.

10.1.1 CONVENTIONAL WBS ISSUES

Conventional work breakdown structures frequently suffer from three fundamental flaws.

1. They are prematurely structured around the product design.

2. They are prematurely decomposed, planned, and budgeted in either too much or too little detail.

3. They are project-specific, and cross-project comparisons are usually difficult or impossible.

Conventional work breakdown structures are prematurely structured around the product design. Figure 10-1 shows a typical conventional WBS that has been structured primarily around the subsystems of its product architecture, then further decomposed into the components of each subsystem. Once this structure is ingrained in the WBS and then allocated to responsible managers with budgets, schedules, and expected deliverables, a concrete planning foundation has been set that is difficult and expensive to change. A WBS is the architecture for the financial plan. Just as software architectures need to encapsulate components that are likely to change, so must planning architectures. To couple the plan tightly to the product structure may make sense if both are reasonably mature. However, a looser coupling is desirable if either the plan or the architecture is subject to change.

```
Management
System requirements and design
Subsystem 1
    Component 11
        Requirements
        Design
        Code
        Test
        Documentation
    . . . (similar structures for other components)
    Component 1N
        Requirements
        Design
        Code
        Test
        Documentation
. . . (similar structures for other subsystems)
Subsystem M
    Component M1
        Requirements
        Design
        Code
        Test
        Documentation
    . . . (similar structures for other components)
    Component MN
        Requirements
        Design
        Code
        Test
        Documentation
Integration and test
    Test planning
    Test procedure preparation
    Testing
    Test reports
Other support areas
    Configuration control
    Quality assurance
    System administration
```

FIGURE 10-1. *Conventional work breakdown structure, following the product hierarchy*

Conventional work breakdown structures are prematurely decomposed, planned, and budgeted in either too little or too much detail. Large software projects tend to be overplanned, and small projects tend to be underplanned. The WBS shown in Figure 10-1 is overly simplistic for most large-scale systems, where six or more levels of WBS elements are commonplace. The management team plans out each element completely and creates a baseline budget and schedule for every task at the same level of detail. On the other hand, most small-scale or in-house developments elaborate their WBSs to a single level only, with no supporting detail. The management team plans and conducts the project with coarse tasking and cost and schedule accountability. Both approaches are out of balance. In general, a WBS elaborated to at least two or three levels makes sense. For large-scale systems, additional levels may be necessary in later phases of the life cycle. The basic problem with planning too much detail at the outset is that the detail does not evolve with the level of fidelity in the plan. For example, it is impossible to lay out accurately in month 1—when the plan is being baselined, and before the architecture and test scenarios have been engineered—details of the test activities that are scheduled 18 months later.

Conventional work breakdown structures are project-specific, and cross-project comparisons are usually difficult or impossible. Most organizations allow individual projects to define their own project-specific structure tailored to the project manager's style, the customer's demands, or other project-specific preferences. With no standard WBS structure, it is extremely difficult to compare plans, financial data, schedule data, organizational efficiencies, cost trends, productivity trends, or quality trends across multiple projects. Each project organizes the work differently and uses different units of measure. Some of the following simple questions, which are critical to any organizational process improvement program, cannot be answered by most project teams that use conventional work breakdown structures.

- What is the ratio of productive activities (requirements, design, implementation, assessment, deployment) to overhead activities (management, environment)?
- What is the percentage of effort expended in rework activities?
- What is the percentage of cost expended in software capital equipment (the environment expenditures)?
- What is the ratio of productive testing versus (unproductive) integration?
- What is the cost of release N (as a basis for planning release N+1)?

10.1.2 EVOLUTIONARY WORK BREAKDOWN STRUCTURES

An evolutionary WBS should organize the planning elements around the process framework rather than the product framework. This approach better accommodates the expected changes in the evolving plan and allows the level of planning fidelity to evolve in a straightforward way. The basic recommendation for the WBS is to organize the hierarchy as follows:

- First-level WBS elements are the workflows (management, environment, requirements, design, implementation, assessment, and deployment). These elements are usually allocated to a single team (as discussed in Chapter 11) and constitute the anatomy of a project for the purposes of planning and comparison with other projects.

- Second-level elements are defined for each phase of the life cycle (inception, elaboration, construction, and transition). These elements allow the fidelity of the plan to evolve more naturally with the level of understanding of the requirements and architecture, and the risks therein.

- Third-level elements are defined for the focus of activities that produce the artifacts of each phase. These elements may be the lowest level in the hierarchy that collects the cost of a discrete artifact for a given phase, or they may be decomposed further into several lower level activities that, taken together, produce a single artifact.

A default WBS consistent with the process framework (phases, workflows, and artifacts) is shown in Figure 10-2. This recommended structure provides one example of how the elements of the process framework can be integrated into a plan. It provides a framework for estimating the costs and schedules of each element, allocating them across a project organization, and tracking expenditures.

The structure shown is intended to be merely a starting point. It needs to be tailored to the specifics of a project in many ways.

- Scale. Larger projects will have more levels and substructures.

- Organizational structure. Projects that include subcontractors or span multiple organizational entities may introduce constraints that necessitate different WBS allocations.

- Degree of custom development. Depending on the character of the project, there can be very different emphases in the requirements, design, and implementation workflows. A business process re-engineering project based primarily on existing components would have much more depth in the requirements element and a fairly shallow design and implementation element. A fully custom development of a one-of-a-kind technical application may require fairly deep design and implementation elements to manage the risks associated with the custom, first-generation components.

A Management
   AA Inception phase management
      AAA   Business case development
      AAB   Elaboration phase release specifications
      AAC   Elaboration phase WBS baselining
      AAD   Software development plan
      AAE   Inception phase project control and status assessments
   AB Elaboration phase management
      ABA   Construction phase release specifications
      ABB   Construction phase WBS baselining
      ABC   Elaboration phase project control and status assessments
   AC Construction phase management
      ACA   Deployment phase planning
      ACB   Deployment phase WBS baselining
      ACC   Construction phase project control and status assessments
   AD Transition phase management
      ADA   Next generation planning
      ADB   Transition phase project control and status assessments
B Environment
   BA Inception phase environment specification
   BB Elaboration phase environment baselining
      BBA   Development environment installation and administration
      BBB   Development environment integration and custom
               toolsmithing
      BBC   SCO database formulation
   BC Construction phase environment maintenance
      BCA   Development environment installation and administration
      BCB   SCO database maintenance
   BD Transition phase environment maintenance
      BDA   Development environment maintenance and administration
      BDB   SCO database maintenance
      BDC   Maintenance environment packaging and transition
C Requirements
   CA Inception phase requirements development
      CAA   Vision specification
      CAB   Use case modeling
   CB Elaboration phase requirements baselining
      CBA   Vision baselining
      CBB   Use case model baselining
   CC Construction phase requirements maintenance
   CD Transition phase requirements maintenance

```
D   Design
    DA   Inception phase architecture prototyping
    DB   Elaboration phase architecture baselining
         DBA    Architecture design modeling
         DBB    Design demonstration planning and conduct
         DBC    Software architecture description
    DC   Construction phase design modeling
         DCA    Architecture design model maintenance
         DCB    Component design modeling
    DD   Transition phase design maintenance
E   Implementation
    EA   Inception phase component prototyping
    EB   Elaboration phase component implementation
         EBA    Critical component coding demonstration integration
    EC   Construction phase component implementation
         ECA    Initial release(s) component coding and stand-alone testing
         ECB    Alpha release component coding and stand-alone testing
         ECC    Beta release component coding and stand-alone testing
         ECD    Component maintenance
    ED   Transition phase component maintenance
F   Assessment
    FA   Inception phase assessment planning
    FB   Elaboration phase assessment
         FBA    Test modeling
         FBB    Architecture test scenario implementation
         FBC    Demonstration assessment and release descriptions
    FC   Construction phase assessment
         FCA    Initial release assessment and release description
         FCB    Alpha release assessment and release description
         FCC    Beta release assessment and release description
    FD   Transition phase assessment
         FDA    Product release assessment and release descriptions
G   Deployment
    GA   Inception phase deployment planning
    GB   Elaboration phase deployment planning
    GC   Construction phase deployment
         GCA    User manual baselining
    GD   Transition phase deployment
         GDA    Product transition to user
```

FIGURE 10-2. *Default work breakdown structure*

- Business context. Contractual projects require much more elaborate management and assessment elements. Projects developing commercial products for delivery to a broad customer base may require much more elaborate substructures for the deployment element. An application deployed to a single site may have a trivial deployment element (such as an internally developed business application) or an elaborate one (such as transitioning from a mission-critical legacy system with parallel operation, to achieve zero downtime).

- Precedent experience. Very few projects start with a clean slate. Most of them are developed as new generations of a legacy system (with a mature WBS) or in the context of existing organizational standards (with preordained WBS expectations). It is important to accommodate these constraints to ensure that new projects exploit the existing experience base and benchmarks of project performance.

The WBS decomposes the character of the project and maps it to the life cycle, the budget, and the personnel. Reviewing a WBS provides insight into the important attributes, priorities, and structure of the project plan. In performing project assessments and software management audits over the past several years, I have found the WBS to be the most valuable source of objective information about the project plan. While the software development plan and the business case provide a context for review, the WBS and the relative budgets allocated among the elements provide the most meaningful indicators of the management approach, priorities, and concerns.

Another important attribute of a good WBS is that the planning fidelity inherent in each element is commensurate with the current life-cycle phase and project state. Figure 10-3 illustrates this idea. One of the primary reasons for organizing the default WBS the way I have is to allow for planning elements that range from planning packages (rough budgets that are maintained as an estimate for future elaboration rather than being decomposed into detail) through fully planned activity networks (with a well-defined budget and continuous assessment of actual versus planned expenditures).

10.2 PLANNING GUIDELINES

Software projects span a broad range of application domains. It is valuable but risky to make specific planning recommendations independent of project context. It is valuable because most people in management positions are looking for a starting point, a skeleton they can flesh out with project-specific details. They know that initial planning guidelines capture the expertise and experience of many other people. Such guidelines are therefore considered credible bases of estimates and instill some confidence in the stakeholders.

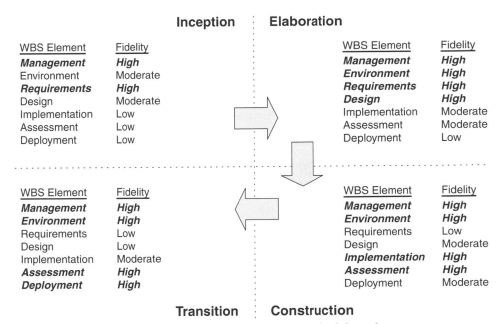

FIGURE 10-3. *Evolution of planning fidelity in the WBS over the life cycle*

Project-independent planning advice is also risky. There is the risk that the guidelines may be adopted blindly without being adapted to specific project circumstances. Blind adherence to someone else's project-independent planning advice is a sure sign of an incompetent management team. There is also the risk of misinterpretation. The variability of project parameters, project business contexts, organizational cultures, and project processes makes it extremely easy to make mistakes that have significant potential impact. Within this book, I have tried to provide an adequate context so that such misinterpretations can be avoided. To temper the project-independent discussions, Appendix D presents a very detailed case study of a specific real-world project. The case study provides a good example of a project that is 90% consistent with the project-independent planning guidelines given here. It also provides examples and rationale for several minor deviations from these guidelines.

Two simple planning guidelines should be considered when a project plan is being initiated or assessed. The first guideline, detailed in Table 10-1, prescribes a default allocation of costs among the first-level WBS elements. The second guideline, detailed in Table 10-2, prescribes the allocation of effort and schedule across the life-cycle phases. Given an initial estimate of total project cost and these two tables, developing a staffing profile, an allocation of staff resources to teams, a top-level project

TABLE 10-1. *WBS budgeting defaults*

FIRST-LEVEL WBS ELEMENT	DEFAULT BUDGET
Management	10%
Environment	10%
Requirements	10%
Design	15%
Implementation	25%
Assessment	25%
Deployment	5%
Total	100%

schedule, and an initial WBS with task budgets and schedules is relatively straightforward. This sort of top-down plan development is a useful planning exercise that should result in a baseline for further elaboration.

What is the source of the data in Table 10-1 and Table 10-2? Unfortunately, it is not a data bank of well-documented case studies of numerous successful projects that followed a modern software process. These data came mostly from my own experience, including involvement with software cost estimation efforts over the past decade that spanned a broad range of software projects, organizations, processes, and technologies.

Table 10-1 provides default allocations for budgeted costs of each first-level WBS element. While these values are certain to vary across projects, this allocation provides a good benchmark for assessing the plan by understanding the rationale for deviations from these guidelines. An important point here is that this is cost allocation, not effort allocation. To avoid misinterpretation, two explanations are necessary.

1. The cost of different labor categories is inherent in these numbers. For example, the management, requirements, and design elements tend to use more personnel who are senior and more highly paid than the other elements use. If requirements and design together consume 25% of the budget

TABLE 10-2. *Default distributions of effort and schedule by phase*

DOMAIN	INCEPTION	ELABORATION	CONSTRUCTION	TRANSITION
Effort	5%	20%	65%	10%
Schedule	10%	30%	50%	10%

(employing people with an average salary of $100/hour), this sum may represent half as many staff hours as the assessment element, which also accounts for 25% of the budget but employs personnel with an average salary of $50/hour.

2. The cost of hardware and software assets that support the process automation and development teams is also included in the environment element.

Table 10-2 provides guidelines for allocating effort and schedule across the life-cycle phases. Although these values can also vary widely, depending on the specific constraints of an application, they provide an average expectation across a spectrum of application domains. Achieving consistency using these specific values is not as important as understanding why your project may be different.

10.3   THE COST AND SCHEDULE ESTIMATING PROCESS

Project plans need to be derived from two perspectives. The first is a forward-looking, top-down approach. It starts with an understanding of the general requirements and constraints, derives a macro-level budget and schedule, then decomposes these elements into lower level budgets and intermediate milestones. From this perspective, the following planning sequence would occur:

1. The software project manager (and others) develops a characterization of the overall size, process, environment, people, and quality required for the project.

2. A macro-level estimate of the total effort and schedule is developed using a software cost estimation model.

3. The software project manager partitions the estimate for the effort into a top-level WBS using guidelines such as those in Table 10-1. The project manager also partitions the schedule into major milestone dates and partitions the effort into a staffing profile using guidelines such as those in Table 10-2. Now there is a project-level plan. These sorts of estimates tend to ignore many detailed project-specific parameters.

4. At this point, subproject managers are given the responsibility for decomposing each of the WBS elements into lower levels using their top-level allocation, staffing profile, and major milestone dates as constraints.

The second perspective is a backward-looking, bottom-up approach. You start with the end in mind, analyze the micro-level budgets and schedules, then sum all these elements into the higher level budgets and intermediate milestones. This approach tends to define and populate the WBS from the lowest levels upward. From this perspective, the following planning sequence would occur:

1. The lowest level WBS elements are elaborated into detailed tasks, for which budgets and schedules are estimated by the responsible WBS element manager. These estimates tend to incorporate the project-specific parameters in an exaggerated way.

2. Estimates are combined and integrated into higher level budgets and milestones. The biases of individual estimators need to be homogenized so that there is a consistent basis of negotiation.

3. Comparisons are made with the top-down budgets and schedule milestones. Gross differences are assessed and adjustments are made in order to converge on agreement between the top-down and the bottom-up estimates.

Milestone scheduling or budget allocation through top-down estimating tends to exaggerate the project management biases and usually results in an overly optimistic plan. Bottom-up estimates usually exaggerate the performer biases and result in an overly pessimistic plan. Iteration is necessary, using the results of one approach to validate and refine the results of the other approach, thereby evolving the plan through multiple versions. This process instills ownership of the plan in all levels of management.

These two planning approaches should be used together, in balance, throughout the life cycle of the project. During the engineering stage, the top-down perspective will dominate because there is usually not enough depth of understanding nor stability in the detailed task sequences to perform credible bottom-up planning. During the production stage, there should be enough precedent experience and planning fidelity that the bottom-up planning perspective will dominate. By then, the top-down approach should be well tuned to the project-specific parameters, so it should be used more as a global assessment technique. Figure 10-4 illustrates this life-cycle planning balance.

10.4 THE ITERATION PLANNING PROCESS

So far, this discussion has dealt only with the application-independent aspects of budgeting and scheduling. Another dimension of planning is concerned with defining the actual sequence of intermediate results. Planning the content and schedule of the major milestones and their intermediate iterations is probably the most tangible form of the overall risk management plan. An evolutionary build plan is important because there are always adjustments in build content and schedule as early conjecture evolves into well-understood project circumstances.

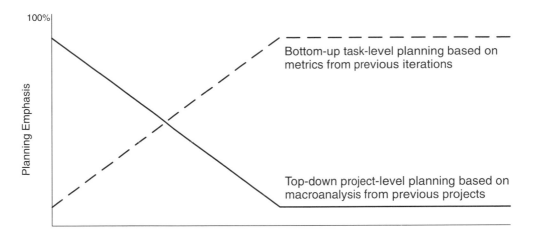

Engineering Stage		Production Stage	
Inception	Elaboration	Construction	Transition

Feasibility iterations   Architecture iterations   Usable iterations   Product releases

Engineering stage planning emphasis:
- Macro-level task estimation for production-stage artifacts
- Micro-level task estimation for engineering artifacts
- Stakeholder concurrence
- Coarse-grained variance analysis of actual vs. planned expenditures
- Tuning the top-down project-independent planning guidelines into project-specific planning guidelines
- WBS definition and elaboration

Production stage planning emphasis:
- Micro-level task estimation for production-stage artifacts
- Macro-level task estimation for maintenance of engineering artifacts
- Stakeholder concurrence
- Fine-grained variance analysis of actual vs. planned expenditures

FIGURE 10-4. *Planning balance throughout the life cycle*

A generic build progression and general guidelines on the number of iterations in each phase are described next. *Iteration* is used to mean a complete synchronization across the project, with a well-orchestrated global assessment of the entire project baseline. Other micro-iterations, such as monthly, weekly, or daily builds, are performed en route to these project-level synchronization points.

- Inception iterations. The early prototyping activities integrate the foundation components of a candidate architecture and provide an executable framework for elaborating the critical use cases of the system. This framework includes existing components, commercial components, and custom prototypes sufficient to demonstrate a candidate architecture and sufficient requirements understanding to establish a credible business case, vision, and software development plan. Large-scale, custom developments may require two iterations to achieve an acceptable prototype, but most projects should be able to get by with only one.

- Elaboration iterations. These iterations result in an architecture, including a complete framework and infrastructure for execution. Upon completion of the architecture iteration, a few critical use cases should be demonstrable: (1) initializing the architecture, (2) injecting a scenario to drive the worst-case data processing flow through the system (for example, the peak transaction throughput or peak load scenario), and (3) injecting a scenario to drive the worst-case control flow through the system (for example, orchestrating the fault-tolerance use cases). Most projects should plan on two iterations to achieve an acceptable architecture baseline. Unprecedented architectures may require additional iterations, whereas projects built on a well-established architecture framework can probably get by with a single iteration.

- Construction iterations. Most projects require at least two major construction iterations: an alpha release and a beta release. An alpha release would include executable capability for all the critical use cases. It usually represents only about 70% of the total product breadth and performs at quality levels (performance and reliability) below those expected in the final product. A beta release typically provides 95% of the total product capability breadth and achieves some of the important quality attributes. Typically, however, a few more features need to be completed, and improvements in robustness and performance are necessary for the final product release to be acceptable. Although most projects need at least two construction iterations, there are many reasons to add one or two more in order to manage risks or optimize resource expenditures.

- Transition iterations. Most projects use a single iteration to transition a beta release into the final product. Again, numerous informal, small-scale iterations may be necessary to resolve all the defects, incorporate beta feedback, and incorporate performance improvements. However, because of the overhead associated with a full-scale transition to the user community, most projects learn to live with a single iteration between a beta release and the final product release.

The general guideline is that most projects will use between four and nine iterations. The typical project would have the following six-iteration profile:

- One iteration in inception: an architecture prototype
- Two iterations in elaboration: architecture prototype and architecture baseline
- Two iterations in construction: alpha and beta releases
- One iteration in transition: product release

Highly precedented projects with a predefined architecture, or very small-scale projects, could get away with a single iteration in a combined inception and elaboration phase and could produce a product efficiently with the overhead of only four iterations. A very large or unprecedented project with many stakeholders may require an additional inception iteration and two additional iterations in construction, for a total of nine iterations. The resulting management overhead may be well worth the cost to ensure proper risk management and stakeholder synchronization.

10.5   PRAGMATIC PLANNING

Even though good planning is more dynamic in an iterative process, doing it accurately is far easier. While executing iteration N of any phase, the software project manager must be monitoring and controlling against a plan that was initiated in iteration N – 1 and must be planning iteration N + 1. The art of good project management is to make trade-offs in the current iteration plan and the next iteration plan based on objective results in the current iteration and previous iterations. This concept seems, and is, overwhelming in early phases or in projects that are pioneering iterative development. But if the planning pump is primed successfully, the process becomes surprisingly easy as the project progresses into the phases in which high-fidelity planning is necessary for success.

Aside from bad architectures and misunderstood requirements, inadequate planning (and subsequent bad management) is one of the most common reasons for project failures. Conversely, the success of every successful project can be attributed in part to good planning. This book emphasizes the importance of three perspectives: planning, requirements, and architecture. The end products associated with these perspectives (a software development plan, requirements specifications, and an architecture description document) are not emphasized. On most successful projects, they are not very important once they have been produced. They are rarely used by most performers on a day-to-day basis, they are not very interesting to the end user, and their paper representations are just the tip of the iceberg with respect to the working details that underlie them.

While a planning document is not very useful as an end item, the act of planning is extremely important to project success. It provides a framework and forcing functions for making decisions, ensures buy-in on the part of stakeholders and performers, and transforms subjective, generic process frameworks into objective processes. A project's plan is a definition of how the project requirements will be transformed into a product within the business constraints. It must be realistic, it must be current, it must be a team product, it must be understood by the stakeholders, and it must be used.

Plans are not just for managers. The more open and visible the planning process and results, the more ownership there is among the team members who need to execute it. Bad, closely held plans cause attrition. Good, open plans can shape cultures and encourage teamwork.

CHAPTER 11

Project Organizations and Responsibilities

Software lines of business and project teams have different motivations. Software lines of business are motivated by return on investment, new business discriminators, market diversification, and profitability. Project teams are motivated by the cost, schedule, and quality of specific deliverables.

Software professionals in both types of organizations are motivated by career growth, job satisfaction, and the opportunity to make a difference. This topic is covered well in *A Discipline for Software Engineering* [Humphrey, 1995].

In the past, most advice on organizations was (rightfully) focused on the project, which is the level where software is developed and delivered. Projects have selfish interests and will rarely invest in any technology or service that does not have a direct impact on the cost, schedule, or quality of that project's deliverables. This chapter recommends and describes organizations for a line of business and for a project. Prescribing organizational hierarchies is clearly a dangerous undertaking in the context of specific organizations and people. Here, generic roles, relationships, and responsibilities are discussed. For any given project or line of business, these recommendations should be only default starting points. Tailoring them to the domain, scale, cultures, and personalities of a specific situation may lead to a variety of different implementations. It may be appropriate, for example, to organize a project or team differently, splitting or merging the roles presented. Nevertheless, these organizational guidelines incorporate many recurring themes of successful projects and should provide a framework for most organizations.

Key Points

▲ Organizational structures form the architecture of the teams.

▲ Organizations engaged in a software line of business need to support projects with the infrastructure necessary to use a common process.

▲ Project organizations need to allocate artifacts and responsibilities clearly across project teams to ensure a balance of global (architecture) and local (component) concerns.

▲ The organization must evolve with the WBS and the life-cycle concerns.

11.1   LINE-OF-BUSINESS ORGANIZATIONS

Figure 11-1 maps roles and responsibilities to a default line-of-business organization. This structure can be tailored to specific circumstances.

The main features of the default organization are as follows:

- Responsibility for process definition and maintenance is specific to a cohesive line of business, where process commonality makes sense. For example, the process for developing avionics software is different from the process used to develop office applications.

- Responsibility for process automation is an organizational role and is equal in importance to the process definition role. Projects achieve process commonality primarily through the environment support of common tools.

- Organizational roles may be fulfilled by a single individual or several different teams, depending on the scale of the organization. A 20-person software product company may require only a single person to fulfill all the roles, while a 10,000-person telecommunications company may require hundreds of people to achieve an effective software organization.

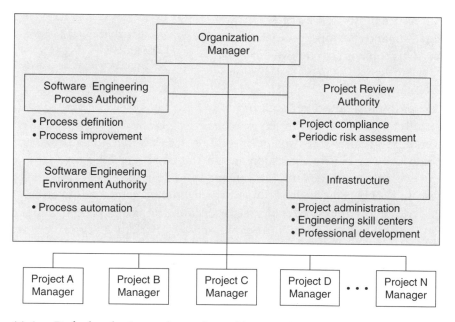

FIGURE 11-1.   *Default roles in a software line-of-business organization*

Software Engineering Process Authority

The Software Engineering Process Authority (SEPA) facilitates the exchange of information and process guidance both to and from project practitioners. This role is accountable to the organization general manager for maintaining a current assessment of the organization's process maturity and its plan for future process improvements. The SEPA must help initiate and periodically assess project processes. Catalyzing the capture and dissemination of software best practices can be accomplished only when the SEPA understands both the desired improvement and the project context. The SEPA is a necessary role in any organization. It takes on responsibility and accountability for the process definition and its maintenance (modification, improvement, technology insertion). The SEPA could be a single individual, the general manager, or even a team of representatives. The SEPA must truly be an authority, competent and powerful, not a staff position rendered impotent by ineffective bureaucracy.

Project Review Authority

The Project Review Authority (PRA) is the single individual responsible for ensuring that a software project complies with all organizational and business unit software policies, practices, and standards. A software project manager is responsible for meeting the requirements of a contract or some other project compliance standard, and is also accountable to the PRA. The PRA reviews both the project's conformance to contractual obligations and the project's organizational policy obligations. The customer monitors contract requirements, contract milestones, contract deliverables, monthly management reviews, progress, quality, cost, schedule, and risk. The PRA reviews customer commitments as well as adherence to organizational policies, organizational deliverables, financial performance, and other risks and accomplishments.

Software Engineering Environment Authority

The Software Engineering Environment Authority (SEEA) is responsible for automating the organization's process, maintaining the organization's standard environment, training projects to use the environment, and maintaining organization-wide reusable assets. The SEEA role is necessary to achieve a significant return on investment for a common process. Tools, techniques, and training can be amortized effectively across multiple projects only if someone in the organization (the SEEA) is responsible for supporting and administering a standard environment. In many cases, the environment may be augmented, customized, or modified, but the existence of an 80% default solution for each project is critical to achieving institutionalization of the organization's process and a good ROI on capital tool investments.

Infrastructure

An organization's infrastructure provides human resources support, project-independent research and development, and other capital software engineering assets. The infrastructure for any given software line of business can range from trivial to highly entrenched bureaucracies. The typical components of the organizational infrastructure are as follows:

- Project administration: time accounting system; contracts, pricing, terms and conditions; corporate information systems integration

- Engineering skill centers: custom tools repository and maintenance, bid and proposal support, independent research and development

- Professional development: internal training boot camp, personnel recruiting, personnel skills database maintenance, literature and assets library, technical publications

An organizational service center promotes a standard environment funded by the line of business and maintained as a capital asset for projects within the organization. The SEEA is a companion group to the SEPA. The SEPA is responsible for process definition and improvement, and the SEEA is responsible for process automation.

It is important that organization managers treat software development environments just as hardware development environments are treated—namely, as capital equipment. There is resistance to this approach in most small-scale or immature organizations, where specific process development and tooling are included as direct project expenses. For most mature software organizations, the process and tooling should be organizational assets, just as they are in other engineering disciplines. As such, they should be funded with capital resources. Financing models can include absorption into overhead or general and administrative costs, or project billing based on usage. In today's software industry, characterized by ingrained accounting methods, project-funded tooling, and software licensing methods, relatively few organizations have transitioned to such a capital investment model for their software environments. These organizations tend to be mature, large-scale software developers that have achieved stable process definitions and have established long-term partnerships with software tool vendors.

11.2 PROJECT ORGANIZATIONS

Figure 11-2 shows a default project organization and maps project-level roles and responsibilities. This structure can be tailored to the size and circumstances of the specific project organization.

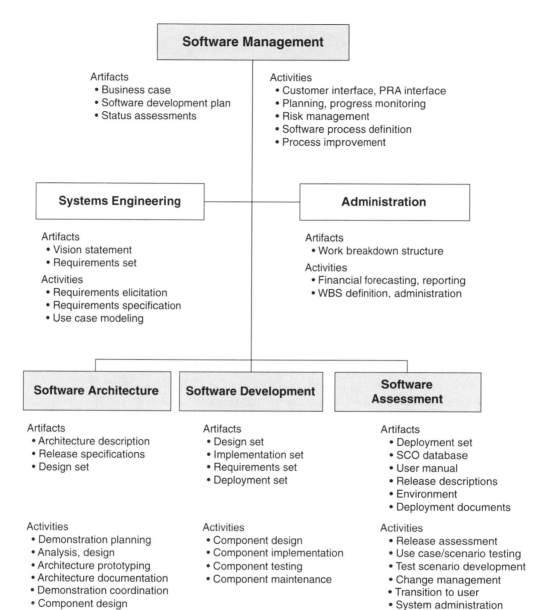

Software Management

Artifacts
• Business case
• Software development plan
• Status assessments

Activities
• Customer interface, PRA interface
• Planning, progress monitoring
• Risk management
• Software process definition
• Process improvement

Systems Engineering

Artifacts
• Vision statement
• Requirements set

Activities
• Requirements elicitation
• Requirements specification
• Use case modeling

Administration

Artifacts
• Work breakdown structure

Activities
• Financial forecasting, reporting
• WBS definition, administration

Software Architecture

Artifacts
• Architecture description
• Release specifications
• Design set

Activities
• Demonstration planning
• Analysis, design
• Architecture prototyping
• Architecture documentation
• Demonstration coordination
• Component design
• Make/buy/reuse analysis

Software Development

Artifacts
• Design set
• Implementation set
• Requirements set
• Deployment set

Activities
• Component design
• Component implementation
• Component testing
• Component maintenance

Software Assessment

Artifacts
• Deployment set
• SCO database
• User manual
• Release descriptions
• Environment
• Deployment documents

Activities
• Release assessment
• Use case/scenario testing
• Test scenario development
• Change management
• Transition to user
• System administration
• Environment configuration
• Environment maintenance
• Toolsmithing

FIGURE 11-2. *Default project organization and responsibilities*

The main features of the default organization are as follows:

- The project management team is an active participant, responsible for producing as well as managing. Project management is not a spectator sport.

- The architecture team is responsible for real artifacts and for the integration of components, not just for staff functions.

- The development team owns the component construction and maintenance activities. The assessment team is separate from development. This structure fosters an independent quality perspective and focuses a team on testing and product evaluation activities concurrent with on-going development.

- Quality is everyone's job, integrated into all activities and checkpoints. Each team takes responsibility for a different quality perspective.

Software Management Team

Most projects are overconstrained. Schedules, costs, functionality, and quality expectations are highly interrelated and require continuous negotiation among multiple stakeholders who have differing goals. The software management team carries the burden of delivering win conditions to all stakeholders. In this regard, the software project manager spends every day worrying about *balance*. Figure 11-3 shows the focus of software management team activities over the project life cycle.

The software management team is responsible for planning the effort, conducting the plan, and adapting the plan to changes in the understanding of the requirements or the design. Toward this end, the team takes ownership of resource management and

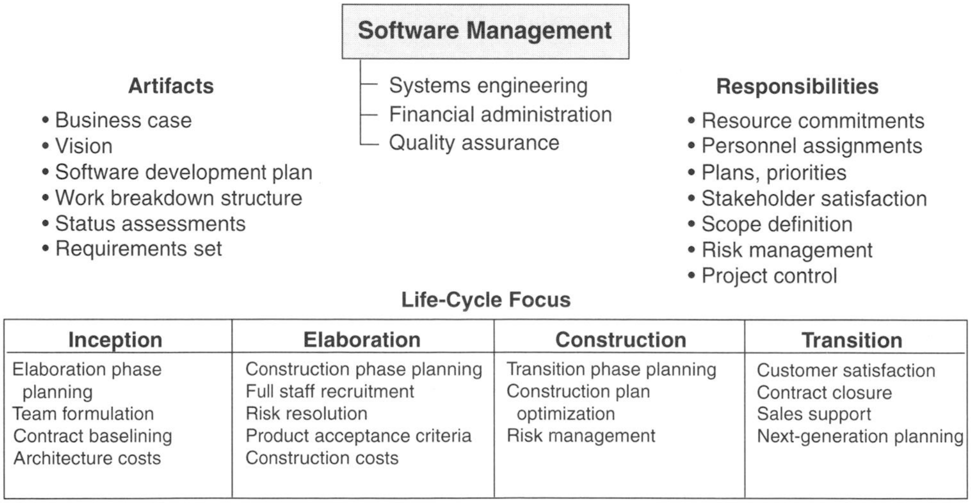

Software Management
- Systems engineering
- Financial administration
- Quality assurance

Artifacts
- Business case
- Vision
- Software development plan
- Work breakdown structure
- Status assessments
- Requirements set

Responsibilities
- Resource commitments
- Personnel assignments
- Plans, priorities
- Stakeholder satisfaction
- Scope definition
- Risk management
- Project control

Life-Cycle Focus

Inception	Elaboration	Construction	Transition
Elaboration phase planning Team formulation Contract baselining Architecture costs	Construction phase planning Full staff recruitment Risk resolution Product acceptance criteria Construction costs	Transition phase planning Construction plan optimization Risk management	Customer satisfaction Contract closure Sales support Next-generation planning

FIGURE 11-3. *Software management team activities*

project scope, and sets operational priorities across the project life cycle. At an abstract level, these activities correspond to managing the expectations of all stakeholders throughout the project life cycle.

The software management team takes ownership of all aspects of quality. In particular, it is responsible for attaining and maintaining a balance among these aspects so that the overall solution is adequate for all stakeholders and optimal for as many of them as possible.

Software Architecture Team

The software architecture team is responsible for the architecture. This responsibility encompasses the engineering necessary to specify a complete bill of materials for the software and the engineering necessary to make significant make/buy trade-offs so that all custom components are elaborated to the extent that construction/assembly costs are highly predictable. Figure 11-4 shows the focus of software architecture team activities over the project life cycle.

For any project, the skill of the software architecture team is crucial. It provides the framework for facilitating team communications, for achieving system-wide qualities, and for implementing the applications. With a good architecture team, an average development team can succeed. If the architecture is weak, even an expert development team of superstar programmers will probably not succeed.

In most projects, the inception and elaboration phases will be dominated by two distinct teams: the software management team and the software architecture team. (Even this distinction may be blurred, depending on scale.) The software development and software assessment teams tend to engage in support roles while preparing for the

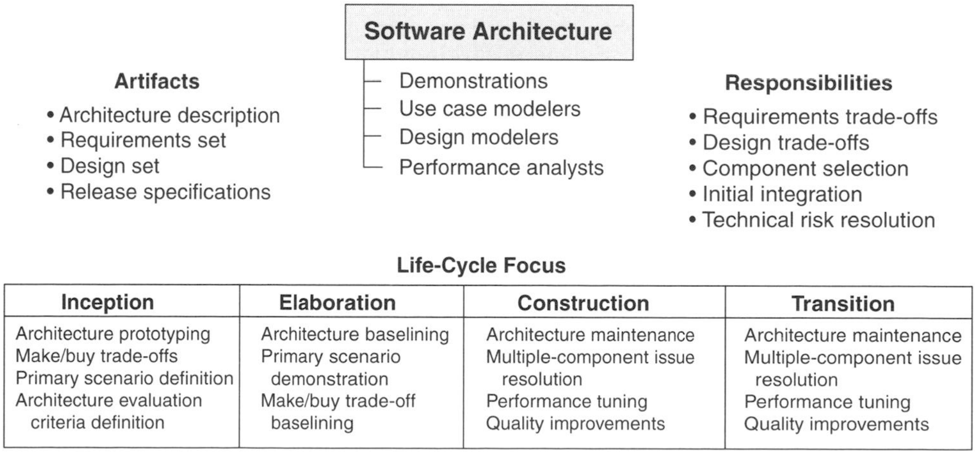

Software Architecture

Artifacts		Responsibilities
• Architecture description	├─ Demonstrations	• Requirements trade-offs
• Requirements set	├─ Use case modelers	• Design trade-offs
• Design set	├─ Design modelers	• Component selection
• Release specifications	└─ Performance analysts	• Initial integration
		• Technical risk resolution

Life-Cycle Focus

Inception	Elaboration	Construction	Transition
Architecture prototyping Make/buy trade-offs Primary scenario definition Architecture evaluation criteria definition	Architecture baselining Primary scenario demonstration Make/buy trade-off baselining	Architecture maintenance Multiple-component issue resolution Performance tuning Quality improvements	Architecture maintenance Multiple-component issue resolution Performance tuning Quality improvements

FIGURE 11-4. *Software architecture team activities*

full-scale production stage. By the time the construction phase is initiated, the architecture transitions into a maintenance mode and must be supported by a minimal level of effort to ensure that there is continuity of the engineering legacy.

To succeed, the architecture team must include a fairly broad level of expertise, including the following:

- Domain experience to produce an acceptable design view (architecturally significant elements of the design model) and use case view (architecturally significant elements of the use case model)

- Software technology experience to produce an acceptable process view (concurrency and control thread relationships among the design, component, and deployment models), component view (structure of the implementation set), and deployment view (structure of the deployment set)

The architecture team is responsible for system-level quality, which includes attributes such as reliability, performance, and maintainability. These attributes span multiple components and represent how well the components integrate to provide an effective solution. In this regard, the architecture team decides how most multiple-component design issues are resolved.

Software Development Team

Figure 11-5 shows the focus of software development team activities over the project life cycle.

Inception	Elaboration	Construction	Transition
Prototyping support Make/buy trade-offs	Critical component design Critical component implementation and test Critical component baseline	Component design Component implementation Component stand-alone test Component maintenance	Component maintenance Component documentation

FIGURE 11-5. *Software development team activities*

The software development team is the most application-specific group. In general, the software development team comprises several subteams dedicated to groups of components that require a common skill set. Typical skill sets include the following:

- Commercial component: specialists with detailed knowledge of commercial components central to a system's architecture

- Database: specialists with experience in the organization, storage, and retrieval of data

- Graphical user interfaces: specialists with experience in the display organization, data presentation, and user interaction necessary to support human input, output, and control needs

- Operating systems and networking: specialists with experience in the execution of multiple software objects on a network of hardware resources, including all the typical control issues associated with initialization, synchronization, resource sharing, name space management, reconfiguration, termination, and interobject communications

- Domain applications: specialists with experience in the algorithms, application processing, or business rules specific to the system

The software development team is responsible for the quality of individual components, including all component development, testing, and maintenance. Component tests should be built as self-documented, repeatable software that is treated like other operational component source code so that it is maintained naturally and is available for automated regression testing. The development team decides how any design or implementation issue local to a single component is resolved.

Software Assessment Team

Figure 11-6 shows the focus of software assessment team activities over the project life cycle.

There are two reasons for using an independent team for software assessment. The first has to do with ensuring an independent quality perspective. This often-debated approach has its pros (such as ensuring that the ownership biases of developers do not pollute the assessment of quality) and cons (such as relieving the software development team of ownership in quality, to some extent). A more important reason for using an independent test team is to exploit the concurrency of activities. Schedules can be accelerated by developing the software and preparing for testing in parallel with development activities. Change management, test planning, and test scenario development can be performed in parallel with design and development.

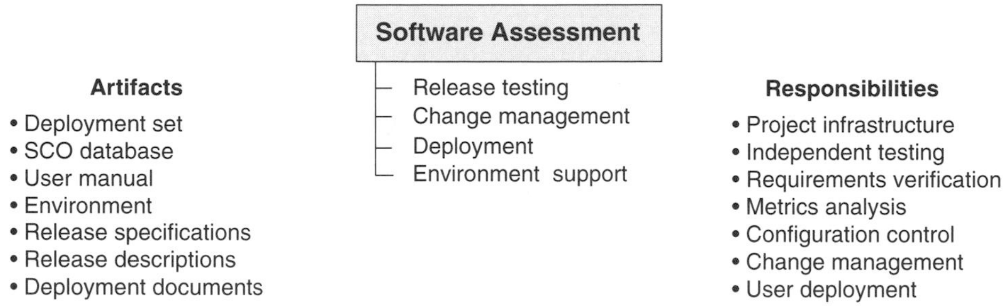

Software Assessment

- Release testing
- Change management
- Deployment
- Environment support

Artifacts

- Deployment set
- SCO database
- User manual
- Environment
- Release specifications
- Release descriptions
- Deployment documents

Responsibilities

- Project infrastructure
- Independent testing
- Requirements verification
- Metrics analysis
- Configuration control
- Change management
- User deployment

Life-Cycle Focus

Inception	Elaboration	Construction	Transition
Infrastructure planning Primary scenario prototyping	Infrastructure baseline Architecture release testing Change management Initial user manual	Infrastructure upgrades Release testing Change management User manual baseline Requirements verification	Infrastructure maintenance Release baselining Change management Deployment to users Requirements verification

FIGURE 11-6. *Software assessment team activities*

A modern process should employ use-case-oriented or capability-based testing (which may span many components) organized as a sequence of builds and mechanized via two artifacts:

1. Release specification (the plan and evaluation criteria for a release)

2. Release description (the results of a release)

Each release may encompass several (perhaps incomplete) components, because integration is proceeding continuously. Evaluation criteria will document what the customer may expect to see at a major milestone, and release descriptions will substantiate the test results. The final iteration(s) will generally be equivalent to acceptance testing and include levels of detail similar to the levels of detail of conventional software test plans, procedures, and reports. These artifacts evolve from fairly brief, abstract versions in early iterations into more detailed and more rigorous documents, with detailed completeness and traceability discussions in later releases. Even for use case testing, test components should be developed in a manner similar to the development of component test cases. For example, rather than develop test procedure documents, a project should generate self-documenting test scenarios that are software programs in their own right. These scenarios should be subjected to change management just like other software and are always maintained up-to-date for automated regression testing.

Some component tests may get elevated to evaluation criteria, with their results documented in release descriptions. Many components may undergo only informal component testing by the development team, with the results captured only within the test software built by a developer. Formal testing for many components will then be subsumed in higher level evaluation criteria (usually capability-oriented or thread-oriented scenarios) and corresponding release descriptions. All components are not created equal: Some of them deserve formal component testing to verify requirements, while others are best tested in the context of capability testing. This judgment must be left to the discretion of the assessment team.

The assessment team is responsible for the quality of baseline releases with respect to the requirements and customer expectations. The assessment team is therefore responsible for exposing any quality issues that affect the customer's expectations, whether or not these expectations are captured in the requirements.

11.3 EVOLUTION OF ORGANIZATIONS

The project organization represents the architecture of the team and needs to evolve consistent with the project plan captured in the work breakdown structure. Figure 11-7 illustrates how the team's center of gravity shifts over the life cycle, with about 50% of the staff assigned to one set of activities in each phase.

A different set of activities is emphasized in each phase, as follows:

- Inception team: an organization focused on planning, with enough support from the other teams to ensure that the plans represent a consensus of all perspectives

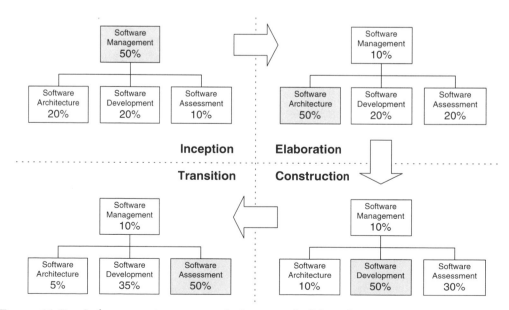

FIGURE 11-7. *Software project team evolution over the life cycle*

- Elaboration team: an architecture-focused organization in which the driving forces of the project reside in the software architecture team and are supported by the software development and software assessment teams as necessary to achieve a stable architecture baseline

- Construction team: a fairly balanced organization in which most of the activity resides in the software development and software assessment teams

- Transition team: a customer-focused organization in which usage feedback drives the deployment activities

It is equally important to elaborate the details of subteams, responsibilities, and work packages, but not until the planning details in the WBS are stable. Defining all the details of lower level team structures prematurely can result in serious downstream inefficiencies.

Process
Automation

Many software development organizations are focused on evolving mature processes to improve the predictability of software management and the performance of their software lines of business (in terms of product quality, time to market, return on investment, and productivity). While process definition and tailoring are necessary, a significant level of process automation is also required in order for modern software development projects to operate profitably.

Automation needs grow depending on the scale of the effort. Just as the construction process varies depending on whether you are building a dollhouse, a single-family home, or a skyscraper, the software process varies across the spectrum from single-person spreadsheet tasks to large-scale, multiple-organization, catastrophic cost-of-failure applications. The techniques, training, time scales, acceptance criteria, and levels of automation differ significantly at opposite ends of the spectrum.

Most software organizations are confronted with the task of integrating their own environment and infrastructure for software development. This process typically results in the selection of more or less incompatible tools that have different information repositories, are supplied by different vendors, work on different platforms, use different jargon, and are based on different process assumptions. Integrating such an infrastructure has proven to be much more problematic than expected.

Key Points

▲ The environment must be a first-class artifact of the process.

▲ Process automation, and change management in particular, are critical to an iterative process. If change is too expensive, the development organization will resist it.

▲ Round-trip engineering and integrated environments promote change freedom and effective evolution of technical artifacts.

▲ Metrics automation is crucial to effective project control.

▲ External stakeholders need access to environment resources to improve interaction with the development team and add value to the process.

Automating the development process and establishing an infrastructure for supporting the various project workflows are important activities of the engineering stage of the life cycle. They include the tool selection, custom toolsmithing, and process automation necessary to perform against the development plan with acceptable efficiency. Evolving the development environment into the maintenance environment is also crucial to any long-lived software development project.

To complicate matters further, it is rare to find stakeholders who treat the environment as a first-class artifact necessary for the continued maintenance of the product. The environment that provides the process automation is a tangible artifact that is critical to the life-cycle cost of the system being developed. The top-level WBS recommended in Chapter 10 recognizes the environment as a first-class workflow.

Section 3.2 introduced three levels of process. Each level requires a certain degree of process automation for the corresponding process to be carried out efficiently:

1. *Metaprocess*: an organization's policies, procedures, and practices for managing a software-intensive line of business. The automation support for this level is called an *infrastructure*. An infrastructure is an inventory of preferred tools, artifact templates, microprocess guidelines, macroprocess guidelines, project performance repository, database of organizational skill sets, and library of precedent examples of past project plans and results.

2. *Macroprocess*: a project's policies, procedures, and practices for producing a complete software product within certain cost, schedule, and quality constraints. The automation support for a project's process is called an *environment*. An environment is a specific collection of tools to produce a specific set of artifacts as governed by a specific project plan.

3. *Microprocess:* a project team's policies, procedures, and practices for achieving an artifact of the software process. The automation support for generating an artifact is generally called a *tool*. Typical tools include requirements management, visual modeling, compilers, editors, debuggers, change management, metrics automation, document automation, test automation, cost estimation, and workflow automation.

While the main focus of process automation is the workflow of a project-level environment, the infrastructure context of the project's parent organization and the tool building blocks are important prerequisites.

12.1   TOOLS: AUTOMATION BUILDING BLOCKS

Many tools are available to automate the software development process. This section provides an overview of the core environment necessary to support the process frame-

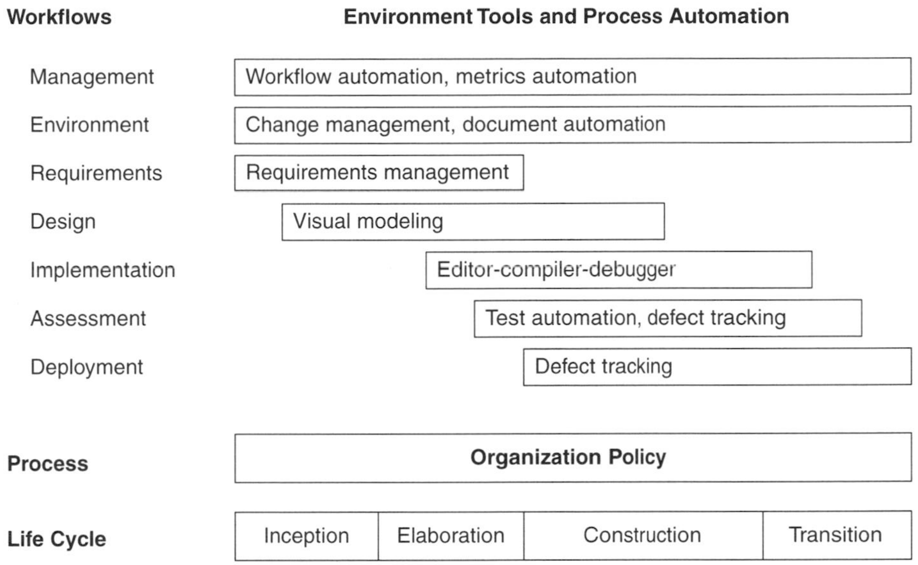

Workflows	Environment Tools and Process Automation
Management	Workflow automation, metrics automation
Environment	Change management, document automation
Requirements	Requirements management
Design	Visual modeling
Implementation	Editor-compiler-debugger
Assessment	Test automation, defect tracking
Deployment	Defect tracking
Process	**Organization Policy**
Life Cycle	Inception · Elaboration · Construction · Transition

FIGURE 12-1. *Typical automation and tool components that support the process workflows*

work. It introduces some of the important tools that tend to be needed universally across software projects and that correlate well to the process framework. (Many other tools and process automation aids are not included.) Most of the core software development tools map closely to one of the process workflows, as illustrated in Figure 12-1.

Each of the process workflows has a distinct need for automation support. In some cases, it is necessary to generate an artifact; in others, it is needed for simple bookkeeping. Some of the critical concerns associated with each workflow are discussed next.

Management

There are many opportunities for automating the project planning and control activities of the management workflow. Software cost estimation tools and WBS tools are useful for generating the planning artifacts. For managing against a plan, workflow management tools and a software project control panel that can maintain an on-line version of the status assessment are advantageous. This automation support can considerably improve the insight of the metrics collection and reporting concepts discussed in Chapter 13. The overall concept of a software project control panel is discussed in Section 13.6.

Environment

Configuration management and version control are essential in a modern iterative development process. Much of the metrics approach recommended in Chapter 13 is dependent on measuring changes in software artifact baselines. Section 12.2 discusses some of the change management automation that must be supported by the environment.

Requirements

Conventional approaches decomposed system requirements into subsystem requirements, subsystem requirements into component requirements, and component requirements into unit requirements. The equal treatment of all requirements drained away engineering hours from the driving requirements, then wasted that time on paperwork associated with detailed traceability that was inevitably discarded later as the driving requirements and subsequent design understanding evolved.

In a modern process, the system requirements are captured in the vision statement. Lower levels of requirements are driven by the process—organized by iteration rather than by lower level component—in the form of evaluation criteria. These criteria are typically captured by a set of use cases and other textually represented objectives. The vision statement captures the contract between the development group and the buyer. This information should be evolving but slowly varying, across the life cycle, and should be represented in a form that is understandable to the buyer. The evaluation criteria are captured in the release specification artifacts, which are transient snapshots of objectives for a given iteration. Evaluation criteria are derived from the vision statement as well as from many other sources, such as make/buy analyses, risk management concerns, architectural considerations, implementation constraints, quality thresholds, and even shots in the dark.

Iterative models allow the customer and the developer to work with tangible, evolving versions of the system. Pragmatically, requirements can—and must—be evolved along with an architecture and an evolving set of application increments. In this way, the customer and the developer have a common, objective understanding of the priorities and the cost/schedule/performance trade-offs associated with those requirements. Rather than focus on consistency, completeness, and traceability of immature requirements specifications, projects need to focus on achieving the proper specification of the project vision and to evolve the lower level specifications through successive sets of evaluation criteria against the evolving design iterations.

The ramifications of this approach on the environment's support for requirements management are twofold:

1. The recommended requirements approach is dependent on both textual and model-based representations. Consequently, the environment should provide integrated document automation and visual modeling for capturing textual specifications and use case models. It is necessary to manage and track changes to either format and present them in human-readable format, whether electronic or paper.

2. Traceability between requirements and other artifacts needs to be automated. The extent of traceability among sets, however, is the subject of a long-standing debate. My opinion is that the requirements set artifacts need a well-defined traceability to the test artifacts, because the overall assessment team is responsible for demonstrating the product's level of compliance with the requirements. However, I do not see any compelling reason to pursue strong traceability relationships between the requirements set artifacts and the other technical artifacts. The problem space description, as represented in the requirements set, and the solution space description, as represented in the other technical artifact sets, often have traceability that is very difficult to represent. This is especially true in component-based architectures that have a large percentage of commercial components. If the process demands tight traceability between the requirements and the design, the architecture is likely to evolve in a way that optimizes requirements traceability rather than design integrity. This effect is even more pronounced if tools are used to automate this process.

Design

The tools that support the requirements, design, implementation, and assessment workflows are usually used together. In fact, the less separable they are, the better. The primary support required for the design workflow is visual modeling, which is used for capturing design models, presenting them in human-readable format, and translating them into source code. An architecture-first and demonstration-based process is enabled by existing architecture components and middleware.

Implementation

The implementation workflow relies primarily on a programming environment (editor, compiler, debugger, linker, run time) but must also include substantial integration with the change management tools, visual modeling tools, and test automation tools to support productive iteration.

Assessment and Deployment

The assessment workflow requires all the tools just discussed as well as additional capabilities to support test automation and test management. To increase change freedom, testing and document production must be mostly automated. Defect tracking is another important tool that supports assessment: It provides the change management instrumentation necessary to automate metrics and control release baselines. It is also needed to support the deployment workflow throughout the life cycle.

12.2 THE PROJECT ENVIRONMENT

The project environment artifacts evolve through three discrete states: the prototyping environment, the development environment, and the maintenance environment.

1. *The prototyping environment* includes an architecture testbed for prototyping project architectures to evaluate trade-offs during the inception and elaboration phases of the life cycle. This informal configuration of tools should be capable of supporting the following activities:

   - Performance trade-offs and technical risk analyses

   - Make/buy trade-offs and feasibility studies for commercial products

   - Fault tolerance/dynamic reconfiguration trade-offs

   - Analysis of the risks associated with transitioning to full-scale implementation

   - Development of test scenarios, tools, and instrumentation suitable for analyzing the requirements

2. *The development environment* should include a full suite of development tools needed to support the various process workflows and to support round-trip engineering to the maximum extent possible.

3. *The maintenance environment* should typically coincide with a mature version of the development environment. In some cases, the maintenance environment may be a subset of the development environment delivered as one of the project's end products.

The transition to a mature software process introduces new challenges and opportunities for management control of concurrent activities and for assessment of tangible progress and quality. Real-world project experience has shown that a highly integrated environment is necessary both to facilitate and to enforce management control of the process. Toward this end, there are four important environment disciplines that are critical to the management context and the success of a modern iterative development process:

1. Tools must be integrated to maintain consistency and traceability. *Round-trip engineering* is the term used to describe this key requirement for environments that support iterative development.

2. *Change management* must be automated and enforced to manage multiple iterations and to enable change freedom. Change is the fundamental primitive of iterative development.

3. Organizational *infrastructures* enable project environments to be derived from a common base of processes and tools. A common infrastructure promotes interproject consistency, reuse of training, reuse of lessons learned, and other strategic improvements to the organization's metaprocess.

4. Extending automation support for *stakeholder environments* enables further support for paperless exchange of information and more effective review of engineering artifacts.

12.2.1 ROUND-TRIP ENGINEERING

As the software industry moves into maintaining different information sets for the engineering artifacts, more automation support is needed to ensure efficient and error-free transition of data from one artifact to another. Round-trip engineering is the environment support necessary to maintain consistency among the engineering artifacts.

Figure 12-2 depicts some important transitions between information repositories. The automated translation of design models to source code (both forward and reverse engineering) is fairly well established. The automated translation of design models to process (distribution) models is also becoming straightforward through technologies such as ActiveX and the Common Object Request Broker Architecture (CORBA).

Compilers and linkers have long provided automation of source code into executable code. As architectures start using heterogeneous components, platforms, and languages, the complexity of building, controlling, and maintaining large-scale webs of components introduces new needs for configuration control and automation of build management. However, today's environments do not support automation to the greatest extent possible. For example, automated test case construction from use case and scenario descriptions has not yet evolved to support anything except the most trivial examples, such as unit test scenarios.

The primary reason for round-trip engineering is to allow freedom in changing software engineering data sources. This configuration control of all the technical

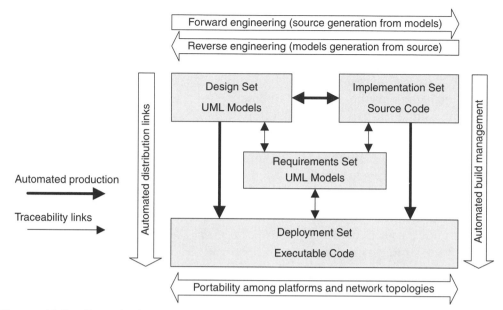

FIGURE 12-2. *Round-trip engineering*

artifacts is crucial to maintaining a consistent and error-free representation of the evolving product. It is not necessary, however, to have bi-directional transitions in all cases. For example, although we should be able to construct test cases for scenarios defined for a given logical set of objects, we cannot "reverse engineer" the objects solely from the test cases. Similarly, reverse engineering of poorly constructed legacy source code into an object-oriented design model may be counterproductive.

Translation from one data source to another may not provide 100% completeness. For example, translating design models into C++ source code may provide only the structural and declarative aspects of the source code representation. The code components may still need to be fleshed out with the specifics of certain object attributes or methods.

12.2.2 CHANGE MANAGEMENT

Change management is as critical to iterative processes as planning. Tracking changes in the technical artifacts is crucial to understanding the true technical progress trends and quality trends toward delivering an acceptable end product or interim release. In conventional software management processes, baseline configuration management techniques for technical artifacts were predominantly a late life-cycle activity. In a modern process—in which requirements, design, and implementation set artifacts are captured in rigorous notations early in the life cycle and are evolved through multiple generations—change management has become fundamental to all phases and almost all activities.

Software Change Orders

The atomic unit of software work that is authorized to create, modify, or obsolesce components within a configuration baseline is called a software change order (SCO). Software change orders are a key mechanism for partitioning, allocating, and scheduling software work against an established software baseline and for assessing progress and quality. The example SCO shown in Figure 12-3 is a good starting point for describing a set of change primitives. It shows the level of detail required to achieve the metrics and change management rigor necessary for a modern software process. By automating data entry and maintaining change records on-line, the change management bureaucracy associated with metrics reporting activities can also be automated.

The level at which an SCO is written is always an issue. What is a discrete change? Is it a change to a program unit or to a component, a file, or a subsystem? Is it a new feature, a defect resolution, or a performance enhancement? Within most projects, the atomic unit of the SCO tends to be easily accepted. In general, an SCO should be written against a single component so that it is easily allocated to a single individual. If resolution requires two people on two different teams, two discrete SCOs should be written.

The basic fields of the SCO are title, description, metrics, resolution, assessment, and disposition.

- *Title.* The title is suggested by the originator and is finalized upon acceptance by the configuration control board (CCB). This field should include a reference to an external software problem report if the change was initiated by an external person (such as a user).

- *Description.* The problem description includes the name of the originator, date of origination, CCB-assigned SCO identifier, and relevant version identifiers of related support software. The textual problem description should provide as much detail as possible, along with attached code excerpts, display snapshots, error messages, and any other data that may help to isolate the problem or describe the change needed.

- *Metrics.* The metrics collected for each SCO are important for planning, for scheduling, and for assessing quality improvement. Change categories are type 0 (critical bug), type 1 (bug), type 2 (enhancement), type 3 (new feature), and type 4 (other), as described later in this section. Upon acceptance of the SCO, initial estimates are made of the amount of breakage and the effort required to resolve the problem. The *breakage* item quantifies the

Title:_____

| **Description** | Name: _____ Date: _____ |
| | Project: _____ |

Metrics

Category: _____ (0/1 error, 2 enhancement, 3 new feature, 4 other)

Initial Estimate   **Actual Rework Expended**

Breakage: _____   Analysis: _____   Test: _____

Rework: _____   Implement: _____   Document: _____

Resolution   Analyst: _____

Software Component: _____

Assessment

Method: _____ (inspection, analysis, demonstration, test)

Tester: _____ Platforms: _____ Date: _____

Disposition   State: _____ Release: _____ Priority _____

Acceptance: _____ Date: _____

Closure: _____ Date: _____

FIGURE 12-3. *The primitive components of a software change order*

volume of change, and the *rework* item quantifies the complexity of change. Upon resolution, the actual breakage is noted, and the actual rework effort is further elaborated. The *analysis* item identifies the number of staff hours expended in understanding the required change (re-creating, isolating, and debugging the problem if the change is type 0 or 1; analysis and prototyping alternative solutions if it is type 2 or 3). The *implement* item identifies the staff hours necessary to design and implement the resolution. The *test* item identifies the hours expended in testing the resolution, and the *document* item identifies all effort expended in updating other artifacts such as the user manual or release description. Breakage quantifies the extent of change and can be defined in units of SLOC, function points, files, components, or classes. In the case of SLOC, a source file comparison program that quantifies differences may provide a simple estimate of breakage. In general, the precision of breakage numbers is relatively unimportant. Changes between 0 and 100 lines should be accurate to the nearest 10, changes between 100 and 1,000 to the nearest 100, and so forth.

- *Resolution.* This field includes the name of the person responsible for implementing the change, the components changed, the actual metrics, and a description of the change. Although the level of component fidelity with which a project tracks change references can be tailored, in general, the lowest level of component references should be kept at approximately the level of allocation to an individual. For example, a "component" that is allocated to a team is not a sufficiently detailed reference.

- *Assessment.* This field describes the assessment technique as either inspection, analysis, demonstration, or test. Where applicable, it should also reference all existing test cases and new test cases executed, and it should identify all different test configurations, such as platforms, topologies, and compilers.

- *Disposition.* The SCO is assigned one of the following states by the CCB:
  - Proposed: written, pending CCB review
  - Accepted: CCB-approved for resolution
  - Rejected: closed, with rationale, such as not a problem, duplicate, obsolete change, resolved by another SCO
  - Archived: accepted but postponed until a later release
  - In progress: assigned and actively being resolved by the development organization

- In assessment: resolved by the development organization; being assessed by a test organization

- Closed: completely resolved, with the concurrence of all CCB members

A priority and release identifier can also be assigned by the CCB to guide the prioritization and organization of concurrent development activities.

Configuration Baseline

A configuration baseline is a named collection of software components and supporting documentation that is subject to change management and is upgraded, maintained, tested, statused, and obsolesced as a unit. With complex configuration management systems, there are many desirable project-specific and domain-specific standards.

There are generally two classes of baselines: external product releases and internal testing releases. A configuration baseline is a named collection of components that is treated as a unit. It is controlled formally because it is a packaged exchange between groups. For example, the development organization may release a configuration baseline to the test organization or even to itself. A project may release a configuration baseline to the user community for beta testing.

Generally, three levels of baseline releases are required for most systems: major, minor, and interim. Each level corresponds to a numbered identifier such as N.M.X, where N is the major release number, M is the minor release number, and X is the interim release identifier. A major release represents a new generation of the product or project, while a minor release represents the same basic product but with enhanced features, performance, or quality. Major and minor releases are intended to be external product releases that are persistent and supported for a period of time. An interim release corresponds to a developmental configuration that is intended to be transient. The shorter its life cycle, the better. Figure 12-4 shows examples of some release name histories for two different situations.

Once software is placed in a controlled baseline, all changes are tracked. A distinction must be made for the cause of a change. Change categories are as follows:

- *Type 0:* critical failures, which are defects that are nearly always fixed before any external release. In general, these sorts of changes represent showstoppers that have an impact on the usability of the software in its critical use cases.

- *Type 1:* a bug or defect that either does not impair the usefulness of the system or can be worked around. Such errors tend to correlate to nuisances in critical use cases or to serious defects in secondary use cases that have a low probability of occurrence.

Typical project release sequence for a large-scale, one-of-a-kind project

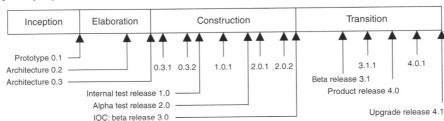

Typical project release sequence for a small commercial product

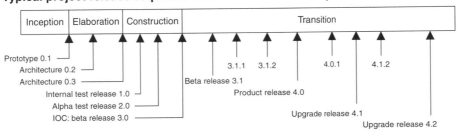

FIGURE **12-4.**   *Example release histories for a typical project and a typical product*

- *Type 2:* a change that is an enhancement rather than a response to a defect. Its purpose is typically to improve performance, testability, usability, or some other aspect of quality that represents good value engineering.

- *Type 3:* a change that is necessitated by an update to the requirements. This could be new features or capabilities that are outside the scope of the current vision and business case.

- *Type 4:* changes that are not accommodated by the other categories. Examples include documentation only or a version upgrade to commercial components.

Table 12-1 provides examples of these changes in the context of two different project domains: a large-scale, reliable air traffic control system and a packaged software development tool.

Configuration Control Board

A CCB is a team of people that functions as the decision authority on the content of configuration baselines. A CCB usually includes the software manager, software architecture manager, software development manager, software assessment manager, and other stakeholders (customer, software project manager, systems engineer, user)

TABLE 12-1. *Representative examples of changes at opposite ends of the project spectrum*

CHANGE TYPE	AIR TRAFFIC CONTROL PROJECT	PACKAGED VISUAL MODELING TOOL
Type 0	Control deadlock and loss of flight data	Loss of user data
Type 1	Display response time that exceeds the requirement by 0.5 second	Browser expands but does not collapse displayed entries
Type 2	Add internal message field for response time instrumentation	Use of color to differentiate updates from previous version of visual model
Type 3	Increase air traffic management capacity from 1,200 to 2,400 simultaneous flights	Port to new platform such as WinNT
Type 4	Upgrade from Oracle 7 to Oracle 8 to improve query performance	Exception raised when interfacing to MSExcel 5.0 due to Windows resource management bug

who are integral to the maintenance of a controlled software delivery system. While CCBs typically take action through board meetings, on-line distribution, concurrence, and approval of CCB actions may make sense under many project circumstances.

The operational concept of an iterative development process must include comprehensive and rigorous change management of the evolving software baselines. The fundamental process for controlling the software development and maintenance activities is described through the sequence of states traversed by an SCO. The [bracketed] words constitute the state of an SCO transitioning through the process.

- [Proposed]. A proposed change is drafted and submitted to the CCB. The proposed change must include a technical description of the problem and an estimate of the resolution effort.

- [Accepted, archived, or rejected]. The CCB assigns a unique identifier and accepts, archives, or rejects each proposed change. Acceptance includes the change for resolution in the next release; archiving accepts the change but postpones it for resolution in a future release; and rejection judges the change to be without merit, redundant with other proposed changes, or out of scope. The CCB verifies that all SCO fields are appropriate and accurate before accepting the SCO, then assigns the SCO to a responsible person in the development organization for resolution.

- [In progress]. The responsible person analyzes, implements, and tests a solution to satisfy the SCO. This task includes updating documentation, release notes, and SCO metrics actuals, and submitting new SCOs, if necessary. Upon achieving a complete solution, the responsible person completes the resolution section of the SCO and submits it to the independent test team for assessment.

- [In assessment]. The independent test team assesses whether the SCO is completely resolved. When the independent test team deems the change to be satisfactorily resolved, the SCO is submitted to the CCB for final disposition and closure.

- [Closed]. When the development organization, independent test organization, and CCB concur that the SCO is resolved, it is transitioned to a closed status.

12.2.3 INFRASTRUCTURES

From a process automation perspective, the organization's infrastructure provides the organization's capital assets, including two key artifacts: a policy that captures the standards for project software development processes, and an environment that captures an inventory of tools. These tools are the automation building blocks from which project environments can be configured efficiently and economically.

Organization Policy

The organization policy is usually packaged as a handbook that defines the life cycle and the process primitives (major milestones, intermediate artifacts, engineering repositories, metrics, roles and responsibilities). The handbook provides a general framework for answering the following questions:

- What gets done? (activities and artifacts)

- When does it get done? (mapping to the life-cycle phases and milestones)

- Who does it? (team roles and responsibilities)

- How do we know that it is adequate? (checkpoints, metrics, and standards of performance)

The need for balance is an important consideration in defining organizational policy. Too often, organizations end up at one of two extremes: no institutionalized process, or too much standardization and bureaucracy. Effective organizational policies have several recurring themes:

- They are concise and avoid policy statements that fill 6-inch-thick documents.

- They confine the policies to the real *shall*s, then enforce them.

- They avoid using the word *should* in policy statements. Rather than a menu of options (*should*s), policies need a concise set of mandatory standards (*shall*s).

- Waivers are the exception, not the rule.

- Appropriate policy is written at the appropriate level.

The last point deserves further discussion. There are many different organizational structures throughout the software development industry. Most software-intensive companies have three distinct levels of organization, with a different policy focus at each level:

- Highest organization level: standards that promote (1) strategic and long-term process improvements, (2) general technology insertion and education, (3) comparability of project and business unit performance, and (4) mandatory quality control

- Intermediate line-of-business level: standards that promote (1) tactical and short-term process improvement, (2) domain-specific technology insertion and training, (3) reuse of components, processes, training, tools, and personnel experience, and (4) compliance with organizational standards

- Lowest project level: standards that promote (1) efficiency in achieving quality, schedule, and cost targets, (2) project-specific training, (3) compliance with customer requirements, and (4) compliance with organizational/business unit standards

Standardization should generally focus on line-of-business units, not on the top-level organization or the projects. Leverage from standardization is generally most effective at the business unit level, where there is the most commonality and reuse across projects, processes, and tools. Standardization of software development techniques and tools across lines of business has proven to be difficult, because the process priorities, tools, techniques, methods, and stakeholder cultures can be very different. Attempting to standardize across domains that have little commonality results in either a highly diluted policy statement or a waiver process that is used too frequently. Standardizing at too high a level is problematic; so is standardizing at too low a level. If all project teams are left to their own devices, every project process and environment will be locally optimized. Over time, the organization's infrastructure for process improvement and growth will erode.

The organization policy is the defining document for the organization's software policies. In any process assessment, this is the tangible artifact that says what you do. From this document, reviewers should be able to question and review projects and

```
I.   Process-primitive definitions
     A.  Life-cycle phases (inception, elaboration, construction, transition)
     B.  Checkpoints (major milestones, minor milestones, status assessments)
     C.  Artifacts (requirements, design, implementation, deployment, management
         sets)
     D.  Roles and responsibilities (PRA, SEPA, SEEA, project teams)
II.  Organizational software policies
     A.  Work breakdown structure
     B.  Software development plan
     C.  Baseline change management
     D.  Software metrics
     E.  Development environment
     F.  Evaluation criteria and acceptance criteria
     G.  Risk management
     H.  Testing and assessment
III. Waiver policy
IV.  Appendixes
     A.  Current process assessment
     B.  Software process improvement plan
```

FIGURE 12-5. *Organization policy outline*

personnel and determine whether the organization does what it says. Figure 12-5 shows a general outline for an organizational policy.

Organization Environment

The organization environment for automating the default process will provide many of the answers to how things get done as well as the tools and techniques to automate the process as much as practical. Some of the typical components of an organization's automation building blocks are as follows:

- Standardized tool selections (through investment by the organization in a site license or negotiation of a favorable discount with a tool vendor so that project teams are motivated economically to use that tool), which promote common workflows and a higher ROI on training

- Standard notations for artifacts, such as UML for all design models, or Ada 95 for all custom-developed, reliability-critical implementation artifacts

- Tool adjuncts such as existing artifact templates (architecture description, evaluation criteria, release descriptions, status assessments) or customizations

- Activity templates (iteration planning, major milestone activities, configuration control boards)

- Other indirectly useful components of an organization's infrastructure

  - A reference library of precedent experience for planning, assessing, and improving process performance parameters; answers for How well? How much? Why?

  - Existing case studies, including objective benchmarks of performance for successful projects that followed the organizational process

  - A library of project artifact examples such as software development plans, architecture descriptions, and status assessment histories

  - Mock audits and compliance traceability for external process assessment frameworks such as the Software Engineering Institute's Capability Maturity Model (SEI CMM)

12.2.4 STAKEHOLDER ENVIRONMENTS

The transition to a modern iterative development process with supporting automation should not be restricted to the development team. Many large-scale contractual projects include people in external organizations that represent other stakeholders participating in the development process. They might include procurement agency contract monitors, end-user engineering support personnel, third-party maintenance contractors, independent verification and validation contractors, representatives of regulatory agencies, and others.

These stakeholder representatives also need access to development environment resources so that they can contribute value to the overall effort. If an external stakeholder team has no environment resources for accepting on-line products and artifacts, the only vehicle for information exchange is paper. This situation will result in the problems described in Chapter 6 as inherent in the conventional process.

An on-line environment accessible by the external stakeholders allows them to participate in the process as follows:

- Accept and use executable increments for hands-on evaluation

- Use the same on-line tools, data, and reports that the software development organization uses to manage and monitor the project

- Avoid excessive travel, paper interchange delays, format translations, paper and shipping costs, and other overhead costs

Figure 12-6 illustrates some of the new opportunities for value-added activities by external stakeholders in large contractual efforts. There are several important reasons for extending development environment resources into certain stakeholder domains.

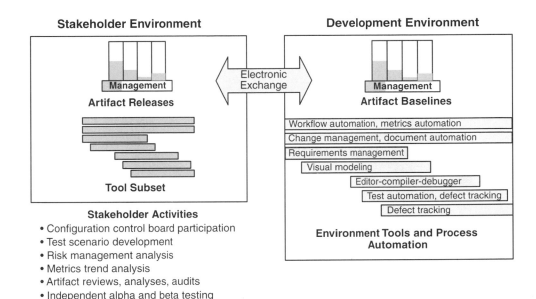

Stakeholder Environment

Development Environment

Management

Artifact Releases

Electronic Exchange

Management

Artifact Baselines

Workflow automation, metrics automation

Change management, document automation

Requirements management

Visual modeling

Editor-compiler-debugger

Test automation, defect tracking

Defect tracking

Tool Subset

Environment Tools and Process Automation

Stakeholder Activities
- Configuration control board participation
- Test scenario development
- Risk management analysis
- Metrics trend analysis
- Artifact reviews, analyses, audits
- Independent alpha and beta testing

FIGURE 12-6. *Extending environments into stakeholder domains*

- Technical artifacts are not just paper. Electronic artifacts in rigorous notations such as visual models and source code are viewed far more efficiently by using tools with smart browsers.

- Independent assessments of the evolving artifacts are encouraged by electronic read-only access to on-line data such as configuration baseline libraries and the change management database. Reviews and inspections, breakage/rework assessments, metrics analyses, and even beta testing can be performed independently of the development team.

- Even paper documents should be delivered electronically to reduce production costs and turnaround time.

Once environment resources are electronically accessible by stakeholders, continuous and expedient feedback is much more efficient, tangible, and useful. In implementing such a shared environment, it is important for development teams to create an open environment and provide adequate resources that accommodate customer access. It is also important for stakeholders to avoid abusing this access, to participate by adding value, and to avoid interrupting development. Internet and intranet technology is making paperless environments economical.

Extending environment resources into stakeholder domains brings up several issues. How much access freedom is supported? Who funds the environment and tool investments? How secure is the information exchange? How is change management synchronized? Some of these cultural changes are discussed in Chapter 17.

CHAPTER 13

Project Control
and Process
Instrumentation

The primary themes of a modern software development process tackle the central management issues of complex software:

1. Getting the design right by focusing on the architecture first

2. Managing risk through iterative development

3. Reducing the complexity with component-based techniques

4. Making software progress and quality tangible through instrumented change management

5. Automating the overhead and bookkeeping activities through the use of round-trip engineering and integrated environments

The fourth item is the subject of this chapter. It is inherently difficult to manage what cannot be measured objectively. This was one of the major issues with the conventional software process, where the intermediate products were predominantly paper documents. Software metrics instrument the activities and products of the software development/integration process. Any software process whose metrics are dominated by manual procedures and human-intensive activities will have limited success. In a modern development process, the most important software metrics are simple, objective measures of how various perspectives of the product and project are changing.

The quality of software products and the progress made toward project goals must be measurable throughout the software development cycle. The goals of software metrics are to provide the development team and the management team with the following:

- An accurate assessment of progress to date

- Insight into the quality of the evolving software product

- A basis for estimating the cost and schedule for completing the product with increasing accuracy over time

13.1 THE SEVEN CORE METRICS

Many different metrics may be of value in managing a modern process. I have settled on seven core metrics that should be used on all software projects. Three are management indicators and four are quality indicators.

MANAGEMENT INDICATORS

- Work and progress (work performed over time)

- Budgeted cost and expenditures (cost incurred over time)

- Staffing and team dynamics (personnel changes over time)

QUALITY INDICATORS

- Change traffic and stability (change traffic over time)

- Breakage and modularity (average breakage per change over time)

- Rework and adaptability (average rework per change over time)

- Mean time between failures (MTBF) and maturity (defect rate over time)

Table 13-1 describes the core software metrics. Each metric has two dimensions: a static *value* used as an objective, and the dynamic *trend* used to manage the achievement of that objective. While metrics values provide one dimension of insight, metrics trends provide a more important perspective for managing the process. Metrics trends with respect to time provide insight into how the process and product are evolving. Iterative development is about managing change, and measuring change is the most important aspect of the metrics program. Absolute values of productivity and quality improvement are secondary issues until the fundamental goal of management has been achieved: predictable cost and schedule performance for a given level of quality.

TABLE 13-1. *Overview of the seven core metrics*

METRIC	PURPOSE	PERSPECTIVES
Work and progress	Iteration planning, plan vs. actuals, management indicator	SLOC, function points, object points, scenarios, test cases, SCOs
Budgeted cost and expenditures	Financial insight, plan vs. actuals, management indicator	Cost per month, full-time staff per month, percentage of budget expended
Staffing and team dynamics	Resource plan vs. actuals, hiring rate, attrition rate	People per month added, people per month leaving
Change traffic and stability	Iteration planning, management indicator of schedule convergence	SCOs opened vs. SCOs closed, by type (0,1,2,3,4), by release/component/subsystem
Breakage and modularity	Convergence, software scrap, quality indicator	Reworked SLOC per change, by type (0,1,2,3,4), by release/component/subsystem
Rework and adaptability	Convergence, software rework, quality indicator	Average hours per change, by type (0,1,2,3,4), by release/component/subsystem
MTBF and maturity	Test coverage/adequacy, robustness for use, quality indicator	Failure counts, test hours until failure, by release/component/subsystem

Appendix C provides a brief derivation and detailed description of these metrics. They have been proven in practice on projects using iterative development. The case study in Appendix D presents a very detailed description of how such metrics can work on a real project.

The seven core metrics can be used in numerous ways to help manage projects and organizations. In an iterative development project or an organization structured around a software line of business, the historical values of previous iterations and projects provide precedent data for planning subsequent iterations and projects. Consequently, once metrics collection is ingrained, a project or organization can improve its ability to predict the cost, schedule, or quality performance of future work activities.

The seven core metrics are based on common sense and field experience with both successful and unsuccessful metrics programs. Their attributes include the following:

- They are simple, objective, easy to collect, easy to interpret, and hard to misinterpret.

- Collection can be automated and nonintrusive.

- They provide for consistent assessments throughout the life cycle and are derived from the evolving product baselines rather than from a subjective assessment.

- They are useful to both management and engineering personnel for communicating progress and quality in a consistent format.

- Their fidelity improves across the life cycle.

The last attribute is important and deserves further discussion. Metrics applied to the engineering stage (dominated by intellectual freedom and risk resolution) will be far less accurate than those applied to the production stage (dominated by implementation activities and change management). Therefore, the prescribed metrics are tailored to the production stage, when the cost risk is high and management value is leveraged. Metrics activity during the engineering stage is geared mostly toward establishing initial baselines and expectations in the production stage plan.

13.2 MANAGEMENT INDICATORS

There are three fundamental sets of management metrics: technical progress, financial status, and staffing progress. By examining these perspectives, management can generally assess whether a project is on budget and on schedule. Financial status is very well understood; it always has been. Most managers know their resource expenditures in terms of costs and schedule. The problem is to assess how much technical progress has been made. Conventional projects whose intermediate products were all paper documents relied on subjective assessments of technical progress or measured the number of documents completed. While these documents did reflect progress in expending energy, they were not very indicative of useful work being accomplished.

The management indicators recommended here include standard financial status based on an earned value system, objective technical progress metrics tailored to the primary measurement criteria for each major team of the organization, and staffing metrics that provide insight into team dynamics.

13.2.1 WORK AND PROGRESS

The various activities of an iterative development project can be measured by defining a planned estimate of the work in an objective measure, then tracking progress (work completed over time) against that plan (Figure 13-1). Each major organizational team should have at least one primary progress perspective that it is measured against. For

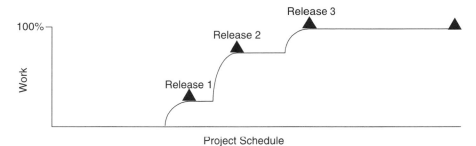

FIGURE **13-1.** *Expected progress for a typical project with three major releases*

the standard teams discussed in Chapter 11, the default perspectives of this metric would be as follows:

- Software architecture team: use cases demonstrated

- Software development team: SLOC under baseline change management, SCOs closed

- Software assessment team: SCOs opened, test hours executed, evaluation criteria met

- Software management team: milestones completed

13.2.2 BUDGETED COST AND EXPENDITURES

To maintain management control, measuring cost expenditures over the project life cycle is always necessary. Through the judicial use of the metrics for work and progress, a much more objective assessment of technical progress can be performed to compare with cost expenditures. With an iterative development process, it is important to plan the near-term activities (usually a window of time less than six months) in detail and leave the far-term activities as rough estimates to be refined as the current iteration is winding down and planning for the next iteration becomes crucial.

Tracking financial progress usually takes on an organization-specific format. One common approach to financial performance measurement is use of an earned value system, which provides highly detailed cost and schedule insight. Its major weakness for software projects has traditionally been the inability to assess the technical progress (% complete) objectively and accurately. While this will always be the case in the engineering stage of a project, earned value systems have proved to be effective for the production stage, where there is high-fidelity tracking of actuals versus plans and predictable results. The other core metrics provide a framework for detailed and realistic quantifiable backup data to plan and track against, especially in the production stage of a software project, when the cost and schedule expenditures are highest.

Modern software processes are amenable to financial performance measurement through an earned value approach. The basic parameters of an earned value system, usually expressed in units of dollars, are as follows:

- Expenditure plan: the planned spending profile for a project over its planned schedule. For most software projects (and other labor-intensive projects), this profile generally tracks the staffing profile.

- Actual progress: the technical accomplishment relative to the planned progress underlying the spending profile. In a healthy project, the actual progress tracks planned progress closely.

- Actual cost: the actual spending profile for a project over its actual schedule. In a healthy project, this profile tracks the planned profile closely.

- Earned value: the value that represents the planned cost of the actual progress.

- Cost variance: the difference between the actual cost and the earned value. Positive values correspond to over-budget situations; negative values correspond to under-budget situations.

- Schedule variance: the difference between the planned cost and the earned value. Positive values correspond to behind-schedule situations; negative values correspond to ahead-of-schedule situations.

Figure 13-2 provides a graphical perspective of these parameters and shows a simple example of a project situation.

The main purpose of the other core metrics is to provide management and engineering teams with a more objective approach for assessing actual progress with greater accuracy. Of all the parameters in an earned value system, actual progress is by far the most subjective assessment. Because most managers know exactly how much cost they have incurred and how much schedule they have used, the variability in making accurate assessments of financial health is therefore centered in the fidelity of the actual progress assessment.

To better understand some of the strengths and weaknesses of an earned value system, consider the development of this book, which was similar in many ways to the development of software. Actual progress could easily be tracked by the current state of each chapter, weight-averaged by the number of pages planned for that chapter.

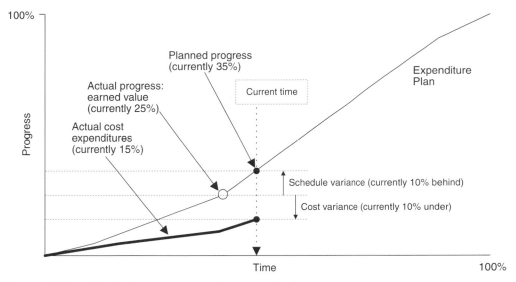

FIGURE **13-2.** *The basic parameters of an earned value system*

I tracked the status of each part (a sequence of related chapters) using the following states and earned values (the percent complete earned):

- 0 to 50%: content incomplete
- 50%: draft content; author has completed first draft text and art
- 65%: initial text baseline; initial text editing complete
- 75%: reviewable baseline; text and art editing complete
- 80%: updated baseline; cross-chapter consistency checked
- 90%: reviewed baseline; author has incorporated external reviewer comments
- 100%: final edit; editor has completed a final cleanup pass

The "percent complete" assessments were assigned subjectively based on my experience writing complex documents. I planned to work for 10 months and spend $10,000 for supporting labor. Table 13-2 illustrates my progress and associated earned value at month 4 of this effort. Although I had drafted about 400 pages of the total 425, I assessed my progress at only 60% complete, taking a weighted average.

If I had plotted a plan for my expenditure profile over time as in Figure 13-2, I could easily have assessed whether I was on schedule and on budget. Figure 13-3 illus-

TABLE 13-2. *Measurement of actual progress of book development (example)*

COMPONENT	PAGES	%	STATUS
Part I	60	75%	Reviewable baseline
Part II	75	75%	Reviewable baseline
Part III	90	65%	Initial text baseline
Part IV	30	65%	Initial text baseline
Part V	130	50%	Draft content
Other (preface, glossary, index)	40	25%	Content incomplete

trates my plan and assessment at month 4, when I was 20% ahead of schedule and 30% under budget.

This example provides a good framework for discussing key attributes of planning and actual progress assessment: establishing an objective basis, developing a suitable work breakdown structure, and planning with appropriate fidelity.

I established objective criteria for percent complete of a given component. While these criteria could be suboptimal for another author, they were accurate for this book. They were based on my experience as an author, my own personal development style, and a well-understood relationship with my technical editor. Similarly, for software projects, the culture of the team, the experience of the team, and the style of the

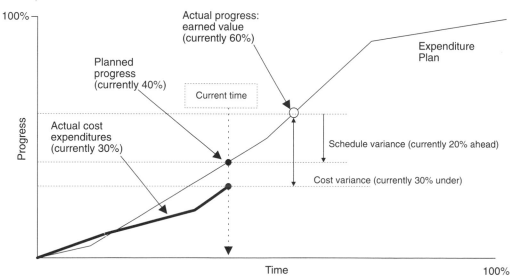

FIGURE 13-3. *Assessment of book progress (example)*

development (the process, its rigor, and its maturity) should drive the criteria used to assess the progress objectively.

I developed a work breakdown structure by breaking down my work by parts (groupings of chapters), which was the easiest approach for tracking progress. Just as with software, this was a natural thing to do once there was a well-established architecture for the book. However, I changed the architecture (the outline and the flow) several times during the first few months. Detailed tracking by component early in the book's development life cycle would have introduced unattractive rework that would have disincentivized me from making architectural improvements. A better work breakdown structure for tracking the entire project's progress (including the contributions of the author, the editor, the artists, the reviewers, the compositors, and the publisher) would be organized by the process, with only the construction progress tracked explicitly by component.

I planned the work with the fidelity appropriate for a single-person project. I chose not to do detailed progress tracking until I had established a full draft content for a given component. I tracked earlier progress through a simple subjective assessment of the level of completeness of first-draft material. The same spirit should be applied to larger projects, using the level of planning fidelity commensurate with the current state of the project and the likelihood of replanning.

13.2.3 STAFFING AND TEAM DYNAMICS

An iterative development should start with a small team until the risks in the requirements and architecture have been suitably resolved. Depending on the overlap of iterations and other project-specific circumstances, staffing can vary. For discrete, one-of-a-kind development efforts (such as building a corporate information system), the staffing profile in Figure 13-4 would be typical. It is reasonable to expect the maintenance team to be smaller than the development team for these sorts of developments. For a commercial product development, the sizes of the maintenance and development teams may be the same. When long-lived, continuously improved products are involved, maintenance is just continuous construction of new and better releases.

Tracking actual versus planned staffing is a necessary and well-understood management metric. There is one other important management indicator of changes in project momentum: the relationship between attrition and additions. Increases in staff can slow overall project progress as new people consume the productive time of existing people in coming up to speed. Low attrition of good people is a sign of success. Engineers are highly motivated by making progress in getting something to work; this is the recurring theme underlying an efficient iterative development process. If this motivation is not there, good engineers will migrate elsewhere. An increase in unplanned attrition—namely, people leaving a project prematurely—is one of the

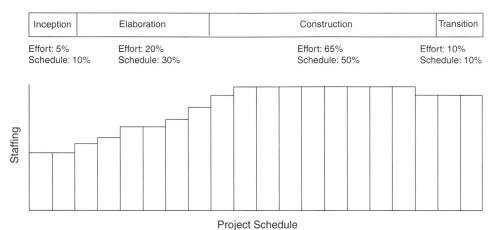

FIGURE 13-4. *Typical staffing profile*

most glaring indicators that a project is destined for trouble. The causes of such attrition can vary, but they are usually personnel dissatisfaction with management methods, lack of teamwork, or probability of failure in meeting the planned objectives.

13.3 QUALITY INDICATORS

The four quality indicators are based primarily on the measurement of software change across evolving baselines of engineering data (such as design models and source code). These metrics are developed more fully in Appendix C.

13.3.1 CHANGE TRAFFIC AND STABILITY

Overall change traffic is one specific indicator of progress and quality. *Change traffic* is defined as the number of software change orders opened and closed over the life cycle (Figure 13-5). This metric can be collected by change type, by release, across all releases, by team, by components, by subsystem, and so forth. Coupled with the work and progress metrics, it provides insight into the stability of the software and its convergence toward stability (or divergence toward instability). *Stability* is defined as the relationship between opened versus closed SCOs. The change traffic relative to the release schedule provides insight into schedule predictability, which is the primary value of this metric and an indicator of how well the process is performing. The next three quality metrics focus more on the quality of the product.

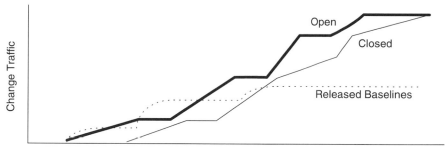

FIGURE 13-5. *Stability expectation over a healthy project's life cycle*

13.3.2 BREAKAGE AND MODULARITY

Breakage is defined as the average extent of change, which is the amount of software baseline that needs rework (in SLOC, function points, components, subsystems, files, etc.). *Modularity* is the average breakage trend over time. For a healthy project, the trend expectation is decreasing or stable (Figure 13-6).

This indicator provides insight into the benign or malignant character of software change. In a mature iterative development process, earlier changes are expected to result in more scrap than later changes. Breakage trends that are increasing with time clearly indicate that product maintainability is suspect.

13.3.3 REWORK AND ADAPTABILITY

Rework is defined as the average cost of change, which is the effort to analyze, resolve, and retest all changes to software baselines. *Adaptability* is defined as the rework trend over time. For a healthy project, the trend expectation is decreasing or stable (Figure 13-7).

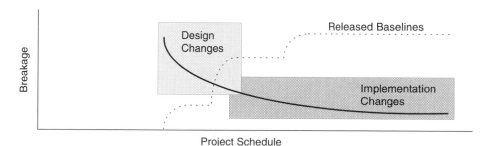

FIGURE 13-6. *Modularity expectation over a healthy project's life cycle*

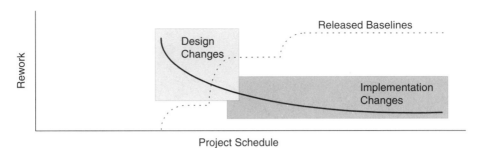

FIGURE 13-7. *Adaptability expectation over a healthy project's life cycle*

Not all changes are created equal. Some changes can be made in a staff-hour, while others take staff-weeks. This metric provides insight into rework measurement. In a mature iterative development process, earlier changes (architectural changes, which affect multiple components and people) are expected to require more rework than later changes (implementation changes, which tend to be confined to a single component or person). Rework trends that are increasing with time clearly indicate that product maintainability is suspect.

13.3.4 MTBF AND MATURITY

MTBF is the average usage time between software faults. In rough terms, MTBF is computed by dividing the test hours by the number of type 0 and type 1 SCOs. *Maturity* is defined as the MTBF trend over time (Figure 13-8).

Early insight into maturity requires that an effective test infrastructure be established. Conventional testing approaches for monolithic software programs focused on achieving complete test coverage of every line of code, every branch, and so forth. In

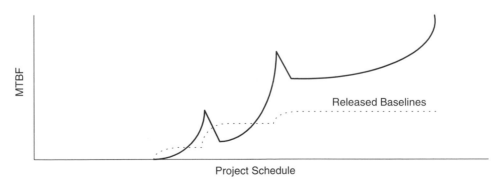

FIGURE 13-8. *Maturity expectation over a healthy project's life cycle*

today's distributed and componentized software systems, such complete test coverage is achievable only for discrete components. Systems of components are more efficiently tested by using statistical techniques. Consequently, the maturity metrics measure statistics over usage time rather than product coverage.

Software errors can be categorized into two types: deterministic and nondeterministic. Physicists would characterize these as Bohr-bugs and Heisen-bugs, respectively. Bohr-bugs represent a class of errors that always result when the software is stimulated in a certain way. These errors are predominantly caused by coding errors, and changes are typically isolated to a single component. Heisen-bugs are software faults that are coincidental with a certain probabilistic occurrence of a given situation. These errors are almost always design errors (frequently requiring changes in multiple components) and typically are not repeatable even when the software is stimulated in the same apparent way. To provide adequate test coverage and resolve the statistically significant Heisen-bugs, extensive statistical testing under realistic and randomized usage scenarios is necessary.

Conventional software programs executing a single program on a single processor typically contained only Bohr-bugs. Modern, distributed systems with numerous interoperating components executing across a network of processors are vulnerable to Heisen-bugs, which are far more complicated to detect, analyze, and resolve. The best way to mature a software product is to establish an initial test infrastructure that allows execution of randomized usage scenarios early in the life cycle and continuously evolves the breadth and depth of usage scenarios to optimize coverage across the reliability-critical components.

As baselines are established, they should be continuously subjected to test scenarios. From this base of testing, reliability metrics can be extracted. Meaningful insight into product maturity can be gained by maximizing test time (through independent test environments, automated regression tests, randomized statistical testing, after-hours stress testing, etc.). This testing approach provides a powerful mechanism for encouraging automation in the test activities as early in the life cycle as practical. This technique could also be used for monitoring performance improvements and measuring reliability.

13.4 LIFE-CYCLE EXPECTATIONS

There is no mathematical or formal derivation for using the seven core metrics. However, there were specific reasons for selecting them:

- The quality indicators are derived from the evolving product rather than from the artifacts.

- They provide insight into the waste generated by the process. Scrap and rework metrics are a standard measurement perspective of most manufacturing processes.

- They recognize the inherently dynamic nature of an iterative development process. Rather than focus on the value, they explicitly concentrate on the trends or changes with respect to time.

- The combination of insight from the current value and the current trend provides tangible indicators for management action.

The actual values of these metrics can vary widely across projects, organizations, and domains. The relative trends across the project phases, however, should follow the general pattern shown in Table 13-3. A mature development organization should be able to describe metrics targets that are much more definitive and precise for its line of business and specific processes.

TABLE 13-3. *The default pattern of life-cycle metrics evolution*

METRIC	INCEPTION	ELABORATION	CONSTRUCTION	TRANSITION
Progress	5%	25%	90%	100%
Architecture	30%	90%	100%	100%
Applications	<5%	20%	85%	100%
Expenditures	Low	Moderate	High	High
Effort	5%	25%	90%	100%
Schedule	10%	40%	90%	100%
Staffing	Small team	Ramp up	Steady	Varying
Stability	Volatile	Moderate	Moderate	Stable
Architecture	Volatile	Moderate	Stable	Stable
Applications	Volatile	Volatile	Moderate	Stable
Modularity	50%–100%	25%–50%	<25%	5%–10%
Architecture	>50%	>50%	<15%	<5%
Applications	>80%	>80%	<25%	<10%
Adaptability	Varying	Varying	Benign	Benign
Architecture	Varying	Moderate	Benign	Benign
Applications	Varying	Varying	Moderate	Benign
Maturity	Prototype	Fragile	Usable	Robust
Architecture	Prototype	Usable	Robust	Robust
Applications	Prototype	Fragile	Usable	Robust

13.5 PRAGMATIC SOFTWARE METRICS

Measuring is useful, but it doesn't do any thinking for the decision makers. It only provides data to help them ask the right questions, understand the context, and make objective decisions. Because of the highly dynamic nature of software projects, these measures must be available at any time, tailorable to various subsets of the evolving product (release, version, component, class), and maintained so that trends can be assessed (first and second derivatives with respect to time). This situation has been achieved in practice only in projects where the metrics were maintained on-line as an automated by-product of the development/integration environment.

The basic characteristics of a good metric are as follows:

1. *It is considered meaningful by the customer, manager, and performer.* If any one of these stakeholders does not see the metric as meaningful, it will not be used. "The customer is always right" is a sales motto, not an engineering tenet. Customers come to software engineering providers because the providers are more expert than they are at developing and managing software. Customers will accept metrics that are demonstrated to be meaningful to the developer.

2. *It demonstrates quantifiable correlation between process perturbations and business performance.* The only real organizational goals and objectives are financial: cost reduction, revenue increase, and margin increase.

3. *It is objective and unambiguously defined.* Objectivity should translate into some form of numeric representation (such as numbers, percentages, ratios) as opposed to textual representations (such as excellent, good, fair, poor). Ambiguity is minimized through well-understood units of measurement (such as staff-month, SLOC, change, function point, class, scenario, requirement), which are surprisingly hard to define precisely in the software engineering world.

4. *It displays trends.* This is an important characteristic. Understanding the change in a metric's value with respect to time, subsequent projects, subsequent releases, and so forth is an extremely important perspective, especially for today's iterative development models. It is very rare that a given metric drives the appropriate action directly. More typically, a metric presents a perspective. It is up to the decision authority (manager, team, or other information processing entity) to interpret the metric and decide what action is necessary.

5. *It is a natural by-product of the process.* The metric does not introduce new artifacts or overhead activities; it is derived directly from the mainstream engineering and management workflows.

6. *It is supported by automation.* Experience has demonstrated that the most successful metrics are those that are collected and reported by automated tools, in part because software tools require rigorous definitions of the data they process.

When metrics expose a problem, it is important to get underneath all the symptoms and diagnose it. Metrics usually display effects; the causes require synthesis of multiple perspectives and reasoning. For example, reasoning is still required to interpret the following situations correctly:

- A low number of change requests to a software baseline may mean that the software is mature and error-free, or it may mean that the test team is on vacation.

- A software change order that has been open for a long time may mean that the problem was simple to diagnose and the solution required substantial rework, or it may mean that a problem was very time-consuming to diagnose and the solution required a simple change to a single line of code.

- A large increase in personnel in a given month may cause progress to increase proportionally if they are trained people who are productive from the outset. It may cause progress to decelerate if they are untrained new hires who demand extensive support from productive people to get up to speed.

Value judgments cannot be made by metrics; they must be left to smarter entities such as software project managers.

13.6   METRICS AUTOMATION

There are many opportunities to automate the project control activities of a software project. For managing against a plan, a software project control panel (SPCP) that maintains an on-line version of the status of evolving artifacts provides a key advantage. This concept was first recommended by the Airlie Software Council [Brown, 1996], using the metaphor of a project "dashboard." The idea is to provide a display panel that integrates data from multiple sources to show the current status of some aspect of the project. For example, the software project manager would want to see a display with overall project values, a test manager may want to see a display focused on metrics specific to an upcoming beta release, and development managers may be interested only in data concerning the subsystems and components for which they are responsible. The panel can support standard features such as warning lights, thresholds, variable scales, digital formats, and analog formats to present an overview of the current situation. It can also provide extensive capability for detailed situation analysis. This automation support can improve management insight into progress and quality trends and improve the acceptance of metrics by the engineering team.

To implement a complete SPCP, it is necessary to define and develop the following:

- Metrics primitives: indicators, trends, comparisons, and progressions

- A graphical user interface: GUI support for a software project manager role and flexibility to support other roles

- Metrics collection agents: data extraction from the environment tools that maintain the engineering notations for the various artifact sets

- Metrics data management server: data management support for populating the metric displays of the GUI and storing the data extracted by the agents

- Metrics definitions: actual metrics presentations for requirements progress (extracted from requirements set artifacts), design progress (extracted from design set artifacts), implementation progress (extracted from implementation set artifacts), assessment progress (extracted from deployment set artifacts), and other progress dimensions (extracted from manual sources, financial management systems, management artifacts, etc.)

- Actors: typically, the monitor and the administrator

Specific monitors (called *roles*) include software project managers, software development team leads, software architects, and customers. For every role, there is a specific panel configuration and scope of data presented. Each role performs the same general use cases, but with a different focus.

- Monitor: defines panel layouts from existing mechanisms, graphical objects, and linkages to project data; queries data to be displayed at different levels of abstraction

- Administrator: installs the system; defines new mechanisms, graphical objects, and linkages; handles archiving functions; defines composition and decomposition structures for displaying multiple levels of abstraction

The whole display is called a panel. Within a panel are graphical objects, which are types of layouts (such as dials and bar charts) for information. Each graphical object displays a metric. A panel typically contains a number of graphical objects positioned in a particular geometric layout. A metric shown in a graphical object is labeled with the metric type, the summary level, and the instance name (such as lines of code, subsystem, server1). Metrics can be displayed in two modes: value, referring to a given point in time, or graph, referring to multiple and consecutive points in time. Only some of the display types are applicable to graph metrics.

Metrics can be displayed with or without control values. A control value is an existing expectation, either absolute or relative, that is used for comparison with a dynamically changing metric. For example, the plan for a given progress metric is a control value for comparing the actuals of that metric. Thresholds are another example of control values. Crossing a threshold may result in a state change that needs to be obvious to a user. Control values can be shown in the same graphical object as the corresponding metric, for visual comparison by the user.

Indicators may display data in formats that are binary (such as black and white), tertiary (such as red, yellow, and green), digital (integer or float), or some other enumerated type (a sequence of possible discrete values such as sun..sat, ready-aim-fire, jan..dec). Indicators also provide a mechanism that can be used to summarize a condition or circumstance associated with another metric, or relationships between metrics and their associated control values.

A trend graph presents values over time and permits upper and lower thresholds to be defined. Crossing a threshold could be linked to an associated indicator to depict a noticeable state change from green to red or vice versa. Trends support user-selected time increments (such as day, week, month, quarter, year). A comparison graph presents multiple values together, over time. Convergence or divergence among values may be linked to an indicator. A progression graph presents percent complete, where elements of progress are shown as transitions between states and an earned value is associated with each state. Trends, comparisons, and progressions are illustrated in Figure 13-9.

Metric information can be summarized following a user-defined, linear structure. (For example, lines of code can be summarized by unit, subsystem, and project.) The project is the top-level qualifier for all data belonging to a set (top-level context). Users can define summary structures for lower levels, select the display level based on previously defined structures, and drill down on a summarized number by seeing the lower level details.

Figure 13-10 illustrates a simple example of an SPCP for a project. In this case, the software project manager role has defined a top-level display with four graphical objects.

1. Project activity status. The graphical object in the upper left provides an overview of the status of the top-level WBS elements. The seven elements could be coded red, yellow, and green to reflect the current earned value status. (In Figure 13-10, they are coded with white and shades of gray.) For example, green would represent *ahead of plan,* yellow would indicate *within 10% of plan,* and red would identify elements that have a greater

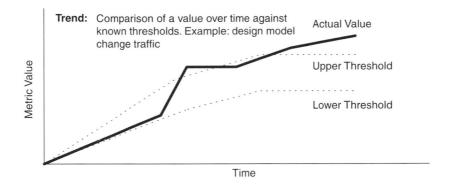

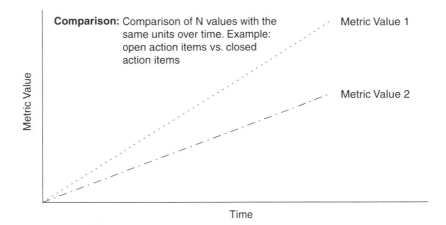

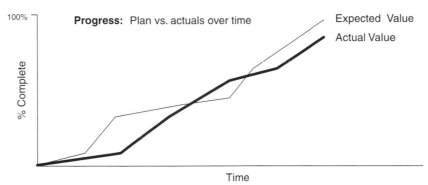

FIGURE 13-9. *Examples of the fundamental metrics classes*

Top-Level WBS Activities

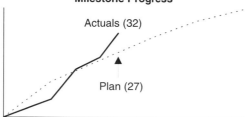

Management		− 4% ↓
Environment		+ 1% ↑
Requirements		+ 6% ↑
Design		− 5% ↓
Implementation		−25% ↓
Assessment		− 2% ↑
Deployment		− 2% ↑

Technical Artifacts

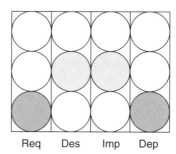

Req   Des   Imp   Dep

Milestone Progress

Actuals (32)

Plan (27)

Action Item Progress

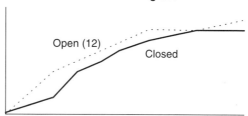

Open (12)

Closed

FIGURE 13-10. *Example SPCP display for a top-level project situation*

than 10% cost or schedule variance. This graphical object provides several examples of indicators: tertiary colors, the actual percentage, and the current first derivative (up arrow means getting better, down arrow means getting worse).

2. Technical artifact status. The graphical object in the upper right provides an overview of the status of the evolving technical artifacts. The Req light would display an assessment of the current state of the use case models and requirements specifications. The Des light would do the same for the design models, the Imp light for the source code baseline, and the Dep light for the test program.

3. Milestone progress. The graphical object in the lower left provides a progress assessment of the achievement of milestones against plan and provides indicators of the current values.

4. Action item progress. The graphical object in the lower right provides a different perspective of progress, showing the current number of open and closed issues.

Figure 13-10 is one example of a progress metric implementation. Although the example is trivial, it provides a view into the basic capability of an SPCP display. The format and content of any project panel are configurable to the software project manager's preference for tracking metrics of top-level interest. Some managers will want only summary data and a few key trends in their top-level display. Others will want many trends and specific details. An SPCP should support tailoring and provide the capability to drill down into the details for any given metric. For example, querying a red light for deployment artifacts would yield the next level of detail in time (a trend chart) or in abstraction (detailed test status for each release, each subsystem, etc.).

The following top-level use case, which describes the basic operational concept for an SPCP, corresponds to a monitor interacting with the control panel:

- Start the SPCP. The SPCP starts and shows the most current information that was saved when the user last used the SPCP.

- Select a panel preference. The user selects from a list of previously defined default panel preferences. The SPCP displays the preference selected.

- Select a value or graph metric. The user selects whether the metric should be displayed for a given point in time or in a graph, as a trend. The default for values is the most recent measurement available. The default for trends is monthly.

- Select to superimpose controls. The user points to a graphical object and requests that the control values for that metric and point in time be displayed. In the case of trends, the controls are shown superimposed with the metric.

- Drill down to trend. The user points to a graphical object displaying a point in time and drills down to view the trend for the metric.

- Drill down to point in time. The user points to a graphical object displaying a trend and drills down to view the values for the metric.

- Drill down to lower levels of information. The user points to a graphical object displaying a point in time and drills down to view the next level of information.

- Drill down to lower level of indicators. The user points to a graphical object displaying an indicator and drills down to view the breakdown of the next level of indicators.

The SPCP is one example of a metrics automation approach that collects, organizes, and reports values and trends extracted directly from the evolving engineering artifacts. Software engineers will accept metrics only if metrics are automated by the environment.

CHAPTER 14

Tailoring the Process

Software management efforts span a broad range of domains. While there are some universal themes and techniques, it is always necessary to tailor the process to the specific needs of the project at hand. A commercial software tool developer with complete control of its investment profile will use a very different process from that of a software integrator on contract to automate the security system for a nuclear power plant. There is no doubt that a mature process and effective software management approaches offer much greater value to the large-scale software integrator than they do to the small-scale tool developer. Neverthe-

Key Points

▲ The process framework must be configured to the specific characteristics of the project.

▲ The scale of the project—in particular, team size—drives the process configuration more than any other factor.

▲ Other key factors include stakeholder relationships, process flexibility, process maturity, architectural risk, and domain experience.

▲ While specific process implementations will vary, the spirit underlying the process is the same.

less, relative to their business goals, the return on investment realized by better software management approaches is worthwhile for any software organization.

14.1 PROCESS DISCRIMINANTS

In tailoring the management process to a specific domain or project, there are two dimensions of discriminating factors: technical complexity and management complexity. Figure 14-1 illustrates these two dimensions of process variability and shows some example project applications. The formality of reviews, the quality control of artifacts, the priorities of concerns, and numerous other process instantiation parameters are governed by the point a project occupies in these two dimensions. Figure 14-2 summarizes the different priorities along the two dimensions.

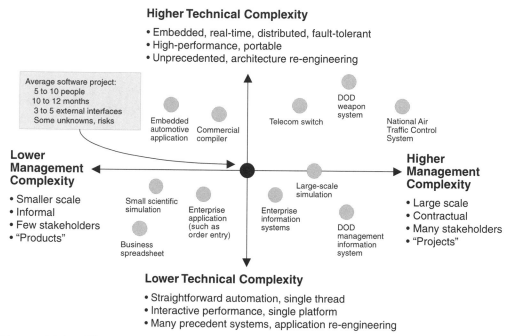

FIGURE 14-1.   *The two primary dimensions of process variability*

A process framework is *not* a project-specific process implementation with a well-defined recipe for success. Judgment must be injected, and the methods, techniques, culture, formality, and organization must be tailored to the specific domain to achieve a process implementation that can succeed. The following discussion about the major differences among project processes is organized around six process parameters: the size of the project and the five parameters that affect the process exponent, and hence economies of scale, in COCOMO II. These are some of the critical dimensions that a software project manager must consider when tailoring a process framework to create a practical process implementation.

14.1.1 SCALE

Perhaps the single most important factor in tailoring a software process framework to the specific needs of a project is the total scale of the software application. There are many ways to measure scale, including number of source lines of code, number of function points, number of use cases, and number of dollars. From a process tailoring perspective, the primary measure of scale is the size of the team. As the headcount increases, the importance of consistent interpersonal communications becomes paramount. Otherwise, the diseconomies of scale can have a serious impact on achievement of the project objectives.

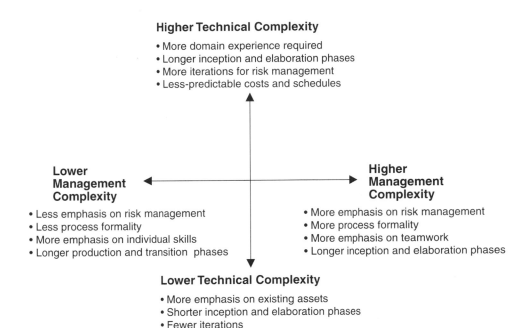

Higher Technical Complexity
- More domain experience required
- Longer inception and elaboration phases
- More iterations for risk management
- Less-predictable costs and schedules

Lower Management Complexity
- Less emphasis on risk management
- Less process formality
- More emphasis on individual skills
- Longer production and transition phases

Higher Management Complexity
- More emphasis on risk management
- More process formality
- More emphasis on teamwork
- Longer inception and elaboration phases

Lower Technical Complexity
- More emphasis on existing assets
- Shorter inception and elaboration phases
- Fewer iterations
- More-predictable costs and schedules

FIGURE **14-2.** *Priorities for tailoring the process framework*

My project experience has demonstrated that five people is an optimal size for an engineering team. Many studies indicate that most people can best manage four to seven things at a time. A simple extrapolation of these results suggests that there are fundamentally different management approaches needed to manage a team of 1 (trivial), a team of 5 (small), a team of 25 (moderate), a team of 125 (large), a team of 625 (huge), and so on. As team size grows, a new level of personnel management is introduced at roughly each factor of 5. This model can be used to describe some of the process differences among projects of different sizes.

Trivial-sized projects require almost no management overhead (planning, communication, coordination, progress assessment, review, administration). There is little need to document the intermediate artifacts. Workflow is single-threaded. Performance is highly dependent on personnel skills.

Small projects (5 people) require very little management overhead, but team leadership toward a common objective is crucial. There is some need to communicate the intermediate artifacts among team members. Project milestones are easily planned, informally conducted, and easily changed. There is a small number of individual workflows. Performance depends primarily on personnel skills. Process maturity is relatively unimportant. Individual tools can have a considerable impact on performance.

Moderate-sized projects (25 people) require moderate management overhead, including a dedicated software project manager to synchronize team workflows and balance resources. Overhead workflows across all team leads are necessary for review, coordination, and assessment. There is a definite need to communicate the intermediate artifacts among teams. Project milestones are formally planned and conducted, and the impacts of changes are typically benign. There is a small number of concurrent team workflows, each with multiple individual workflows. Performance is highly dependent on the skills of key personnel, especially team leads. Process maturity is valuable. An environment can have a considerable impact on performance, but success can be achieved with certain key tools in place.

Large projects (125 people) require substantial management overhead, including a dedicated software project manager and several subproject managers to synchronize project-level and subproject-level workflows and to balance resources. There is significant expenditure in overhead workflows across all team leads for dissemination, review, coordination, and assessment. Intermediate artifacts are explicitly emphasized to communicate engineering results across many diverse teams. Project milestones are formally planned and conducted, and changes to milestone plans are expensive. Large numbers of concurrent team workflows are necessary, each with multiple individual workflows. Performance is highly dependent on the skills of key personnel, especially subproject managers and team leads. Project performance is dependent on average people, for two reasons:

1. There are numerous mundane jobs in any large project, especially in the overhead workflows.

2. The probability of recruiting, maintaining, and retaining a large number of exceptional people is small.

Process maturity is necessary, particularly the planning and control aspects of managing project commitments, progress, and stakeholder expectations. An integrated environment is required to manage change, automate artifact production, and maintain consistency among the evolving artifacts.

Huge projects (625 people) require substantial management overhead, including multiple software project managers and many subproject managers to synchronize project-level and subproject-level workflows and to balance resources. There is significant expenditure in overhead workflows across all team leads for dissemination, review, coordination, and assessment. Intermediate artifacts are explicitly emphasized to communicate engineering results across many diverse teams. Project milestones are very formally planned and conducted, and changes to milestone plans typically cause malignant replanning. There are very large numbers of concurrent team workflows, each with multiple individual workflows. Performance is highly dependent on the skills of key personnel, especially subproject managers and team leads. Project performance is still dependent on average people.

Software process maturity and domain experience are mandatory to avoid risks and ensure synchronization of expectations across numerous stakeholders. A mature, highly integrated, common environment across the development teams is necessary to manage change, automate artifact production, maintain consistency among the evolving artifacts, and improve the return on investment of common processes, common tools, common notations, and common metrics.

Table 14-1 summarizes some key differences in the process primitives for small and large projects.

TABLE 14-1. *Process discriminators that result from differences in project size*

PROCESS PRIMITIVE	SMALLER TEAM	LARGER TEAM
Life-cycle phases	Weak boundaries between phases	Well-defined phase transitions to synchronize progress among concurrent activities
Artifacts	Focus on technical artifacts Few discrete baselines Very few management artifacts required	Change management of technical artifacts, which may result in numerous baselines Management artifacts important
Workflow effort allocations	More need for generalists, people who perform roles in multiple workflows	Higher percentage of specialists More people and teams focused on a specific workflow
Checkpoints	Many informal events for maintaining technical consistency No schedule disruption	A few formal events Synchronization among teams, which can take days
Management discipline	Informal planning, project control, and organization	Formal planning, project control, and organization
Automation discipline	More ad hoc environments, managed by individuals	Infrastructure to ensure a consistent, up-to-date environment available across all teams Additional tool integration to support project control and change control

14.1.2 STAKEHOLDER COHESION OR CONTENTION

The degree of cooperation and coordination among stakeholders (buyers, developers, users, subcontractors, and maintainers, among others) can significantly drive the specifics of how a process is defined. This process parameter can range from cohesive to adversarial. Cohesive teams have common goals, complementary skills, and close communications. Adversarial teams have conflicting goals, competing or incomplete skills, and less-than-open communications.

A product that is funded, developed, marketed, and sold by the same organization can be set up with a common goal (for example, profitability). A small, collocated organization can be established that has a cohesive skill base and excellent day-to-day communications among team members.

It is much more difficult to set up a large contractual effort without some contention across teams. A development contractor rarely has all the necessary software or domain expertise and frequently must team with multiple subcontractors, who have competing profit goals. Funding authorities and users want to minimize cost, maximize the feature set, and accelerate time to market, while development contractors want to maximize profitability. Large teams are almost impossible to collocate, and synchronizing stakeholder expectations is challenging. All these factors tend to degrade team cohesion and must be managed continuously. Table 14-2 summarizes key differences in the process primitives for varying levels of stakeholder cohesion.

TABLE 14-2. *Process discriminators that result from differences in stakeholder cohesion*

PROCESS PRIMITIVE	FEW STAKEHOLDERS, COHESIVE TEAMS	MULTIPLE STAKEHOLDERS, ADVERSARIAL RELATIONSHIPS
Life-cycle phases	Weak boundaries between phases	Well-defined phase transitions to synchronize progress among concurrent activities
Artifacts	Fewer and less detailed management artifacts required	Management artifacts paramount, especially the business case, vision, and status assessment
Workflow effort allocations	Less overhead in assessment	High assessment overhead to ensure stakeholder concurrence
Checkpoints	Many informal events	3 or 4 formal events
		Many informal technical walkthroughs necessary to synchronize technical decisions
		Synchronization among stakeholder teams, which can impede progress for weeks
Management discipline	Informal planning, project control, and organization	Formal planning, project control, and organization
Automation discipline	(insignificant)	On-line stakeholder environments necessary

14.1.3 PROCESS FLEXIBILITY OR RIGOR

The degree of rigor, formality, and change freedom inherent in a specific project's "contract" (vision document, business case, and development plan) will have a substantial impact on the implementation of the project's process. For very loose contracts such as building a commercial product within a business unit of a software company (such as a Microsoft application or a Rational Software Corporation development tool), management complexity is minimal. In these sorts of development processes, feature set, time to market, budget, and quality can all be freely traded off and changed with very little overhead. For example, if a company wanted to eliminate a few features in a product under development to capture market share from the competition by accelerating the product release, it would be feasible to make this decision in less than a week. The entire coordination effort might involve only the development manager, marketing manager, and business unit manager coordinating some key commitments.

On the other hand, for a very rigorous contract, it could take many months to authorize a change in a release schedule. For example, to avoid a large custom development effort, it might be desirable to incorporate a new commercial product into the overall design of a next-generation air traffic control system. This sort of change would require coordination among the development contractor, funding agency, users (perhaps the air traffic controllers' union and major airlines), certification agencies (such as the Federal Aviation Administration), associate contractors for interfacing systems, and others. Large-scale, catastrophic cost-of-failure systems have extensive contractual rigor and require significantly different management approaches. Table 14-3 summarizes key differences in the process primitives for varying levels of process flexibility.

14.1.4 PROCESS MATURITY

The process maturity level of the development organization, as defined by the Software Engineering Institute's Capability Maturity Model [SEI, 1993; 1993b; 1995], is another key driver of management complexity. Managing a mature process (level 3 or higher) is far simpler than managing an immature process (levels 1 and 2). Organizations with a mature process typically have a high level of precedent experience in developing software and a high level of existing process collateral that enables predictable planning and execution of the process. This sort of collateral includes well-defined methods, process automation tools, trained personnel, planning metrics, artifact templates, and workflow templates. Tailoring a mature organization's process for a specific project is generally a straightforward task. Table 14-4 summarizes key differences in the process primitives for varying levels of process maturity.

TABLE 14-3.   *Process discriminators that result from differences in process flexibility*

PROCESS PRIMITIVE	FLEXIBLE PROCESS	INFLEXIBLE PROCESS
Life-cycle phases	Tolerant of cavalier phase commitments	More credible basis required for inception phase commitments
Artifacts	Changeable business case and vision	Carefully controlled changes to business case and vision
Workflow effort allocations	(insignificant)	Increased levels of management and assessment workflows
Checkpoints	Many informal events for maintaining technical consistency	3 or 4 formal events Synchronization among stakeholder teams, which can impede progress for days or weeks
Management discipline	(insignificant)	More fidelity required for planning and project control
Automation discipline	(insignificant)	(insignificant)

TABLE 14-4.   *Process discriminators that result from differences in process maturity*

PROCESS PRIMITIVE	MATURE, LEVEL 3 OR 4 ORGANIZATION	LEVEL 1 ORGANIZATION
Life-cycle phases	Well-established criteria for phase transitions	(insignificant)
Artifacts	Well-established format, content, and production methods	Free-form
Workflow effort allocations	Well-established basis	No basis
Checkpoints	Well-defined combination of formal and informal events	(insignificant)
Management discipline	Predictable planning Objective status assessments	Informal planning and project control
Automation discipline	Requires high levels of automation for round-trip engineering, change management, and process instrumentation	Little automation or disconnected islands of automation

TABLE 14-5. *Process discriminators that result from differences in architectural risk*

PROCESS PRIMITIVE	COMPLETE ARCHITECTURE FEASIBILITY DEMONSTRATION	NO ARCHITECTURE FEASIBILITY DEMONSTRATION
Life-cycle phases	More inception and elaboration phase iterations	Fewer early iterations More construction iterations
Artifacts	Earlier breadth and depth across technical artifacts	(insignificant)
Workflow effort allocations	Higher level of design effort Lower levels of implementation and assessment	Higher levels of implementation and assessment to deal with increased scrap and rework
Checkpoints	More emphasis on executable demonstrations	More emphasis on briefings, documents, and simulations
Management discipline	(insignificant)	(insignificant)
Automation discipline	More environment resources required earlier in the life cycle	Less environment demand early in the life cycle

14.1.5 ARCHITECTURAL RISK

The degree of technical feasibility demonstrated before commitment to full-scale production is an important dimension of defining a specific project's process. There are many sources of architectural risk. Some of the most important and recurring sources are system performance (resource utilization, response time, throughput, accuracy), robustness to change (addition of new features, incorporation of new technology, adaptation to dynamic operational conditions), and system reliability (predictable behavior, fault tolerance). The degree to which these risks can be eliminated before construction begins can have dramatic ramifications in the process tailoring. Table 14-5 summarizes key differences in the process primitives for varying levels of architectural risk.

14.1.6 DOMAIN EXPERIENCE

The development organization's domain experience governs its ability to converge on an acceptable architecture in a minimum number of iterations. An organization that has built five generations of radar control switches may be able to converge on an adequate baseline architecture for a new radar application in two or three prototype release iterations. A skilled software organization building its first radar application may require four or five prototype releases before converging on an adequate baseline. Table 14-6 summarizes key differences in the process primitives for varying levels of domain experience.

TABLE 14-6. *Process discriminators that result from differences in domain experience*

PROCESS PRIMITIVE	EXPERIENCED TEAM	INEXPERIENCED TEAM
Life-cycle phases	Shorter engineering stage	Longer engineering stage
Artifacts	Less scrap and rework in requirements and design sets	More scrap and rework in requirements and design sets
Workflow effort allocations	Lower levels of requirements and design	Higher levels of requirements and design
Checkpoints	(insignificant)	(insignificant)
Management discipline	Less emphasis on risk management Less-frequent status assessments needed	More-frequent status assessments required
Automation discipline	(insignificant)	(insignificant)

14.2 EXAMPLE: SMALL-SCALE PROJECT VERSUS LARGE-SCALE PROJECT

An analysis of the differences between the phases, workflows, and artifacts of two projects on opposite ends of the management complexity spectrum shows how different two software project processes can be. The following gross generalizations are intended to point out some of the dimensions of flexibility, priority, and fidelity that can change when a process framework is applied to different applications, projects, and domains.

Table 14-7 illustrates the differences in schedule distribution for large and small projects across the life-cycle phases. A small commercial project (for example, a 50,000 source-line Visual Basic Windows application, built by a team of five) may require only 1 month of inception, 2 months of elaboration, 5 months of construction, and 2 months of transition. A large, complex project (for example, a 300,000 source-line embedded avionics program, built by a team of 40) could require 8 months

TABLE 14-7. *Schedule distribution across phases for small and large projects*

| | ENGINEERING | | PRODUCTION | |
DOMAIN	INCEPTION	ELABORATION	CONSTRUCTION	TRANSITION
Small commercial project	10%	20%	50%	20%
Large, complex project	15%	30%	40%	15%

of inception, 14 months of elaboration, 20 months of construction, and 8 months of transition. Comparing the ratios of the life cycle spent in each phase highlights the obvious differences.

The biggest difference is the relative time at which the life-cycle architecture milestone occurs. This corresponds to the amount of time spent in the engineering stage compared to the production stage. For a small project, the split is about 30/70; for a large project, it is more like 45/55.

One key aspect of the differences between the two projects is the leverage of the various process components in the success or failure of the project. This reflects the importance of staffing or the level of associated risk management. Table 14-8 lists the workflows in order of their importance.

The following list elaborates some of the key differences in discriminators of success. None of these process components is unimportant, although some of them are more important than others.

- Design is key in both domains. Good design of a commercial product is a key differentiator in the marketplace and is the foundation for efficient new product releases. Good design of a large, complex project is the foundation for predictable, cost-efficient construction.

- Management is paramount in large projects, where the consequences of planning errors, resource allocation errors, inconsistent stakeholder expectations, and other out-of-balance factors can have catastrophic consequences for the overall team dynamics. Management is far less important in a small team, where opportunities for miscommunications are fewer and their consequences less significant.

- Deployment plays a far greater role for a small commercial product because there is a broad user base of diverse individuals and environments.

TABLE 14-8.   *Differences in workflow priorities between small and large projects*

RANK	SMALL COMMERCIAL PROJECT	LARGE, COMPLEX PROJECT
1	Design	Management
2	Implementation	Design
3	Deployment	Requirements
4	Requirements	Assessment
5	Assessment	Environment
6	Management	Implementation
7	Environment	Deployment

A large, one-of-a kind, complex project typically has a single deployment site. Legacy systems and continuous operations may pose several risks, but in general these problems are well understood and have a fairly static set of objectives.

Another key set of differences is inherent in the implementation of the various artifacts of the process. Table 14-9 provides a conceptual example of these differences.

TABLE 14-9. *Differences in artifacts between small and large projects*

ARTIFACT	SMALL COMMERCIAL PROJECT	LARGE, COMPLEX PROJECT
Work breakdown structure	1-page spreadsheet with 2 levels of WBS elements	Financial management system with 5 or 6 levels of WBS elements
Business case	Spreadsheet and short memo	3-volume proposal including technical volume, cost volume, and related experience
Vision statement	10-page concept paper	200-page subsystem specification
Development plan	10-page plan	200-page development plan
Release specifications and number of releases	3 interim release specifications	8 to 10 interim release specifications
Architecture description	5 critical use cases, 50 UML diagrams, 20 pages of text, other graphics	25 critical use cases, 200 UML diagrams, 100 pages of text, other graphics
Software	50,000 lines of Visual Basic code	300,000 lines of C++ code
Release description	10-page release notes	100-page summary
Deployment	User training course Sales rollout kit	Transition plan Installation plan
User manual	On-line help and 100-page user manual	200-page user manual
Status assessment	Quarterly project reviews	Monthly project management reviews

LOOKING
FORWARD

Part I presented several perspectives on conventional software management. It objectively described a conventional project profile, conventional software economics, and conventional principles of software management. Parts II and III described a process framework and the management disciplines necessary to make a state change to a modern software process. Part IV completes the presentation of a modern software management framework. It revisits three of the Part I descriptions of conventional results and describes the performance of the modern software management process.

The material in Part IV is mostly conjecture, including an expectation (Chapter 15), some hypotheses (Chapter 16), and some heuristics (Chapter 17). Chapter 15 sets forth the expected profile of a well-managed iterative development project and describes how it would differ from conventional project experience. Chapter 16 presents some hypothetical observations about next-generation software economics. Chapter 17 highlights some of the cultural changes necessary in transitioning to modern software management techniques. These presentations follow the same format as Part I so that the discriminating differences are clear.

CHAPTER 15

Modern Project Profiles

Chapter 1 presented five recurring issues of conventional projects. A modern process framework exploits several critical approaches for resolving these issues:

1. *Protracted integration and late design breakage* are resolved by forcing integration into the engineering stage. This is achieved through continuous integration of an architecture baseline supported by executable demonstrations of the primary scenarios.

2. *Late risk resolution* is resolved by emphasizing an architecture-first approach, in which the high-leverage elements of the system are elaborated early in the life cycle.

3. The analysis paralysis of a *requirements-driven functional decomposition* is avoided by organizing lower level specifications along the content of releases rather than along the product decomposition (by subsystem, by component, etc.).

4. *Adversarial stakeholder relationships* are avoided by providing much more tangible and objective results throughout the life cycle.

5. The conventional *focus on documents and review meetings* is replaced by a focus on demonstrable results and well-defined sets of artifacts, with more-rigorous notations and extensive automation supporting a paperless environment.

225

The ways in which healthy modern projects resolve these five issues are discussed in more detail next. Because the resolutions of issues 4 and 5 are tightly coupled, they are discussed together in Section 15.4. Sections 15.5 and 15.6 discuss modern projects in the context of my top 10 software management principles and an alternative set of software best practices.

15.1 CONTINUOUS INTEGRATION

Iterative development produces the architecture first, allowing integration to occur as the verification activity of the design phase and enabling design flaws to be detected and resolved earlier in the life cycle. This approach avoids the big-bang integration at the end of a project by stressing continuous integration throughout the project. Figure 15-1 illustrates the differences between the progress profile of a healthy modern project and that of a typical conventional project, which was introduced in Figure 1-2. The architecture-first approach forces integration into the design phase through the construction of demonstrations. The demonstrations do not eliminate the design breakage; instead, they make it happen in the engineering stage, when it can be resolved efficiently in the context of life-cycle goals. The downstream integration nightmare, late patches, and shoe-horned software fixes are avoided. The result is a more robust and maintainable design.

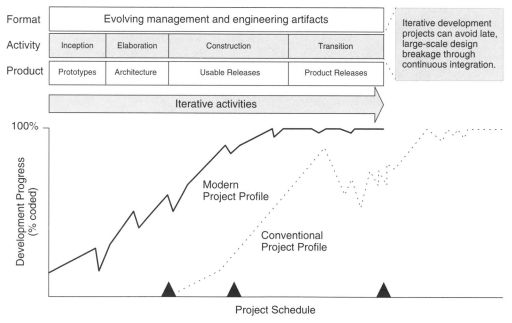

FIGURE 15-1. *Progress profile of a modern project*

TABLE 15-1. *Differences in workflow cost allocations between a conventional process and a modern process*

SOFTWARE ENGINEERING WORKFLOWS	CONVENTIONAL PROCESS EXPENDITURES	MODERN PROCESS EXPENDITURES
Management	5%	10%
Environment	5%	10%
Requirements	5%	10%
Design	10%	15%
Implementation	30%	25%
Assessment	40%	25%
Deployment	5%	5%
Total	100%	100%

The continuous integration inherent in an iterative development process also enables better insight into quality trade-offs. System characteristics that are largely inherent in the architecture (performance, fault tolerance, maintainability) are tangible earlier in the process, when issues are still correctable without jeopardizing target costs and schedules. A recurring theme of successful iterative development projects is a cost profile very different from that experienced by conventional processes.

Table 15-1 identifies the differences in a modern process profile from the perspective of the cost distribution among the various project workflows. This table is a simple combination of Table 1-1 (a typical conventional allocation) and Table 10-1 (a default modern allocation). In my experience, the primary discriminator of a successful modern process is inherent in the overall life-cycle expenditures for assessment and testing. Conventional projects, mired in inefficient integration and late discovery of substantial design issues, expend roughly 40% or more of their total resources in integration and test activities. Modern projects with a mature, iterative process deliver a product with only about 25% of the total budget consumed by these activities.

15.2 EARLY RISK RESOLUTION

The engineering stage of the life cycle (inception and elaboration phases) focuses on confronting the risks and resolving them before the big resource commitments of the production stage. Conventional projects usually do the easy stuff first, thereby demonstrating early progress. A modern process attacks the important 20% of the requirements, use cases, components, and risks. This is the essence of my most important principle: architecture first. Defining the architecture rarely includes simple steps for which visible progress can be achieved easily. The effect of the overall life-cycle philosophy on the 80/20 lessons learned over the past 30 years of software management experience provides a useful risk management perspective.

- **80% of the engineering is consumed by 20% of the requirements.** Strive to understand the driving requirements completely before committing resources to full-scale development. Do not strive prematurely for high fidelity and full traceability of the requirements.

- **80% of the software cost is consumed by 20% of the components.** Elaborate the cost-critical components first so that planning and control of cost drivers are well understood early in the life cycle.

- **80% of the errors are caused by 20% of the components.** Elaborate the reliability-critical components first so that assessment activities have enough time to achieve the necessary level of maturity.

- **80% of software scrap and rework is caused by 20% of the changes.** Elaborate the change-critical components first so that broad-impact changes occur when the project is nimble.

- **80% of the resource consumption (execution time, disk space, memory) is consumed by 20% of the components.** Elaborate the performance-critical components first so that engineering trade-offs with reliability, changeability, and cost-effectiveness can be resolved as early in the life cycle as possible.

- **80% of the progress is made by 20% of the people.** Make sure that the initial team for planning the project and designing the architecture is of the highest quality. An adequate plan and adequate architecture can then succeed with an average construction team. An inadequate plan or inadequate architecture will probably not succeed, even with an expert construction team.

Figure 15-2 compares the risk management profile of a modern project with the profile for a typical conventional project presented in Figure 1-3.

15.3 EVOLUTIONARY REQUIREMENTS

Conventional approaches decomposed system requirements into subsystem requirements, subsystem requirements into component requirements, and component requirements into unit requirements. The organization of requirements was structured so that traceability was simple. With an early life-cycle emphasis on requirements first, design second, then complete traceability between requirements and design

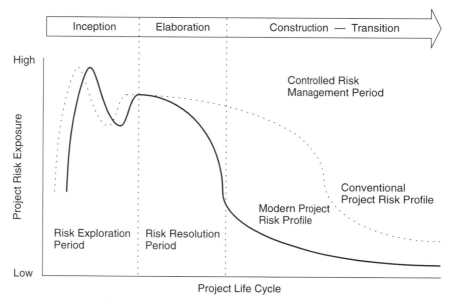

FIGURE 15-2. *Risk profile of a typical modern project across its life cycle*

components, the natural tendency was for the design structure to evolve into an organization that closely paralleled the structure of the requirements organization. It was no surprise that functional decomposition of the problem space led to a functional decomposition of the solution space.

Most modern architectures that use commercial components, legacy components, distributed resources, and object-oriented methods are not trivially traced to the requirements they satisfy. There are now complex relationships between requirements statements and design elements, including 1 to 1, many to 1, 1 to many, conditional, time-based, and state-based.

Top-level system requirements are retained as the vision, but lower level requirements are captured in evaluation criteria attached to each intermediate release. These artifacts, illustrated in Figure 15-3, are intended to evolve along with the process, with more and more fidelity as the life cycle progresses and requirements understanding matures. This is a fundamental difference from conventional requirements management approaches, in which this fidelity was pursued far too early in the life cycle.

15.4   TEAMWORK AMONG STAKEHOLDERS

Many aspects of the classic development process cause stakeholder relationships to degenerate into mutual distrust, making it difficult to balance requirements, product features, and plans. A more iterative process, with more-effective working relationships

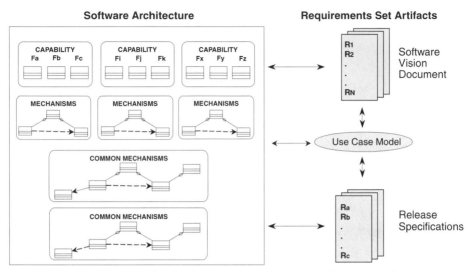

FIGURE 15-3. *Organization of software components resulting from a modern process*

between stakeholders, allows trade-offs to be based on a more objective understanding by everyone. This process requires that customers, users, and monitors have both applications and software expertise, remain focused on the delivery of a usable system (rather than on blindly enforcing standards and contract terms), and be willing to allow the contractor to make a profit with good performance. It also requires a development organization that is focused on achieving customer satisfaction and high product quality in a profitable manner.

The transition from the exchange of mostly paper artifacts to demonstration of intermediate results is one of the crucial mechanisms for promoting teamwork among stakeholders. Major milestones provide tangible results and feedback from a usage point of view. As Table 15-2 shows, designs are now guilty until proven innocent: The project does not move forward until the objectives of the demonstration have been achieved. This prerequisite does not preclude the renegotiation of objectives once the demonstration and major milestone results permit further understanding of the trade-offs inherent in the requirements, design, plans, and technology.

In Table 15-2, the apparent results may still have a negative connotation. A modern iterative process that focuses on demonstrable results (rather than just briefings and paper) requires all stakeholders to be educated in the important distinction between apparently negative results and evidence of real progress. For example, a design flaw discovered early, when the cost to resolve it is tenable, can often be viewed as positive progress rather than as a major issue.

TABLE 15-2. *Results of major milestones in a modern process*

APPARENT RESULT	REAL RESULT
Early demonstrations expose design issues and ambiguities in a tangible form.	Demonstrations expose the important assets and risks of complex software systems early, when they can be resolved within the context of life-cycle goals.
The design is noncompliant (so far).	Understanding of compliance matures from important perspectives (architecturally significant requirements and use cases).
Driving requirements issues are exposed, but detailed requirements traceability is lacking.	Requirements changes are considered in balance with design trade-offs.
The design is considered "guilty until proven innocent."	Engineering progress and issues are tangible, for incorporation into the next iteration's plans.

15.5 TOP 10 SOFTWARE MANAGEMENT PRINCIPLES

My top 10 software management principles were introduced in Chapter 4 as a backdrop to the software process framework and its underlying tenets. To summarize a modern project profile, the following paragraphs revisit each of these principles and describe the project expectation associated with the successful application of each principle. In essence, the list provides a concise, top-level description of the features and benefits of a modern process as viewed by a software project manager.

1. **Base the process on an *architecture-first* approach.** An early focus on the architecture results in a solid foundation for the 20% of the stuff (requirements, components, use cases, risks, errors) that drives the overall success of the project. Getting the architecturally important components to be well understood and stable before worrying about the complete breadth and depth of the artifacts should result in scrap and rework rates that decrease or remain stable over the project life cycle.

2. **Establish an *iterative life-cycle process* that confronts risk early.** A more dynamic planning framework supported by an iterative process results in better risk management and more predictable performance. Resolving the critical issues first results in a predictable construction phase with no surprises, as well as minimal exposure to sources of cost and schedule unpredictability.

3. **Transition design methods to emphasize *component-based development*.** The complexity of a software effort is mostly a function of the number of human-generated artifacts. Making the solution smaller reduces management complexity.

4. Establish a ***change management environment.*** The dynamics of iterative development, including concurrent workflows by different teams working on shared artifacts, necessitate highly controlled baselines.

5. Enhance change freedom through tools that support ***round-trip engineering.*** Automation enables teams to spend more time on engineering and less time on overhead tasks.

6. Capture design artifacts in rigorous, ***model-based notation.*** An engineering notation for design enables complexity control, objective assessment, and automated analyses.

7. Instrument the process for ***objective quality control*** and progress assessment. Progress and quality indicators are derived directly from the evolving artifacts, providing more-meaningful insight into trends and correlation with requirements.

8. Use a ***demonstration-based approach*** to assess intermediate artifacts. Integration occurs early and continuously throughout the life cycle. Intermediate results are objective and tangible.

9. Plan intermediate releases in groups of usage scenarios with ***evolving levels of detail.*** Requirements, designs, and plans evolve in balance. Useful software releases are available early in the life cycle.

10. Establish a ***configurable process*** that is economically scalable. Methods, techniques, tools, and experience can be applied straightforwardly to a broad domain, providing improved return on investment across a line of business.

Throughout this book I have emphasized the importance of balance. From numerous perspectives, the software project manager's paramount objective is to maintain the proper balance of emphasis across the 10 principles. Figure 15-4 summarizes this balance theme in the context of the fundamental software economics equation.

15.6 SOFTWARE MANAGEMENT BEST PRACTICES

Many software management best practices have been captured by various authors and industry organizations. One of the most visible efforts has been the Software Acquisition Best Practices Initiative, sponsored by the U.S. Department of Defense to "improve and restructure our software acquisition management process." Brown summarized the initiative [Brown, 1996], which has three components: the Airlie Software Council (composed of software industry gurus), seven different issue panels

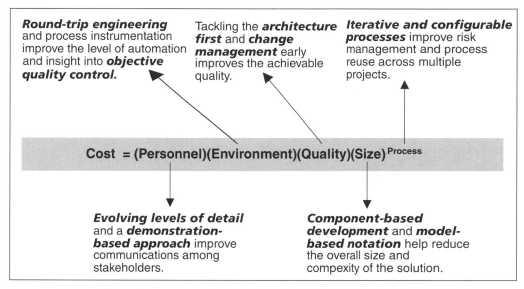

FIGURE 15-4. *Balanced application of modern principles to achieve economic results*

(composed of industry and government practitioners), and a program manager's panel (composed of experienced industry project managers). Each component produced recommendations and results, and reviewed the work of the other components.

The Airlie Software Council was "purposely structured to include highly successful managers of large-scale software projects, internationally recognized authors, prominent consultants, and executives responsible for software development at major companies." One of the Council's products was a set of nine best practices. The Council attempted to focus on the practices that would have the greatest effect in improving the software management discipline for large-scale software projects and controlling the complexities therein.

The nine best practices are described next, with my commentary on how they resonate with the process framework, management disciplines, and top 10 principles that I have recommended. (Quotations are presented in *italics*.)

1. *Formal risk management.*

   ▲ Using an ***iterative process*** that confronts risk is more or less what this is saying.

2. *Agreement on interfaces.*

   ▲ While we may use different words, this is exactly the same intent as my ***architecture-first*** principle. Getting the architecture baselined forces the project to gain agreement on the various external interfaces and the important internal interfaces, all of which are inherent in the architecture.

3. Formal inspections.

▲ The assessment workflow throughout the life cycle, along with the other engineering workflows, must balance several different defect removal strategies. The least important strategy, in terms of breadth, should be formal inspection, because of its high costs in human resources and its low defect discovery rate for the critical architectural defects that span multiple components and temporal complexity.

4. Metric-based scheduling and management.

▲ This important principle is directly related to my **model-based notation** and **objective quality control** principles. Without rigorous notations for artifacts, the measurement of progress and quality degenerates into subjective estimates.

5. Binary quality gates at the inch-pebble level.

▲ This practice is easy to misinterpret. Too many projects have taken exactly this approach early in the life cycle and have laid out a highly detailed plan at great expense. Three months later, when some of the requirements change or the architecture changes, a large percentage of the detailed planning must be rebaselined. A better approach would be to maintain fidelity of the plan commensurate with an understanding of the requirements and the architecture. Rather than inch pebbles, I recommend establishing milestones in the engineering stage followed by inch pebbles in the production stage. This is the primary message behind my **evolving levels of detail** principle.

6. Programwide visibility of progress versus plan.

▲ This practice—namely, open communications among project team members—is obviously necessary. None of my principles traces directly to this practice. It seems so obvious, I let it go without saying.

7. Defect tracking against quality targets.

▲ This important principle is directly related to my **architecture-first** and **objective quality control** principles. The make-or-break defects and quality targets are architectural. Getting a handle on these qualities early and tracking their trends are requirements for success.

8. Configuration management.

▲ The Airlie Software Council emphasized configuration management as key to controlling complexity and tracking changes to all artifacts. It also recognized that automation is important because of the volume and dynamics of modern, large-scale projects, which make manual methods cost-prohibitive and error-prone. The same reasoning is behind my **change management** principle.

9. *People-aware management accountability.*

   ▲ This is another management principle that seems so obvious, I let it go without saying.

There is significant overlap and commonality of spirit between my top principles and the Airlie Software Council's best practices. However, I think the Council omitted some important principles: configurability and component-based, model-based, demonstration-based development. This omission is surprising, because my rationale for including component-based and model-based principles was to reduce the complexity of development. This is exactly the stated purpose of the Airlie Software Council. The demonstration-based principle is in my top 10 primarily to force integration to occur continuously throughout the life cycle and to promote better stakeholder relationships through a more meaningful medium of communications. Because the Airlie Software Council was focused on a particular domain—namely, large-scale, nationally important systems—configurability was less important.

The two Airlie Software Council practices I would not have included are inspections and binary quality gates at the inch-pebble level. Although they are useful, they are overemphasized in practice, and there are other important principles that should have been included.

CHAPTER 16

Next-Generation Software Economics

Next-generation software economics is being practiced by some advanced software organizations. Many of the techniques, processes, and methods described in this book's process framework have been practiced for several years. However, a mature, modern process is nowhere near the state of the practice for the average software organization. This chapter introduces several provocative hypotheses about the future of software economics. A general structure is proposed for a cost estimation model that would be better suited to the process framework in this book. I think this new approach would improve the

Key Points

▲ Next-generation software economics should reflect better economies of scale and improved return on investment profiles. These are the real indicators of a mature industry.

▲ Further technology advances in round-trip engineering are critical to making the next quantum leap in software economics.

▲ Future cost estimation models need to be based on better primitive units defined from well-understood software engineering notations such as the Unified Modeling Language.

accuracy and precision of software cost estimates, and would accommodate dramatic improvements in software economies of scale. Such improvements will be enabled by advances in software development environments. Finally, I look again at Boehm's benchmarks of conventional software project performance and describe, in objective terms, how the process framework should improve the overall software economics achieved by a project or organization.

16.1 NEXT-GENERATION COST MODELS

Software experts hold widely varying opinions about software economics and its manifestation in software cost estimation models: Source lines of code versus function points. Economy of scale versus diseconomy of scale. Productivity measures versus

237

quality measures. Java versus C++. Object-oriented versus functionally oriented. Commercial components versus custom development. All these topics represent industry debates surrounded by high levels of rhetoric. The passionate overhype or underhype, depending on your perspective, makes it difficult to separate facts from exaggeration. Energetic disagreement is an indicator of an industry in flux, in which many competing technologies and techniques are maturing rapidly. One of the results, however, is a continuing inability to predict with precision the resources required for a given software endeavor. Accurate estimates are possible today, although honest estimates are imprecise. It will be difficult to improve empirical estimation models while the project data going into these models are noisy and highly uncorrelated, and are based on differing process and technology foundations.

Some of today's popular software cost models are not well matched to an iterative software process focused on an architecture-first approach. Despite many advances by some vendors of software cost estimation tools in expanding their repertoire of up-to-date project experience data, many cost estimators are still using a conventional process experience base to estimate a modern project profile. This section provides my perspective on how a software cost model should be structured to best support the estimation of a modern software process. There are cost models and techniques in the industry that can support subsets of this approach. My software cost model is all theory; I have no empirical evidence to demonstrate that this approach will be more accurate than today's cost models. Even though most of the methods and technology necessary for a modern management process are available today, there are not enough relevant, completed projects to back up my assertions with objective evidence.

A next-generation software cost model should explicitly separate architectural engineering from application production, just as an architecture-first process does. The cost of designing, producing, testing, and maintaining the architecture baseline is a function of scale, quality, technology, process, and team skill. There should still be some diseconomy of scale (exponent greater than 1.0) in the architecture cost model because it is inherently driven by research and development-oriented concerns. When an organization achieves a stable architecture, the production costs should be an exponential function of size, quality, and complexity, with a much more stable range of process and personnel influence. The production stage cost model should reflect an economy of scale (exponent less than 1.0) similar to that of conventional economic models for bulk production of commodities. Figure 16-1 summarizes an hypothesized cost model for an architecture-first development process.

Next-generation software cost models should estimate large-scale architectures with economy of scale. This implies that the process exponent during the production stage will be less than 1.0. My reasoning is that the larger the system, the more opportunity there is to exploit automation and to reuse common processes, components, and architectures.

$$\text{Effort} = F(T_{Arch}, S_{Arch}, Q_{Arch}, P_{Arch}) + F(T_{App}, S_{App}, Q_{App}, P_{App})$$

$$\text{Time} = F(P_{Arch}, \text{Effort}_{Arch}) + F(P_{App}, \text{Effort}_{App})$$

where:

T = technology parameter (environment automation support)
S = scale parameter (such as use cases, function points, source lines of code)
Q = quality parameter (such as portability, reliability, performance)
P = process parameter (such as maturity, domain experience)

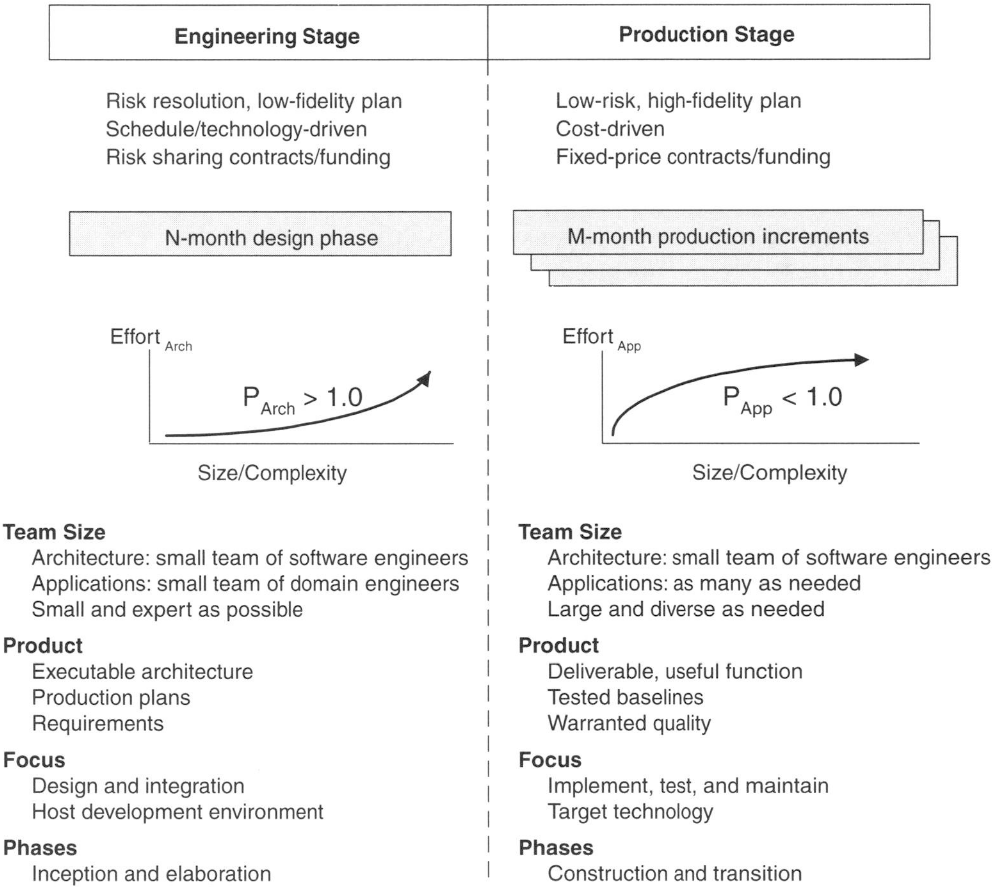

Engineering Stage	Production Stage
Risk resolution, low-fidelity plan	Low-risk, high-fidelity plan
Schedule/technology-driven	Cost-driven
Risk sharing contracts/funding	Fixed-price contracts/funding
N-month design phase	M-month production increments

Effort_{Arch} $P_{Arch} > 1.0$ Size/Complexity

Effort_{App} $P_{App} < 1.0$ Size/Complexity

Team Size
Architecture: small team of software engineers
Applications: small team of domain engineers
Small and expert as possible

Product
Executable architecture
Production plans
Requirements

Focus
Design and integration
Host development environment

Phases
Inception and elaboration

Team Size
Architecture: small team of software engineers
Applications: as many as needed
Large and diverse as needed

Product
Deliverable, useful function
Tested baselines
Warranted quality

Focus
Implement, test, and maintain
Target technology

Phases
Construction and transition

FIGURE 16-1. *Next-generation cost models*

In the conventional process, the minimal level of automation that supported the overhead activities of planning, project control, and change management led to labor-intensive workflows and a diseconomy of scale. This lack of management automation was as true for multiple-project, line-of-business organizations as it was for individual projects. Next-generation environments and infrastructures are moving to automate and standardize many of these management activities, thereby requiring a lower percentage of effort for overhead activities as scale increases.

Reusing common processes across multiple iterations of a single project, multiple releases of a single product, or multiple projects in an organization also relieves many of the sources of diseconomy of scale. Critical sources of scrap and rework are eliminated by applying precedent experience and mature processes. Establishing trustworthy plans based on credible project performance norms and using reliable components reduce other sources of scrap and rework. While most reuse of components results in reducing the size of the production effort, the reuse of processes, tools, and experience has a direct impact on the economies of scale.

Another important difference in this cost model is that architectures and applications have different units of mass (scale versus size) and are representations of the solution space. Scale might be measured in terms of architecturally significant elements (classes, components, processes, nodes), and size might be measured in SLOC or megabytes of executable code. These measures differ from measures of the problem space such as discrete requirements or use cases. The problem space description certainly drives the definition of the solution space. However, there are many solutions to any given problem, as illustrated in Figure 16-2, each with a different value proposition. Cost is a key discriminator among potential solutions. Cost estimates that are more accurate and more precise can be derived from specific solutions to problems. Therefore, the cost estimation model must be governed by the basic parameters of a

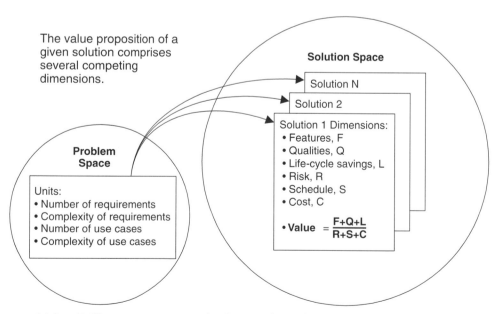

FIGURE 16-2. *Differentiating potential solutions through cost estimation*

candidate solution. If none of the value propositions is an acceptable solution to the problem, further candidate solutions need to be pursued or the problem statement needs to change.

The debate between function point zealots and source line zealots is a good indicator of the need for measures of both scale and size. I think function points are more accurate at quantifying the scale of the architecture required, while SLOC more accurately depicts the size of the components that make up the total implementation. The beauty of using SLOC is that collection can be easily automated and precision can be easily achieved. However, the accuracy of SLOC as a measure of size is ambiguous and can lead to misinterpretation when SLOC is used in absolute comparisons among different projects and organizations. This is particularly true in the early phases of projects if SLOC is used to represent scale. Many projects have used SLOC as a successful measure of size in the later phases of the life cycle, when the most important measures are the relative changes from month to month as the project converges on releasable versions.

The value of function points is that they are better at depicting the overall scale of the solution, independently of the actual size and implementation language of the final realization. Function points are not easily extracted from any rigorous representation format, however, so automation and change tracking are difficult or ambiguous.

A rigorous notation for design artifacts is a necessary prerequisite to improvements in the fidelity with which the scale of a design can be estimated. In the future, I expect there will be an opportunity to automate a new measure of scale derived directly from design representations in UML.

I expect two major improvements in next-generation software cost estimation models:

1. Separation of the engineering stage from the production stage will force estimators to differentiate between architectural scale and implementation size. This will permit greater accuracy and more-honest precision in life-cycle estimates.

2. Rigorous design notations such as UML will offer an opportunity to define units of measure for scale that are more standardized and therefore can be automated and tracked. These measures can also be traced more straightforwardly into the costs of production.

Quantifying the scale of the software architecture in the engineering stage is an area ripe for research. Over the next decade, two breakthroughs in the software process seem possible, both of them realized through technology advances in the supporting environment. The first breakthrough would be the availability of integrated tools that automate the transition of information between requirements, design, implementation, and deployment elements. These tools would allow more comprehensive

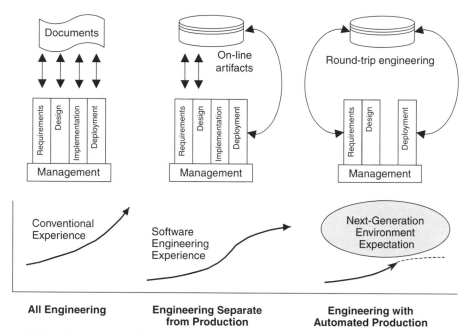

FIGURE 16-3. *Automation of the construction process in next-generation environments*

round-trip engineering among the engineering artifacts. The second breakthrough would focus on collapsing today's four sets of fundamental technical artifacts into three sets by automating the activities associated with human-generated source code, thereby eliminating the need for a separate implementation set. This technology advance, illustrated in Figure 16-3, would allow executable programs to be produced directly from UML representations without human intervention. Visual modeling tools can already produce code subsets from UML models, but producing complete subsets is still in the future.

While the first breakthrough would be risky but straightforward, the second one would be a major paradigm shift. When a software engineering team can produce implementation and deployment artifacts in an error-free, automated environment, the software development process can change dramatically, as it did when chip production transitioned to an automated "printing" process.

16.2 MODERN SOFTWARE ECONOMICS

Chapter 1 introduced Boehm's top 10 software metrics [Boehm, 1987] as an objective presentation of the current state of the software management practice. That framework can be used to summarize some of the important themes in an economic context and speculate on how a modern software management framework should perform.

There are not enough project data to prove my assertions, but I believe that these expected changes provide a good description of what an organizational manager should strive for in making the transition to a modern process. (Quotations are presented in *italics*.)

1. *Finding and fixing a software problem after delivery costs 100 times more than finding and fixing the problem in early design phases.*

   ▲ Modern processes, component-based development technologies, and architecture frameworks are explicitly targeted at improving this relationship. In many domains, and for software problems local to an individual component, advances in encapsulation techniques should reduce the impact on resources significantly, perhaps by an order of magnitude. Nevertheless, an architecture-first approach will likely yield tenfold to hundredfold improvements in the resolution of architectural errors. Consequently, the iterative process places a huge premium on early architecture insight and risk-confronting activities.

2. *You can compress software development schedules 25% of nominal, but no more.*

   ▲ This metric should remain valid for the engineering stage of the life cycle, when the intellectual content of the system is evolved. However, if the engineering stage is successful at achieving a consistent baseline—including architecture, construction plans, and requirements—schedule compression in the production stage should be more flexible. Whether a line-of-business organization is amortizing the engineering stage across multiple projects or a project organization is amortizing the engineering stage across multiple increments, there should be much more opportunity for concurrent development.

3. *For every $1 you spend on development, you will spend $2 on maintenance.*

   ▲ It is difficult to generalize about this metric, because there are many different maintenance models. The comparison of absolute numbers makes little sense except for one-of-a-kind projects. A better way to measure this ratio would be the productivity rates between development and maintenance. (Appendix C describes this maintainability measurement.) One interesting aspect of iterative development is that the line between development and maintenance has become much fuzzier. A mature iterative process and a good architecture can reduce scrap and rework levels considerably. Given the overall homogenization of development and maintenance activities, my gut tells me that this metric should change to a one-for-one relationship, where development productivity will be similar to maintenance productivity.

4. *Software development and maintenance costs are primarily a function of the number of source lines of code.*

▲ This metric says that the size of the product is the primary cost driver, and the fundamental unit of size is a line of code. While this was obvious in previous generations of software technology, it is becoming much less obvious in today's component-based technologies. Commercial components, reuse, and automatic code generators can seriously pollute the meaning of a source line of code. Construction costs will still be driven by the complexity of the bill of materials. The use of more components, more types of components, more sources of components, and more custom components will necessitate more integration labor and will drive up costs. The use of fewer components, fewer types, fewer sources, and more industrial-strength tooling will drive down costs. Unfortunately, the component industry is still too immature to agree on standards for a bill of materials that could improve the fidelity of its cost estimations. Therefore, the next-generation cost models should become less sensitive to the number of source lines and more sensitive to the discrete numbers of components and their ease of integration.

5. *Variations among people account for the biggest differences in software productivity.*

▲ For any engineering venture in which intellectual property is the real product, the dominant productivity factors will be personnel skills, teamwork, and motivations. To the extent possible, a modern process encapsulates the requirements for high-leverage people in the engineering stage, when the team is relatively small. The production stage, when teams typically are much larger, should then operate with far less dependency on scarce expertise.

6. *The overall ratio of software to hardware costs is still growing. In 1955, it was 15:85; in 1985, 85:15.*

▲ I'm not sure what this metric looks like today. The popularity of the personal computer and the differences in post-1985 versus pre-1985 software costs, particularly personal computer software tools, have undoubtedly changed the relationship. The main impact of this metric on software economics is that hardware continues to get cheaper. Processing cycles, storage, and network bandwidth continue to offer new opportunities for automation. Consequently, software environments are playing a much more important role. From a modern process perspective, I can see the environment doing much more of the bookkeeping and analysis activities that were previously done by humans. Configuration control and quality assurance analyses are already largely automated, and the next frontier is automated production and automated testing.

7. Only about 15% of software development effort is devoted to programming.

▲ In the past 10 years there has been a noticeable shift away from investments in languages and compilers, Java and Ada 95 notwithstanding. Modern technology investments have transitioned into process maturity (for example, the SEI CMM), visual modeling (such as UML), automated software quality (such as test automation), components (such as ActiveX, Java, and CORBA), configuration management, metrics, and other aspects of software engineering. The amount of programming that goes on in a software development project is still roughly 15%. The difference is that modern projects are programming at a much higher level of abstraction. An average staff-month of programming produced perhaps 200 machine instructions in the 1960s and 1,000 machine instructions in the 1970s and 1980s. Programmer productivity in the 1990s can produce tens of thousands of machine instructions in a single month, even though only a few hundred human-generated source lines may be produced.

8. Software systems and products typically cost 3 times as much per SLOC as individual software programs. Software-system products (i.e., system of systems) cost 9 times as much.

▲ This diseconomy of scale should be greatly relieved with a modern process and modern technologies. Under certain circumstances—such as a software line of business producing discrete, customer-specific software systems with a common architecture, common environment, and common process—an economy of scale is achievable.

9. Walkthroughs catch 60% of the errors.

▲ I have emphasized the need for this metric to be banished from the top 10. Human inspections and walkthroughs will not expose the critical issues; they will only help resolve them. This metric should be replaced by the following: While the environment catches most of the first-level inconsistencies and errors, the really important architectural issues can be exposed only through demonstration and early testing and resolved through human scrutiny.

10. 80% of the contribution comes from 20% of the contributors.

▲ This relationship is timeless and constitutes the background philosophy to be applied throughout the planning and conduct of a modern software management process.

Modern Process Transitions

Successful software management is hard work. Technical breakthroughs, process breakthroughs, and new tools will make it easier, but management discipline will continue to be the crux of software project success. New technological advances will be accompanied by new opportunities for software applications, new dimensions of complexity, new avenues of automation, and new customers with different priorities. Accommodating these changes will perturb many of our ingrained software management values and priorities. However, striking a balance among requirements, designs, and plans will remain the

> **Key Points**
>
> ▲ The transition to modern software processes and technologies necessitates several culture shifts that will not always be easy to achieve.
>
> ▲ Lessons learned in transitioning organizations to a modern process have exposed several recurring themes of success that represent important culture shifts from conventional practice.
>
> ▲ A significant transition should be attempted on a significant project. Pilot projects do not generally attract top talent, and top talent is crucial to the success of any significant transition.

underlying objective of future software management endeavors, just as it is today.

The software management framework I have presented in this book is not revolutionary; numerous projects have been practicing some of these disciplines for years. However, many of the techniques and disciplines suggested herein will necessitate a significant paradigm shift. Some of these changes will be resisted by certain stakeholders or by certain factions within a project or organization. It is not always easy to separate cultural resistance from objective resistance. This chapter summarizes some of the important culture shifts to be prepared for in order to avoid as many sources of friction as possible in transitioning successfully to a modern process.

17.1   CULTURE SHIFTS

Several culture shifts must be overcome to transition successfully to a modern software management process. For some of these adjustments, it will be difficult to distinguish between objective opposition and stubborn resistance. Nevertheless, there are general indications of a successful transition to a modern culture. This section discusses several of the rough indicators to look for in order to differentiate projects that have made a genuine cultural transition from projects that have only put up a facade. Many of these indicators are derived directly from the process framework described in earlier chapters; others are second-order effects.

- **Lower level and mid-level managers are performers.** There should be no "pure managers" in an organization or suborganization with 25 or fewer people. The need for pure managers arises only when personnel resources exceed this level. Hands-on management skills vary, but competent managers typically spend much of their time performing, especially with regard to understanding the status of the project firsthand and developing plans and estimates. Above all, the person managing an effort should plan it. This does not mean the manager should approve the plan; it means the manager should participate in developing it. In independent project assessments I have performed, a good indicator of trouble ahead is a manager who did not author the plan nor take ownership of it. The stakeholders affected by this transition are software project managers.

- **Requirements and designs are fluid and tangible.** The conventional process focused too much on producing documents that attempted to describe the software product and focused too little on producing tangible increments of the products themselves. Major milestones were defined solely in terms of specific documents. Development organizations for large contractual projects were driven to produce tons of paper in order to meet milestones and receive progress payments, rather than spend their energy on tasks that would have reduced risk and produced quality software. An iterative process requires actual construction of a sequence of progressively more comprehensive systems that demonstrate the architecture, enable objective requirements negotiations, validate the technical approach, and address resolution of key risks. Ideally, all stakeholders would be focused on these "real" milestones, with incremental deliveries of useful functionality rather than speculative paper descriptions of the end-item vision. The transition to a less document-driven environment will be embraced by the engineering teams; it will probably be resisted by traditional contract monitors.

- **Ambitious demonstrations are encouraged.** The purpose of early life-cycle demonstrations is to expose design flaws, not to put up a facade. Stakeholders must not overreact to early mistakes, digressions, or immature designs. Evaluation criteria in early release plans are goals, not requirements. If early engineering obstacles are overemphasized, development organizations will set up future iterations to be less ambitious. On the other hand, stakeholders should not tolerate lack of follow-through in resolving issues. If negative trends are not addressed with vigor, they can cause serious downstream perturbations. Open and attentive follow-through is necessary to resolve issues. The management team is most likely to resist this transition (especially if the project was oversold), because it will expose any engineering or process issues that were easy to hide using the conventional process. Customers, users, and the engineering team will embrace this transition for exactly the same reason.

- **Good and bad project performance is much more obvious earlier in the life cycle.** In an iterative development, success breeds success, and early failures are extremely risky to turn around. Real-world project experience has shown time and again that it is the early phases that make or break a project. It is therefore of paramount importance to ensure that the very best team possible performs the planning and architecture phases. If these phases are done right and with good teams, projects can be completed successfully by average teams evolving the applications into the final product. If the planning and architecture phases are not performed adequately, all the expert programmers and testers in the world probably will not achieve success. No one should resist early staffing with the right team. However, most organizations have scarce resources for these sorts of early life-cycle roles and are hesitant to make the necessary staff allocations.

- **Early increments will be immature.** External stakeholders, such as customers and users, cannot expect initial deliveries to perform up to specification, to be complete, to be fully reliable, or to have end-target levels of quality or performance. On the other hand, development organizations must be held accountable for, and demonstrate, tangible improvements in successive increments. The trends will indicate convergence toward specification. Objectively quantifying changes, fixes, and upgrades will indicate the quality of the process and environment for future activities. Customers and users will have difficulty accepting the flaws of early releases, although they should be impressed by later increments. Management and the development team will accept immaturity as a natural part of the process.

- **Artifacts are less important early, more important later.** It is a waste of time to worry about the details (traceability, thoroughness, and completeness) of the artifact sets until a baseline is achieved that is useful enough and stable enough to warrant time-consuming analyses of these quality factors.

Otherwise, a project will squander early engineering cycles and precious resources adding content and quality to artifacts that may quickly become obsolete. While the development team will embrace this transition whole-heartedly, traditional contract monitors will resist the early de-emphasis on completeness.

- **Real issues are surfaced and resolved systematically.** Successful projects recognize that requirements and designs evolve together, with continuous negotiation, trade-off, and bartering toward best value, rather than blindly adhering to an ambiguous contract statement. On a healthy project that is making progress, it should be easy to differentiate between real and apparent issues. Depending on the situation, this culture shift could affect almost any team.

- **Quality assurance is everyone's job, not a separate discipline.** Many organizations have a separate group called quality assurance. I am generally against the concept of separate quality assurance activities, teams, or artifacts. Quality assurance should be woven into every role, every activity, every artifact. True quality assurance is measured by tangible progress and objective data, not by checklists, meetings, and human inspections. The software project manager or designee should assume the role of ensuring that quality assurance is properly integrated into the process. The traditional policing by a separate team of inspectors is replaced by the self-policing teamwork of an organization with a mature process, common objectives, and common incentives. Traditional managers and quality assurance personnel will resist this transition. Engineering teams will embrace it.

- **Performance issues arise early in the life cycle.** Early performance issues have surfaced on almost every successful project I know of. These issues are a sign of an immature design but a mature design process. Stakeholders will usually be concerned over early performance issues. Development engineers will embrace the emphasis on early demonstrations and the ability to assess and evaluate performance trade-offs in subsequent releases.

- **Investments in automation are necessary.** Because iterative development projects require extensive automation, it is important not to underinvest in the capital environment. It is also important for stakeholders to acquire an integrated environment that permits efficient participation in an iterative development. Otherwise, interactions with the development organization will degenerate to paper exchange and many of the issues of the conventional process. These investments may be opposed by organization managers overly focused on near-term financial results or by project personnel who favor the preference of the individual project over the global solution that serves both the project and the organization goals.

- **Good software organizations should be more profitable.** In the commercial software domain, this is not an issue. In most of the software contracting domain, especially government contracts, it is definitely an issue. As part of the adversarial nature of the acquisition and contracting process, there is considerable focus on ensuring that contractor profits are within a certain acceptable range (typically 5% to 15%). Occasionally, excellent contractor performance, good value engineering, or significant reuse results in potential contractor profit margins in excess of the acceptable initial bid. As soon as customers (or their users or engineering monitors) become aware of such a trend, it is inevitable that substantial pressure will be exerted to apply these "excess" resources to out-of-scope changes until the margin is back in the acceptable range.

  As a consequence, the simple profit motive that underlies commercial transactions and incentivizes efficiency is replaced by complex contractual incentives (and producer-consumer conflicts) that are usually suboptimal. Very frequently, contractors see no economic incentive to implement major cost savings, and certainly there is little incentive to take risks that may have a large return. On the other hand, contractors can easily consume large amounts of money (usually at a small profit margin) without producing results and with little accountability for poor performance.

  For the software industry to prosper, good contractors should be rewarded (more profit) and bad contractors should be punished (less profit). A customer who gets a good product at a reasonable price should be happy that the contractor also made a good profit. Allowing contractors who perform poorly to continue doing so is not good for anyone. This is one area in which the commercial domain is far more effective than the government contracting domain.

17.2 DENOUEMENT

In summary, the conventional software process was characterized by the following:

- Sequentially transitioning from requirements to design to code to test
- Achieving 100% completeness of each artifact at each life-cycle stage
- Treating all requirements, artifacts, components, and so forth, as equals
- Achieving high-fidelity traceability among all artifacts at each stage in the life cycle

A modern iterative development process framework is characterized by the following:

- Continuous round-trip engineering from requirements to test at evolving levels of abstraction

- Achieving high-fidelity understanding of the drivers (the 20%) as early as practical

- Evolving the artifacts in breadth and depth based on risk management priorities

- Postponing completeness and consistency analyses until later in the life cycle

A modern process framework attacks the primary sources of the diseconomy of scale inherent in the conventional software process. Figure 17-1 illustrates the next generation of software project performance by depicting the development progress versus time, where progress is defined as percent coded (demonstrable in its target form). (The figure follows the same presentation format as Figures 1-2 and 15-1.)

My goal in this book has been to explain how to move onto the upper, shaded region, with a modern process supported by an advanced, fully integrated environment and a component-based architecture. Organizations that succeed should be capable of deploying software products that are constructed largely from existing components in 50% less time, with 50% fewer development resources, and maintained by teams 50% the size of those required by today's systems.

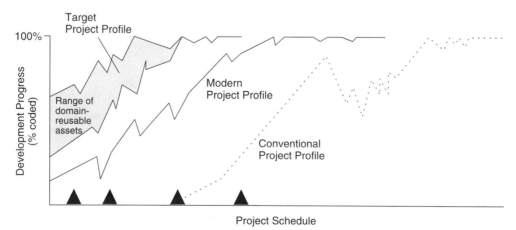

FIGURE 17-1. *Next-generation project performance*

As an organization transitions to new techniques and technologies, there is always apprehension and concern about failing. Maintaining the status quo and relying on existing methods is usually considered the safest path. In the software industry, where most organizations succeed on only a small percentage of their projects, maintaining the status quo is not always safe. When an organization decides to make a transition, these two pieces of conventional wisdom are usually offered by internal champions as well as external change agents: (1) Pioneer any new techniques on a small pilot program. (2) Be prepared to spend more resources—money and time—on your first project that makes the transition. I see both recommendations as counterproductive.

Small pilot programs outside the mainstream have their place, but they rarely achieve any paradigm shift of consequence. Trying a new little technique, tool, or method on a very rapid, small-scale effort—less than 3 months, say, and only a few people—can frequently show good results, initial momentum, or proof of concept. The problem with pilot programs is that they are almost never on the critical path of the organization. Consequently, they do not merit "A" players, adequate resources, or management attention.

The most successful organizational paradigm shifts I have seen resulted from sets of circumstances similar to these: The organizations took their most critical project and highest caliber personnel, gave them adequate resources, *and* demanded better results. If, on the other hand, an organization expects a new method, tool, or technology to have an adverse impact on the results of the trailblazing project, that expectation is almost certain to come true. Why? Because no organization manager would knowingly cause an adverse impact on the most important projects in the organization, and that is where the organization's best people will be assigned. Therefore, the trailblazing project will be a noncritical project staffed with noncritical personnel of whom less is expected. This low expectation is often a self-fulfilling prophecy.

A better way to transition to a more mature iterative development process that supports automation technologies and modern architectures is to take the following shot:

- *Ready.* Do your homework. Analyze modern approaches and technologies. Define (or improve, or optimize) your process. Support it with mature environments, tools, and components. Plan thoroughly.

- *Aim.* Select a critical project. Staff it with the right team of complementary resources and demand improved results.

- *Fire.* Execute the organizational and project-level plans with vigor and follow-through.

CASE STUDIES AND BACKUP MATERIAL

The foundations of the material presented in the first four parts of this book span numerous efforts by many people, projects, and organizations. Most of my opinions and recommendations are based on lessons learned from project applications. This part contains detailed appendixes that provide some historical perspectives and some detailed explanations of relevant practices.

- Appendix A summarizes three different perspectives of the state of software management practice in the mid-1990s.

- Appendix B summarizes the evolution of the COCOMO model from its inception through the current version, COCOMO II. This topic provides a context for my views on the evolution of software economics.

- Appendix C provides further detail on the derivation of and rationale behind the change metrics recommended in Chapter 13.

- Appendix D is a thorough case study of a successful large-scale, complex software project. It is a rich source of real-world examples that can serve as performance benchmarks for other projects. While any project case study will present some topics that interest only a narrow community, many topics provide universally interesting results. This project's culture, approach, and results are a model of a well-managed, mature software process.

- Appendix E assesses the process presented in this book using the Software Engineering Institute's Maturity Questionnaire. It provides a rough description of the maturity, consistency, and completeness of the process framework against a well-accepted benchmark of process assessment.

The State of the Practice in Software Management

Three important analyses performed in the mid-1990s yielded similar insights into the state of the software engineering industry. They concluded that the success rate for software projects is very low. This appendix summarizes the results of those analyses.

Patterns of Software Systems Failure and Success

This book [Jones, 1996] is a thorough presentation of the state of the software industry. Jones analyzed the results of thousands of

> **Key Points**
>
> ▲ Many software industry management practices in the 1990s still reflect an immature process characterized by excessive scrap and rework.
>
> ▲ About 10% of conventional projects succeed, where success is defined as meeting the customer's expectations in cost, schedule, quality, and feature set *and* making a profit.
>
> ▲ Software management factors are the primary discriminators of project success and failure.

projects grouped into six subindustries: systems software, information systems, commercial software, outsource software, military software, and end-user software. Table A-1 summarizes his overall assessment of the root causes of software project success and failure.

Jones makes an interesting observation about this table:

> *It is both interesting and significant that the first six out of sixteen [sic] technology factors associated with software disasters are specific failures in the domain of project management, and three of the other technology deficiencies can be indirectly assigned to poor management practices.*

Jones also identifies the cultural and people factors that discriminate successful projects from failures. These are presented in Table A-2.

TABLE A-1. *Technologies used on software projects*

TECHNOLOGIES ON UNSUCCESSFUL PROJECTS	TECHNOLOGIES ON SUCCESSFUL PROJECTS
No historical software measurement data*	Accurate software measurement*
Failure to use automated estimating tools*	Early use of estimating tools*
Failure to use automated planning tools*	Continuous use of planning tools*
Failure to monitor progress or milestones*	Formal progress reporting*
Failure to use effective architecture*	Formal architecture planning*
Failure to use effective development methods*	Formal development methods*
Failure to use design reviews	Formal design reviews
Failure to use code inspections	Formal code inspections
Failure to include formal risk management*	Formal risk management*
Informal, inadequate testing	Formal testing methods
Manual design and specification	Automated design and specifications
Failure to use formal configuration control*	Automated configuration control*
More than 30% creep in user requirements*	Less than 10% creep in user requirements*
Inappropriate use of 4GLs	Use of suitable languages
Excessive and unmeasured complexity	Controlled and measured complexity
Little or no reuse of certified materials	Significant reuse of certified materials
Failure to define database elements	Formal database planning

*Project management factors

The patterns of success and failure are evaluated from many different perspectives. The differences among the six subindustries and among projects of different scale are described in detail by Jones. One striking message is the commonality of these factors across all domains.

While I agree with most of the overall message summarized in the two tables, my opinion differs somewhat on the relative importance of the various factors and the implementation details associated with applying some technologies successfully. For example, the top three factors in Table A-1 may be the most common characteristics, but I do not think they are the most important discriminators of success and failure. My views are presented in Chapter 4.

TABLE A-2. *Social factors observed on software projects*

UNSUCCESSFUL PROJECTS	SUCCESSFUL PROJECTS
Excessive schedule pressure	Realistic schedule expectation
Executive rejection of estimates	Executive understanding of estimates
Severe friction with clients	Cooperation with clients
Divisive corporate politics	Congruent management goals
Poor team communications	Excellent team communications
Naive senior executives	Experienced senior executives
Project management malpractice	Capable project management
Unqualified technical staff	Capable technical staff
Generalists used for critical tasks: quality assurance, testing, planning, estimating	Specialists used for critical tasks: quality assurance, testing, planning, estimating

"Chaos"

This report [Standish Group, 1995] focuses on the commercial software industry and reaches these conclusions:

- U.S. companies would spend $81 billion on canceled software projects in 1995.
- 31% of software projects studied were canceled before they were completed.
- 53% of software projects overran by more than 50%.
- Only 9% of software projects for large companies were delivered on time and within budget. For medium-sized and small companies, the numbers improved to 16% and 28%, respectively.

The report characterizes the top 10 reasons for success and the top 10 reasons that projects are risky. (It calls risky projects "challenged.") These factors are summarized in Table A-3. Most of the "Chaos" report deals with the issues and obstacles perceived by managers of corporate information systems. Although there is only a minor treatment of possible solutions, the report recommends curing the disease, which is a highly process-oriented approach, rather than just resolving the symptoms.

The report states:

> *Research at The Standish Group also indicates that smaller time frames, with delivery of software components early and often, will increase the success rate.*

TABLE A-3.   *Factors that affect the success of software projects*

SUCCESSFUL PROJECTS	% OF RESPONSES	CHALLENGED PROJECTS	% OF RESPONSES
User involvement	15.9	Lack of user input	12.8
Executive management support	13.9	Incomplete requirements	12.3
Clear statement of requirements	13.0	Changing requirements	11.8
Proper planning	9.6	Lack of executive support	7.5
Realistic expectations	8.2	Technology incompetence	7.0
Smaller project milestones	7.7	Lack of resources	6.4
Competent staff	7.2	Unrealistic expectations	5.9
Ownership	5.3	Unclear objectives	5.3
Clear vision and objectives	2.9	Unrealistic time frames	4.3
Hard-working, focused staff	2.4	New technology	3.7
Other	13.9	Other	23.0

Shorter time frames result in an iterative process of design, prototype, develop, test, and deploy small elements. This process is known as growing software, as opposed to the old concept of developing software. Growing software engages the user earlier, each component has an owner or a small set of owners, and expectations are realistically set. In addition, each software component has a clear and precise statement and set of objectives. Software components and small projects tend to be less complex. Making the projects simpler is a worthwhile endeavor because complexity causes only confusion and increased cost.

The "Chaos" report reflects the predominant beliefs among software managers, namely that the primary reasons for success and failure center on the requirements management process. The data imply that if organizations understand *what* they are building (the requirements), then *how* it gets built (the process) is not a big issue. But that is far from true: Requirements management activities typically consume only about 10% of life-cycle resources; the other 90% must also be performed successfully. Because requirements management activities dominate the early life cycle, they are an easy scapegoat. In contrast to what the data imply, the recommendations in the report for making the problem smaller are quite insightful and are consistent with the spirit of a modern iterative process.

*Report of the Defense Science Board Task Force on Acquiring Defense
Software Commercially*

This report [Defense Science Board, 1994] presents the following conclusions:

- Current Department of Defense practice was not compatible with commercial business practices.

- DOD program management approaches discouraged the use of commercial practices.

- There was a shortfall of sufficiently qualified software personnel at all levels of DOD.

- DOD had not fully identified the pros and cons of using commercial components.

- DOD did not emphasize architecture.

- DOD did not adequately promote technology transfer with the commercial market.

The report states that although DOD had performed numerous studies of software projects (18 were enumerated), the majority of the recommendations from these studies had not been implemented.

The principal reasons that DOD software projects get into trouble are identified as follows:

- Poor requirements definition

- Inadequate software process management

- Lack of integrated product teams

- Ineffective subcontractor management

- Lack of consistent attention to process

- Too little attention to software architecture

- Poorly defined, inadequately controlled interfaces

- Software upgrades to fix hardware deficiencies

- Focus on innovation rather than cost and risk

- Limited or no tailoring of military standards

These primary recommendations are made:

- Exploit commercial practices (such as iterative development and architecture-first processes).
- Exploit commercial components and technologies.
- Invest more in software education for DOD people.

The report discusses ways to resolve the risks it identifies. It does not overhype the need to do a better job of defining and controlling requirements, as many previous DOD studies had done. This topic is mentioned and then discussed with appropriate emphasis, balanced with many other equally important factors. The "Chaos" report pins most of the blame for unsuccessful projects on requirements management deficiencies. The Department of Defense would have agreed in the late 1980s, but seems to have matured to a more balanced self-assessment and understanding of both the symptoms and the disease.

The COCOMO Cost Estimation Model

Several software cost models are in use today. One popular, open, and well-documented software cost model is the COnstructive COst MOdel (COCOMO) developed by Barry Boehm. The evolution of COCOMO provides an interesting window for observing the evolution of software engineering economics over the past 20 years.

The COCOMO estimating equations follow this simple form:

$$\text{Effort} = C1 \ EAF \ (\text{Size})^{P1}$$
$$\text{Time} = C2 \ (\text{Effort})^{P2}$$

where:

Effort = number of staff-months

    C1 = a constant scaling coefficient for effort

  EAF = an effort adjustment factor that characterizes the domain, personnel, environment, and tools used to produce the artifacts of the process

  Size = size of the end product (in human-generated source code), measured by the number of delivered source instructions (DSI) required to develop the required functionality

Key Points

▲ The history of the COCOMO model provides insight into the evolution of software economics priorities.

▲ The original COCOMO model was well suited for conventional software project cost estimation in the 1980s.

▲ Ada COCOMO improved on the original version, particularly through a parameterized exponent that reflected modern process improvements and their impact on economies of scale.

▲ COCOMO II is better suited for estimating modern software development projects. It provides more natural support to modern processes and technologies and a more up-to-date basis of project experience.

P1 = an exponent that characterizes the economies of scale inherent in the process used to produce the end product, in particular the ability of the process to avoid non-value-adding activities (rework, bureaucratic delays, communications overhead)

Time = total number of months

C2 = a constant scaling coefficient for schedule

P2 = an exponent that characterizes the inherent inertia and parallelism in managing a software development effort

B.1 COCOMO

The original COCOMO model [Boehm, 1981] was one of the minor breakthroughs in software engineering during the early 1980s. It was a breakthrough partly because of its inherent technology contribution but primarily because it provided a well-defined framework for communication of trade-offs and priorities associated with software cost and schedule management. As a naïve graduate student at UCLA in 1980, I first encountered the COCOMO model as the subject of a new graduate-level course taught by Boehm. At the same time, I was working at TRW as a lead designer on a software-intensive proposal for which we needed to plan and defend the software cost and schedule estimates. A huge benefit offered by the COCOMO model was the ability to make an estimate, reference a credible basis for it, reason about its strengths and weaknesses, and negotiate with stakeholders. Since then, I have used COCOMO to rationalize technology insertions, process improvements, project architecture changes, and new management approaches. In these activities, I became experienced with its strengths and weaknesses, as well as its use and misuse.

The original COCOMO model was based on a database of 56 projects. Its three modes reflected the differences in process across a range of software domains. These modes were identified as organic, semidetached, and embedded. Organic mode projects were characterized by in-house, less-complex developments that had flexible processes. Features, qualities, cost, and schedule could be freely changed with minimal overhead. Embedded mode systems represented typical defense community projects: Complexity, reliability, and real-time issues were dominant, and the contractual nature of the business resulted in a highly rigorous process. Features, qualities, costs, and schedules were tightly controlled, and changes required approvals by many stakeholders. Semidetached mode projects represented something in between.

Basic Effort and Schedule Estimating Formulas

These were the original COCOMO cost estimation relationships:

Organic mode $\quad\quad$ Effort $= 3.2$ EAF $(\text{Size})^{1.05}$

$\quad\quad\quad\quad\quad\quad\quad$ Time (in months) $= 2.5$ $(\text{Effort})^{0.38}$

Semidetached mode $\qquad$ Effort $= 3.0$ EAF $(Size)^{1.12}$
Time (in months) $= 2.5$ $(Effort)^{0.35}$

Embedded mode $\qquad$ Effort $= 2.8$ EAF $(Size)^{1.2}$
Time (in months) $= 2.5$ $(Effort)^{0.32}$

where:

Effort $=$ number of staff-months
EAF $=$ product of 15 effort adjustment factors (Table B-1)
Size $=$ number of delivered source instructions (in units of thousands of lines of code)

The effort adjustment factor (EAF) multiplier represents the combined effects of multiple parameters. These parameters allow the project to be characterized and normalized against the projects in the COCOMO database. Each parameter is assessed as very low, low, nominal, high, or very high. The effect of each parameter setting is a multiplier that typically ranges from 0.5 to 1.5. The product of these 15 effects is used as the coefficient in the cost equation.

TABLE B-1. *COCOMO project characterization parameters*

IDENTIFIER	EFFORT ADJUSTMENT FACTOR	PARAMETER RANGE	POTENTIAL IMPACT
RELY	Required reliability	0.75 – 1.40	1.87
DATA	Database size	0.94 – 1.16	1.23
CPLX	Product complexity	0.70 – 1.65	2.36
TIME	Execution time constraint	1.00 – 1.66	1.66
STOR	Main storage constraint	1.00 – 1.56	1.56
VIRT	Virtual machine volatility	0.87 – 1.30	1.49
TURN	Computer turnaround time	0.87 – 1.15	1.32
ACAP	Analyst capability	1.46 – 0.71	2.06
AEXP	Applications experience	1.29 – 0.82	1.57
PCAP	Programmer capability	1.42 – 0.70	2.03
VEXP	Virtual machine experience	1.21 – 0.90	1.34
LEXP	Language experience	1.14 – 0.95	1.20
MODP	Use of modern practices	1.24 – 0.82	1.51
TOOL	Use of software tools	1.24 – 0.83	1.49
SCED	Required development schedule	1.23 – 1.10	1.23

Assumptions

Several assumptions are inherent in the COCOMO formulas. Delivered source instructions include all (noncomment) lines of computer-processed code. The development life cycle starts at the beginning of product design and ends with acceptance test at the conclusion of the integration and test phase. (The requirements analysis effort and schedule are estimated separately as an additional percentage of the development estimate.) The activities include only direct-charged project efforts and exclude typical overhead activities such as administrative support, facilities, and capital equipment. A staff-month consists of 152 hours. The project will be well managed. The project will experience stable requirements.

Life-Cycle Description

The COCOMO life cycle includes five basic phases: plans and requirements, product design, detailed design, code and unit test, and integration and test. COCOMO provides recommendations for distributing the effort and schedule across the basic phases of the conventional waterfall model. These recommendations vary somewhat with mode and scale; Table B-2 provides a typical profile for a large, embedded mode project. COCOMO estimates the effort and schedule to develop the solution (product design through integration and test). Formulating the problem (plans and requirements) is estimated as an additional percentage over and above the development effort and schedule.

Software Work Breakdown Structure

Most conventional work breakdown structures are organized around the product subsystems at the higher levels and around the detailed activities at the lower levels. The standard activities estimated by COCOMO and included in the software WBS are requirements analysis, product design, programming, test planning, verification and validation, project office functions (management and administration), configuration management and quality assurance, and manuals. COCOMO also recommends

TABLE B-2. *Effort and schedule partition across conventional life-cycle phases*

ACTIVITY	EFFORT (%)	SCHEDULE (%)
Plans and requirements	(+8)	(+36)
Product design	18	36
Detailed design	25	18
Code and unit test	26	18
Integration and test	31	28

TABLE B-3.   *Default effort allocations across COCOMO WBS activities*

ACTIVITY	BUDGET (%)
Requirements analysis	4
Product design	12
Programming	44
Test planning	6
Verification and validation	14
Project office	7
Configuration management and quality assurance	7
Manuals	6

a top-level distribution of effort across the activities of the WBS. Again, these profiles are dependent on mode and scale. Table B-3 identifies the expected expenditure profile among the activities in the WBS for a large, embedded mode project. An important caveat is that in COCOMO, the "programming" activity includes detailed design, coding, unit testing, and integration.

A Typical COCOMO Project Profile

The following discussion focuses on a specific example project in order to illuminate some of the project planning implications. Assume a large, 100,000 source-line (100-KDSI) mission-critical system (for example, control of a power plant) built under contract for a government agency. Figure B-1 illustrates the COCOMO-estimated profile for this project. COCOMO would estimate 900 staff-months for development plus 72 staff-months for requirements specification for this project. The schedule required would be 22 months from initiation of design through test, plus 8 months for requirements.

B.2   Ada COCOMO

In the mid-1980s, TRW confronted the challenge of transitioning several projects to Ada. In some cases, a government mandate was the forcing function. (These projects tended to struggle.) In other cases, the project engineers believed that Ada technology was critical to a competitive bid and successful performance. (These projects tended to succeed.) I developed the first prototype of Ada COCOMO on an internal research and development project in 1985. The purpose of this effort was to provide a framework for convincing TRW management and a government customer that the cost benefits of using Ada on a specific large-scale project were significant, and that proposing

Example: 100,000-SLOC project that requires 972 staff-months of effort and 30 months of schedule

Effort

$$= 2.8 \text{ EAF (KDSI)}^{1.2}$$
$$= 2.8 \ (1.28) \ (100)^{1.2}$$

= 900 staff-months of development effort

+ <u>72</u> staff-months for plans, requirements

= **972 staff-months** of total effort

Cost Driver	Setting	Effect
Language experience	Nominal	1.0
Schedule constraint	Nominal	1.0
Database size	Nominal	1.0
Turnaround time	Nominal	1.0
Virtual machine experience	Nominal	1.0
Virtual machine volatility	Nominal	1.0
Use of software tools	High	0.88
Modern programming practices	Nominal	1.0
Storage constraint	Nominal	1.0
Applications experience	Low	1.10
Timing constraint	Nominal	1.0
Required reliability	High	1.15
Product complexity	High	1.15
Personnel/team capability	Nominal	1.0

> The total EAF (1.28 in this example) is the product of all the individual cost-driver effects.

Time

$$= 2.5 \text{ (Effort)}^{0.32}$$
$$= 2.5 \ (900)^{0.32}$$

= 22 months of development schedule

+ <u>8</u> months for plans, requirements

= **30 months**

Effort adjustment factor = 1.28

Staffing Profile and Activity Mix

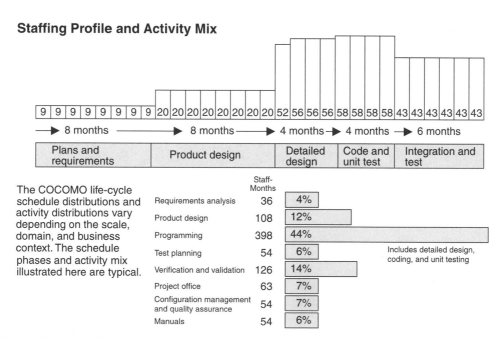

The COCOMO life-cycle schedule distributions and activity distributions vary depending on the scale, domain, and business context. The schedule phases and activity mix illustrated here are typical.

	Staff-Months	
Requirements analysis	36	4%
Product design	108	12%
Programming	398	44%
Test planning	54	6%
Verification and validation	126	14%
Project office	63	7%
Configuration management and quality assurance	54	7%
Manuals	54	6%

Includes detailed design, coding, and unit testing

FIGURE B-1. *Profile of a conventional project*

Ada on this project was a winning competitive strategy. It was also the lowest risk software approach for delivering the system on budget and on schedule with the required quality. (The project was CCPDS-R, the next-generation missile warning system presented as a case study in Appendix D.)

This initial development of Ada COCOMO was just one of the activities in a three-pronged approach:

1. Develop a set of architectural foundation components in Ada to measure compiler performance and provide a reusable set of foundation components for command and control systems such as CCPDS-R.

2. Develop a next-generation process description to exploit iterative development techniques and an architecture-first, demonstration-based approach. This Ada process model [Royce, Walker, 1990b] was a major step toward a modern process for use in defense domain projects.

3. Develop an Ada version of COCOMO to describe the cost and schedule benefits of this new technology and process.

The results of this effort were critical to TRW's approach to CCPDS-R, and the development of Ada COCOMO was key to selling the whole approach both to management and to the government customer. This initial version was then formalized within TRW under Boehm's leadership [Boehm and Royce, Walker, 1988]. Several other project experiences were incorporated, the parameters were tuned, and the process focus was expanded by introducing the concept of a parameterized exponent.

The primary improvement in Ada COCOMO was to eliminate the three modes of COCOMO (organic, semidetached, and embedded) and allow the exponent to be parameterized to reflect the economy of scale contributions inherent in a modern iterative development process. Several minor modifications tailored the other parameters to the technology advances inherent in the Ada environment.

The Ada COCOMO cost estimation relationship was as follows:

$$\text{Effort} = 2.8 \text{ EAF } (\text{Size})^{\text{P}}$$
$$\text{Time} = 2.5 (\text{Effort})^{0.32}$$

where:

Effort = number of staff-months

EAF = product of 19 effort adjustment factors (Table B-4)

Size = number of delivered source instructions (in units of thousands of lines of code)

P = process exponent

Time = total number of months

TABLE B-4. *Ada COCOMO improvements to the effort adjustment factors*

IDENTIFIER	EFFORT ADJUSTMENT FACTOR	Ada COCOMO PERTURBATIONS
RELY	Required reliability	Changes to underlying effects (positive impact)
DATA	Database size	No change
CPLX	Product complexity	Changes to underlying effects (positive impact)
RUSE	Required level of reuse	New effect for complexity of reusable components
SECU	Security constraints	New effect for classified projects
TIME	Execution time constraint	No change
STOR	Main storage constraint	No change
VIRT	Virtual machine volatility	Deleted (split into two new factors)
VMVH	Host VM volatility	New effect accommodating host aspects of VIRT
VMVT	Target VM volatility	New effect accommodating target aspects of VIRT
TURN	Computer turnaround time	New level of interactive response (positive impact)
ACAP	Analyst capability	Changes to underlying effects (more impact)
AEXP	Applications experience	No change
PCAP	Programmer capability	Changes to underlying effects (less impact)
VEXP	Virtual machine experience	No change
LEXP	Language experience	Changes to underlying effects (more impact)
MODP	Use of modern practices	Changes to underlying effects (more impact)
TOOL	Use of software tools	New levels of automation support
SCED	Required development schedule	Changes to underlying effects (less impact)

The EAF multiplier again represents the combined effects of multiple parameters. In Ada COCOMO, however, there were several changes to reflect general improvements to COCOMO, Ada-specific effects, and the effects of a more iterative process. This adjustment resulted in two new cost drivers (RUSE and SECU), one split cost driver (VIRT was split into host and target components: VMVH and VMVT), and several new ratings or changes to the underlying effects of a cost driver.

One of the foundations of Ada COCOMO was the use of the Ada process model. It was not necessary to use the Ada language in order to use the primary techniques of this process model. However, at the time it was developed, there was so much Ada underhype and overhype within the defense software market that the process description was coupled to the use of Ada. This approach had its pros and cons. In retrospect, the Ada process model can be viewed as an intermediate state between the conventional process and the modern process framework described in this book. Ada process model strategies are summarized here to provide an understanding of the process parameterization of the Ada COCOMO exponent.

One critical strategy of the Ada process model was to emphasize the preliminary design review (PDR) milestone, which was required by the applicable military standard, as an architecture review supported by an executable demonstration of capabilities. This overarching goal led to several substrategies that exploited the techniques, tools, and technologies of the Ada environment:

- A small core design team with expertise in software architecture and the applications domain

- An early focus on executable architecture skeletons for demonstrating critical components and system-level threads and for exposing risk

- Incremental and separate detailed design walkthroughs for components and builds rather than a monolithic critical design review (CDR) across the whole system

- Continuous integration via Ada compilation and architecture-first development

- Test program and requirements verification focused on engineering string tests (now called use cases) and component stand-alone tests

- Self-documenting Ada code and big-picture descriptions instead of massive, detailed design documents that describe the as-built design

- Automated metrics derived from the evolving code baselines

The Ada COCOMO process exponent ranged from 1.04 to 1.24 and was defined from the combined effects of the following four parameters:

1. Ada process model experience. This process maturity rating ranged from "no familiarity" with the process to "successfully employed on multiple projects."

2. Design thoroughness at PDR. This parameter characterized the level of design detail inherent in the design baseline demonstrated at PDR. It ranged from "little thoroughness (20%)" to "complete thoroughness (100%)."

3. Risks eliminated at PDR. This parameter assessed the level of uncertainty inherent in the project at PDR, after which full-scale development is initiated. It ranged from "little risk resolution (20%)" to "complete resolution (100%)."

4. Requirements volatility during development. This parameter ranged from "many large changes" to "no changes," characterizing the amount of process turbulence confronted by the project.

The actual exponent for Ada COCOMO was determined by summing the ratings for each parameter across a scale from 0.00 to 0.05. The embedded mode exponent (1.20) from the original COCOMO would relate to an Ada COCOMO process with a 0.04 rating on each of the process parameters $[1.04 + (4 \times 0.04)]$. In terms of the process parameters just described, this would correspond to (1) little familiarity with the Ada process model, (2) some design thoroughness at PDR (40%), (3) some risks eliminated by PDR (40%), and (4) frequent but moderate requirements changes.

These four parameters were aimed primarily at characterizing the process and its ability to relieve the diseconomies of scale inherent in the conventional process. By keeping the design team smaller and establishing a more tangible architecture description by PDR, the process attempted to optimize interpersonal communications, avoid late downstream rework, and encourage earlier requirements convergence.

B.3   COCOMO II

The COCOMO II project [Boehm *et al.*, 1995; Horowitz, 1997] is an effort being performed by the USC Center for Software Engineering, with the financial and technical support of numerous industry affiliates. (They include AT&T Bell Labs, Bellcore, DISA, EDS, E-Systems, Hewlett-Packard, Hughes, IDA, IDE, JPL, Litton Data Systems, Lockheed Martin, Loral, MDAC, Motorola, Northrop-Grumman, Rational, Rockwell, SAIC, SEI, SPC, TASC, Teledyne, Texas Instruments, TRW, USAF Rome Labs, US Army Research Lab, and Xerox.) The objectives of this project are threefold:

1. To develop a software cost and schedule estimation model for the life-cycle practices of the 1990s and 2000s

2. To develop a software cost database and tool support for improvement of the cost model

3. To provide a quantitative analytic framework for evaluating software technologies and their economic impact

USC speculates that the post-2000 software marketplace will include five distinct populations:

1. End-user programmers (55 million) generating spreadsheets or database queries

2. Component developers (600,000) generating end-user applications and composition aids

3. Component integrators (700,000) building applications rapidly from existing GUI builders, database/object managers, middleware, and domain-specific components

4. System integrators (700,000) dealing with larger scale systems, unprecedented systems, few-of-a-kind applications, embedded systems requiring up-front engineering, and other substantial custom software development

5. Infrastructure developers (750,000) developing domain-independent components such as operating systems, database management systems, networks, and user interface frameworks

End users are not targeted by COCOMO II because they tend to do very rapid, small-scale efforts for which simple activity-based estimation is adequate. Projects that require teams of people working over months or years are the primary target market for software cost estimation models.

The COCOMO II strategy is to preserve the openness of the original COCOMO model, tailor it to the marketplace just described, key the inputs and outputs to the level of information available, and enable the model to be tailored to various project process strategies. In particular, this generation of COCOMO provides range estimates rather than point estimates. These vary over the life cycle from early, coarse-grained inputs and wide-ranging estimates to later, fine-grained inputs and more-precise estimates. Figure B-2 illustrates the estimation accuracy over the life cycle.

To support this strategy, COCOMO II defines three different models for cost estimation. Figure B-3 maps these models to the phases of an iterative life cycle. The models correspond to the level of fidelity and uncertainty appropriate for the current phase of the life cycle. The post-architecture model corresponds closely to the traditional COCOMO model, where it was assumed that the project had stable requirements, plans, and candidate architecture at the outset. Projects then followed a waterfall process through delivery with little requirements volatility. The post-architecture model provides for fine-grained estimates of the project once it has a requirements baseline, an architecture baseline, and a plan for the construction phase. The early design model provides for coarser grained estimates in the elaboration

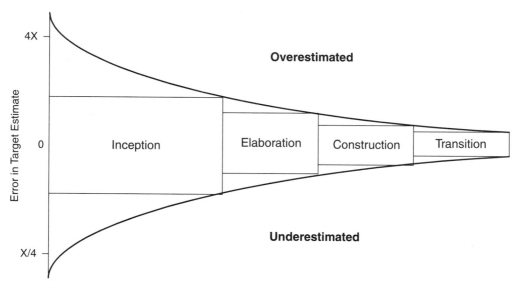

FIGURE B-2. *Software estimation over a project life cycle*

phase of the life cycle, and the applications composition model allows for very rough order-of-magnitude estimates during the inception phase of a project.

The applications composition model corresponds to exploratory work typically done during prototyping efforts and feasibility analyses. The estimating equation is a simple linear relationship of object points and domain complexity.

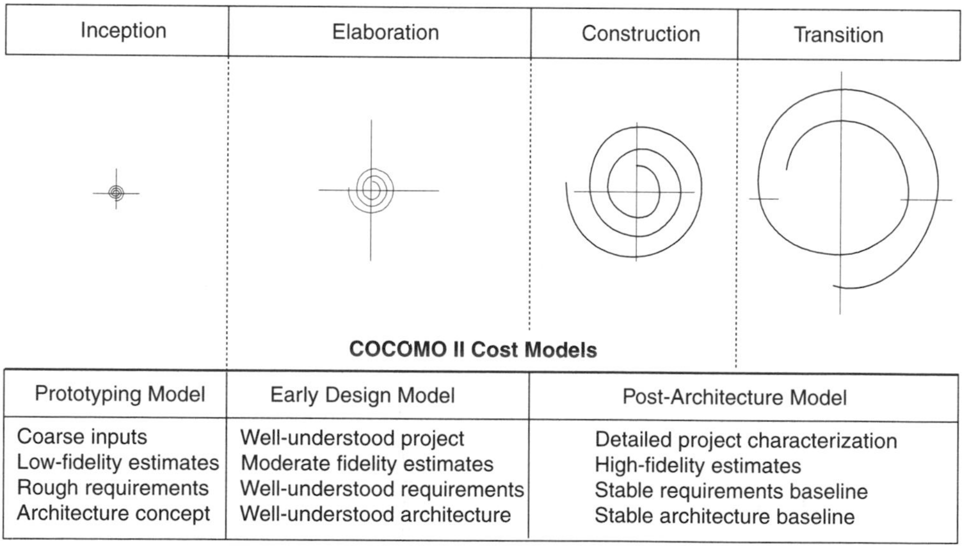

Inception	Elaboration	Construction	Transition

COCOMO II Cost Models

Prototyping Model	Early Design Model	Post-Architecture Model	
Coarse inputs	Well-understood project	Detailed project characterization	
Low-fidelity estimates	Moderate fidelity estimates	High-fidelity estimates	
Rough requirements	Well-understood requirements	Stable requirements baseline	
Architecture concept	Well-understood architecture	Stable architecture baseline	

FIGURE B-3. *COCOMO II estimation over a project life cycle*

The early design model corresponds to the level of detail available in the engineering stage of a project, during which the architecture, requirements, and plans are being synthesized. The overall cost estimate equation is as follows:

$$\text{Effort} = 2.45 \ E_{\text{Arch}} \ (\text{Size})^P$$

where:

$$\text{Effort} = \text{number of staff-months}$$
$$E_{\text{Arch}} = \text{product of seven early design effort adjustment factors (Table B-5)}$$
$$\text{Size} = \text{number of function points (preferred) or KSLOC}$$
$$P = \text{process exponent}$$

The early design phase parameters are composites of the post-architecture parameters. They provide a simpler estimating method for the early life cycle when there are substantially more unknowns.

The post-architecture cost estimating equation is as follows:

$$\text{Effort} = 2.45 \ E_{\text{App}} \ (\text{Size})^P$$

where:

$$\text{Effort} = \text{number of staff-months}$$
$$E_{\text{App}} = \text{product of 17 post-architecture effort adjustment factors (Table B-6)}$$
$$\text{Size} = \text{number of KSLOC (preferred) or function points}$$
$$P = \text{process exponent}$$

TABLE B-5. *Early design model effort adjustment factors*

IDENTIFIER	COMPOSITE EFFORT ADJUSTMENT FACTORS
Product complexity	RELY-DATA-CPLX-DOCU
Required reuse	RUSE
Platform difficulty	TIME-STOR-PVOL
Personnel experience	AEXP-PEXP-LTEX
Personnel capability	ACAP-PCAP-PCON
Facilities	TOOL-SITE
Schedule	SCED

TABLE B-6. *COCOMO II post-architecture model updates to Ada COCOMO and COCOMO*

IDENTIFIER	EFFORT ADJUSTMENT FACTOR	COCOMO II PERTURBATIONS
RELY	Required reliability	No change from COCOMO
DATA	Database size	No change from COCOMO
CPLX	Product complexity	No change from COCOMO
RUSE	Required reuse	No change from Ada COCOMO
DOCU	Documentation	Added; suitability of documentation to the life-cycle needs
TIME	Execution time constraint	No change from COCOMO
STOR	Main storage constraint	No change from COCOMO
PVOL	Platform volatility	Combined VMVH and VMVT parameters of Ada COCOMO into platform volatility
ACAP	Analyst capability	No change from COCOMO
AEXP	Applications experience	No change from COCOMO
PCAP	Programmer capability	No change from COCOMO
PEXP	Platform experience	Expanded platform experience from virtual machine experience
PCON	Personnel continuity	New parameter
LTEX	Language/tool experience	Changed to include both tool and language experience
SITE	Multiple-site development / Team communications	New parameter for degree of collocation and degree of automation among teams
TOOL	Use of software tools	No change from COCOMO
SCED	Required development schedule	No change from COCOMO

The E coefficients represent the combined effects of multiple parameters. The post-architecture model uses parameters similar to those used by the conventional COCOMO model. These parameters allow the development environment to be characterized and normalized with the parameters in the COCOMO II project database (currently 83 projects). The effect of each parameter setting (very low, low, nominal, high, very high) is a multiplier that typically ranges from 0.5 to 1.5. The product of these 17 effects is used to compute the effort in the cost equation.

The name of the post-architecture model describes the product of the early design phase—namely, the architecture. The use of function points is recommended to quantify size for the early design phase, because function points are better suited to early phases when the structure (and hence the SLOC estimates) for the software solution is relatively unknown. The use of SLOC is recommended to quantify size for the post-architecture model. This approach seems to be a good technical compromise between the SLOC zealots and the function point zealots.

COCOMO II uses the same exponent for the early design and the post-architecture models. The process exponent can range from (1.01..1.26) and is defined as the combined effects of the following five parameters:

1. Application precedentedness: the degree of domain experience of the development organization

2. Process flexibility: the degree of contractual rigor, ceremony, and change freedom inherent in the project contract, life-cycle activities, and stakeholder communications

3. Architecture risk resolution: the degree of technical feasibility demonstrated before commitment to full-scale production

4. Team cohesion: the degree of cooperation and shared vision among stakeholders (buyers, developers, users, and maintainers, among others)

5. Process maturity: the maturity level of the development organization, as defined by the Software Engineering Institute's Capability Maturity Model

The COCOMO II exponent parameterization is an evolutionary upgrade of the Ada COCOMO approach with a more solid basis. Table B-7 summarizes the parameter ratings. The actual exponent for COCOMO II is determined by summing the effects for each parameter. The combined impact of these process parameters can be very high. The COCOMO II team has yet to permit an actual economy of scale to be achieved (that is, the value of P is never less than 1.0). They believe that economy of scale is achievable through corresponding reductions in size resulting from use of commercial components, reusable components, CASE tools, and object-oriented technologies.

Another interesting upgrade in COCOMO II is the schedule estimating equation, which is now a function of both the effort estimate and the process parameters. The resulting impact of a better process is a reduction in both effort and schedule.

Overall, COCOMO II is a good improvement over conventional cost models, many of which are grossly out of date. It is a good match for iterative development, modern technology, and the management process described in this book. However, it is also immature, and its project database still comprises diverse projects from numerous organizations. It is hard to believe that it will be any more reliable than the original COCOMO model.

TABLE B-7. *COCOMO II process exponent parameters*

PARAMETER	VERY LOW (0.00)	LOW (0.01)	NOMINAL (0.02)	HIGH (0.03)	VERY HIGH (0.04)	EXTRA HIGH (0.05)
Precedentedness	Thoroughly unprecedented	Largely unprecedented	Somewhat unprecedented	Generally familiar	Largely familiar	Thoroughly familiar
Development flexibility	Rigorous	Occasional relaxation	Some relaxation	General conformity	Some conformity	General goals
Architecture risk resolution	Little 20%	Some 40%	Often 60%	Generally 75%	Mostly 90%	Full 100%
Team cohesion	Very difficult interactions	Some difficult interactions	Basically cooperative	Largely cooperative	Highly cooperative	Seamless interactions
Process maturity	Level 1	Level 2	Level 2+	Level 3	Level 4	Level 5

Change Metrics

Measurement of software progress and quality is an extremely complex undertaking because of the large number of product, project, and personnel parameters that have an impact on software development efforts. It is probably impossible to specify a set of absolute definitions of software measurement that will satisfy most projects. However, several aspects of software measurement are generally applicable to almost all software projects.

This is the basic hypothesis of this metrics approach:

Key Points

▲ One of the most important characteristics of good software is its ease of change.

▲ Measuring and assessing the scrap and rework effort in a succession of software baselines provides useful insight into the convergence toward, or divergence from, acceptable quality and progress.

▲ Metrics extracted directly from the evolving technical artifacts provide a foundation for process instrumentation that enables consistent, accurate, and precise project control.

The most important characteristic of software is that it is "soft": The easier the software is to change, the easier it is to achieve any of its other required characteristics.

The core metrics are therefore centered on measurements of software change trends (scrap and rework) in the software artifacts throughout the life cycle. To manage most serious software efforts, the software project manager needs several context-independent metrics (for comparison with general expectations) and several context-dependent metrics.

I developed much of this material in 1987 to rationalize the metrics program used for the CCPDS-R project, which is presented as a case study in Appendix D. The material was published [Royce, Walker, 1990] after three years of field experience had demonstrated its usefulness and resulted in several refinements. There have been many other attempts over the past 20 years to define measures of software quality. For several reasons, none has really caught on in practice, although there are some recurring themes that overlap my recommendations fairly well. Some recurring obstacles are the need for subjectivity and the cost of human resources required to collect and interpret metrics.

C.1 OVERVIEW

My approach to metrics is similar to that of DeMarco, who proposes to measure software quality through the absence of spoilage [DeMarco, 1982]. To remain technology- and project-independent, his definitions are purposely vague; mine are quite explicit. Consistency of application is important for accurate interpretation, just as it is with cost estimation techniques. Software cost estimation has subjective inputs and objective outputs. My approach will define objective inputs, which may require subjective interpretation within the context of a specific project.

One effective way to assess software quality over a life cycle is by measuring rework in the configured baselines. The unit of measurement can be source lines of code, function points, object points, files, components, or some other measure of the software size. This discussion uses SLOC as the primitive size metric because it is used predominantly by the industry, is the easiest measure to understand, and best matches the case study data in Appendix D.

In some cases, the software quality assessment derived from an objective collection of change metrics will require context-dependent assessment. Judgment is needed to assess quality using any metric. The same metrics should be used to assess quality during development (trend-oriented) and following development (value-oriented). For example, the volume of rework following product delivery is an objective measure of quality or lack of quality. The amount of rework following the first configuration baseline during development is ambiguous without further context. Zero rework might be interpreted as a perfect baseline (which is unlikely), an inadequate test program, or an unambitious first build.

Software Quality

It is extremely difficult to make this concept objective. Only two mechanisms are available for defining customer expectations of quality: software requirements specifications for function and performance, and an approved expenditure plan that quantifies cost and schedule goals. These artifacts, which basically correspond to the contract, are traditionally the lowest quality products produced by a project because they must be agreed upon early in the life cycle, when there are still too many unknowns. A modern, iterative process and objective software metrics should provide better insight into the extent to which function, performance, cost, and schedule comply with customer expectations.

Software Change Orders

SCOs, discussed at length in Chapter 12, constitute direction to proceed with changing a configured software component. (SCOs are often called software problem reports, but *problem* has a negative connotation, and not all changes are motivated by problems.) The change may be needed to rework a poor-quality component (type 0 or 1, a fix), to rework a component to achieve better quality (type 2, an enhancement), or to accommodate a customer-directed change in requirements (type 3, a scope change). The difference between a fix and an enhancement is inherent in the reason for the change. Assuming that the unchanged component is compliant, if the reason for the change is to improve cost-effectiveness, increase testability, increase usability, or improve efficiency in some other way, the rework is type 2. Both type 0 or 1 and type 2 rework should increase the quality of the end product. However, type 0 or 1 also indicates inadequate quality in a current baseline. In practice, differentiating between type 0 or 1 and type 2 may be quite subjective. As discussed later, most of the metrics are insensitive to the categorization, but if the differentiation is consistently applied, it can provide useful insight. Collection and analysis of change metrics focus on type 0, 1, and 2 SCOs, which are collected and analyzed together.

Type 3 SCOs typically reflect a requirements change that redefines the customer expectations. Such changes have a broader impact and therefore require various levels of software and systems engineering as well as highly varying levels of regression testing. Because of this wide range of variability, type 3 SCOs are analyzed separately in these metrics. The data derived from type 0, 1, and 2 SCOs should provide a solid basis for estimating maintainability and the effort required for type 3 SCOs.

Source Lines of Code

Whether SLOC provides a good metric for measuring software volume has always been controversial. (DeMarco calls this *bang*.) Jones identifies some of the precautions necessary when dealing with SLOC [Jones, 1994]. He goes so far as to say that "using lines of code for normalization of data involving multiple or different languages should be considered an example of professional malpractice." One point everyone agrees on is that whatever is used must be defined objectively and consistently to be of value for comparison. How the absolute unit of SLOC is defined is not as important as defining it consistently across all projects and all areas of a specific project. Requiring the use of a common counting tool forces standardization on a given definition.

Configuration Control Board

The CCB is the governing body responsible for authorizing changes to a configured baseline product. At a minimum, members include the software development manager, the software assessment manager, and, for a contractual effort, a customer representative. The CCB decides on all proposed changes to configured products and approves all SCOs. The CCB is responsible for collecting the software quality metrics, analyzing trends objectively and subjectively, and proposing changes to the development process, tools, products, or personnel to improve future quality.

Configured Baseline

A configured baseline is a set of products that are subjected to change control through the CCB. Configured baselines may represent intermediate products that have completed design, development, and informal test, or final products that have completed formal test.

C.2   METRICS DERIVATION

This section defines and describes in detail the necessary statistics to be collected, the metrics derived from these statistics, and some general guidelines for their interpretation. Appendix D provides detailed examples of a real-world application to illustrate further how such metrics can be used to manage and control a project. The derivations are not an obvious top-down progression; rather, they resulted from substantial trial and error, numerous empirical analyses, intuition, and heuristics.

The raw statistics to be collected include numbers and types of software changes, SLOC damaged, and SLOC fixed. The challenges are to find the right filtering techniques for the raw rework statistics that identify useful trends, and to uncover objective measures to quantify progress (intermediate attributes during development) and quality (attributes of the end product). The final objective is to quantify the product's modularity, adaptability, maturity, and maintainability. Modularity and adaptability are intuitively easy to define as a function of rework; maturity and maintainability are more subtle.

- Modularity. This metric measures the average extent of breakage or scrap. It identifies the need to quantify the scrap (volume of SLOC damaged) and the number of instances of rework (number of SCOs). In effect, modularity is defined as a measure of breakage localization, with a lower value being better.

- Adaptability. This metric measures the average complexity of breakage as measured in rework. It identifies the need to quantify the rework (effort required for resolution) and the number of instances of rework (number of

SCOs). Adaptability quantifies the ease of change, with a lower value being better.

- Maturity. Intuitively, maturity corresponds to the level of trustworthiness of the product. Objectively, this metric measures the defect rate. The goal is to be defect-free—namely, to achieve infinite maturity. The trust increases primarily through extended usage. Because software is intellectual property, not comprised of physical matter, it does not wear out. Software should mature over time, meaning that its users (test team, beta users, users of a released product) should experience defects less frequently with each subsequent release of the product. This statement assumes constant functionality and performance in new releases. The expectation of increasing maturity in new releases is valid even when functionality and performance change. Similarly, there should be noticeable trends in release maturity across the development life cycle of a healthy iterative development effort. A simple indicator of the defect rate would require measuring the number of defects (type 0 and 1 SCOs) and the amount of usage time. From these parameters, the mean time between failures (MTBF) can be derived for a given release. Higher vales of maturity are better, reflecting the average time between defects perceived by a user.

- Maintainability. Theoretically, the maintainability of a product is related to the productivity with which the maintenance team can operate. Productivity is so difficult to compare among projects, however, that this definition is intuitively unsatisfying. The ratio of the productivity of rework to the productivity of development provides a value that is independent of productivity yet reflects the development complexity. The ratio normalizes the project productivity differences and provides a relatively comparable metric. Consequently, maintainability is defined as the ratio of rework productivity to development productivity. Intuitively, this value identifies a product that can be changed three times as efficiently as it was developed (maintainability = 0.33) as having better (lower) maintainability than a product that can be changed twice as efficiently (maintainability = 0.5) as it was developed, independent of the absolute maintenance productivity realized. The statistics needed to compute these values are the total development effort, total SLOC, total rework effort, and total reworked SLOC.

While these values provide useful objective measures of end products, their intermediate values as a function of time also provide insight during development into the expected end-product values. Once a project has gained some experience with maintenance of early increments, this experience should be useful for predicting the rework inherent in remaining increments.

This brief derivation was relatively simple. It is not necessary to deal with these metrics as a complete set, although multiple perspectives are needed by project management to achieve accuracy. Subsets, or different sets, are also useful. Most of the analysis, mathematics, and data collection inherent in these metrics should be automated so that practitioners need only interpret the results and understand their basis.

C.2.1 COLLECTED STATISTICS

Some specific statistics must be collected over the software project life cycle to implement the proposed metrics. These statistics, identified in Table C-1, include the following:

- Total SLOC ($SLOC_T$). This statistic tracks the estimated total size of the product under development. This value may change significantly over the life of the development as early requirements unknowns are resolved and design solutions mature. This total should also include reused software, which is part of the delivered product and subject to change by the development team.
- Configured SLOC ($SLOC_C$). This statistic tracks the transition of software components from a maturing design state into a controlled configuration. For any given project, this statistic will provide insight into progress and

TABLE C-1. *Definitions of collected statistics*

COLLECTED STATISTICS	DEFINITION
Total SLOC	$SLOC_T$ = total size in SLOC
Configured SLOC	$SLOC_C$ = current baseline SLOC
Critical defects	SCO_0 = number of type 0 SCOs
Normal defects	SCO_1 = number of type 1 SCOs
Improvements	SCO_2 = number of type 2 SCOs
New features	SCO_3 = number of type 3 SCOs
Number of SCOs	$N = SCO_0 + SCO_1 + SCO_2$
Open rework (breakage)	B = cumulative broken SLOC due to SCO_0, SCO_1, and SCO_2
Closed rework (fixes)	F = cumulative fixed SLOC
Rework effort	E = cumulative effort expended fixing SCO_0, SCO_1, and SCO_2
Usage time	UT = hours that a given baseline has been operating under realistic usage scenarios

stability of the development team. For projects with reused software, there will be an early contribution to $SLOC_C$ and thus immediate progress and quality metrics.

- Defects (SCO_0 and SCO_1). Changes to resolve software errors constitute an important statistic from which the reliability and maturity of a baseline can be derived. The expectation is that the highest incidence of uncovering errors occurs immediately after a release and decreases with time as the software matures.

- Improvements (SCO_2). Another stimulus for changing a baseline, improvements are also key to assessment of the quality and the progress toward producing quality. The expectation for improvements is inversely proportional to defects. Because the defect rate starts high and damps out, improvements start low (the focus is on defects) and increase. This phenomenon is loosely based on the assumption that a fixed team is working the test and maintenance activities. It is captured by the following relationship:

Effort (defects) + Effort (improvements) = Constant

Differentiation between defects and improvements is somewhat subjective. The change metrics defined herein are not particularly sensitive to either type because they rely on the sum of the impacts from both types. However, the difference between defects and improvements can have a significant impact on the maturity measures described in Section C.2.2.

- New features (SCO_3). Type 3 changes reflect an update to the stakeholder expectations for new features or capabilities outside the scope of the current contract. The statistics for type 3 changes are analyzed separately because they reflect new work rather than rework.

- Number of SCOs (N). Because an SCO is a discrete unit of change, it is important for its definition to be consistent throughout all domains where the metrics will be compared. What is the level at which changes are documented and tracked? Most projects converge on a fairly loose definition of an SCO based on size, breadth of impact on individuals and teams, and CCB culture. This loose approach will work for the individual project, but if every project uses a different definition, comparability across projects is compromised. In general, SCOs should affect a single component and should be allocated to a single individual or team leader. With this simple standard, more-precise definitions of these primitives are unnecessary. Imprecise primitives work fine, and greater precision adds little value. As more and more metrics collection is supported by automated tools, there will be further homogenization of the overall measurement techniques and primitive units.

- Open rework (B). Theoretically, all rework corresponds to an increase in quality. The rework is necessary either to remove an instance of "bad" quality (SCO_0 and SCO_1) or to enhance a component to improve life-cycle cost effectiveness (SCO_2). To assess quality trends accurately, the dynamics of the rework must be evaluated in the context of the life-cycle phase. A certain amount of rework is necessary on a large software engineering effort; early rework is considered a sign of healthy progress in a modern process model. Continuous rework, late rework, or zero rework due to the absence of a configured baseline are generally indicators of negative quality. Interpretation of this statistic requires project context. In general, however, rework should ultimately approach zero at product delivery. To provide a consistent collection process that can be automated, rework can be defined as the number of SLOC estimated to change due to an SCO. The absolute accuracy of the estimates is generally unimportant. Because open rework is tracked with an estimate and closed rework is tracked separately with actuals, the values continually correct themselves and remain consistent.

- Closed rework (F). Whereas the breakage statistics estimate the damage done, the repair statistics identify the actual damage that was fixed. Upon resolution, the corresponding breakage estimate is updated to reflect the actual required repair that remains in the baseline. Although the actual SLOC fixed (F) will never be absolutely accurate, it will be relatively accurate for assessing trends. Because "fixed" can take on several different meanings depending on what is added, deleted, or changed, a consistent set of guidelines is necessary. Changed SLOC will increase B and F without a change to $SLOC_C$. Added code will increase B, F, and $SLOC_C$, although not in the same proportions. Deleted code (an infrequent occurrence) with no corresponding addition could increase B and reduce $SLOC_C$. Given the volume of changes and the need for only roughly accurate data for identifying trends, the accuracy and precision of the raw data are relatively unimportant.

- Rework effort (E). The total effort expended in resolving SCOs is another necessary perspective for tracking the complexity of rework. Activities should be limited to technical requirements, software engineering, design, development, and functional test. Higher level systems engineering, management, configuration control, verification testing, and system testing should be excluded, because these activities tend to be more a function of company, customer, or project attributes, independent of quality. The goal here is to normalize the widely varying bureaucratic activities out of the metrics.

- Usage time (UT). This important statistic corresponds to the number of hours that a given baseline has been operating under realistic usage scenarios. For some systems, this statistic corresponds to straight time measurements; for many others, automated tests can simulate one day of usage in a one-hour test. For example, most transaction processing systems have an expected average load that they process daily. If this average load can be packaged in a test scenario and executed against the product baseline in one hour, it counts as 24 hours of usage time. As another example, consider a development tool that is used by humans operating at human speeds of several keystrokes per second. If automated GUI test tools can support scripts of interactions that can be tested against the product at a tenfold higher rate, then every hour of test time counts as 10 hours of usage time. Defining the mapping of test time to usage time is generally straightforward. This is also a great requirements analysis exercise that frequently uncovers ambiguities in the understanding of usage scenarios among different stakeholders.

C.2.2 END-PRODUCT QUALITY METRICS

The end-product quality metrics (Table C-2) provide insight into the maintainability of the software products with respect to type 0, 1, and 2 SCOs. Type 3 SCOs are explicitly not included, because they redefine the inherent target quality of the system and tend to require more global system and software engineering as well as some major reverification of system-level requirements. Because these types of changes are dealt with in extremely diverse ways by different customers and projects, they would tend to cloud the meanings and comparability of the data.

The following metrics data should be very helpful in determining and planning the amount of effort necessary to implement type 3 SCOs. They are also useful when applied against subsets of the product such as components or releases. The word *product* is used as the basis of what is being measured.

TABLE C-2. *End-product quality metrics*

METRIC	DEFINITION
Scrap ratio	$B/SLOC_T$, percentage of product scrapped
Rework ratio	$E/Effort_{Development}$, percentage of rework effort
Modularity	B/N, average breakage per SCO
Adaptability	E/N, average effort per SCO
Maturity	$UT/(SCO_0 + SCO_1)$, mean time between defects
Maintainability	(scrap ratio)/(rework ratio), maintenance productivity

- Scrap ratio. This metric provides a value for comparison with historical projects, future increments, or future projects. It defines the percentage of the product that had to be reworked during its life cycle.

- Rework ratio. This value identifies the percentage of effort spent in rework compared to the total effort. It probably provides the best indicator of rework (or maintenance) productivity.

- Modularity. This value identifies the average amount of SLOC broken per SCO, which reflects the inherent ability of the integrated product to localize the impact of change. To the maximum extent possible, CCBs should ensure that SCOs are written for single source changes and applied consistently across the project.

- Adaptability. This value provides insight into the ease with which the product can be changed. While a low number of changes is generally a good indicator of a quality process, the magnitude of effort per change is usually more important.

- Maturity. This value provides an indicator of the current mean time between failures (MTBF) for the product. While the ultimate goal for maturity is always infinity (namely, zero defects), every project must settle for less. Once a product has been released to its user community, the MTBF is generally fixed and stable. Throughout the development life cycle, however, maintenance actions are expected to improve the maturity over the life of a single release, and the trends across multiple releases should show improvement toward the project's end goals for maturity.

- Maintainability. This value identifies the relationship of maintenance cost to development cost. It provides a fair normalization for comparisons among different projects. Because the maintainability numerator is in terms of effort and its denominator is in terms of SLOC, it is a ratio of productivities (effort per SLOC). A simple mathematical rearrangement will show that maintainability (or the quality of maintenance, Q_M) is equivalent to the following:

$$Q_M = \text{Productivity}_{\text{Maintenance}}/\text{Productivity}_{\text{Development}}$$

For example, if the (scrap ratio) = (rework ratio), the productivity of modification is equivalent to the productivity of development and $Q_M = 1$. Intuitively, a value of 1 represents a "poor" level of maintainability because it should be easier to change existing software than to develop an alternative from scratch. The fact that conventional projects tended to spend $2 on maintenance for every $1 of development [Boehm, 1987] can serve as a benchmark of what would constitute a "good" level of maintainability. Consider a software line of business with an average product life span of 16 years and an average yearly breakage rate of 12%. If $Q_M = 1$, there would be about a 1:2 ratio between development expenditures and maintenance expenditures, or a maintainability that is roughly the norm for the software industry. A maintainability value much less than 1 would, in most cases, indicate a highly maintainable product, at least with respect to development cost and conventional experience.

These descriptions identify idealized trends for these metrics. Real project situations will never be ideal. It is important, however, for stakeholders to understand the extent to which the metrics vary from the ideal. The application of these metrics across project increments should be useful for the project as a whole and for comparisons with other projects.

C.2.3 IN-PROGRESS INDICATORS

The in-progress indicators are defined in Table C-3. Relative expectations are described next and illustrated in Figures C-1 and C-2.

- Rework stability. This metric quantifies the difference between total rework and closed rework. Its importance is to indicate whether the resolution rate is keeping up with the breakage rate. Figure C-1 shows an example of a healthy project in which the resolution rate does not diverge (except for short periods of time) from the breakage rate. The breakage rate should also be tracked relative to the $SLOC_C$ delivery rate, because the level of effort devoted to testing and maintenance varies over the life cycle. This is the purpose of the next metric.

TABLE C-3. *Definitions of in-progress indicators*

INDICATOR	DEFINITION
Rework stability	B–F, breakage minus fixes plotted over time
Rework backlog	$(B–F)/SLOC_C$, currently open rework
Modularity trend	Modularity plotted over time
Adaptability trend	Adaptability plotted over time
Maturity trend	Maturity plotted over time

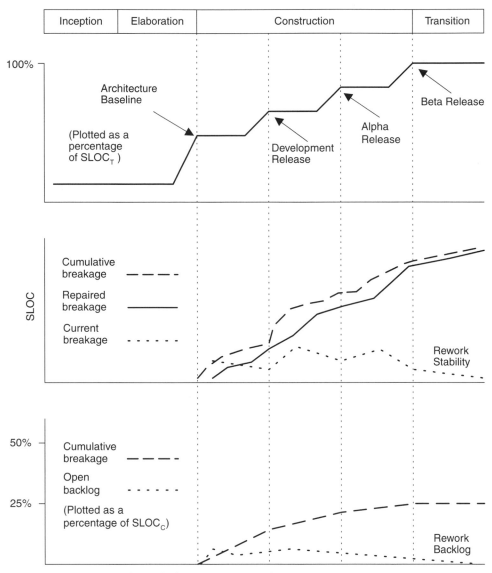

FIGURE C-1. *Expected trends for in-progress indicators*

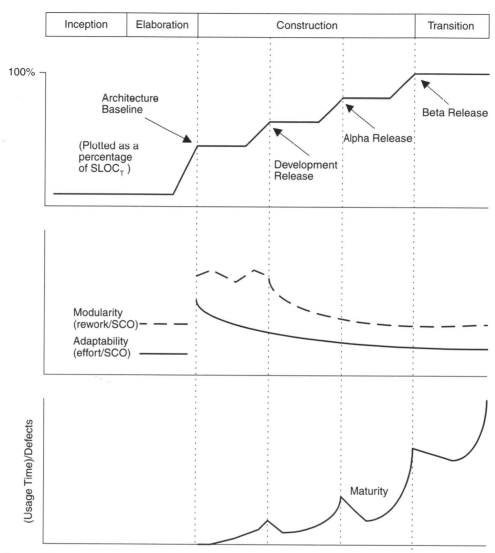

FIGURE C-2. *Expectations for quality trends*

- Rework backlog. The rework backlog is the percentage of the existing product baseline, $SLOC_C$, that is currently in need of repair. In general, the backlog should rise to some manageable level following establishment of the first baseline, as testing uncovers necessary changes. Rework backlog should remain relatively stable throughout the test program until it drops to zero. Large changes or sustained growth in backlog from month to month should be scrutinized. Sustained increases may indicate instability and divergence from plan.

- Modularity trend. Changes in this value show how the extent of change is evolving over a project's life cycle. The general trend provides insight into quality (how well the architecture accommodates change localization) and management (schedule convergence and downstream change risks). Most trivial changes get caught and implemented in stand-alone test activities. This value addresses the nontrivial changes that creep into configuration baselines. While it is difficult to quantify what constitutes a good trend, the following rule of thumb is typical on successful projects: The average SCO should affect the equivalent of a single program unit (the lowest level of separately compilable code elements). For example, the average breakage per SCO for software written in C++ (in which the average program unit is about 50 lines of code) should be about 50 at project completion. In a mature iterative development process, the earlier changes (design changes that affect multiple components and people) are expected to require more rework than later changes (implementation changes, which tend to be confined to a single component or person). Modularity trends that are increasing with time clearly indicate that the product architecture is degrading.

- Adaptability trend. This value provides a mechanism for assessing trends in the complexity of change, as opposed to the extent of change. When changes are easy to implement, a project is more likely to increase the number of changes, thereby increasing quality. With the conventional process, it was more expensive to incorporate changes later in the life cycle. In a modern iterative process, the objective is to establish a robust process and architecture so that making changes is easier, and the results are more predictable, later in the life cycle. Rework trends may only stabilize rather than continue to get simpler over time. Nevertheless, this is a critical difference from the conventional process. A good trend is difficult to quantify in absolute terms. In practice, successful projects tend to experience an average cost of change of less than one staff-week.

- Maturity trend. It is easy to explain the expectation for this value for a single release. However, most modern software projects consist of several iterations and increments with overlapping activities and release schedules. Assessing the maturity of a whole system is far more complex than assessing the maturity of a given release. The expectation for an individual release would be a relatively immature product (frequently experienced defects) that shows rapidly improving maturity as fixes are incorporated in maintenance updates. The expectation for the simple project example illustrated in Figure C-2 is that with each subsequent release, the whole baseline encounters fewer defects and more usage time. Consequently, the reliability growth should be getting better and better. Exponential growth, shown in the figure, may be unrealistic for most systems. Linear growth may be more realistic. "Your mileage may vary," but a healthy process and architecture should not experience a sustained decrease in maturity, and short-term decreases should have an obvious cause.

C.3   PRAGMATIC CHANGE METRICS

Section 13.1 describes some goals of a successful metrics program. These goals are reiterated next and discussed in terms of whether the metrics described here meet these goals.

- **Metrics must be simple, objective, easy to collect, easy to interpret, and hard to misinterpret.** The number of statistics to be maintained in an SCO database to implement this metrics approach is small: fewer than 10. They are simple counts and can have simple definitions, although in practice many of the units of these counts are ambiguous. Depending on the discipline, consistency, and level of automation inherent in an organization's process, the definition and collection of these metrics may be relatively easy. On the other hand, an ad hoc organization with diverse software projects may find it very difficult to converge on acceptable practices. The various perspectives provided by these metrics have a straightforward interpretation in most cases. Most trends are obviously good or bad. Most values are context-dependent, but with data from multiple projects in a common context, it should be easy to reason about similarities and differences.

- **Metrics collection must be automated and nonintrusive, that is, not interfere with the activities of developers.** All the collected data and analysis required in this metrics approach can be, and have been, automated. While engineers simply follow their normal workflows for generating artifacts, the configuration control system can be instrumented to collect and process all the data required to extract the metrics and trends.

- **Metrics must provide consistent assessments throughout the life cycle, especially in early phases, when efforts to improve quality have a high pay-off.** The approach described here is derived from a software maintenance perspective. However, an iterative development process can be viewed as a merging of the development and maintenance activities into a more common set of life-cycle activities that use the same techniques and tools. From this perspective, an iterative approach can be seen as simply accelerating the establishment of baselines so that baseline changes, and their inherent progress and insight into quality, can be used to better instrument the process. With conventional technologies, this would have been a manual, error-prone activity. With today's advanced change management automation and round-trip engineering support among various engineering artifacts, change freedom is improved and the transition to an iterative process is technically feasible and economically advantageous.

- **Metrics, both values and trends, must be used actively by management and engineering personnel for communicating progress and quality in a consistent format.** These metrics deal with tangible measurements of evolving software artifacts. They are derived directly from the evolving baselines of the product, not from separate documentation or subjective judgments. Software engineers will accept and use these objective metrics to avoid bad technical and management decisions. As far as managers are concerned, they will acclimate to any objective measures. The metrics presented are straightforward: Most stakeholders can understand them, they can be automated, and they can be compared with the metrics from other projects if used judiciously.

CCPDS-R
Case Study

This appendix presents a detailed case study of a successful software project that followed many of the techniques presented in this book. *Successful* here means on budget, on schedule, and satisfactory to the customer. The Command Center Processing and Display System-Replacement (CCPDS-R) project was performed for the U.S. Air Force by TRW Space and Defense in Redondo Beach, California. The entire project included systems engineering, hardware procurement, and software development, with each of these three major activities consuming about one-third of the total cost. The schedule spanned 1987 through 1994.

The software effort included the development of three distinct software systems totaling more than one million source lines of code. This case study focuses on the initial software development, called the Common Subsystem, for which about 355,000 source lines were developed. The Common Subsystem effort also produced a reusable architecture, a mature process, and an integrated environment for efficient development of the two software subsystems of roughly similar size that followed. This case study therefore represents about one-sixth of the overall CCPDS-R project effort.

Although this case study does not coincide exactly with the management process presented in this book nor with all of today's modern technologies, it used most of the same techniques and was managed to the same spirit and priorities. TRW delivered

> **Key Points**
>
> ▲ An objective case study is a true indicator of a mature organization and a mature project process. The software industry needs more case studies like CCPDS-R.
>
> ▲ The metrics histories were all derived directly from the artifacts of the project's process. These data were used to manage the project and were embraced by practitioners, managers, and stakeholders.
>
> ▲ CCPDS-R was one of the pioneering projects that practiced many modern management approaches.
>
> ▲ This appendix provides a practical context that is relevant to the techniques, disciplines, and opinions provided throughout this book.

the system on budget and on schedule, and the users got more than they expected. TRW was awarded the Space and Missile Warning Systems Award for Excellence in 1991 for "continued, sustained performance in overall systems engineering and project execution." A project like CCPDS-R could be developed far more efficiently today. By incorporating current technologies and improved processes, environments, and levels of automation, this project could probably be built today with equal quality in half the time and at a quarter of the cost.

D.1   CONTEXT FOR THE CASE STUDY

I worked full time on the CCPDS-R project for 6 years, so this appendix is written from firsthand experience. My responsibilities included managing the development of the foundation technologies, developing the technical and cost proposals, conducting the software engineering exercise, and managing the software engineering activities through the early operational capability milestone.

I have tried to provide an accurate portrayal of the CCPDS-R project. While the data presented are mostly historical fact, all the subjective comments and value judgments are mine. The data were derived from published papers, internal TRW guidebooks, contract deliverable documents—all available from the actual artifacts of the CCPDS-R project—and my own personal experience. In a few minor cases, I have edited the data to remove unnecessary precision and eliminate inconsistencies within source documents produced at different points in the life cycle. My goal was to produce a relatively consistent description while excluding some of the minutia that would require detailed and irrelevant explanation.

Although the software industry can claim many successful projects (not enough, but many), good case studies are lacking. There are very few well-documented projects with objective descriptions of what worked, what didn't, and why. This was one of my primary motivations for providing the level of detail contained in this appendix. It is heavy in project-specific details, approaches, and results, for three reasons:

1. Generating the case study wasn't much work. CCPDS-R is unique in its detailed and automated metrics approach. All the data were derived directly from the historical artifacts of the project's process.

2. This sort of objective case study is a true indicator of a mature organization and a mature project process. The absolute values of this historical perspective are only marginally useful. However, the trends, lessons learned, and relative priorities are distinguishing characteristics of successful software development.

3. Throughout previous chapters, many management and technical approaches are discussed generically. This appendix provides in a real-world example at least one relevant benchmark of performance.

> My comments on relevance with the techniques, disciplines, and opinions discussed in previous chapters are provided in shaded boxes.

D.2 COMMON SUBSYSTEM OVERVIEW

The CCPDS-R project produced a large-scale, highly reliable command and control system that provides missile warning information used by the National Command Authority. The procurement agency was Air Force Systems Command Headquarters, Electronic Systems Division, at Hanscom Air Force Base, Massachusetts. The primary user was US Space Command, and the full-scale development contract was awarded to TRW's Systems Integration Group in 1987. The CCPDS-R contract called for the development of three subsystems:

1. The Common Subsystem was the primary missile warning system within the Cheyenne Mountain Upgrade program. It required about 355,000 source lines of code, had a 48-month software development schedule, and laid the foundations for the subsystems that followed (reusable components, tools, environment, process, procedures). The Common Subsystem included a primary installation in Cheyenne Mountain, with a backup system deployed at Offutt Air Force Base, Nebraska.

2. The Processing and Display Subsystem (PDS) was a scaled-down missile warning display system for all nuclear-capable commanders-in-chief. The PDS software (about 250,000 SLOC) was fielded on remote, read-only workstations that were distributed worldwide.

3. The STRATCOM Subsystem (about 450,000 SLOC) provided both missile warning and force management capability for the backup missile warning center at the command center of the Strategic Command.

Overall Software Acquisition Process

The CCPDS-R acquisition included two distinct phases: a concept definition (CD) phase and a full-scale development (FSD) phase. The CD phase proposal was competed for by five major bidders, and two firm-fixed-price contracts of about $2 million each were awarded. The winning contractors also invested their own discretionary resources to discriminate themselves with the best-value FSD phase proposal. Figure D-1 summarizes the overall acquisition process and the products of each phase.

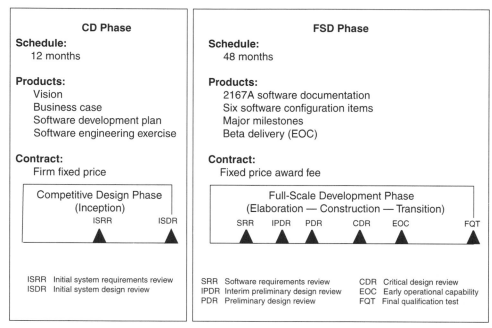

FIGURE D-1. *CCPDS-R life-cycle overview*

The CD phase was very similar in intent to the inception phase. The primary products were a system specification (a vision document), an FSD phase proposal (a business case, including the technical approach and a fixed-price-incentive and award-fee cost proposal), and a software development plan. The CD phase also included a system design review, technical interchange meetings with the government stakeholders (customer and user), and several contract-deliverable documents. These events and products enabled the FSD source selection to be based on demonstrated performance of the contractor-proposed team as well as the FSD proposal.

From a software perspective, there was one additional source selection criterion included in the FSD proposal activities: a software engineering exercise. This was a unique but very effective approach for assessing the abilities of the two competing contractors to perform software development. The Air Force was extremely concerned with the overall software risk of this project: Recent projects had demonstrated dismal software development performance. The Air Force acquisition authorities had also been frustrated with previous situations in which a contractor's crack proposal team was not the team committed to perform after contract award, and contractor proposals exaggerated their approaches or capabilities beyond what they could deliver.

CCPDS-R was also a very large software development activity and was one of the first projects to use the Ada programming language. There was serious concern that the Ada development environments, contractor processes, and contractor training programs might not be mature enough to use on a full-scale development effort. The purpose of the software engineering exercise was to demonstrate that the contractor's proposed software process, Ada environment, and software team were in place, were mature, and were demonstrable.

The software engineering exercise occurred immediately after the FSD proposals were submitted. The customer provided both bidders with a simple two-page specification of a "missile warning simulator." This simulator had some of the same fundamental requirements as the CCPDS-R full-scale system, including a distributed architecture, a flexible user interface, and the basic processing scenarios of a simple CCPDS-R missile warning thread. The exercise requirements included the following:

- Use the proposed software team.

- Use the proposed software development techniques and tools.

- Use the FSD-proposed software development plan.

- Conduct a mock design review with the customer 23 days after receipt of the specification.

The software engineering exercise would provide objective evidence of the credibility of each contractor's proposed software development approach.

The results produced by TRW's CCPDS-R team were impressive. They demonstrated to the customer that the team was prepared, credible, and competent at conducting the proposed software approach. Approximately 12 staff-months were expended in the effort (12 people full-time for 23 days).

A detailed plan was established that included an activity network, responsibility assignments, and expected results for tracking progress. The plan included two architecture iterations and all the milestones and artifacts proposed in the software development plan. The exercise produced the following results:

- Four primary use cases were elaborated and demonstrated.

- A software architecture skeleton was designed, prototyped, and documented, including two executable, distributed processes; five concurrent tasks (separate threads of control); eight components; and 72 component-to-component interfaces.

- A total of 4,163 source lines of prototype components were developed and executed. Several thousand lines of reusable components were also integrated into the demonstration.

- Three milestones were conducted and more than 30 action items resolved.

- Production of 11 documents (corresponding to the proposed artifacts) demonstrated the automation inherent in the documentation tools.

- The Digital Equipment Corporation VAX/VMS tools, Rational R1000 environment, LaTeX documentation templates, and several custom-developed tools were used.

- Several needed improvements to the process and the tools were identified. The concept of evolving the plan, requirements, process, design, and environment at each major milestone was considered potentially risky but was implemented with rigorous change management.

This exercise proved to be a discriminating factor in the CCPDS-R contract award. TRW had proposed an architecture-first, demonstration-based approach and had demonstrated its operational concept successfully under realistic, albeit small-scale and accelerated, conditions. Despite submitting a bid that was more than 20% higher than that of their competitor, TRW's approach was selected as the best value and lowest risk. Award of the contract to TRW was due, in large part, to successful performance on the software engineering exercise and TRW's ability to demonstrate a much more credible, lower risk process under realistic conditions.

> The software engineering exercise served the same purpose as an SEI Software Capability Evaluation (Appendix E). Each bidder's proposal provided a software development plan—the "say what you do" part of an organizational process. The exercise demonstrated that the proposing organization could perform as advertised.

D.3   PROJECT ORGANIZATION

In preparing for the CCPDS-R project, TRW placed a strong emphasis on evolving the right team. The CD phase team represented the essence of the architecture team (Section 11.2), which is responsible for an efficient engineering stage. This team had the following primary responsibilities:

- Analyze and specify the project requirements
- Define and develop the top-level architecture
- Plan the FSD phase software development activities
- Configure the process and development environment
- Establish trust and win-win relationships among the stakeholders

The CD phase team was small and expert, with little, if any, organizational hierarchy. One of its exceptional attributes was its complement of talent. All necessary skills were covered, and there was very little competition among personnel.

The FSD phase team was formed by transitioning many of the CD phase team members into leadership positions and expanding the number of personnel to the necessary levels for full-scale development. Figure D-2 illustrates the software organization evolution and FSD software responsibilities.

> The organizational structure and responsibilities for CCPDS-R were very similar to those recommended in Figure 11-2. The staffing levels evolved as prescribed in Table 10-2.

D.4   COMMON SUBSYSTEM PRODUCT OVERVIEW

The Common Subsystem software comprised six computer software configuration items (CSCIs). (*CSCI* is government jargon for a set of components that is managed, configured, and documented as a unit and allocated to a single team for development.) CSCIs are defined and described in DOD-STD-2167A [DOD, 1988]. The CSCIs were identified as follows:

1. Network Architecture Services (NAS). This foundation middleware provided reusable components for network management, interprocess communications, initialization, reconfiguration, anomaly management, and instrumentation of software health, performance, and state. This CSCI was designed to be reused across all three CCPDS-R subsystems.

2. System Services (SSV). This CSCI comprised the software architecture skeleton, real-time data distribution, global data types, and the computer system operator interface.

3. Display Coordination (DCO). This CSCI comprised user interface control, display formats, and display population.

4. Test and Simulation (TAS). This CSCI comprised test scenario generation, test message injection, data recording, and scenario playback.

5. Common Mission Processing (CMP). This CSCI comprised the missile warning algorithms for radar, nuclear detonation, and satellite early warning messages.

6. Common Communications (CCO). This CSCI comprised external interfaces with other systems and message input, output, and protocol management.

Table D-1 summarizes the distinguishing characteristics of each CSCI.

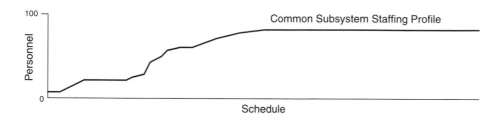

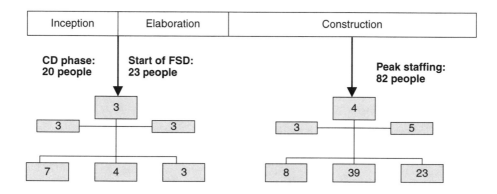

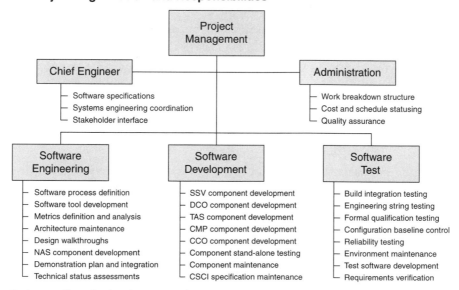

FIGURE D-2. *Full-scale development phase project organization*

TABLE D-1. *CSCI summary*

CSCI	SIZE (SLOC)	COMPLEXITY	ASSETS (+) AND CHALLENGES (−)
NAS	20,000	Very high	+ Experienced, superior team; second-generation product
			− Reusable across subsystems; high performance, reliability
SSV	160,000	High	+ Some tool-produced code; stable NAS primitives
			− Numerous global interfaces, types, components
DCO	70,000	Moderate	+ Flexible display design; tool-produced formats
			− Tough performance requirement; continuous change
TAS	10,000	Low	+ Simple application; some off-line processing
			− Offsite team; limited environment resources
CMP	15,000	Moderate	+ Domain experience; straightforward processing
			− Offsite team; stringent performance requirements; numerous stakeholders involved in approving algorithm design
CCO	80,000	High	+ Skilled people; precedent domain experience
			− Stringent performance requirements; unstable external interface
Total	355,000	High	Large scale, high performance, high reliability

The Software Architecture Skeleton

The CCPDS-R software process was tailored to exploit Ada and reusable middleware components in order to construct a distributed architecture rapidly. The NAS CSCI provided these primitive components and was initially developed on independent research and development funding before the CCPDS-R contract was awarded. These components were a first-generation middleware solution that enabled a true component-based development approach to distributed architectures. The instantiation of the NAS generic tasks, processes, sockets, and circuits into a run-time infrastructure was called a software architecture skeleton (SAS). The software engineering associated with the Common Subsystem SAS was the focus of the early builds and demonstrations. This is an excellent example of an architecture-first process.

The SAS encompasses the declarative view of the solution, including all the top-level control structures, interfaces, and data types passed across these interfaces. In the CCPDS-R definition of an architecture, this view included the following:

- All Ada main programs

- All Ada tasks and task attributes

- All sockets (asynchronous task-to-task communications), socket attributes, and connections to other sockets

- Data types for objects passed across sockets

- NAS components for initialization, state management of processes and tasks, interprocess communications, fault handling, health and performance monitoring, instrumentation, network management, logging, and network control

Even though a SAS will compile, it will not really execute many scenarios (except to come up and idle) unless software is added that reads messages, processes them, and writes them within application tasks. The purpose of a SAS is to provide the structure and interface network for integrating components into threads of capability. There are two important aspects of SAS verification and assessment: compilation and execution. Merely constructing and compiling all the SAS objects together is an important and nontrivial assessment that will provide substantial feedback about the consistency and quality of the SAS. Constructing components and executing stimuli and response threads within the SAS provide further feedback about structural integrity and run-time semantics.

The SAS, then, provides the forum for integration and architecture evolution. It is important to construct the SAS early and to evolve it into a stable baseline in which change is managed and measured for feedback about architecture stability. CCPDS-R installed its first SAS baseline (after three informal iterations) around month 13, just before the preliminary design review (PDR) milestone; all subsequent change was performed via rigorous configuration control. The SAS underwent numerous changes after its first baseline. These changes were scrutinized closely as the project progressed, but the SAS dynamics converged on an acceptable architecture with solid substantiation early in the life cycle. The SAS was useful in assessing the volatility in the overall software interfaces and captured the conceptual architecture of the Common Subsystem.

Figure D-3 provides a perspective of the software architecture stability. The graphs show that there was significant architectural change over the first 20 months of the project, after which the architecture remained pretty stable. The large spike in processes and tasks around month 5 corresponded to an attempt at a much more

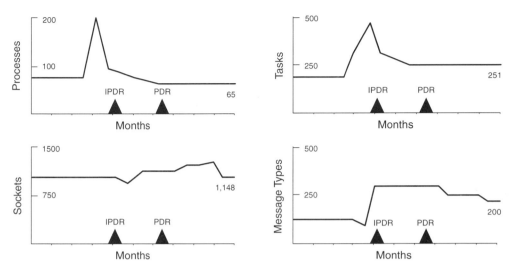

FIGURE D-3. *Common Subsystem SAS evolution*

distributed approach. As this architecture experimentation exposed the design trade-offs in distribution strategies, the SAS process design was changed back to the original number of processes, but the SAS task-level design converged on an increased number of tasks. The basic problems being examined by the architecture team were the trade-offs in concurrency, operating system process overhead, run-time library tasking overhead, paging, context switching, and the mix of interprocess, intertask, and internode message exchange. The complexity of such run-time interactions made modeling and simulation ineffective. Only the early run-time demonstrations of multiple distribution configurations allowed the architecture team to achieve the understanding of technical trade-offs necessary to select an adequate solution. If the change in the distribution design had occurred very late in the project, the impact could have been immense. Because sockets and messages were fairly simple to change and corresponded to lower level application interfaces, changes to these numbers continued at a low level through the critical design review (CDR) milestone.

The freedom to experiment with an architecture proved to be very valuable to the achievement of an adequate architecture baseline early in the life cycle. This was enabled primarily by the flexibility of the NAS CSCI.

CCPDS-R was seriously committed to an architecture-first approach. The "architecture" description of CCPDS-R was centered on the process view, as described in Chapter 7. This was due primarily to the stringent run-time performance requirements and the risks associated with a first-generation distributed architecture.

D.5 PROCESS OVERVIEW

CCPDS-R software development followed a standard Department of Defense life cycle after contract award, with a software requirements review, preliminary design review, critical design review, and final qualification test. The life cycles of the 12-month competitive design phase and full-scale development phase are easily mapped to the phases of the iterative process framework presented in Chapter 5. Figure D-4 illustrates this mapping.

To manage this large software effort, six incremental builds were defined. Figure D-4 summarizes the build content and overlap, and the individual build metrics and microprocess are further described in Section D.5.1. The conclusion of each build corresponded to a new baseline of the overall Common Subsystem. From a macroprocess view, the initial milestones focused on achieving a baseline architecture. The PDR baseline required three major architecture iterations, the conclusions of which coincided with the milestones for the software requirements review (SRR), interim PDR (IPDR), and PDR:

1. The SRR demonstration: initial feasibility of the foundation components, and basic use cases of initialization and interprocess communications

2. The IPDR demonstration: the feasibility of the architectural infrastructure under the riskiest use cases, including the following:

    • A peak data load missile warning scenario of a mass raid from the Soviet Union

    • A peak control load scenario of a system failover and recovery from the primary thread of processing to a backup thread of processing with no loss of data

3. The PDR demonstration: adequate achievement of the peak load scenarios and the other primary use cases within a full-scale architectural infrastructure, including the other critical-thread components

The CDR demonstration updated the architecture baseline to represent the equivalent of an alpha test capability for the complete architectural infrastructure and the critical-thread scenarios. This was a usable system in that it provided a set of complete use cases sufficient for the user to perform a subset of the mission.

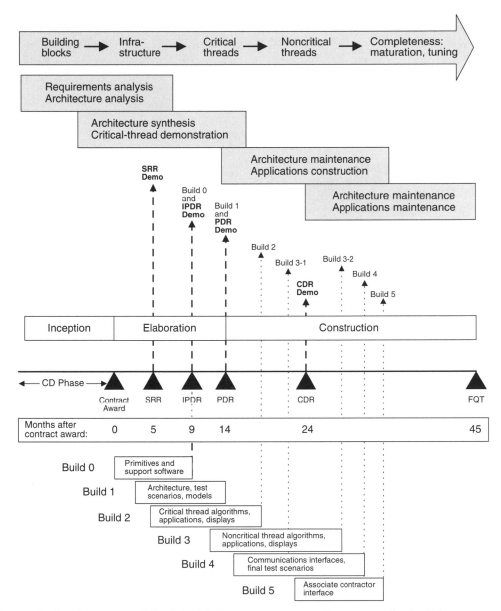

FIGURE D-4. *Overview of the CCPDS-R macroprocess, milestones, and schedule*

The overall CCPDS-R software process had a well-defined macroprocess similar to the life-cycle phases described in Figure 5-1. Each major milestone was accompanied by a major demonstration of capability and typically included contributions from several of the on-going builds. It would be more accurate to call the design process used on the project incremental rather than iterative, although, as with any large-scale system, it was clearly both.

D.5.1 RISK MANAGEMENT: BUILD CONTENT

Planning the content and schedule of the Common Subsystem builds resulted in a useful and accurate representation of the overall risk management plan. The importance of a sound build plan was well understood by the management team, and it was carefully thought out early in the inception phase. The management team set the expectation for reallocating build content as the life cycle progressed and more-accurate assessments of complexity, risk, personnel, and engineering trade-offs were achieved. This evolutionary plan was important, and there were several adjustments in build content and schedule as early conjecture evolved into objective fact.

Figure D-5 illustrates the detailed schedule and CSCI content of the Common Subsystem. The details of its build content are as follows:

- Build 0. This build comprised the foundation components necessary to build a software architecture skeleton. The intertask/interprocess communications, generic task and process executives, and common error reporting components were included. This build was also the conclusion of the research and development project executed in parallel with the CD (inception) phase. These NAS components were the cornerstone of the architectural framework and were built to be reusable across all three CCPDS-R subsystems. They represented very complex, high-risk components with stringent performance, reliability, and reusability demands.

- Build 1. This build was essentially the "architecture." It included a complete set of instantiated tasks (300), processes (70), interconnections (1,000), states, and state transitions for the structural solution of the CCPDS-R software architecture. To achieve a cycling architecture, this build also added all the NAS components for initialization, state management (reconfiguration), and instrumentation. A trivial user interface and the capability to inject test scenarios into the architecture were added to support the initial demonstration. Upon completion of build 1, only a few critical use cases were demonstrable: initializing the architecture, injecting

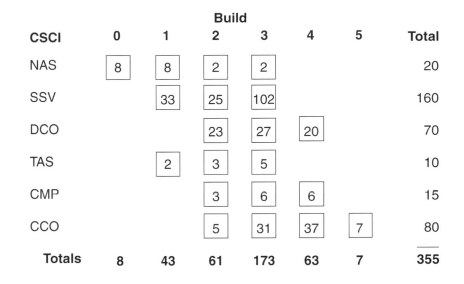

CSCI	**Build**						Total
	0	**1**	**2**	**3**	**4**	**5**	
NAS	8	8	2	2			20
SSV		33	25	102			160
DCO			23	27	20		70
TAS		2	3	5			10
CMP			3	6	6		15
CCO			5	31	37	7	80
Totals	**8**	**43**	**61**	**173**	**63**	**7**	**355**

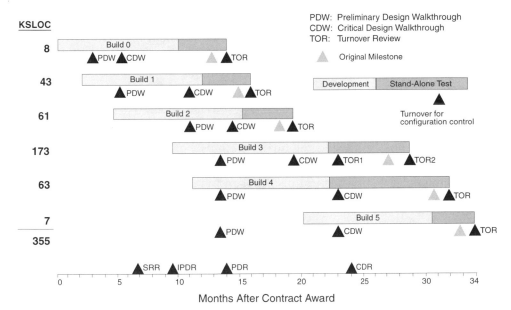

FIGURE D-5. *Common Subsystem builds*

a scenario to drive the data flow through the system, and orchestrating reconfigurations such as primary thread switchover to backup thread.

- Build 2. This was the first build of mission-critical components and achieved the initial capability to execute real mission scenarios. The three primary risks inherent in the mission scenarios were the timeliness of the display database distribution, the performance (resource consumption and accuracy) of the missile warning radar algorithms, and the performance of the user interface for several complex displays. Upon completion of build 2, several mission-oriented use cases could be executed, including the worst-case data processing thread and the worst-case control processing thread (primary-to-backup switchover).

- Build 3. This build contained the largest volume of code, including display format definitions, global type definitions, and representation specifications needed for validation of external interface transactions. Although the code was voluminous, much of it was produced automatically in a cookbook manner by constructing code generation tools. The remaining components allocated to build 3 included the external communications interface protocol handling, the completed user-system interface for the mission operators, the user-system interface for the computer support positions, the system services for mission reconfigurations, database resets, off-line data reduction, and the nuclear detonation algorithms. Although initially planned as one large build, this increment was later split into two more manageable releases, builds 3-1 and 3-2.

- Build 4. This build provided the final installment of missile warning algorithms for satellite early warning systems, the final installment of mission management and mission status displays, and the final installment of external communications interface processing.

- Build 5. In the middle of the Common Subsystem schedule, build 5 was added to coincide with a particular external interface (being built on a separate contract), the schedule for which had slipped so that it was not going to be available during its originally planned build (build 4). Consequently, the external interface was scheduled into an entirely new build.

The build sequence defined on CCPDS-R is a good example of the typical build sequence recommended in Section 10.4.

D.5.2 THE INCREMENTAL DESIGN PROCESS

The individual milestones within a build included a preliminary design walkthrough (PDW), a critical design walkthrough (CDW), and a turnover review (TOR). The schedules for these milestones were flowed down from, and integrated with, the higher level project milestones (SRR, IPDR, PDR, and CDR). Figure D-6 provides an overview of a build's life cycle and the focus of activities.

Within a build, a well-defined sequence of design walkthroughs took place. These walkthroughs were informal, detailed, technical peer reviews of intermediate design products. They were attended by interested reviewers, including other designers, testers, and even stakeholders outside the software organization (customer, user, project systems engineering personnel). Attendance was usually kept to a small number of knowledgeable people, typically 10 to 20. The explicit focus of these reviews was the important components, the architectural interfaces, and the driving issues— namely, the 20% of the stuff that deserved scrutiny. Coverage across all requirements and components was not required.

The design walkthroughs were informal and highly interactive, and there was plenty of open critique. No dry runs were necessary. Technical issues were noted as action items and tracked to closure. PDWs and CDWs usually lasted one or two days, with each of the participating CSCI managers responsible for presenting appropriate material.

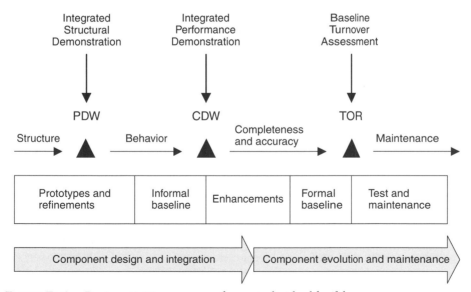

FIGURE D-6. *Basic activities sequence for an individual build*

Preliminary Design Walkthroughs

Initial prototyping and design work was concluded with a PDW and a basic capability demonstration. The walkthrough focused on the structural attributes of the components within the build. The basic agenda was tailored for each build, but it generally included the following topics for each CSCI:

- Overview: CSCI overview, interfaces, components, and metrics
- Components: walkthrough of each major component, showing its source code interface, allocated system requirements specification (SRS) requirements, current metrics, operational concept for key usage scenarios, stand-alone test plan, and erroneous conditions and responses
- Demonstration: focused on exercising the control interfaces across the components within the integrated architecture

Critical Design Walkthroughs

A build's design work was concluded with a CDW and a capability demonstration that exposed the key performance parameters of components within the build. While the PDW focused on the declarative view of the design, the CDW focused on the completeness of the components and the behavioral perspective of operating within the allocated performance requirements. The basic agenda was tailored for each build, but it generally included the following topics for each CSCI:

- CSCI overview: interfaces, components, and metrics; summary of changes since PDW; disposition of all PDW action items; build integration test scenarios
- Components: walkthrough of each major component, showing its source code interface, allocated SRS requirements, current metrics, operational concept for key usage scenarios, stand-alone test plan, and erroneous conditions and responses
- Demonstration: focused on exercising the critical performance threads

Code Walkthroughs

Detailed code walkthroughs were also used to disseminate projectwide expertise and ensure the development of self-documenting source code. Some authors generated source code that demonstrated excellent levels of readability worthy of being assessed as self-documenting. The CSCI managers and the software chief engineer coordinated the need for code walkthroughs and their allocation among various authors to meet the following objectives:

- Better dissemination of self-documenting source code style
- Identification of coding issues not easily caught by compilers and source code analysis tools
  - Object naming, coding style, and commenting style: Does it promote readability?
  - Unnecessarily complex objects or methods: Are there simpler approaches?
  - Reuse: Is custom software being built where reusable components exist?
  - Potential performance issues: Are there potentially inefficient implementations?
- Reduction of the amount of source code needed for review in the larger design walkthroughs
- Exposure of inexperienced personnel to the products of experts and vice versa

The typical code review involved a single reviewer limited to two hours of detailed analysis using on-line source code browsing tools. The result of the review was confined to a one-page description of relevant comments to the author, the CSCI manager, and the software chief engineer. The software chief engineer was responsible for noting global trends, identifying improvements needed in code analysis tools, and raising lessons learned to the appropriate walkthrough or other technical exchange forum.

Turnover Reviews

Turnover reviews were not really reviews; they were typically a one-month activity during which components were completed with stand-alone testing and turned over for configuration control, build integration testing, and engineering string testing.

The checkpoints used on CCPDS-R for the incremental design process are good examples of the minor milestones described in Section 9.2. The mixture of walkthroughs and inspections was focused on the 20% of components that had a potential high return on human resource investment. In general, the real value of design walkthroughs and inspections was communications among project subteams and methodical coordination of processes. Very few serious quality flaws were uncovered in these meetings (as opposed to the demonstration activities), but the technical interchange was well mechanized by these checkpoints.

D.5.3 COMPONENT EVOLUTION

CCPDS-R used Ada as a uniform life-cycle format for design evolution. This uniformity allowed for software development progress metrics to be extracted directly from the evolving source files. The use of Ada as a design language was based on a special design package containing objects that had names prefixed by the string *TBD* (to be defined). This package of TBD objects included predefined TBD types, TBD constants, TBD values, and a TBD procedure for depicting source lines of code associated with comments that together would act as placeholders for as-yet undefined code segments. In particular, there was the following procedure declaration:

```
TBD_Statements (Number_Of_Statements: In Integer);
```

This declaration required that a parameter depict the number of statements estimated for a given code segment described with proper comments. Source lines with calls to a TBD object were counted as ADL (Ada design language) lines; source lines with no TBD references were counted as Ada source lines. Table D-2 provides an example of a typical component evolution.

The basic component evolution would look like this:

- At creation, only the interface (the specification part) would be defined with Ada source lines and corresponding comments. The estimated SLOC count for the component would typically be specified by a single TBD_Statements line.

- At PDW, the substructure of the component would be fleshed out along with most component declarations and estimates of the subordinate program units using multiple calls to TBD_Statements. At this time, there would generally be about 30% of the SLOC in Ada and 70% in ADL.

- By CDW, most of the program unit interfaces and declarations would be fully fleshed out in Ada, with some detailed processing still using TBD_Statements as placeholders. In general, CDW-level components would be about 70% Ada and 30% ADL. A guideline also stated that by CDW, there would be no calls to TBD_Statements with values greater than 25.

- By turnover, the string TBD would not appear anywhere in the source files. This would correspond to a complete implementation.

TABLE D-2. *A typical component evolution from creation through turnover*

VIEW	PROGRAM UNIT	TYPE	Ada	ADL	TOTAL	%
Creation view	Total package		6	122	128	5
	Inm_Erm_Procedures	Package	2	122	124	2
PDW view	Total package		47	101	148	32
	Inm_Erm_Procedures	Package	24	19	43	56
	All_Node_Connections	Procedure	3	19	22	14
	Create_Inm_Erm_Circuits	Procedure	4	8	12	33
	On_Node_Connections	Procedure	3	7	10	30
	Perform_Reconfiguration	Procedure	6	2	8	75
	Perform_Shutdown	Procedure	4	3	7	57
	Process_Error_Messages	Procedure	3	43	46	7
CDW view	Total package		87	48	135	65
	Inm_Erm_Procedures	Package	30	11	41	73
	All_Node_Connections	Procedure	16	0	16	100
	Create_Inm_Erm_Circuits	Procedure	8	4	12	67
	On_Node_Connections	Procedure	9	0	9	100
	Perform_Reconfiguration	Procedure	6	2	8	75
	Perform_Shutdown	Procedure	6	1	7	86
	Process_Error_Messages	Procedure	12	30	42	29
Turnover view	Total package		137	0	137	100
	Inm_Erm_Procedures	Package	42	0	42	100
	All_Node_Connections	Procedure	16	0	16	100
	Create_Inm_Erm_Circuits	Procedure	12	0	12	100
	On_Node_Connections	Procedure	9	0	9	100
	Perform_Reconfiguration	Procedure	8	0	8	100
	Perform_Shutdown	Procedure	7	0	7	100
	Process_Error_Messages	Procedure	43	0	43	100

These guidelines were violated occasionally, but the evolution of most components followed this pattern pretty well. There were also detailed style standards that formed the basis of early code walkthroughs and the requirements for an automated code auditor that checked for numerous standards violations before turnover.

One of the by-products of the use of Ada as a design language for CCPDS-R was that the evolving source files were always in a uniform representation format from which the current work accomplished (source lines of Ada) and the current work pending (TBD_Statements) could be easily extracted. Although the Ada source lines were not necessarily complete—inasmuch as further design evolution might cause change—they represented a relatively accurate assessment of work accomplished. The complete set of design files across the development teams could be processed at any time to gain insight into development progress. A metrics tool was developed that scanned Ada source files and compiled statistics on the amount of completed Ada and TBD_Statements. It produced outputs such as those listed in Table D-3.

This metrics tool and the CCPDS-R coding standards allowed collection of metrics by CSCI and by build so that progress could be monitored from several perspectives. The development progress metrics described in Section D.7.1 were derived monthly from the outputs of this tool and were presented at the various design walkthroughs by each component designer to display the summary metrics and hierarchy of the component being discussed.

This metrics tool allowed management to extract some key measures of progress directly from the evolving source baselines. The software engineers simply adhered to the software standards in fleshing out their source files and maintaining them in compilable formats. Once a month, all source code was processed by the tools and integrated into various perspectives for communicating progress. The resulting metrics were useful not only to the managers but also to the engineers for communicating why they needed more resources or why they needed to reprioritize certain activities. As described in Chapter 13, acceptance by both manager and practitioner, and extraction directly from the evolving artifacts, were crucial to the success of this metrics approach.

TABLE D-3. *NAS CSCI metrics summary at month 10*

ELEMENTS	TOTAL	DESIGNED	CODED
Top-level components	40	39	33
Lower level components	13	13	10
Total program units	494	484	459
	Source lines: 18,494	ADL: 1,858	Ada: 16,636
		10% TBD	90% complete

D.5.4 THE INCREMENTAL TEST PROCESS

Although the overall test requirements were extremely complex, the CCPDS-R build structure accommodated a manageable and straightforward test program. Substantial informal testing occurred as a natural by-product of the early architecture demonstrations and the requirement that all components be maintained in a compilable format.

Because compilable Ada was used as the primary format throughout the life cycle, most conventional integration issues—such as data type consistency, program unit obsolescence, and program unit dependencies—were caught and resolved in compilation.

The informal testing inherent in the demonstration activities was far from sufficient to verify that requirements were satisfied and reliability expectations were met for this mission-critical, nationally important system. A highly rigorous test sequence was devised with five different test activities: stand-alone test, build integration test, reliability test, engineering string test, and final qualification test.

1. Stand-Alone Test (SAT). The development teams were responsible for stand-alone testing of components before delivery into a formal, configuration-controlled test baseline used for all other test activities. SAT typically tested a single component (which may comprise several lower level components) in a stand-alone environment. This level of testing corresponds to completeness and boundary condition tests to the extent possible in a stand-alone context.

2. Build Integration Test (BIT). This was mostly a smoke test to ensure that previously demonstrated capabilities still operated as expected. A BIT sequence is the primary quality assessment vehicle for closing out a turn-over review. A given build turnover may take days or weeks, depending on its size or the percentage of new componentry. The purpose of BIT is not to verify requirements but to establish a stable, reliable baseline. It is very informal, dynamic, and focused on exposing errors and inconsistencies. BITs validate the following:

   - Previously demonstrated threads can be repeated successfully.

   - Previously defined deficiencies have been resolved.

   - Interfaces across components are completely tested.

   - The baseline is stable enough for efficient requirements verification testing.

3. Reliability Test. One of the outputs of the BIT process and a turnover review was a stable test baseline that was subjected to extensive after-hours stress testing for long periods of time under randomized but realistic test scenarios. This sort of testing was designed to help uncover potentially

insipid, transient errors of major design consequence. Reliability testing logged as much test time as possible while resources were otherwise mostly idle (on nights and weekends).

4. Engineering String Test (EST). These tests focused on verifying specific subsets of requirements across multiple CSCIs through demonstration and test of use case realizations (called capability threads).

5. Final Qualification Test (FQT). These tests were equivalent to ESTs except that they represented the set of requirements that could not be verified unless the whole system was present. For example, a 50% reserve capacity requirement could not be verified until FQT, when the whole system was operational.

The overall subsystem build plan was driven by allocating all reliability-critical components (components that could cause type 0 errors) to build 0, 1, or 2. Figure D-7 illustrates the overall flow of test activities and test baselines supporting this build plan. The sequence of baselines allowed maximum time for the early-build, critical-thread components to mature. These components were also subjected to much more extensive testing, increasing trustworthiness in their readiness for operational use. Sufficient test time was logged to derive an empirical software mean time between

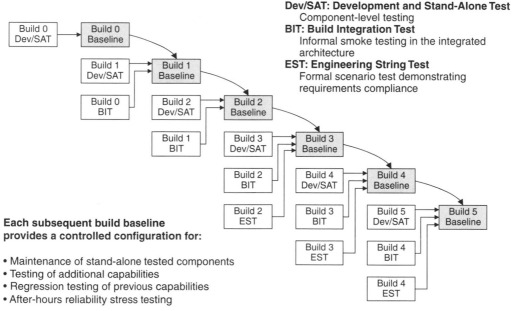

FIGURE D-7. *Incremental baseline evolution and test activity flow*

failures (MTBF) that was demonstrable and acceptable to the customer. For example, early builds of the Common Subsystem contained all the components for processing thread state management, fault isolation, fault recovery, operating system interfaces, and real-time data distribution. Roughly 90% of the components that could expose the system to critical failures, causing mission degradation, were encapsulated.

> The CCPDS-R build sequence and test program are good examples of confronting the most important risks first. A stable architecture was also achieved early in the life cycle so that substantial reliability testing could be performed. This strategy allowed useful maturity metrics, such as those presented in Section 13.3, to be established to demonstrate a realistic software MTBF to the customer.

D.5.5 DOD-STD-2167A Artifacts

CCPDS-R software development was required to comply with DOD-STD-2167A, which is now obsolete. Without going into detail about the documentation required, this section summarizes the basic documentation approach used on the project. Data item descriptions in 2167A specified document format and content. Substantial tailoring was allowed to match the development approach and to accommodate the use of Ada both as a design language and the implementation language. Primary tailoring included the following:

1. Use of the evolving Ada source files as the single homogeneous life-cycle design format and evolution of these files in a self-documenting manner. This technique exploited Ada's readability features and avoided the extra effort involved in preparing separate, detailed design descriptions that inevitably diverge from the implementation.

2. Organization of the test sequences and deliverable documents around the build content driven by subsets of use cases (referred to as engineering strings and scenarios) rather than by CSCI. This string-based testing spanned components in multiple CSCIs. It was organized by build and mechanized via a software test plan, software test procedure, and software test report documentation sequence. These document sequences were provided for each BIT (one for each build), each EST (for builds 2, 3, and 4), and FQT (one final all-encompassing test sequence). Each test sequence involved components from several (incomplete) CSCIs because integration was proceeding continuously.

3. Building of separate unit test documentation as self-documented, repeatable software. This was treated like other operational source code so that it

was maintained homogeneously and up-to-date for automated regression testing. The same concept was used for the BIT and EST scenario testing: Rather than develop test procedure documents, the CCPDS-R process generated self-documenting test scenarios that were software programs in their own right. Because they were subjected to change management just like other software, they were always maintained up-to-date for automated regression testing.

Table D-4 summarizes the software documentation that resulted from 2167A tailoring and the corresponding artifacts recommended in Chapter 6. The 2167A approach was tremendously inefficient, even with tailoring (although it was far more efficient than the approach used for most conventional projects). It was clear from the outset that the documentation burden was tremendous, but straying from convention was considered too risky. Table D-4 focuses only on software documentation, excluding documents that supported the systems engineering concerns (safety, human factors engineering, reliability) and the operational community (cutover plan, logistical support, training). Those documents also required input and support from the software organization, even though the primary responsibility for them resided elsewhere within the CCPDS-R project.

One of the key artifacts in Table D-4 is the software development file (SDF). For CCPDS-R, this was an organized directory of on-line information, rather than a document, most of which was maintained as compilable, self-documenting Ada source code. The SDF had several sections of content that evolved as described in Table D-5.

> CCPDS-R evolved an approach to artifacts that is very similar to the approach presented in Chapter 6. Initially, most artifacts were paper-based. After the customer showed far more interest in the demonstration artifacts and the configuration baselines of the product components and test components, the demand for paper documents subsided—not enough, but somewhat. One big improvement was the transition to a completely electronic SDF, in which the design and coding standards promoted self-documenting artifacts. Separate artifacts to document the design and code were no longer necessary. One long-standing issue for CCPDS-R was the need for a higher level, graphical design description. This was provided in the system design document and in software top-level design documents using ad hoc text and graphics to represent the design. These representations were ambiguous, frequently out of date, and difficult to understand. The use of Unified Modeling Language notation, an architecture approach such as that presented in Chapter 7, visual modeling tools, and support for round-trip engineering would have improved the design representation approach considerably and would have eliminated a lot of wasted effort.

TABLE D-4. *CCPDS-R software artifacts*

NO.	CONTRACT-DELIVERABLE DOCUMENT	ARTIFACT COUNTERPART (CHAPTER 6)
1	System specification	Vision statement
6	Software requirements specification (SRS)	End-item release specifications 1 for each CSCI
1	System design document (SDD)	Architecture description
6	Software top-level design document (STLDD)	UML design models 1 for each CSCI
42	Software development file (SDF)	Implementation set artifacts 1 per component
6	Software product specification (SPS)	Final implementation set artifacts Deployment set artifacts 1 for each CSCI
4	Demonstration plan (not required by 2167A)	Major milestone release specifications 1 for each major demonstration
4	Demonstration report (not required by 2167A)	Major milestone release description 1 for each major demonstration
9	Test data file (TDF)	Release descriptions 1 for each build's BIT, EST, and FQT test sequences
4	Software test plan (STP)	Release specifications Design set artifacts, test models
4	Software test procedure (STPR)	Implementation set artifacts
4	Software test report (STR)	Release descriptions
1	Software development plan (SDP)	Software development plan
1	Software standards and procedures manual (SSPM)	Software development plan
48	Project management review (PMR)	Status assessments
3	Software user manual (SUM)	User manual 1 for each operational role

TABLE D-5. *Software development file evolution*

SECTION	PDW STATUS	CDW STATUS	TOR STATUS
Requirements	Summarized	Allocated	Traced
Component overview	Complete	Complete	Complete
Top-level program unit	Ada	Ada	Ada baselines
Subordinate units	Ada/ADL	Ada/ADL	Ada baselines
SAT plan	Draft	Complete	Complete
SAT test code	Some demonstration	Draft	Ada baselines
SAT test results	Some demonstration	Some demonstration	Ada baselines
SCO log	None	None	Initial
Metrics	Initial metrics	Updated metrics	Updated metrics
Code auditor results	None	Initial	Complete
Notes/waivers	None	None	As needed

D.6 DEMONSTRATION-BASED ASSESSMENT

Conventional design reviews define standards for review topics that result in tremendously broad reviews, only a small portion of which is really important or understood by a diverse audience. For example, reviewing all requirements in equal detail is inefficient and unproductive. All requirements are not created equal; some are critical to design evolution of the architecture, while others are critical only to a few components. The CCPDS-R software review process improved the efficiency of design evolution, review, and stakeholder concurrence in two ways: by allocating the technical breadth and depth of review to smaller scale design walkthroughs, and by focusing the major milestone reviews on the important design trade-offs. Moreover, focusing the design review on an executable demonstration provided a more understandable and concrete review vehicle for a diverse set of stakeholders.

Many conventional projects built demonstrations or benchmarks of stand-alone design issues (for example, a user-system interface mockup or a critical algorithm). However, the "design baseline" was usually represented on paper in design review presentations and design documents. Although it was easy for stakeholders to accept these artifacts as valid, they were ambiguous and not amenable to straightforward change management. Given the typical design review attitude that the design was "innocent until proven guilty," these representational formats made it easy to put up a credible facade and assert that the design was not guilty. In contrast, the CCPDS-R software design review process was demonstration-based, requiring tangible evidence that the architecture and design progress were leading to an acceptable quality product. The design review demonstrations provided such evidence by demonstrating an executable version of the current architecture under the critical scenarios of usage.

Numerous qualities of the evolving architecture baseline should be made visible at any given design review. At a minimum, these demonstrations provide acute insight into the integrity of the architecture and its subordinate components, the run-time performance risks, and the understanding of the system's operational concept and key use cases.

On the CCPDS-R project, lessons learned from informal design walkthroughs (and their informal demonstrations) were tracked via action items. Major milestone design reviews provided both a briefing and a demonstration. The briefing summarized the overall design and the important results of the design walkthroughs, and presented an overview of the demonstration goals, scenarios, and expectations. The demonstration at the design review was a culmination of the real design review process conducted by the software development team. The sequence of demonstration activities included the development of a plan, definition of a set of evaluation criteria, integration of components into an executable capability, and generation of test drivers, scenarios, and throw-away components. Although the demonstration plans were not elaborate (typically 15 to 35 pages), they captured the purpose of the demonstration, the actual evaluation criteria for assessing the results, the scenarios of execution, and the overall hardware and software configuration that would be demonstrated.

There is an interesting difference in the evolving insight into run-time performance when using a demonstration-based approach for design review. While the conventional approach almost always started with an optimistic assessment and then got worse, a modern demonstration-based approach frequently starts with a pessimistic assessment and then gets better.

The following key lessons were learned in the CCPDS-R demonstration activities:

- **Early construction of test scenarios has a high ROI.** The early investment in building some of the critical test scenarios served two invaluable purposes. First, it forced a certain important subset of the requirements to be "implemented" in very tangible form. These test scenarios caused several interactions and negotiations with the users that increased the understanding of requirements early in the life cycle. Second, these implementation activities got the test team involved early in building an environment for demonstration and testing that was highly mature by the time the project reached full-scale testing.

- **Demonstration planning and execution expose the important risks.** Negotiating the content of each demonstration and the associated evaluation criteria served to focus the architecture team, management team, and external stakeholders on the critical priorities of the early requirements and architecture activities. Rather than deal with the full elaboration and traceability of all 2,000 requirements, the team focused on understanding the 20 or so design drivers.

- **Demonstration infrastructure, instrumentation, and scaffolding have a high ROI.** At the outset of the project, there was a concern that these demonstrations would require a significant investment in throw-away components that were needed only for the purpose of the demonstration. In most cases, very little of this work ended up being thrown away. Most efforts resulted in components that were reused in later stand-alone tests, build integration tests, or engineering string tests. As one benchmark of the level of throw-away components, the IPDR demonstration amounted to 72,000 SLOC. Of this, only about 2,000 SLOC (smart stubs and dummy messages) were thrown away.

- **Demonstration activities expose the crucial design trade-offs.** The integration of the demonstration provided timely feedback on the important design attributes and the level of design maturity. The demonstration efforts typically involved 10 to 12 designers integrating components into the architecture. They ran into numerous obstacles, built numerous workarounds, and performed several component redesigns and a few architecture redesigns. Most of this work occurred over the period of a month, much of it late at night. What was really going on in these all-night integration-debug-rebuild-redesign efforts was very detailed, very effective design review. I coordinated these activities, gaining a first-hand understanding of what the architectural strengths and weaknesses were, which components were mature, which components were fragile, and what the priorities must be in post-demonstration improvements.

- **Early performance issues drive early architecture improvements.** The first two demonstrations contained extensive functionality and demonstrated run-time performance that was significantly less than required. The demonstration evaluation criteria were close to the end-item performance requirements. In retrospect, this was counterproductive because it led to an early expectation on the part of contract monitors that demonstration evaluation criteria and requirements would be too closely aligned. Although the customer and TRW management were initially quite anxious about this situation, the straightforward resolutions and substantial progress made in subsequent demonstrations ameliorated their concerns.

The implementation of demonstrations as the predominant intermediate product of an organic development effort is well understood. Section 9.1 describes demonstrations with little discussion of multiple-stakeholder coordination. In the context of multiple stakeholders in a contractual situation, however, the implementation of a demonstration-based assessment can be subtly difficult. The next few sections provide detailed perspectives to illuminate some of the CCPDS-R experience.

The IPDR Demonstration

The interim PDR major milestone demonstration of the Common Subsystem had three critical objectives:

1. Tangible assessment of the software architecture design integrity through construction of a prototype SAS

2. Tangible assessment of the critical requirements understanding through construction of the worst-case missile warning scenario

3. Exposure of the architectural risks associated with the peak missile warning scenario (the worst-case data processing performance corresponding to a mass missile raid from the Soviet Union) and the fault detection and recovery scenario (the worst-case control processing associated with a failure in the primary processing thread and a real-time switchover to a hot backup processing thread)

The CCPDS-R software culture is evident in these objectives. The demonstrations were not set up to be cakewalks that would impress the customer with perfect results and minimal open issues. (Neither were the walkthroughs, project management reviews, nor major milestones.) These demonstrations were always honest engineering activities with ambitious goals, open discussion of trade-offs, and a show-me approach to substantiating assertions about progress and quality. The results of a demonstration were apt to change requirements, plans, and designs equally; all three of these dimensions evolved during the life cycle.

Demonstration activities generally spanned a six-month period, with the first three months focused on planning. Only a few people across the stakeholder teams participated in specifying the formal evaluation criteria. Figure D-8 summarizes the schedule for the IPDR demonstration; it includes details of the intense integration period in the two months before the demonstration.

The first three months of planning, which encompassed a draft plan, government review and comment, and final plan production, could have been achieved in one week with a collocated team of all interested stakeholders. The review sequence that occurred was a requirement of the contract. Because this was the first time that TRW or the customer had used a demonstration-based approach, both were unsure of the best process and agreed on an overly conservative approach. This demonstration was the first attempt at constructing a full-scale SAS. Consequently, this was the first (and worst-case) major integration effort for the Common Subsystem. The subsequent demonstrations tended to have shorter, but equally intense, integration activities lasting 4 or 5 weeks.

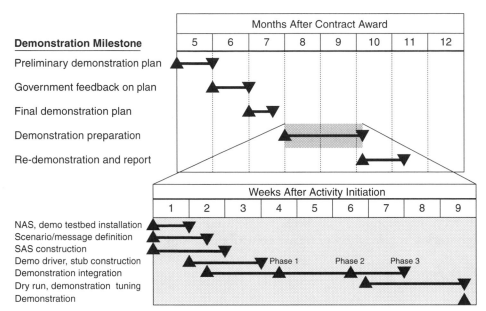

FIGURE D-8. *CCPDS-R first demonstration activities and schedule*

IPDR Demonstration Scope

The basic scope of the IPDR demonstration was defined in the CCPDS-R statement of work:

> *The contractor shall demonstrate the following capabilities at the NORAD Demo 1: system services, system initialization, system failover and recovery, system reconfiguration, test message injection, and data logging.*

These capabilities were fairly well understood by the customer and TRW. They represented the key components and use cases necessary to meet the objectives.

1. System services were the NAS software components of general utility to be reused across all three subsystems. These components were the foundation of the architectural infrastructure. They included the interprocess communications services, generic applications control (generic task and process executives), NAS utilities (list routines, name services, string services), and common error reporting and monitoring services. These components were all building blocks needed to demonstrate any executable thread.

2. Data logging (SSV CSCI) was a capability needed to instrument some of the results of the demonstration and was a performance concern.

3. Test message injection (TAS CSCI) components permitted messages to be injected into any object in the system so that there was a general test driver capability.

4. System initialization was the fundamental use case (called phase 1 in Figure D-8) that would illustrate the existence of a consistent software architecture skeleton and error-free operation of a substantial set of the system services. One of the perceived performance risks was the requirement to initialize a large distributed software architecture, including both custom and commercial components, within a given time.

5. The second scenario (phase 2) was to inject the peak message traffic load into the architecture and cause all the internal message traffic to cascade through the system in a realistic way. Executing this scenario required all the software objects to have smart, but simple, message processing stubs to be "modeled." These simple Ada programs completed the thread with dummy message traffic by reading and writing messages as expected under a peak load. Prototype message processing software was constructed to accept incoming messages and forward them through the strings of components that made up the SAS. This included all significant expected traffic, from receipt of external sensor messages through missile warning display updates, across both primary and backup threads. It also included all overhead traffic associated with status monitoring, error reporting, performance monitoring, and data logging.

6. System failover and recovery (phase 3) was one of the riskiest scenarios, because it required a very sophisticated set of state management and state transition control interfaces to be executed across a logical network of hundreds of software objects. The basic operation of this use case was to inject a simulated fault into a primary thread operational object to exercise the following sequence of events: fault detection, fault notification, orchestrated state transition from primary thread to backup thread, shutdown of primary thread. All these network state transitions needed to occur without interruption of service to the missile warning operators. Reconfiguration, in this specific case, meant recovering from a degraded mode. Following the system failover defined above, a new backup thread would be initialized so that there was minimum exposure to single-point failures. In the delivered system, repair immediately followed failover.

IPDR Demonstration Evaluation Criteria

The essential IPDR evaluation criteria were derived from the requirements, the risk assessments, and the evolving design trade-offs:

- All phases:
  - No critical errors shall occur.
- Phase 1:
  - The system shall initialize itself in less than 10 minutes.
  - The system shall be initialized from a single terminal.
  - After initialization is complete, the number of processes, tasks, and sockets shall match exactly the expected numbers in the then-current SAS baseline.
- Phase 2:
  - Averaged over the worst-case minute of the 20-minute peak scenario, the total processor utilization for each node shall be less than 30%.
  - There shall be no error reports of duplicate or lost messages.
  - All displayed data shall be received within 1 second from its injection time.
  - The message injection process shall maintain an injection rate matching the intended scenario rate.
  - The data logs shall show no unexpected state transitions or error reports and shall log all injected messages.
- Phase 3:
  - The operator shall be capable of injecting a fault into any object.
  - An error report shall be received within 2 seconds of the injection of a fault.
  - The switchover from the primary to backup thread shall be completed within 2 seconds of the fault injection with no loss of data.
  - The shutdown of the failed primary thread and reinitialization as a new backup thread shall be completed in less than 5 minutes from failure.
  - The data logs shall match the expected state transitions with no fatal errors reported other than the injected fault.

There were 23 other evaluation criteria for less important visibility into detailed capabilities and intermediate results. They are not listed because they require much more explanation.

IPDR Demonstration Results

The results of the IPDR demonstration were fruitful. Of the 37 evaluation criteria, 31 were considered satisfactory. Six criteria were not met, including three of the essential criteria just discussed. These were considered very serious issues that required immediate redesign and re-demonstration. Of most concern was excessive processor utilization during the peak load scenario. While the threshold was 30%, actual utilization was 54%. This corresponded to the essential overhead of the architectural infrastructure, operating system, and networking software. Because this was always a perceived risk of the CCPDS-R reusable middleware design, it received extensive attention. Five distinct action items for performance analysis were created, as well as an action item to demonstrate the performance improvement at the next project management review after the five action items were resolved.

Greatly simplified, the five action items were as follows:

1. Update the scenario. The actual test scenario used as the peak load was in fact about 33% worse than the real peak load. The internal message traffic threads were worse than the true worst case (for example, each message caused an "alarm" that resulted in redundant and unnecessary message traffic). The IPDR demonstration forced TRW, the customer, and the user to converge on a better understanding of the real worst-case mission scenario in tangible and objective terms. It also forced the architecture team to understand better the message traffic patterns and the optimization trade-offs. The return on investment realized from this activity was never quantified, but it was certainly enormous.

2. Tune the interprocess communications (IPC) buffering parameters. The NAS components had many options for optimizing performance. Even though numerous local optimizations were made over the final month of integration activities, there was a definite need for a more global analysis to take advantage of lessons learned in exploiting the patterns of message traffic.

3. Enhance network transactions. The node-to-node message traffic was an obvious bottleneck because the current version of the operating system (DEC VMS 4.7) did not exploit the symmetric multiprocessing capability of the VAX processors. The pending upgrade to VMS 5.0 would provide a substantial increase to this component of the overall performance.

4. Improve performance of the IPC component. An obvious bottleneck in the NAS interprocess communications component had an impact on one of the performance optimization features. The demonstration team identified this as a design flaw that needed resolution. (A prototype solution was already in progress.)

5. Improve reliability in the IPC component. The IPDR demonstration exposed another serious design flaw: Erroneous behavior could occur under a very intense burst of messages. The overly stressful scenario made this flaw obvious. In a system with the stringent reliability requirements of CCPDS-R, it had to be fixed, even though it might never occur in operation. Although fixing this sort of problem was mildly painful at the time, it could have caused malignant breakage and immense scrap and rework if the flaw had gone undetected until late in the project.

The five action items accurately represented the critical issues that were still unresolved at the time of the demonstration. There was tremendous anxiety on the part of TRW management and the customer; both had expected the demonstration to conclude with no open issues. Nevertheless, both parties were pleased with the demonstration process and the unprecedented insight they had achieved into the true design progress, design trade-offs, requirements understanding, and risk assessment. The overall anxiety of the stakeholders was significantly relieved after the closure of the action items and the re-demonstration that occurred about one month after the IPDR demonstration. While the original objective of 30% processor utilization still had not been achieved, the team had demonstrated the flexibility of the architecture and the opportunities for optimization, and succeeded in reducing the overall utilization from 54% to 35%. This positive trend was sufficient for everyone to feel comfortable that the performance requirement would ultimately be met through straightforward engineering optimizations and operating system upgrades.

These were the visible and formal results of the IPDR demonstration. As the responsible manager for the process, the architecture, and this demonstration, I also observed many intangible results. Over a period of 8 weeks of late-night integration and debug sessions—during which priorities were coordinated, design issues were resolved, workarounds were brainstormed, stakeholders were placated with on-going status reports, and the engineering teams were motivated toward an ambitious objective—many lessons were learned:

1. Very effective design review was occurring throughout the period. The demonstration was the result of the engineering team's review, presented to the stakeholders as tangible evidence of progress. Although we ended up with only five open issues, 50 or more design issues had been opened, resolved, and closed during the 8-week integration activity. This early resolution of defects—in the requirements specification, the process, the tools,

and the design—had undocumented but extensive return on investment by avoiding a tremendous amount of late downstream breakage that could have occurred had we not resolved these issues in this early demonstration.

2. Through day-to-day participation in this activity, I gained detailed insight into where the design was weak, where it was robust, and why. For example, when we uncovered issues in some components, the responsible designer delivered a resolution within hours. In other components, there was recurring resistance and resolutions frequently took days. By the time the demonstration activity concluded, I knew very well where change was easy (usually indicating well-designed components) and where it was difficult (for numerous reasons). These lessons helped in structuring the risk profile for future planning, personnel allocation, and test priorities.

3. The demonstration served as a strong team-building exercise in which there was a very tangible goal and the engineers were working in the forum they preferred: getting stuff to work.

4. The detailed technical understanding and objective discussions of design trade-offs proved invaluable to developing a trustworthy relationship with all stakeholders, including the customer, the user, and TRW management. We were armed with facts and figures, not subjective speculation.

Government Response to the IPDR Demonstration

The formal IPDR demonstration represented a major paradigm shift from conventional design reviews. Consequently, there was a fair amount of tension and anxiety between TRW and the Air Force in converging on detailed evaluation criteria for the demonstration. The following paragraphs, with quotations presented in *italics*, were extracted verbatim from the final plan TRW submitted. This is a good summary of some of the concerns likely to show up when an organization takes on this process for the first time. It also provides insight into the spirit of the demonstration.

> *After careful evaluation of the Government's Preliminary Demo 1 Plan comments, the following observations summarize this submittal of the Demo 1 Plan and the modifications that have been made from the previous version:*
>
> 1. *This submittal has eliminated all requirements references to avoid making any allusion to an intent of satisfying, proving, or demonstrating any requirements. These requirements verification activities are performed by the test organization in a very rigorous and traceable fashion. The demonstration activity is intended to be an engineering-intensive activity, streamlined through minimal documentation, to provide early insight into the*

design feasibility and progress. TRW intends to maximize the usefulness of the demonstration as an engineering activity and to avoid turning it into a less useful documentation-intensive effort.

2. *Several government comments requested further details on requirements, designs, etc. This information is not necessary in the Demo Plan. It is redundant with other documents (SRS, SDD, design walkthrough packages) or it is provided in the informal test procedures delivered 2 weeks prior to the demonstration. Providing more information in a single document (and in every document) may make the reviewer's job easier but it would also be excessive, more time-consuming, and counterproductive to produce, thereby reducing the technical content of the engineering product being reviewed.*

3. *In light of the government's concern over the relationship of the demonstration to the requirements, the evaluation criteria provided in this plan should be carefully scrutinized. We feel that the evaluation criteria are explicit, observable, and insightful with respect to determining design feasibility, especially at such an early point in the life cycle. Although we are open to constructive modification of these evaluation criteria, we feel that modifying them to relate more closely to the System Specification or SRS requirements would be inappropriate. The requirements perspective and our demonstration perspective are different and difficult to relate.*

4. *The source code for the components being demonstrated has not been delivered with the plan as required in the statement of work. The total volume for the demonstrated components is roughly 1 to 2 feet thick, and it is still changing at a rapid rate. Instead of delivering all the source code, interested reviewers may request specific components for review. All source code will be browseable at the contractor facility during the demonstration.*

As mentioned before, the government's overall response to the IPDR demonstration was very positive, although the five critical action items were an unexpected outcome and initially caused intense concern. After TRW demonstrated resolution of these action items one month later, the government response was overwhelmingly positive. The objective insight, open discussion of trade-offs, and understandability of the design issues, requirements issues, and performance issues resulted in exceptional relationships among the stakeholders. The customer and the user representatives requested encore demonstrations to their upper management, and there was a sense of success among stakeholders in which they could all take ownership. This event proved to be very important: From this point on, everyone wanted to maintain the project's reputation as a flagship example of how to do software right.

D.7   CORE METRICS

The CCPDS-R metrics approach was first developed solely to manage the project and meet the needs of the contract. While it achieved these goals, it also resulted in a great case study. CCPDS-R was nowhere near perfect; numerous mistakes were made all along the way. This was true of the metrics program, too: It measured some of the wrong things, measured some things in the wrong way, struggled with early interpretations, and used some manual methods where automation was needed. Nevertheless, these metrics activities led to more teamwork, better processes, better understanding of risks, and, ultimately, better products produced with more efficiency. Early in the project, there was resistance from management, from practitioners, and even from contract monitors. After the first year, following several improvements in interpretation, automation, presentation, and definition, there was nearly universal support. All parties used the objective data from the metrics program to substantiate their plans, their risks, their design directions, and their results.

All the Common Subsystem metrics presented here were extracted directly from the monthly project management reviews. None of these data were created after the fact. Although the CCPDSR-R metrics program was a contractual requirement, the government did not define the actual metrics to be used. This was left up to the contractor so that the project team would take ownership of the metrics program selected.

TRW formulated a metrics program with four objectives:

1. Provide data for assessing current project trends and identifying the need for management attention

2. Provide data for planning future builds and subsystems

3. Provide data for assessing the relative complexity of meeting the software end-item quality requirements

4. Provide data for identifying where process improvements are needed and substantiating the need

The following sections contain explicit examples of the metrics recommended in Chapter 13. There are several instances of progress metrics as well as the quality indicators of scrap, rework, and maturity. The basis for automation, which required some interesting technical approaches embedded directly in the evolving design and code artifacts, is also described.

D.7.1 Development Progress

Measuring development progress accurately with several concurrent builds in various states was a complex undertaking for the Common Subsystem management team. Significant effort went into devising a consistent approach that would provide accurate insight into subsystem-level status and build status. The goal was a balanced assessment that included the following:

- The Ada/ADL metrics. These data provided good insight into the direct indicators of technical progress. By themselves, these metrics were fairly accurate at depicting the true progress in design and implementation. They were generally weak at depicting the completed contract deliverables and financial status.

- Earned value metrics. These data provided good insight into the financial status and contract deliverables. They were generally weak indicators of true technical progress.

As with most software metrics, both of these perspectives initially were somewhat inaccurate assessments of absolute progress. They were, however, excellent assessments of relative progress when tracked periodically (in this case, monthly). As experience was gained with these metrics, the absolute assessments became well-tuned predictors of success or risk. The overall assessment was crammed into one chart, as illustrated in Figure D-9. The figure depicts the top-level progress summary for each build and for the Common Subsystem as a whole. The length of shading within each build relative to the dashed line (corresponding to the current month) identifies whether progress was ahead of or behind schedule. For example, Figure D-9 displays month 17 status: Build 2 SAT testing is one month behind schedule, build 3 design work is one month ahead of schedule, the Common Subsystem design effort is on schedule, and Common Subsystem SAT testing is one month behind schedule. The shading was a judgment by the software chief engineer, who combined the monthly progress metrics and the monthly financial metrics into a consolidated (and somewhat subjective) assessment.

Monthly collection of metrics provided detailed management insight into build progress, code growth, and other indicators. The metrics were collected by build and by CSCI to provide multiple perspectives. Individual CSCI managers collected and assessed their metrics before the metrics were incorporated into a project-level summary. This process was objective, efficient, and meaningful. Although the lowest level estimates of TBD_Statements were certainly subjective, they were being determined by the most knowledgeable people: the actual designers. They were being maintained in the evolving source code format because this was the format in which the designers

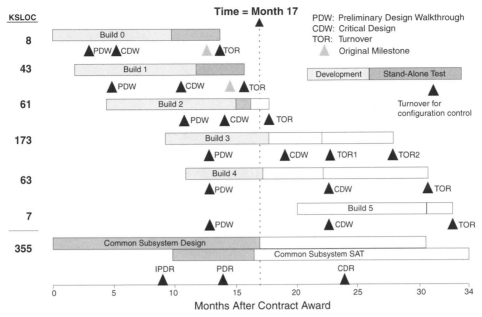

FIGURE D-9. *Development progress summary*

preferred to work, increasing the likelihood that the artifact would be kept up-to-date. This process also assured consistent and uniform communication of progress across the project.

Figure D-10 illustrates the monthly progress assessments for the Common Subsystem and each build. The planned evolution was based roughly on weight-averaging the SLOC counts for each build with the guidelines described in Section D.5.3: 30% done by PDW and 70% done by CDW. Overall, the Common Subsystem performed very close to its plan, with one exception. The progress achieved at IPDR (significantly ahead of plan) reflected the unexpected positive impact of the source code generation tools, particularly for the SAS generation of 50,000+ SLOC.

Performance against plans varied for the individual builds. In general, each build tracked its plan fairly well. The progress of the subsystem and each build was assessed monthly with internal management and the customer in the project management reviews. The progress metrics provided an objective mechanism and consistent language for explaining perturbations to the plan, perturbations to the architecture, issues in requirements, issues in design, scheduling risks, and other management topics. The objectivity of the approach was a key contributor to the nonadversarial relationships that evolved among all stakeholders.

Everyone understood that although the metrics were not very precise early in the life cycle, they were accurate. The absolute values were rarely important. The relative

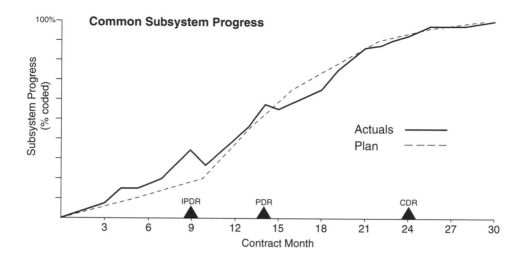

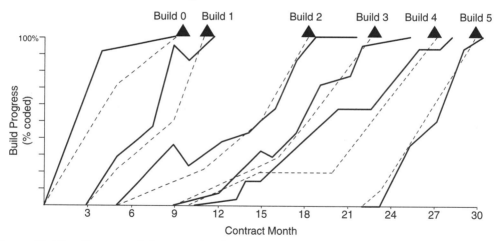

FIGURE D-10. *Common Subsystem development progress*

trends were most important, and, as the process evolved, the precision of all metrics improved over time. By PDR, the metrics data had become a cornerstone of project communications.

D.7.2 TEST PROGRESS

The test organization was responsible for build integration tests and requirements verification testing (some SATs, ESTs, and FQT). Build integration testing proved to

TABLE D-6. *SCO characteristics for build 2 BIT testing*

PROBLEM SOURCE	MINOR (<1 HOUR)	MODERATE (<1 DAY)	MAJOR (>1 DAY)	TOTAL
Requirement interpretation	5			5
Inadequate stand-alone test	3	4	2	9
Interface problem	9	2	1	12
Inadequate performance	1			1
Desired enhancement (not a problem)	3			3
Inconsistent configuration	3	2		5
Totals	24	8	3	35

be less effective than expected for uncovering problems. BITs were intended to carry out a complete set of integration test procedures from the most basic capability to off-nominal boundary conditions. Much of this work, particularly the basic threads, was redundant with demonstration integration efforts. Consequently, the BITs were frequently redundant with demonstration preparation and were less cost-effective than if the demonstration preparation activities had been combined with BIT and made a responsibility of the test organization. Table D-6 summarizes the build 2 BIT results, which reflect a highly integrated product state. Nevertheless, more effort had been allocated to BIT planning, preparation, and conduct than was necessary. The merging of the demonstration preparation and BIT activities would have enabled fewer people to do a better job. This approach would have enabled more integration (as part of demonstration activities) before turnover and more efficient regression testing after turnover to ensure that all previous issues were resolved.

Table D-7 and Figure D-11 provide perspectives on the progress metrics used to plan and track the CCPDS-R test program. The figure plots the progress against the plan for requirements verification tests. SATs, ESTs, and FQTs were sources of test cases used by the software organization. SATs were the responsibility of the development teams but had to be executed in the formal configuration management environment and witnessed (peer-reviewed) by the test personnel. ESTs consisted of functionally related groups of scenarios that demonstrated requirements spanning multiple components. FQTs were tests for requirements compliance that could not be demonstrated until a complete system existed. Quantitative performance requirements (QPRs) spanned all CSCIs.

Formal SAT testing (requirements verification done in stand-alone tests) was more difficult than planned. This was primarily due to excessive design detail in the software requirements specifications and in the project review and signoff procedures.

TABLE D-7. *Requirements verification work by test type and CSCI*

TEST TYPE	NAS	SSV	DCO	TAS	CMP	CCO	QPR	TOTAL
Build 0/1 SAT	42			5				47
Build 2 SAT	11	52	63	15	12			153
Build 3/4/5 SAT		65	62	18	198	46		389
EST 1/2	131	39	77	94				341
EST 3	32	49	117	42				240
EST 4	16	172	219	5	4	6		422
EST5/FQT	5	105	84	42	54	207	46	543
Totals	237	482	622	221	268	259	46	2,135

Formal SAT testing was scrutinized by the government and required fairly long lead times for review. The government required overly detailed test procedures for numerous design details that should not have been treated as requirements. In the heat of development, the SAT procedures were rarely available 30 to 60 days before turnover, as required by the contract for any requirements verification test. The formal SAT process was one of the main reasons that the turnover reviews were consistently completed later than planned.

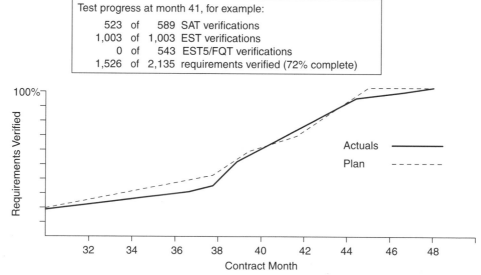

FIGURE D-11. *Common Subsystem test progress*

D.7.3 STABILITY

Figure D-12 illustrates the overall rate of configuration baseline changes. It shows the cumulative number of SLOC that were broken (checked out of the baseline for rework because of an identified defect, enhancement, or other change) and the number of SLOC repaired (checked back into the baseline with fixes, enhancements, or other changes). Breakage rates that diverged from repair rates resulted in management attention, reprioritization of resources, and corrective actions taken to ensure that the test organization (driving the breakage) and development organization (driving the repair) remained in relative equilibrium. Overall, the situation shown depicts a very healthy project.

D.7.4 MODULARITY

Figure D-13 identifies the total breakage as a ratio of the entire software subsystem. This metric identifies the total scrap generated by the Common Subsystem software development process as about 25% of the whole product. Industry averages for software scrap run in the 40% to 60% range. The initial configuration management baseline was established around the time of PDR, at month 14. There were 1,600 discrete changes processed against configuration baselines thereafter.

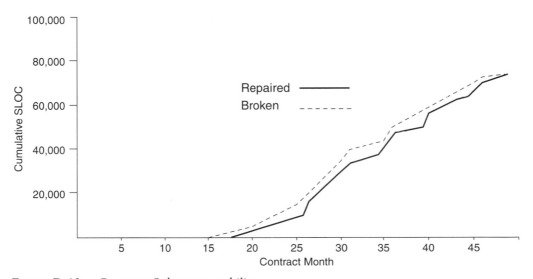

FIGURE D-12. *Common Subsystem stability*

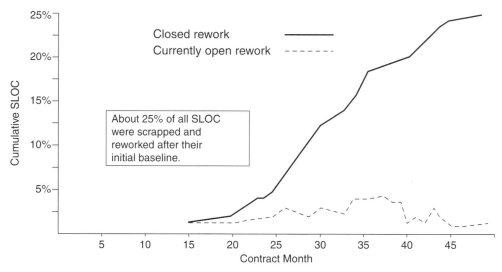

FIGURE D-13. *Common Subsystem modularity*

D.7.5 ADAPTABILITY

Over the entire Common Subsystem, about 5% of the total effort was expended in rework activities against software baselines. The average cost of change was about 24 hours per SCO. These values provide some insight into the ease with which the software baselines could be changed. The level of adaptability achieved by CCPDS-R was roughly four times better than the typical project, in which rework costs over the development life cycle usually exceed 20% of the total cost.

Figure D-14 plots the average cost of change across the Common Subsystem schedule. The 1,600+ SCOs processed against the evolving configuration baseline by FQT resulted in a fairly stable cost of change. CCPDS-R is one of the few counterexamples of "the later you are in the life cycle, the more expensive things are to fix."

Most of the early SCO trends (shown in the box labeled "Design Changes" in Figure D-14) were changes that affected multiple people and multiple components (that is, interface or architectural changes). The later SCO trends (shown in "Implementation Changes") were usually localized to a single person and a single component. The final phase of SCOs reflected an uncharacteristic increase in breakage, the result of a large engineering change proposal that completely changed the input message set to the Common Subsystem. This was one area of the software design that was not as easy to change as we might have hoped. Although the design was very robust and adaptable for numerous premeditated change scenarios, an overhaul of the message set was never foreseen nor accommodated in the design.

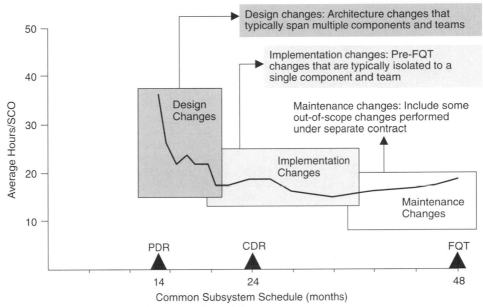

FIGURE D-14. *Common Subsystem adaptability*

D.7.6 MATURITY

CCPDS-R had a specific reliability requirement, for which the software had a specific allocation. The independent test team constructed an after-hours, automated test suite that exercised the evolving software baselines with randomized message scenarios. This strategy resulted in extensive test time being logged under realistic conditions from which a credible software MTBF could be substantiated. The reliability-critical components, forced by the iteration plan into the earliest baselines, were subjected to the most reliability stress testing. This plan ensured early insight into maturity and software reliability issues. Figure D-15 illustrates the results.

With modern distributed architectures, this sort of statistical testing is both necessary for ensuring maximum coverage and useful for uncovering significant issues of races, deadlocks, resource overruns, memory leakage, and other Heisen-bugs. Executing randomized and accelerated scenarios for long periods of time (running all night or over a long weekend) enables early insight into overall system resource integrity.

D.7.7 COST/EFFORT EXPENDITURES BY ACTIVITY

Table D-8 provides the overall cost breakdown for the CCPDS-R Common Subsystem. These data were extracted from the final WBS cost collection runs and were structured as recommended in Section 10.1. The next-level elements are described in Table D-9.

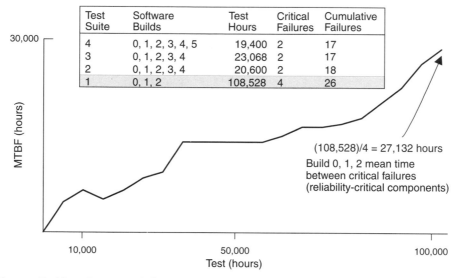

Test Suite	Software Builds	Test Hours	Critical Failures	Cumulative Failures
4	0, 1, 2, 3, 4, 5	19,400	2	17
3	0, 1, 2, 3, 4	23,068	2	17
2	0, 1, 2, 3, 4	20,600	2	18
1	0, 1, 2	108,528	4	26

(108,528)/4 = 27,132 hours
Build 0, 1, 2 mean time between critical failures (reliability-critical components)

FIGURE D-15. *Common Subsystem maturity*

TABLE D-8. *Common Subsystem cost expenditures by top-level WBS element*

WBS ELEMENT	COST (%)	ACTIVITIES AND ARTIFACTS
Management and administration	9	Deliverable plans, administrative support, financial administration, customer interface, contracts, overall control and leadership
Process/product specification	7	Technical requirements, demonstration plans and evaluation criteria, iteration plans, software process, metrics analysis
Software engineering	11	Architecture engineering, design walkthrough coordination, NAS CSCI development, metrics definition and assessment, demonstration planning and integration
Development	38	Development, testing, documentation, and maintenance of application components
Testing, assessment, and deployment	24	Release management; formal test preparation, conduct, and reporting; test scenario development; change management; deployment
Infrastructure	11	System administration, hardware and software resources, toolsmithing, tool integration
Total software activities	100	Cost expenditures, including hardware and software tools (in the infrastructure element), travel, and other direct costs

TABLE D-9. *Common Subsystem lower level WBS elements*

WBS ELEMENT	COST (%)	ACTIVITIES AND ARTIFACTS
Software project management	6	Customer interface, contracts, administration
Software engineering	5	Requirements coordination, chief engineer
Specifications	4	CSCI SRS development
Demonstrations	3	Plans, integration, reports
Tools/metrics	3	Tools, metrics collection
NAS CSCI	3	Middleware, 20 KSLOC
Integration and test management	4	Test coordination, management
BIT testing	3	Integration smoke testing
EST testing	9	Formal test plans, testing, reports
FQT testing	6	Formal test plans, testing, reports
Configuration management and testbed control	3	Release management, integration
Environment	11	Hardware, software, system administration
Development management	5	CSCI applications management
SSV CSCI	11	Architecture, system software, 160 KSLOC
DCO CSCI	9	Display interface applications, 70 KSLOC
CCO CSCI	9	Communications applications, 80 KSLOC
TAS CSCI	2	Test and exercise applications, 10 KSLOC
CMP CSCI	4	Mission algorithm applications, 15 KSLOC
Total software activities	100	All software-related expenses

These are some noteworthy data points:

- The percentages in Table D-8 are roughly traceable to the percentages in Chapter 10. However, some of the management elements in Table D-9 were split across elements in Table D-8 to extract the activities at the project management level.

- The overall test team effort is relatively low compared with the effort typically expended on projects that used the conventional process. The main reason is that the architecture team delivered an integrated software product to the test and assessment team, which was responsible primarily for testing the integrated quality of the evolving product.

- CCPDS-R used an efficient environment that represented 11% of the total cost of the effort.

- Overall maintenance (total rework effort expended) was only 5% of the total cost. Although this is not shown explicitly in the tables, it was tracked in the individual CSCI WBS elements.

To compare varying levels of productivity in a fairly normalized manner, individual CSCI costs can be compared with each other as well as with the other metrics. These comparisons need to be tempered by management understanding of subjective attributes such as team competence, requirements volatility, CSCI complexity, and other noncomparable factors.

> The top-level WBS tracks pretty closely with the process workflows of Section 8.1 and the effort allocations recommended in Table 10-2.

D.8 OTHER METRICS

Preceding sections of this case study have described specific approaches and metrics. This section summarizes some other, more global perspectives of CCPDS-R project performance: software size evolution, subsystem process improvements, SCO resolution profile, and CSCI productivities and quality factors.

D.8.1 SOFTWARE SIZE EVOLUTION

The software sizes of the Common Subsystem and the individual CSCIs were tracked monthly and were derived directly from the evolving metrics files. There was a large amount of code growth from the original contract bid (150,000 SLOC) to the delivered product (355,000 SLOC), with no substantial increase in the software development budget. There were two reasons for this level of code growth:

1. The method for counting source lines was changed around month 8 to provide a better balance in estimating the engineering effort and to be consistent with the counting method embraced by Ada COCOMO.

2. Several automatic code generation tools were developed that output verbose source code with fewer human-generated input lines. These tools were used for the straightforward generation of display formats, message validation processing, and socket/circuit bookkeeping functions. They represented about 14,000 SLOC of tools, which required another 20,000 lines

of input data files. The output of these tools was about 200,000 SLOC of operational software. In gross terms, these code generation tools resulted in about a fivefold return on investment.

The total code growth is summarized in Table D-10.

The primary reason for the increase in SLOC was the change in the counting rules. At contract award, a simple semicolon count was being used. This approach transitioned to the following counting procedure, which was implemented with a simple tool used by all personnel on the project:

- Within an Ada specification part, each carriage return counted as one SLOC. Four coding standards allowed the SLOC counting to be consistent:

  1. Each parameter of a subprogram declaration is listed on a separate line. The effort associated with design of a subprogram interface is generally proportional to the number of parameters.

  2. For custom enumeration types (such as socket names and system states) and record types, each enumeration or field is listed on a separate line. Custom types usually involve custom design and engineering, resulting in an increased number of SLOC.

  3. For predefined enumeration types (such as keyboard keys and compass directions), enumerations are listed on the fewest number of lines possible without loss of readability. These types generally require no custom engineering.

  4. Initialization of composite objects (such as records and arrays) is listed with one component per line. Each of these assignments represents a custom statement; an "others" clause is typically used for non-custom assignments.

TABLE **D-10.** *Common Subsystem CSCI sizes*

CSCI	CONTRACT AWARD	DELIVERED	AUTOMATICALLY PRODUCED
NAS	20,000	20,000	
SSV	18,000	160,000	140,000
DCO	48,000	70,000	18,000
TAS	17,000	10,000	4,000
CMP	23,000	15,000	
CCO	24,000	80,000	40,000
Totals	150,000	355,000	202,000

- Within Ada bodies, each semicolon counts as one SLOC. Generic instantiations count one line for each generic parameter.

This definition treats declarative (specification) design much more sensitively than it does executable (body) design. Although this definition caused many heated debates, within the project and externally, it served as quite good enough. It was not important to have the perfect definition; it was very important to have a consistent and adequate definition.

Two components drove the change in the definition of SLOC. First, the SAS packages in SSV contained a network definition that consisted of all the process definitions, task definitions, socket definitions, and socket connections. These packages contained numerous record definitions, custom-enumerated types, and record and array field initializations in specification parts. The source code for these elements consisted of more than 50,000 carriage returns but only a few hundred semicolons. Because the engineering effort involved with these packages was much more like the effort associated with 50,000 SLOC, there was a need to change. The second component, with similar rationale, was the system global message types. These packages numbered some 300 different record types that represented the majority of data exchanged across SAS objects.

Because of the variety of different categories of SLOC developed on CCPDS-R, a method was devised for normalizing the different categories so that budgets could be properly allocated and productivities compared. The result was an extension of the COCOMO technique for incorporating reuse, called equivalent source lines of code (ESLOC). In essence, ESLOC converts the standard COCOMO measure of SLOC into a normalized measure that is comparable on an effort-per-line basis. The need for this new measure arises in budget allocation and productivity analysis for mixtures of newly developed, reused, and tool-produced source code. For example, a 10,000-SLOC display component that is automatically produced from a tool by specifying 1,000 lines of display formatting script should not be allocated the same budget as a newly developed 10,000-SLOC component. Table D-11 defines the conversion of SLOC to ESLOC on CCPDS-R.

TABLE D-11.   *SLOC-to-ESLOC conversion factors*

SLOC FORMAT	DESIGN NEW = 40%	IMPLEMENT NEW = 20%	TEST NEW = 40%	ESLOC
Commercial	0%	0%	0%	0%
New	40%	20%	40%	100%
Reused	20%	5%	30%	55%
Automated	0%	0%	40%	40%
Tool input	30%	10%	10%	50%

The rationale for these conversion factors included many factors:

- Commercial off-the-shelf components do not result in any contribution to the ESLOC count. The integration of these components scales up with the amount of newly developed interfacing software.

- New software must be developed from scratch. It requires complete design, implementation, and test efforts, and has an ESLOC multiplier of 100% (one-for-one conversion).

- Reused components represent code that was previously developed for a different application but is applicable to the component with some modification. While there are many ways to assess the relative cost of reuse, and each instance is best handled individually, this conversion provides a simple rule of thumb as a default. In general, reused software requires 50% of the design effort, 25% of the implementation effort, and 75% of the test effort. Normalized across the 40/20/40 allocations of new software, this results in a total of 55%.

- Automated components usually require a separate source notation (the tool input format below) as input to a tool that then automatically produces the resulting SLOC. Because automated source code becomes part of the end product, it needs to be fully tested. However, the design and implementation effort is set to zero. If the tool that automates the source code production must be developed, its SLOC count should be included in the new category. The resulting conversion factor is a 40% SLOC-to-ESLOC ratio.

- Tool input can take on many diverse forms. CCPDS-R had input files for the architecture definition (a long but straightforward table of names, attributes, and relationships), display definitions (display object types, locations, and attributes), and message validation. These higher level abstraction formats were converted using 75% of the design effort (simple, high-level notations), 50% of the implementation effort (repetitive, high-level syntax and semantics), and 25% of the test effort (which focused on the generated code, not this code). The resulting conversion factor is a 50% SLOC-to-ESLOC ratio.

All in all, the development of a few code production tools reduced the total ESLOC of the Common Subsystem by 78,000 lines, as summarized in Table D-12. ESLOC was analyzed solely to ensure that the overall staffing and budget allocations, negotiated with each CSCI lead, were relatively fair. These ESLOC estimates were input to cost modeling analyses that incorporated the relative complexity of each CSCI and the other COCOMO effort adjustment factors.

TABLE D-12. *Common Subsystem CSCI sizes in ESLOC*

CSCI	DELIVERED SLOC	TOOL-PRODUCED	TOOL INPUTS	DEVELOPED TOOLS	SIZE (ESLOC)
NAS	20,000				20,000
SSV	160,000	140,000	20,000	15,000	101,000
DCO	70,000	18,000	6,000	6,000	68,800
TAS	10,000	4,000			7,600
CMP	15,000				15,000
CCO	80,000	40,000	12,000	3,000	65,000
Totals	355,000	202,000	38,000	24,000	277,400

All this code counting stuff may appear confusing when summarized in a couple of pages. However, over the first year of the project, these analyses and definitions were highly scrutinized and well understood. They provided a useful perspective for discussing several of the engineering trade-offs being evaluated. After the first year, the SLOC counts were very stable and well correlated to the schedule estimating analyses performed throughout the project life cycle. On one hand, the CCPDS-R code counting process is a good example of why SLOC is a problematic metric for measuring software size. On the other hand, CCPDS-R is an example of a complex system in which SLOC metrics worked very effectively.

> This section on software size is a good example of the issues associated with transitioning to component-based development. While projects can and must deal with heterogeneous measurements of size, there is no industry-accepted approach. Consequently, project managers need to analyze carefully such important metrics definitions.

D.8.2 SUBSYSTEM PROCESS IMPROVEMENTS

One of my main themes in this book is that real process improvements should be evident in subsequent project performance. Because it comprised three separate projects, CCPDS-R provides a perfect case study for illustrating this trend. Overall, the Common Subsystem subsidized much of the groundwork for the PDS and STRATCOM subsystems—namely, the process definition, the tools, and the reusable architecture primitives. With each successive subsystem, productivity and quality improved significantly. This is the expectation for a mature software process such as the one developed and evolved on CCPDS-R. It is always difficult to compare productivities across projects, but CCPDS-R subsystems had consistent measures of human-generated SLOC and homogeneous processes, teams, and techniques. The consistent metrics approach produced a comparable set of measures. The normalized unit of measure chosen to compare productivities was the cost per SLOC. The absolute costs are irrelevant; the relative costs among subsystems are not. The PDS Subsystem was delivered at 40% of the cost per SLOC of the Common Subsystem, and the STRATCOM Subsystem at 33%. This is one of the real indicators of a level 3 or level 4 process.

Table D-13 summarizes the SCO traffic across all CSCIs at month 58. By this time, the Common Subsystem was well beyond its FQT and had processed quite a few SCOs in a maintenance mode to accommodate engineering change proposals. The PDS and STRATCOM subsystems were well into their test phases. For completeness, the table provides entries for support, test, and operating system/vendor. (Tracking of commercial product change orders was similar to SCO tracking.) Support included code generation tools, configuration management tools, metrics tools, and stand-alone test drivers; test included software drivers used for requirements verification.

Table D-13 shows that the values of the modularity metric (average scrap per change) and the adaptability metric (average rework per change) were generally much better in the subsequent subsystems (PDS and STRATCOM) than they were in the Common Subsystem. The one exception was the SCG CSCI, a special communications capability needed in the STRATCOM Subsystem that did not have a counterpart in the other subsystems and was uniquely complex.

> CCPDS-R demonstrated the true indicator of a mature process, as described in Section E.2. With each subsequent subsystem, performance—as measured by quality, productivity, or time to market—improved. CCPDS-R was subjected to numerous SEI software capability evaluations over its lifetime, and the project's process maturity contributed to a level 3 or higher assessment. These performance improvements were not due solely to a mature process. Stakeholder teamwork and project investments in architecture middleware and process automation were probably equally important to overall project success.

D.8.3 SCO RESOLUTION PROFILE

The average change costs evolved over time into a fairly constant value of 16 hours per change. This effort included analysis time, redesign, recode, and retest of the resolution. The profile of changes shown in Figure D-16 provides another interesting perspective.

TABLE D-13. *CCPDS-R subsystem changes by CSCI*

CSCI	TOTAL SCOs	OPENED SCOs	CLOSED SCOs	REJECTED SCOs	AVERAGE SCRAP (SLOC/SCO)	AVERAGE REWORK (HOURS/SCO)
Common Subsystem						
NAS	236	1	197	38	30	15
SSV	1,200	16	1,004	180	24	16
DCO	526	10	434	82	30	15
TAS	255	0	217	38	40	11
CMP	123	2	105	16	24	35
CCO	435	1	406	28	64	22
PDS Subsystem						
PSSV	297	11	231	55	25	8
PDCO	167	10	126	31	25	21
PCO	73	0	72	1	20	10
STRATCOM Subsystem						
SSSV	531	30	401	100	18	10
SDCO	339	11	286	42	16	14
STAS	60	0	50	10	20	9
SMP	326	17	299	10	30	9
SCO	180	1	160	19	40	8
SCG	61	6	51	4	85	27
Other						
Support	648	2	546	100	Not tracked	Not tracked
Test	376	1	356	19	Not tracked	Not tracked
Operating system/vendor	223	13	161	49	Not tracked	Not tracked
Totals	6,056	132	5,102	822	32	13

D.8.4 CSCI PRODUCTIVITIES AND QUALITY FACTORS

Table D-14 summarizes some of the CCPDS-R CSCI quality and productivity data. Productivities for the CSCIs are not absolute; for comparison purposes, they are normalized relative to the overall subsystem productivity. The subsystem productivity is based on a total effort of approximately 1,800 staff-months. This includes all management, development, and test resources. The individual productivities of each CSCI

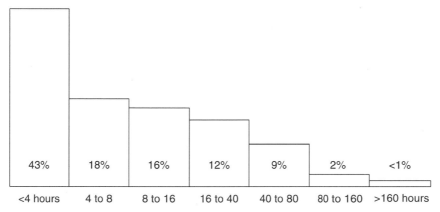

FIGURE D-16. *Common Subsystem SCO change profile*

were normalized. Productivities are described from two perspectives: SLOC per staff-month and ESLOC per staff-month. These data and my own experience lead me to the following conclusions:

- NAS was an extremely complex software engineering problem, requiring and achieving both high performance and reusability. It had an exceptional team, was based on an existing prototype, and had adequate schedule.

TABLE D-14. *Common Subsystem CSCI summary*

CSCI	COMPLEXITY	SLOC	PRODUCTIVITY (STAFF-MONTHS) SLOC	ESLOC	SCRAP (SLOC/SCO)	REWORK (HOURS/SCO)
NAS: complex middleware	Very high	20,000	260	260	30	15
SSV: architecture, systems software	High	160,000	320	200	24	16
DCO: display, user interface	Moderate	70,000	170	160	30	15
TAS: test and simulation	Low	10,000	110	75	40	11
CMP: mission algorithms	Moderate	15,000	100	100	24	35
CCO: external communications	High	80,000	170	140	64	22
Total: missile warning subsystem	High	355,000	200	160	24	16

- SSV had very high absolute productivity because the automatically generated code, from custom CASE tools, was contained mostly within this CSCI. The above-average team on SSV also contributed to the high productivity.

- DCO was fairly average on all counts but accommodated substantial requirements volatility in the display interface without a contract amendment. The design of this CSCI and the performance of the team were far better than these numbers would indicate.

- TAS had a very low productivity despite being the simplest and most well-understood software. The main reason was that the plan for task resources was far less ambitious than the plans for other teams. Another reason was that the TAS team was located off-site, with highly constrained development environment resources.

- CMP had a very high cost of change and low productivity for no obvious technical reason. To ensure technical integrity, the inherent missile warning algorithm changes were closely scrutinized by many stakeholders. The coordination of this process resulted in very high overhead in CMP productivity and changes.

- CCO had the worst quality metrics. This was due primarily to a design that did not foresee a major message set change and therefore resulted in fairly broad and hard-to-resolve breakage. The CCO team was also perhaps the most difficult to transition (culturally) to the process, metrics, and demonstration approach used on CCPDS-R.

Overall, this level of productivity and quality was approximately double TRW's standard for previous command center software projects.

D.9 PEOPLE FACTORS

CCPDS-R used two unique approaches to managing its people. The first was the core team concept, which focused on leveraging the skills of a few experts across the entire team. The second was targeted at actively avoiding attrition. CCPDS-R was TRW's first large Ada project, and management was concerned that personnel trained by the project would become attractive targets for opportunities elsewhere inside and outside the company. To incentivize people to remain on the project for a long time, the CCPDS-R project instituted an award fee flowdown program.

As a result of the overall management approach to CCPDS-R, there was very little attrition of people across the Common Subsystem, with most of the engineering team transitioning to new assignments at planned points in the life cycle. Contrary to initial expectations, the PDS and STRATCOM subsystems were overlapped enough with the Common Subsystem that most of the people employed were new to the project. The one instance of attrition was the transition of the core architecture team (five NAS experts) back to internally funded research and development projects to productize the NAS CSCI into a commercially available middleware product. This occurred around the time of the CDR milestone.

D.9.1 CORE TEAM

The core team of the CCPDS-R software organization was established early in the concept definition phase to deal explicitly with the important 20% of the software engineering activities that had a high return on investment. In particular, this team of fewer than 10 individuals was responsible for the following:

1. Developing the highest leverage components (mostly within the NAS CSCI). These components resolved many of the difficult computer science issues such as real-time scheduling, interprocess communications, run-time configuration management, error processing, and distributed systems programming. As a result of encapsulating these complex issues in a small number of high-leverage components, the mainstream components were simpler and far less dependent on expert personnel.

2. Setting the standards and procedures for design walkthroughs and software artifacts. In general, the core team represented the frontline pioneers for most of the software activities. This team was generally the first team to conduct any given project workflow and built the first version of most artifacts. Consequently, the core team was intimately involved with setting precedent, whether it was the standards for a given activity or the format/content of a given artifact.

3. Disseminating the culture throughout the software organization. The core team was truly a single, tight-knit team during the inception phase and for most of the elaboration phase. As the process and architecture stabilized, the team started to migrate, with several of its members taking on technical leadership roles on the various development and assessment teams. During construction and transition, a few members of the core team still maintained the architecture integrity across the entire project. However, there was also a set of globally minded individuals with strong relationships to the architecture team who became immersed in other areas of development and assessment. These team and personnel transitions proved to be an invaluable mechanism for maintaining a common culture.

> This core team concept is similar in purpose to the architecture team described in Section 11.2.

D.9.2 AWARD FEE FLOWDOWN PLAN

During the mid-1980s, software expertise was at a premium. TRW software integration business and the general software industry were growing rapidly. Both TRW management and the government customer were acutely concerned about recruiting and retaining a stable, quality software team for the CCPDS-R project. The project also needed to obtain and develop as much Ada experience as possible, and Ada experience was a scarce resource during the early stages of CCPDS-R. TRW proposed an innovative profit sharing approach to enhance the project's ability to attract and retain a complementary team.

The basic premise of the CCPDS-R award fee flowdown plan was that employees would share in the profitability of the project. (Award fees are contract payments over and above the cost basis. They are tied to project performance against predefined criteria.) TRW management agreed to allocate a substantial portion of the award fee pool at each major milestone to be given directly to project employees. This additional compensation was to be distributed to the individuals based on their relative contribution and their longevity on the project. The implementation of the award fee flowdown plan was intended to achieve the following objectives:

- Reward the entire team for excellent project performance
- Reward different peer groups relative to their overall contribution
- Substantially reward the top performers in every peer group
- Minimize attrition of good people

The resulting plan was fairly complex but straightforward to implement. In the end, this plan achieved its goals in minimizing attrition, especially in the early phases of the life cycle, when the loss of key people could have been devastating. In retrospect, the one flaw in the plan was that the early award fees (at PDR and CDR) were far less substantial than the later award fees. As a result, the teams responsible for the construction and transition phases received more award fee flowdown than did the teams working on the inception and elaboration phases.

This was the basic operational concept of the plan:

- Management defined the various peer groups (systems engineering, software engineering, business administration, and administration).

- Every 6 months, the people within each peer group ranked one another with respect to their contribution to the project. The manager of each peer group also ranked the entire team. The manager compiled the results into a global performance ranking of the peer group.

- Each award fee was determined by the customer at certain major milestones. Half of each award fee pool was distributed to project employees.

- The algorithm for distributions to project employees was fairly simple. The general range of additional compensation relative to each employee's salary was about 2% to 10% each year.

  - The distribution to each peer group was made relative to the average salary and total number of people within the group. The differences in employees' salaries within each group defined the relative differences in what was expected of the employees in terms of contributions toward overall project success.

  - The distribution within a peer group had two parts. Half of the total peer group pool was distributed equally among all members. The other half was distributed to the top performers within the peer group as defined by the group's self-ranking. Management had some discretion in the amounts and ranges.

The true impact of this award fee flowdown plan is hard to determine. I think it made a difference in the overall teamwork and in retaining the critical people. The peer rankings worked well in discriminating the top performers. While there were always a few surprises, the peer rankings matched management perceptions pretty closely. The end results of CCPDS-R speak for themselves. Overall, TRW shared a little less than 10% of its overall profit with project employees. CCPDS-R was a very profitable project for TRW and a good value for the Air Force customer. The return on this investment would be considered very high by all stakeholders.

D.10   CONCLUSIONS

TRW and the Air Force have extensively documented the successes of architecture-first development on CCPDS-R. This project achieved twofold increases in productivity and quality along with on-budget, on-schedule deliveries of large mission-critical systems. The success of CCPDS-R is due, in large part, to the balanced use of modern technologies, modern tools, and an iterative development process that is substantially similar to the process described in this book. Table D-15 summarizes the numerous dimensions of improvement incorporated into the CCPDS-R project. The resulting efficiencies were largely attributable to a major reduction in the software scrap and

TABLE D-15. *CCPDS-R technology improvements*

PARAMETER	MODERN SOFTWARE PROCESS	CCPDS-R APPROACH
Environment	Integrated tools	DEC/Rational/custom tools
	Open systems	VAX/DEC-dependent
	Hardware performance	Several VAX family upgrades
	Automation	Custom-developed change management system, metrics tools, code auditors
Size	Reuse, commercial components	Common architecture primitives, tools, processes across all subsystems
	Object oriented	Message-based, object-oriented architecture
	Higher level languages	100% Ada
	CASE tools	Custom automatic code generators for architecture, message input/output, display format source code
	Distributed middleware	Early investment in NAS development for reuse across multiple subsystems
Process	Iterative development	Demonstration, multiple builds, early delivery
	Process maturity models	Level 3 process before SEI CMM definition
	Architecture first	Executable architecture baseline at PDR
	Acquisition reform	Excellent customer/contractor/user teamwork; highly tailored 2167A for iterative development
	Training	Mostly on-the-job training and internal mentoring

rework (less than 25%) enabled by an architecture-first focus, an iterative development process, an enlightened and open-minded customer, and the use of modern environments, languages, and tools.

Overall, the Common Subsystem subsidized much of the groundwork for the PDS and STRATCOM subsystems—namely, the process definition, the tools, and the reusable architecture primitives. This investment paid significant returns on the subsequent subsystems, in which productivity and quality improved. This is the economic expectation of a mature software process such as that developed and evolved on CCPDS-R.

CCPDS-R adhered to DOD-STD-2167A and delivered all the required contract deliverable documents in the Common Subsystem. As the stakeholders gained experience in the new iterative process and demonstration-based reviews, the pressure to deliver ineffective documentation was reduced. The customer and user were far more concerned with the evolving capability than they were with delivered paper.

One of the primary (and subtle) improvements that was enabled by the CCPDS-R software approach was the teamwork between the customer, user, and contractor. Continuous bartering, negotiation, and interpretation of the contract deliverables were productive in making real progress and ensuring that each phase of the life cycle resulted in a win-win situation for all stakeholders.

The level of requirements volatility was moderate, with numerous user interface changes, missile warning algorithm changes, and other requirements changes accommodated throughout the project. On the design side, TRW also incorporated numerous architectural changes, technology insertions, and other design changes from the original technical proposal. Requirements were continuously evolved with designs and were stabilized after CDR as test-to baselines. There was one late, major contract scope change, which was normalized out of most of the data in this case study to provide a more readable presentation. This change occurred around month 35 and involved a complete overhaul of the input message formats into the system. With the intense focus on performance, many components were built with some tight dependencies on the input message formats. Unlike many of the architectural changes, algorithm changes, and display changes, this sort of change was simply not foreseen. Consequently, performance optimizations during design sacrificed some ease of changeability in the message formats. The breakage caused by this change was not as localized as it could have been but was straightforwardly absorbed with predictable performance. The late uptick in rework trends (maintenance changes depicted in Figure D-14) was a result of incorporating this major change. All stakeholders were pleased with the resulting solution.

The requirements volatility described above would have killed most projects using a conventional management approach. CCPDS-R maintained good project performance and nonadversarial relationships among stakeholders throughout the life cycle while continuously absorbing a moderate level of requirements volatility. While this is very difficult to quantify and qualify, I think it was the most significant accomplishment of the entire project.

As discussed in Chapter 15, successful projects tend to provide a balance across the breadth of technologies required. Too great a focus on any technology will not result in success. A balanced effort across the majority of the technologies is necessary to succeed on a large project. CCPDS-R is a perfect example. There was a heavy investment in developing the right process, integrating tools into an effective environment, and developing the architecture components necessary to implement a demonstration-based approach. All stakeholders (developers, managers, customers, and users) were engaged in nonadversarial relationships and working toward a common set of goals.

The CCPDS-R team was successful all along the way. While many people and organizations contributed to the project, the following individuals had a major impact on the overall management approach: Tom Bostelaar, Charles Grauling, Tom Herman, Terry Krupp, Steve Patay, Patti Shishido, and Mike Springman (all from TRW); Gerry LaCroix (Mitre); Paul Heartquist and Bill Wenninger (U.S. Air Force). The project management skill of Don Andres, at TRW, was critical to executing a new software process with a lot of good ideas and to achieving success under the game conditions of a large-scale, nationally important project with tremendous scrutiny from multiple government organizations.

Process Improvement and Mapping to the CMM

The Software Engineering Institute's Capability Maturity Model (SEI CMM) provides a well-known benchmark of software process maturity [SEI, 1993; 1993b; 1995]. The CMM has become a popular vehicle in many domains for assessing the maturity of an organization's software process. This appendix assumes a basic understanding of the CMM and discusses the current state of the CMM as it is generally practiced in the industry. Background on the underlying software process maturity framework is given in *Managing the Software Process* [Humphrey, 1989].

Key Points

▲ The Capability Maturity Model is a good perspective from which to assess the process framework presented in this book. Appropriately implemented and adopted with conviction, the process framework should achieve a level 3 or 4 maturity.

▲ The real indicators of a mature process are predictable results and project performance that demonstrates improvement on subsequent activities.

▲ Having a mature process in place is far more important than merely passing an audit.

▲ A mature process would pass a surprise audit. If an organization says what it does and does what it says, there is no need to prepare for an audit.

E.1 CMM OVERVIEW

The CMM defines five levels of software process maturity based on an organization's support for certain "key" process areas (KPAs). A level 1 (initial) process describes an organization with an immature or undefined process. Level 2 (repeatable), level 3 (defined), level 4 (managed), and level 5 (optimizing) maturities describe organizations with higher levels of software process maturity. The associated KPAs for these levels are summarized as follows:

- Level 2 KPAs: requirements management, software project planning, software project tracking and oversight, software subcontract management, software quality assurance, software configuration management

- Level 3 KPAs: organizational process focus, organizational process definition, training program, integrated software management, software product engineering, intergroup coordination, peer reviews

- Level 4 KPAs: process measurement and analysis, quality management, defect prevention

- Level 5 KPAs: technology innovation, process change management

The goal for most organizations is to achieve a level 3 process. A software capability evaluation (SCE) is commonly used to assess an organization's maturity. An SCE determines whether the organization "says what it does and does what it says" by evaluating the organization's software process (usually in the form of policy statements) and project practices. The organization policy—capturing the "say what you do"—and project implementations—demonstrating the "do what you say"—are evaluated under the KPA framework. The evaluation process is not perfect, but it is a good relative indicator of software process maturity.

A typical SCE uses the SEI Maturity Questionnaire [SEI, 1998] as part of a thorough audit. The evaluation includes detailed analyses, interviews, and other forms of assessment. The questionnaire is generally used as an entry point to provide context for initiating the evaluation.

There have been many different assessments of the distribution of software organizations across the five levels. Table E-1 approximates this distribution for the software industry around 1995.

One of the key drawbacks of the SEI CMM is that the KPAs focus primarily on the document artifacts of the conventional process, such as design, requirements, and traceability documents, as well as subcontracts, contracts, plans, and reports. Very few of the KPAs actually address the evolving engineering artifacts (requirements models, design models, source code, or executable code), the level of process automation in the environment, or the software architecture process. In other words, many of

TABLE E-1. *Industry distribution across maturity levels*

CMM MATURITY LEVEL	FREQUENCY	BASIC PERFORMANCE LEVEL
1 Initial	70%	Unpredictable, high risk
2 Repeatable	15%	Treading water, but surviving
3 Defined	<10%	Stable, predictable, progressing
4 Managed	<5%	Very predictable, trustworthy
5 Optimizing	<1%	Continuously improving

my top 10 principles for a modern process are not addressed at the levels they deserve. Another drawback is the inherent depiction of configuration management and quality assurance as disciplines that are separate from, rather than integral to, all activities of the process.

In practice, the real indicator of process maturity is the level of predictability in project performance. Correlating project performance to the five levels of CMM maturity should demonstrate the following trends:

- Level 1 has random (unpredictable) performance.

- Level 2 achieves repeatable performance from project to project.

- Level 3 shows better performance on successive projects in terms of cost, schedule, or quality.

- Level 4 demonstrates project performance that improves on subsequent projects either substantially in one dimension of performance or significantly across multiple dimensions (for example, cost and quality).

- Level 5 corresponds to off-scale performance on subsequent projects or substantial improvement across all dimensions. Level 5 organizations almost always occupy a very narrow niche.

Figure E-1 summarizes the project performance expected for successive projects of an organization at a given maturity level.

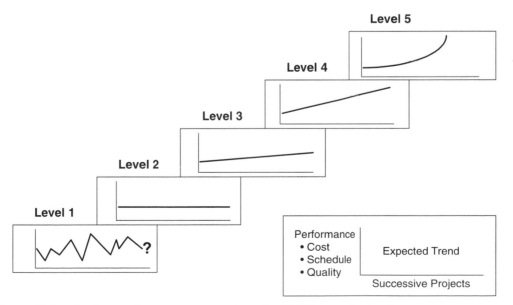

FIGURE E-1. *Project performance expectations for CMM maturity levels*

Many organizations can put up the facade necessary to be assessed at level 3. Consequently, a level 3 process is not necessarily a good process. On the other hand, a really good process should easily achieve a level 3 rating. From my field experience with dozens of software process assessments and software capability evaluations, I have learned some other indicators of a truly mature process:

- Objective understanding of current maturity

- Objective understanding of project performance in quantifiable terms of cost and quality

- Real project performance improvement

- Minimal time needed to prepare for an evaluation

A mature organization and mature projects know the process and follow it. They do not need to spend time preparing for an audit. If you think your organization is a level 3, answer this: Could it withstand a surprise audit?

E.2   PRAGMATIC PROCESS IMPROVEMENT

This section contains some descriptive and prescriptive thoughts about the general themes of process improvement. My goal is to instill a proper balance of hope and fear about the promises of process improvement.

- Process maturity. Compliance with quality process frameworks such as the SEI CMM does not necessarily result in the development of quality products. However, a truly high-quality process that produces quality products will be assessed as mature. One drawback of most process frameworks is that they specify a statically defined quality assurance program as someone's separate job rather than integrate quality assurance dynamically into all jobs.

- Cost of a mature process. A mature process does *not* cost more money. On the contrary, it always saves money in the long run. Because improving an immature process changes their spending profiles, organizations usually perceive a near-term cost for process improvement. The important point here is that selling process improvement to in-process projects, which are dominated by near-term cost concerns, is very difficult. Process improvement is sellable, however, to organizations that are more concerned with long-term business pursuits, and to long-term projects still in the planning stage.

- Software metrics. Objective measures are required for assessing the quality of a software product and the progress of the work—two different perspectives of a software effort. Architects are more concerned with quality indicators, while managers are usually more concerned with progress indicators. The success of any software process whose metrics are collected manually will be limited. The most important software metrics are simple, objective measures of how various perspectives of the product/project are changing. Absolute measures are usually much less important than relative changes with respect to time. Because of the dynamic nature of software projects, these measures must be available at any time, be tailorable to various subsets of the evolving product (subsystem, release, version, component, team), and be maintained so that trends can be assessed (first and second derivatives). Such continuous availability has been achieved in practice only when the metrics were maintained on-line as an automated by-product of the development environment.

- Process tailoring. Different software efforts require different processes. While there are some universal themes and techniques, there are also situation-dependent differences in techniques, priorities, ceremony, and emphasis. Different software development situations have different needs that span a range of good processes. An organization's internal process for product development will not be exactly the same as the process used by projects developing large operational systems on contract with an external customer.

- Process versus method. A project management process deals with different concerns than a technical method does. The former is characterized by iterative development, demonstration-based evaluation, and risk management, the latter by object-oriented techniques, architectural approaches, and UML representations. Although a bad management process will probably never be saved by a good method, a good management process can succeed with most technical methods. Clearly, some methods are better than others. The result of a good design method coupled with a good management process is profound. This is the goal.

E.3   MATURITY QUESTIONNAIRE

The remainder of this section provides an SEI CMM perspective of the process framework presented in this book. I have used the SEI Maturity Questionnaire [SEI, 1998] as a scenario for evaluating the completeness of the process framework from a well-accepted benchmark of process maturity. In the pages that follow, each quoted question is presented in *italics*, followed by my generic response with references to the artifacts, activities, and checkpoints of the process framework.

In some responses, such as those associated with training, the process framework does not prescribe a specific approach. These responses are organization-specific, which means that an organization would need a mechanism specific to its internal practices and culture.

Requirements Management, Level 2

1. *Are system requirements allocated to software used to establish a baseline for software engineering and management use?*

   ▲ Software requirements are captured in the vision statement and in the use case model. Each iteration is accompanied by a release specification that captures the objectives for intermediate milestones. All these artifacts are baselined and are subjected to change management discipline.

2. *As the systems requirements are allocated to software change, are the necessary adjustments to software plans, work products, and activities made?*

   ▲ In an iterative development, each new iteration is accompanied by new release specifications and updates to the technical artifacts. The purpose of type 3 software change orders (SCOs) is to address changes caused by changes in requirements.

3. *Does the project follow a written organizational policy for managing the system requirements allocated to software?*

   ▲ An organizational policy should include an explicit approach for defining and managing all the project artifacts, including the requirements set artifacts.

4. *Are the people in the project who are charged with managing the allocated requirements trained in the procedures for managing allocated requirements?*

   ▲ Training is an organization-specific issue.

5. *Are measurements used to determine the status of the activities performed for managing the allocated requirements (e.g., total number of requirements changes that are proposed, open, approved, and incorporated into the baseline)?*

   ▲ Type 3 SCOs should be tracked and reported in periodic status assessments.

6. *Are the activities for managing allocated requirements on the project subjected to SQA review?*

   ▲ Quality assurance is the responsibility of all teams. The independent test organization, which has primary responsibility for software quality assurance, does not merely review the management of allocated requirements; it actively participates in generating the release specifications, release description, and traceability to the requirements set. The Configuration Control Board (CCB) also reviews change requirements captured in the SCOs. Requirements set artifacts are also "reviewed" through the engineering activities associated with evolving use case models, design set artifacts, implementation set artifacts, and demonstrations of deployment set artifacts.

Software Project Planning, Level 2

1. *Are estimates (e.g., size, cost, and schedule) documented for use in planning and tracking the software project?*

   ▲ The WBS defines the cost baseline and plan. The business case and software development plan define the schedule baseline and iteration content, as well as the size baseline, from several perspectives. The status assessments provide the tracking mechanism for comparing progress and quality against the baseline plans and adjustments to plans. At lower levels, SCOs document detailed estimates, plans, and actuals.

2. *Do the software plans document the activities to be performed and the commitments made for the software project?*

   ▲ The business case and software development plan describe the high-level activities to be performed and are signed off by the software project manager as a commitment. The WBS documents the cost baselines and commitments for all levels of management. SCOs also document lower level activities and commitments.

3. *Do all affected groups and individuals agree to their commitments related to the software project?*

   ▲ The work breakdown structure (WBS) provides the mechanism for negotiating commitments between the software project manager and subordinate managers. SCOs and the CCB provide a mechanism for negotiating lower level commitments.

4. *Does the project follow a written organizational policy for planning a software project?*

   ▲ Organizational policy should provide the organizational baseline from which projects are planned. The organization's infrastructure should also provide access to precedent experience and default planning benchmarks.

5. *Are adequate resources provided for planning the software project (e.g., funding and experienced individuals)?*

   ▲ The software project manager, who is accountable for the plan, should create it and take ownership in its success. The business case contains the expectations and commitments necessary for the organization to determine the return on investment

(ROI) for the effort. The adequacy of planning resources is not specified by policy. A good target benchmark is that about 10% of a project's effort should be allocated to planning and management activities. While the determination of adequate resources is project-specific, these assessments would come under the scrutiny of the organization's Project Review Authority (PRA) and would be reviewed at each major milestone.

6. *Are measurements used to determine the status of the activities for planning the software project (e.g., completion of milestones for the project planning activities as compared to the plan)?*

   ▲ The progress metrics are specifically designed to provide insight into the critical perspectives of plan versus actuals (development progress, test progress, evaluation criteria passed, scenarios executed, SLOC developed, SCOs closed versus opened, etc.).

7. *Does the project manager review the activities for planning the software project on both a periodical and an event-driven basis?*

   ▲ The status assessments ensure that the software project manager is held accountable for addressing the necessary management indicators and assessing risk periodically. Major milestones and release descriptions provide a similar forcing function for event-driven assessments.

Software Project Tracking and Oversight, Level 2

1. *Are the project's actual results (e.g., schedule, size, and cost) compared with estimates in the software plans?*

   ▲ Status assessments compare planned results with actual results for progress indicators. The release descriptions compare planned quality indicators (evaluation criteria) with actual results. SCOs also document planned versus actual results for detailed change management.

2. *Is corrective action taken when actual results differ significantly from the project's software plans?*

   ▲ Failed evaluation criteria should be addressed in release descriptions and subsequent iterations. Other deviations from plan are addressed in status assessments, where follow-through is required and tracked.

3. *Are changes in the software commitments agreed to by all affected groups and individuals?*

   ▲ Changes in commitment are negotiated through the evolving WBS, software development plans, and status assessments. Low-level commitments are also addressed by CCBs, tracked on SCOs, and accounted for in release descriptions.

4. *Does the project follow a written organizational policy for both tracking and controlling its software development activities?*

▲ Organizational policy should define the standard status assessment format for a certain set of topics so that cross-project comparisons are possible.

5. *Is someone on the project assigned specific responsibilities for tracking software work products and activities (e.g., effort, schedule, and budget)?*

▲ The software project manager is the responsible individual. Status assessments provide the mechanism for ensuring periodic review and accountability in conjunction with a WBS baseline.

6. *Are measurements used to determine the status of the activities for software tracking and oversight (e.g., total effort expended in performing tracking and oversight activities)?*

▲ WBS expenditures and progress metrics provide the mechanism for tracking the status of activities and enable instrumentation and oversight of the entire software effort.

7. *Are the activities for software project tracking and oversight reviewed with senior management on a periodic basis (e.g., project performance, open issues, risks, and action items)?*

▲ This is exactly the purpose of the business case (which is updated at life-cycle phase transitions), status assessments, and major milestone reviews.

Software Subcontract Management, Level 2

While subcontracting is not specifically addressed by the process framework, all the techniques, tools, and mechanisms are assumed to be flowed down to subcontractors so that the process remains homogeneous. If this cannot be done, or if the prime contractor cannot define a well-partitioned piece of work to be performed by a mature subcontractor, subcontracting should be avoided. To manage risks effectively, the number and complexity of organizational interfaces must be managed. All subcontracting decisions should be documented in the business case.

1. *Is a documented procedure used for selecting subcontractors based on their ability to perform the work?*

▲ Organizational policy should require all personnel on a project, including software subcontractors, to follow a single development plan. Projects should employ subcontractors that have been assessed as having a process that is at least as mature as that of the project's parent organization. (In other words, a level 3 organization should not employ a level 2 subcontractor.)

2. *Are changes to subcontracts made with the agreement of both the prime contractor and the subcontractor?*

   ▲ Common sense suggests this would always be the case.

3. *Are periodic technical interchanges held with subcontractors?*

   ▲ Subcontractors following the same development plan would participate in the same technical interchanges, major milestones, and status assessments.

4. *Are the results and performance of the software subcontractor tracked against their commitments?*

   ▲ Subcontractors following the same development plan would be tracked against their commitments in the same way that the prime contractor is tracked.

5. *Does the project follow a written organizational policy for managing software subcontracts?*

   ▲ Policy documents require that subcontractors follow the process that the prime contractor follows.

6. *Are the people responsible for managing software subcontracts trained in managing software subcontracts?*

   ▲ Training is an organization-specific issue.

7. *Are measurements used to determine the status of the activities for managing software subcontracts (e.g., schedule status with respect to planned delivery dates and effort expended for managing the subcontract)?*

   ▲ Subcontractors should be managed in the same homogeneous way as the prime contractor.

8. *Are the software subcontract activities reviewed with the project manager on both a periodic and event-driven basis?*

   ▲ Subcontractors should be managed by the software project manager in the same way as the rest of the project team. All subcontractor commitment decisions are documented in the business case, which is updated at life-cycle phase transitions.

Software Quality Assurance, Level 2

All activities and all people are involved in SQA. The use of an independent assessment team is recommended to enable quality assessment activities, such as testing and metrics analysis, to be performed concurrently (for schedule efficiency) and independently (for diversity of technical perspective). Accountability for quality resides in the various teams within an organization. For the purpose of answering this questionnaire, however, the activities of the independent assessment team correlate most closely to the CMM definition of SQA.

1. *Are SQA activities planned?*

   ▲ The software development plan describes the test activities, metrics, and quality control activities. The WBS captures many of the details of the plan. Release specifications are also mechanisms for planning the SQA activities.

2. *Do SQA activities provide objective verification that software products and activities adhere to applicable standards, procedures, and requirements?*

   ▲ Release specifications identify the objectives of an iteration. Software development plans identify the project standards and procedures. Release specifications also describe the quality of intermediate products from the perspective of objective pass/fail criteria. CCBs and SCOs verify that low-level standards and procedures are checked and tracked. Automated tools within the environment (compilers, documentation production, change management) should be burdened with assuring that products adhere to applicable standards.

3. *Are the results of SQA reviews and audits provided to affected groups and individuals (e.g., those who performed the work and those who are responsible for the work)?*

   ▲ All the process checkpoints and CCB activities are SQA reviews. Intermediate results are documented periodically in release descriptions. All SCOs are addressed by the CCB with participation by affected groups.

4. *Are issues of noncompliance that are not resolved within the project addressed by senior management (e.g., deviations from applicable standards)?*

   ▲ This is one of the explicit purposes of PRA approval of the development plans and status assessments. Periodic PRA reviews address any proposed deviations from organizational policy as the project progresses.

5. *Does the project follow a written organizational policy for implementing SQA?*

   ▲ Organizational policy and software development plans should provide the written SQA policies for the organization and projects, respectively.

6. *Are adequate resources provided for performing SQA activities (e.g., funding and a designated manager who will receive and act on software noncompliance items)?*

▲ The adequacy of SQA resources is not specified by policy. A good target benchmark is that about 25% of a project's effort should be allocated to assessment team activities (testing, assessment, metrics, CCB). While the determination of adequate resources and individuals is project-specific, these assessments would clearly come under the scrutiny of the PRA.

7. *Are measurements used to determine the cost and schedule status of the activities performed for SQA (e.g., work completed, effort, and funds expended compared to the plan)?*

▲ The WBS provides the baseline, and the periodic status assessments track actuals versus plan for all activities.

8. *Are activities for SQA reviewed with senior management on a periodic basis?*

▲ This is one of the explicit purposes of PRA reviews and PRA approval of the software development plan.

Software Configuration Management, Level 2

All activities and all people are involved with SCM, just as they are with SQA. An independent assessment team assumes primary responsibility for configuration control activities, including SCO database maintenance, CCB administration, and baseline management. These activities should be performed concurrently (for schedule efficiency) and independently (for diversity of technical perspective). In general, SCM activities are practiced by all software engineers and are supported primarily by the software engineering environment. For the purpose of answering this questionnaire, the activities of the assessment team correlate most closely to the CMM definition of SCM.

1. *Are software configuration management activities planned for the project?*

▲ The software development plan should document the SCM activities and support them with automation.

2. *Has the project identified, controlled, and made available the software work products through the use of configuration management?*

▲ SCOs and all artifacts are configuration-controlled.

3. *Does the project follow a documented procedure to control changes to configuration items/units?*

▲ SCOs provide the on-line mechanism for change control as documented in the organizational policy and software development plan.

4. Are standard reports on software baselines (e.g., software configuration control board minutes and change request summary and status reports) distributed to affected groups and individuals?

▲ Status assessments, which contain the CCB results in the form of standard metrics, should be available to all stakeholders and project teams.

5. Does the project follow a written organizational policy for implementing software configuration management activities?

▲ This is provided by the organizational policy and software development plans.

6. Are project personnel trained to perform the software configuration management activities for which they are responsible?

▲ Training is an organization-specific issue. In general, everyone in the software organization practices configuration management as enforced by the environment. The formal configuration management activities of the independent test group are primarily administrative control and reporting.

7. Are measurements used to determine the status of activities for software configuration management (e.g., effort and funds expended for software configuration management activities)?

▲ The WBS provides the baseline, and the periodic status assessments track actuals versus plan for all activities.

8. Are periodic audits performed to verify that software baselines conform to the documentation that defines them (e.g., by the SCM group)?

▲ CCBs are the most frequent audits that verify consistency on an SCO-by-SCO basis. Release descriptions provide an integrated quality, completeness, and consistency audit of the interim baselines created for major milestones.

Organization Process Focus, Level 3

1. Are the activities for developing and improving the organization's and project's software processes coordinated across the organization (e.g., via a software engineering process group)?

▲ All development plans and status assessments are reviewed and approved by the Software Engineering Process Authority (SEPA). These mechanisms provide for coordination and consistency across the organization.

2. Is your organization's software process assessed periodically?

▲ The SEPA is responsible for periodic assessments such as trend analyses. These assessments should be planned and quantified in an appendix to the organizational policy.

3. *Does your organization follow a documented plan for developing and improving its software process?*

▲ The SEPA should document this plan as an appendix to the organizational policy.

4. *Does senior management sponsor the organization's activities for software process development and improvements (e.g., by establishing long-term plans, and by committing resources and funding)?*

▲ The extent to which senior management sponsors these activities should be easy to evaluate from the composition of the SEPA and details of the organizational policy. Another indicator of management sponsorship is the extent to which the organization's process is backed up with capital investments in automation.

5. *Do one or more individuals have full-time or part-time responsibility for the organization's software process activities (e.g., a software engineering process group)?*

▲ The SEPA has this responsibility. Whether this is a single person part-time or a team of people full-time depends on the specific organization.

6. *Are measurements used to determine the status of the activities performed to develop and improve the organization's software process (e.g., effort expended for software process assessment and improvement)?*

▲ The organizational policy should address the ROI of the SEPA activities and should be updated periodically.

7. *Are the activities performed for developing and improving software processes reviewed periodically with senior management?*

▲ The organization general manager should be required to approve all periodic updates to the organizational policy.

Organization Process Definition, Level 3

1. *Has your organization developed, and does it maintain, a standard software process?*

▲ The organizational policy defines the standard software process and is updated periodically.

2. *Does the organization collect, review, and make available information related to the use of the organization's standard software process (e.g., estimates and actual data on software size, effort, and cost; productivity data; and quality measurements)?*

   ▲ The SEPA attends all status assessments and maintains a library of organizational assets, including status assessment results, software development plans, past project perfomance data, and other standard organizational tools and components.

3. *Does the organization follow a written policy for both developing and maintaining its standard software process?*

   ▲ Organizational policy defines the standard process and its maintenance.

4. *Do individuals who develop and maintain the organization's standard software process receive the required training to perform these activities?*

   ▲ Training is an organization-specific issue.

5. *Are measurements used to determine the status of the activities performed to define and maintain the organization's standard software process (e.g., status of schedule milestones and the cost of process definition activities)?*

   ▲ An appendix to the organizational policy should address the ROI of the SEPA activities.

6. *Are the activities and work products for developing and maintaining the organization's standard software process subject to SQA review and audit?*

   ▲ The activities and work products are continuously reviewed by practitioners. The organization general manager should convene the appropriate review authority as necessary to ensure that the organizational process collateral is adequate. The SEPA is the chief organizational SQA authority. The buck stops there unless the general manager intervenes.

Training Program, Level 3

1. *Are training activities planned?*

   ▲ Training is an organization-specific issue.

2. *Is training **provided** for developing the skills and knowledge needed to perform software managerial and technical roles?*

   ▲ Training is an organization-specific issue.

3. *Do members of the software engineering group and other software-related groups **receive** the training necessary to perform their roles?*

▲ Training is an organization-specific issue.

4. *Does your organization follow a written organizational policy to meet its training needs?*

▲ Training is an organization-specific issue.

5. *Are adequate resources provided to implement the organization's training program (e.g., funding, software tools, appropriate training facilities)?*

▲ Training is an organization-specific issue.

6. *Are measurements used to determine the quality of the training program?*

▲ Training is an organization-specific issue.

7. *Are training program activities reviewed with senior management on a periodic basis?*

▲ Training is an organization-specific issue.

Integrated Software Management, Level 3

1. *Was the **project's** defined software process developed by tailoring the **organization's** standard software process?*

▲ The organizational policy specifies the mandatory mechanisms, the starting point, and the degrees of freedom for establishing a project process. The project process is reviewed and approved by the SEPA.

2. *Is the project planned and managed in accordance with the project's defined software process?*

▲ The software project manager authors and approves the software development plan and is held accountable for the plan through periodic PRA reviews.

3. *Does the project follow a written organizational policy requiring that the software project be planned and managed using the organization's standard software process?*

▲ The organizational policy is the written policy.

4. *Is training required for individuals tasked to tailor the organization's standard software process to define a software process for a new project?*

▲ Training is an organization-dependent issue. The software project manager should author the software development plan.

5. *Are measurements used to determine the effectiveness of the integrated software management activities (e.g., frequency, causes and magnitude of replanning efforts)?*

▲ Projects use status assessments, including required metrics, to assess progress and quality performance. The metrics are collected and analyzed by the SEPA and PRA to determine effectiveness and any improvements required.

6. *Are the activities and work products used to manage the software project subjected to SQA review and audit?*

▲ The software development plan is reviewed by both the PRA and the SEPA (organizational SQA).

Software Product Engineering, Level 3

1. *Are the software work products produced according to the project's defined software process?*

▲ The software project manager is responsible for compliance with the software development plan. Any deviations from plan or standards (or both) are reviewed periodically through status assessments and are accommodated as appropriate in subsequent iterations or product baselines.

2. *Is consistency maintained across software work products (e.g., is the documentation tracing allocated requirements through software requirements, design, code, and test cases maintained)?*

▲ The CCB provides continuous attention to change management traceability. Release descriptions are a mechanism for assessing consistency and completeness of the work products of a major milestone. Traceability among the engineering sets (use case models, design models, source code, and executable components) is maintained by the environment. The extent to which such information is summarized or detailed to ensure completeness depends on the scale of the project and the stakeholder concerns (for example, safety), and is captured in release descriptions.

3. *Does the project follow a written organizational policy for performing the software engineering activities (e.g., a policy which requires the use of appropriate methods and tools for building and maintaining software products)?*

▲ The organizational policy requires specific activities and a standard environment for the purpose of standardizing methods or tools across projects. Many of the methods and tools are left open to project-specific selection.

4. *Are adequate resources provided for performing the software engineering tasks (e.g., funding, skilled individuals, and appropriate tools)?*

▲ The adequacy of software engineering resources is not specified by policy. A good benchmark is that about 50% of a project's effort should be allocated to software engineering tasks: 10% in requirements, 15% in design, and 25% in component implementation. The determination of adequate resources and individuals is project-specific and should be scrutinized by the PRA.

5. *Are measurements used to determine the functionality and quality of the software products (e.g., numbers, types, and severity of defects identified)?*

▲ The explicit purpose of the metrics required and reported in status assessments is to assess progress and quality.

6. *Are the activities and work products for engineering software subjected to SQA reviews and audits (e.g., is required testing performed, are allocated requirements traced through the software requirements, design, code, and test cases)?*

▲ All the engineering sets (technical artifacts) are evolved and updated at each major milestone. SCOs, CCBs, and release descriptions force continuous attention to traceability.

Intergroup Coordination, Level 3

This set of questions is specifically supported by a focus on architecture. Intergroup coordination is specifically associated with software architecture because architecture encompasses the intercomponent and human-to-human interfaces.

1. *On the project, do the software engineering group and other engineering groups collaborate with the customer to establish the system requirements?*

▲ The project vision statement and the release specifications are the responsibility of the software architecture group. They are negotiated with the customer and are evolved at each iteration.

2. *Do the engineering groups agree to the commitments as represented in the overall project plan?*

▲ The software development plans, release specifications, and WBS define the commitments and plans.

3. *Do the engineering groups identify, track, and resolve intergroup issues (e.g., incompatible schedules, technical risks, or system-level problems)?*

▲ Demonstrations are the mechanism for productive and tangible engineering coordination at an architectural level. CCBs provide intergroup resolution on the level of SCOs. Proper scheduling of architecture demonstrations enables integration issues to be resolved as early in the life cycle as possible. Proper scheduling also enhances early resolution of important intergroup issues.

4. *Is there a written organizational policy that guides the establishment of interdisciplinary engineering teams?*

▲ CCBs, PRAs, and demonstration teams are established interdisciplinary engineering teams.

5. *Do the support tools used by different engineering groups enable effective communication and coordination (e.g., compatible word processing systems, database systems, and problem tracking systems)?*

▲ Standard work breakdown structures, standard environments, and the SCO database enable the various engineering groups to coordinate within a common framework. Within a project, the artifacts developed by all teams should use common notations, methods, and tools.

6. *Are measures used to determine the status of the intergroup coordination activities (e.g., effort expended by the software engineering group to support other groups)?*

▲ Tracking the efforts of the architecture team provides insight into the stability of the architecture. Stability is a good indicator of effective intergroup coordination. Because the architecture team is separate, with explicit WBS elements, tracking can be achieved more easily through the defined management and quality metrics reported in the periodic status assessments.

7. *Are the activities for intergroup coordination reviewed with the project manager on both a periodic and event-driven basis?*

▲ A good architecture-first approach plans the first iterations to expose any significant issues in intergroup coordination. Periodic status assessments and major milestone events provide tangible and objective insight into intergroup coordination through observation of architecture metrics.

Peer Reviews, Level 3

The process framework does not specifically call for peer reviews in the classic sense. However, there are several mechanisms whose purpose is exactly that of classic peer reviews. These mechanisms include demonstrations (global integration peer reviews), CCBs (change management peer reviews), status assessments (management peer reviews), and conventional peer reviews (code walkthroughs, inspections), as incorporated by project software development plans.

1. *Are peer reviews planned?*

   ▲ CCBs, status assessments, and demonstrations should be planned and followed through in a systematic way.

2. *Are actions associated with defects that are identified during peer reviews tracked until they are removed?*

   ▲ All defects, independent of source, are tracked via SCOs, and the metrics are reported in the status assessments.

3. *Does the project follow a written organizational policy for performing peer reviews?*

   ▲ Organizational policy should require CCBs, demonstrations, and status assessments. It should also specify that other forms of peer reviews be defined in the project's software development plan.

4. *Do participants of peer reviews receive the training required to perform their roles?*

   ▲ Training is an organization-specific issue.

5. *Are measurements used to determine the status of peer review activities (e.g., number of peer reviews performed, effort expended on peer reviews, and number of work products reviewed compared to the plan)?*

   ▲ CCBs provide extensive change management metrics. Release descriptions require the same ROI metrics to be collected for demonstrations. The SEPA periodically assesses the ROI of organizational trend analyses from status assessment data.

6. *Are peer review activities and work products subject to SQA review and audit (e.g., planned reviews are conducted and follow-up actions are tracked)?*

   ▲ Software project managers, CCBs, and PRAs provide continuous follow-through.

Quantitative Process Management, Level 4

1. *Does the project follow a documented plan for conducting quantitative process management?*

   ▲ An appendix to the organizational policy should define the plan for quantitative process improvement. Status assessments evaluate collected metrics in the context of organizational norms maintained by the SEPA.

2. *Is the performance of the **project's** defined software process controlled quantitatively (e.g., through the use of quantitative analytic methods)?*

▲ The data are collected and reported to the SEPA through status assessments. These metrics are fed back into the planning of each subsequent iteration.

3. *Is the process capability of the **organization's** standard software process known in quantitative terms?*

▲ An appendix to the organizational policy should define the current process assessment and the plan for process improvement in quantitative terms.

4. *Does the project follow a written organizational policy for measuring and controlling the performance of the project's defined software process (e.g., projects plan for how to identify, specify, and control special causes of variation)?*

▲ The software development plan should define a metrics program for measuring and controlling the software process. It should also require that this process (and its control mechanisms) be evolved and improved as the project progresses.

5. *Are adequate resources provided for quantitative process management activities (e.g., funding, software support tools, and organizational measurement program)?*

▲ The adequacy of process management resources is not specified by policy. A good benchmark is that a team about the size of the square root of the number of active projects is sufficient.

6. *Are measurements used to determine the status of the quantitative process management activities (e.g., cost of quantitative process management activities and accomplishment of milestones for quantitative process management activities)?*

▲ An appendix to the organizational policy should address the ROI of the SEPA activities.

7. *Are the activities for quantitative process management reviewed with the project manager on both a periodic and event-driven basis?*

▲ Status assessments and major milestones provide periodic and event-driven reviews of quantitative process management data.

Software Quality Management, Level 4

1. *Are the activities for managing software quality planned for the project?*

▲ Release specifications identify the expectations for the quality metrics. These specifications are established for each iteration and are documented in status assessments (in-progress snapshots) and release descriptions (major milestone baselines).

2. *Does the project use measurable and prioritized goals for managing the quality of its software products (e.g., functionality, reliability, maintainability, and usability)?*

   ▲ This is the purpose of the release specifications and associated demonstrations, release descriptions, and metrics.

3. *Are measurements of quality compared to goals for software product quality to determine if the quality goals are satisfied?*

   ▲ The project vision statement, release specifications, and release descriptions track the achievement of quality goals. Status assessments also provide periodic insight into the achievement of a certain minimum set of quality indicators.

4. *Does the project follow a written organizational policy for managing software quality?*

   ▲ Organizational policy defines the mechanisms for managing software quality (release specifications, release descriptions, quality metrics, PRAs, and CCB/SCOs).

5. *Do members of the software engineering group and other software-related groups receive required training in software quality management (e.g., training in collecting measurement data and benefits of quantitatively managing product quality)?*

   ▲ Training is an organization-specific issue.

6. *Are measurements used to determine the status of the activities for managing software quality (e.g., the costs of poor quality)?*

   ▲ The scrap and rework metrics provide proven indicators of process performance in achieving quality and of the costs associated with reworking inadequate quality in intermediate products.

7. *Are the activities performed for software quality management reviewed with senior management on a periodic basis?*

   ▲ Quality activities and metrics should be reviewed periodically with senior management.

Defect Prevention, Level 5

1. *Are defect prevention activities planned?*

   ▲ Not addressed.

2. *Does the project conduct causal analysis meetings to identify common causes of defects?*

▲ Not addressed.

3. *Once identified, are common causes of defects prioritized and systematically eliminated?*

   ▲ Not addressed.

4. *Does the project follow a written organizational policy for defect prevention activities?*

   ▲ Not addressed.

5. *Do members of the software engineering group and other software-related groups receive required training to perform their defect prevention activities (e.g., training in defect prevention methods and the conduct of task kick-off or causal analysis meetings)?*

   ▲ Training is an organization-specific issue.

6. *Are measurements used to determine the status of defect prevention activities (e.g., the time and cost for identifying and correcting defects and the number of action items proposed, open, and completed)?*

   ▲ Projects must use a set of metrics for determining the effectiveness and status of defects. Defect prevention activities are not specifically addressed or formalized, but the primitives are well defined via the management and quality metrics. PRA reviews, SCOs, and CCBs provide mechanisms for practicing defect prevention.

7. *Are the activities and work products for defect prevention subjected to SQA review and audit?*

   ▲ All status assessments and PRA reviews are provided to the SEPA (for organization SQA). Status assessments are distributed to project personnel and stakeholders, and SCO data are reviewed in CCBs to verify that all personnel are contributing to the SQA of defect prevention data.

Technology Change Management, Level 5

1. *Does the organization follow a plan for managing technology changes?*

   ▲ Not addressed.

2. *Are new technologies evaluated to determine their effect on quality and productivity?*

   ▲ Not addressed.

3. *Does the organization follow a documented procedure for incorporating new technologies into the **organization's** standard software process?*

▲ Not addressed.

4. *Does senior management sponsor the organization's activities for managing technology change (e.g., by establishing long-term plans and commitments for funding, staffing, and other resources)?*

   ▲ Not addressed.

5. *Do process data exist to assist in the selection of new technology?*

   ▲ Not addressed.

6. *Are measurements used to determine the status of the organization's activities for managing technology change (e.g., the effect of implementing technology changes)?*

   ▲ Not addressed.

7. *Are the organization's activities for managing technology change reviewed with senior management on a periodic basis?*

   ▲ Not addressed.

Process Change Management, Level 5

1. *Does the organization follow a documented procedure for developing and maintaining plans for software process improvement?*

   ▲ The organizational policy should include an appendix on process improvement.

2. *Do people throughout your organization participate in software process improvement activities (e.g., on teams to develop software process improvements)?*

   ▲ The SEPA and PRAs participate. Other participation is organization-specific.

3. *Are improvements continually made to the organization's standard software process and the project's defined software processes?*

   ▲ Each new iteration of a project is an opportunity to inject process improvements into the software development plan. Organizational policy also requires periodic reassessment and improvement.

4. *Does the organization follow a written policy for implementing software process improvements?*

   ▲ The written policy should be included as an appendix to the organizational policy.

5. *Is training in software process improvement required for both management and technical staff?*

   ▲ Training is an organization-specific issue.

6. *Are measurements made to determine the status of the activities for software process improvement (e.g., the effect of implementing each process improvement compared to its defined goals)?*

   ▲ The organizational policy and SEPA should be required to assess the ROI of organizational improvement activities periodically.

7. *Are software process improvement efforts reviewed with senior management on a periodic basis?*

   ▲ The general manager of the organization should be responsible for approving all changes to the organizational policy.

E.4   QUESTIONS NOT ASKED BY THE MATURITY QUESTIONNAIRE

To assess the maturity of an organization's process, I would ask several other sets of questions that are not currently addressed by the CMM key process areas. Whereas the preceding responses track directly to the Maturity Questionnaire, the following questions correspond to other policies, mechanisms, and approaches of a modern process for which the CMM provides little motivation. These additions to the Questionnaire would help in the evaluation of additional discriminators of a successful modern process framework.

Personnel Accountability, Level 2

One important goal of controlled software management is clear delineation of responsibility and mechanisms for accountability. Consequently, the following questions should also be asked in an assessment of an organization's process implementation:

1. Does the organization define a role for maintaining its process description and assets?

2. Does the SEPA role have a track record of influencing projects and corporate strategy?

3. Do software project managers author their development plans?

4. Do software project managers present their status assessments themselves?

Environment Automation, Level 3

An organization that lacks a significant level of automation is unlikely to have a truly mature process. Answers to the following questions will help in evaluating an organization's automation level:

1. Does the organizational policy define a minimum core environment?
2. Does the environment support metrics collection as a natural by-product of the process?
3. Is documentation an automated, homogeneous by-product of software engineering (as opposed to a separate, heterogeneous artifact)?
4. Is round-trip engineering adequately supported by automation?
5. Are test artifacts developed and maintained with the same tools, techniques, and change management as the product artifacts?
6. Is the regression testing adequately supported by automation?
7. Are randomized scenarios and after-hours tests used to ensure statistical test coverage?
8. Are the language editors, configuration management environment, compiler, and debugger integrated?

Architecture Engineering, Level 3

An organization that lacks a significant and systematic focus on architecture is unlikely to have a truly mature process. Answers to the following questions will help in evaluating this perspective:

1. Is instrumentation available for providing objective insight into the execution characteristics of demonstrations (as opposed to being custom-developed on each project)?
2. Are peer inspections focused on the truly critical components?
3. Is there a well-articulated definition of architecture?
4. Is there a rigorous design notation from which design progress, design volatility, and design qualities can be objectively assessed?
5. Does the architecture team exhibit expertise in both the domain knowledge and the relevant software engineering disciplines?

Change Management, Level 3

In an iterative development process, the management of changes and the extent of change freedom are key indications of process maturity.

1. Are software changes defined unambiguously in terms of type and priority?

2. Are measurements of change collected, reported, and analyzed?

3. Are roles and responsibilities for maintaining the change management database defined and enforced?

4. Is there a mechanism for verifying that the originator of a change request is satisfied with the change implementation?

5. Is there a track record of changes as well as demonstrated change avoidance for risk management purposes?

Predictability, Level 3

The best indication of a mature process is predictable results.

1. Does the organization maintain plan versus actual data?

2. Is there a documented correlation between plan versus actuals on recent projects?

3. Are historical plans and actuals used in current projects?

4. Is there a track record of action where plan and actuals diverge?

Integrated Economics, Level 4

The appropriate economic motivations should be woven into an organization's process.

1. Are there sufficient organizational standards to define the metrics primitives so that measurements across projects are comparable?

2. Are measurements from previous iterations used systematically in the planning of subsequent iterations?

3. Does the SEPA assess the current state of the organization's process maturity?

4. Are the process improvement activities of an organization measured against the return on investment?

5. Do software project managers generally believe that the SEPA adds value to their project?

E.5   OVERALL PROCESS ASSESSMENT

The responses given here suggest that an organization that has implemented the process framework described in this book would be at least a strong SEI level 3, and arguably a level 4. A sure sign that an organization has achieved this level of maturity would be its ability to (1) expand on the responses of this document with more-detailed explanations of organization-specific and project-specific implementations, and (2) back up each response with specific examples from experience in the field. If the process of preparing for such a process audit requires more than 1 or 2 staff-weeks, the organization's Software Engineering Process Authority is probably more a facade than a useful factor in the organization's operation. The collateral needed for a process audit should be a natural by-product of the project management process.

Glossary

Adaptability   The rework trend over time

Architecture   The significant structure and behavior of a system, including all engineering specifications necessary to determine a complete bill of materials with a high level of confidence

Architecture first   An approach that requires a demonstrable balance to be achieved among the driving requirements, the architecturally significant design decisions, and the life-cycle plans before the resources for full-scale development are committed

Artifact   A discrete, cohesive collection of information, typically developed and reviewed as a single entity

Assessment workflow   The activities associated with assessing the trends in process and product quality

Breakage   The average extent of change, which is the amount of software baseline that needs rework; measured in source lines of code, function points, components, subsystems, files, or other units

Budgeted cost   The planned expenditure profile over the life cycle of the project

Business case   Cost, revenue, schedule, and profit expectations

Change management   Tracking changes to the technical artifacts in order to maintain control and understand the true technical progress and quality trends toward delivering an acceptable end product or interim release

Change traffic   The number of software change orders opened and closed over the life cycle

Component   A cohesive unit of software, either in source code or executable format, with a defined interface and behavior

Component-based development   A management and engineering paradigm that emphasizes the use of existing components over the development of custom components

Configurable process   A life-cycle framework suitable for a broad spectrum of applications

Configuration baseline   A named collection of software components and supporting documentation that is subject to change management and is upgraded, maintained, tested, statused, and obsolesced as a unit

Configuration Control Board   A team of people that functions as the decision authority on the content of configuration baselines

Construction phase   The third phase of the life cycle, focused on the construction of a usable product that is mature enough to transition to the user community

Conventional process   A waterfall software development process that transitions sequentially from requirements analysis to design to coding to unit testing to integration testing to system verification

Demonstration   A set of software components that executes threads of relevant use cases

Deployment artifacts   Project-specific documents for transitioning the product into operational status (for example, computer system operations manuals, software installation manuals, plans and procedures for cutover from a legacy system, site surveys)

Deployment set   Machine-processable languages and associated files

Deployment workflow   The activities associated with transitioning the end products to the user

Design model   Design notations (for example, UML) at varying levels of abstraction to represent the components of the solution space and their identities, attributes, static relationships, dynamic interactions, and so forth

Design set   Models of the solution space

Design workflow   The activities associated with modeling the solution and evolving the architecture and design artifacts

Development environment   A full suite of development tools needed to support all the various process workflows and round-trip engineering

Elaboration phase   The second phase of the life cycle, focused on the elaboration of an architecture baseline consistent with a production plan and a requirements vision

Engineering stage   The early life-cycle activities that evolve the plans, the requirements, and the architecture together, resolving the development risks; typically operates with a diseconomy of scale

Environment   The process automation support for producing the life-cycle artifacts; should include requirements management, visual modeling, document automation, host/target programming tools, automated regression testing, and continuous and integrated change management and defect tracking

Environment workflow   The activities associated with automating the production of life-cycle artifacts and evolving the maintenance environment

Evolving levels of detail   The evolution of project artifacts commensurate with the current level of requirements and architecture understanding

Executable code   Machine language notations, executable software, and the build scripts, installation scripts, and executable target-specific data necessary to use the product in its target environment

Expenditure profile   Cost expended over time

Implementation set   Human-readable programming language and associated source files

Implementation workflow   The activities associated with programming the components and evolving the implementation and deployment set artifacts

Inception phase   The first phase of the life cycle, focused on the inception of a product vision and its corresponding business case

Initial operational capability milestone   A review conducted late in the construction phase to assess the readiness of the software to begin the transition into customer or user sites and to authorize the start of system qualification testing

Inspection   A human review of an artifact

Iteration   A distinct sequence of activities within a single phase, resulting in a release; includes a well-defined plan and a well-documented result

Iterative life-cycle process   A process that refines the problem understanding, an effective solution, and an effective plan over several iterations to ensure a balanced treatment of all stakeholder objectives

Life cycle   One complete pass through the four phases (inception, elaboration, construction, and transition); the span of time between the beginning of the inception phase and the end of the transition phase

Life-cycle architecture milestone   A review conducted at the end of the elaboration phase to demonstrate an executable architecture to all stakeholders and achieve agreement on the detailed plan for the construction phase

Life-cycle objectives milestone   A review conducted at the end of the inception phase to present a recommendation to all stakeholders on how to proceed with development; includes a plan, estimated cost and schedule, and expected benefits and cost savings

Maintenance environment   A mature version of the development environment

Maintenance stage   The evolution of the software product after its initial development life cycle

Major milestone   Systemwide event held at the end of each development phase to provide visibility to systemwide issues, synchronize the management and engineering perspectives, and verify that the goals of the phase have been achieved

Management set   Artifacts for capturing the project plans, intermediate states, and histories

Management workflow   The activities associated with planning and controlling the life-cycle process and ensuring win conditions for all stakeholders

Maturity   MTBF trend over time

Mean time between failures (MTBF)   The average usage time between type 0 (critical) software faults

Minor milestone   Iteration-focused event conducted to review the content of a given iteration in detail and to authorize continued work

Model-based notation   Semantically rich graphical and textual design notations (for example, UML)

Modern process   An iterative software development process that develops an architecture first, then evolves useful releases of capability within that architecture until an acceptable product release is achieved

Modularity   The average breakage trend over time

Objective quality control   Life-cycle assessment of the process and all intermediate products using well-defined measures derived directly from the evolving engineering artifacts and integrated into all activities and teams

Organizational policy   An artifact that defines the life cycle and the process primitives: major milestones, intermediate artifacts, engineering repositories, metrics, and roles and responsibilities

Phase   The span of time between two major milestones of the process, during which a well-defined set of objectives is met, artifacts are completed, and the decision is made whether to move into the next phase

Product   The subset of deployment artifacts delivered to end users

Product release milestone   A review conducted at the end of the transition phase to assess the completion of the software and its transition to the support organization, if applicable

Production stage   The late life-cycle activities to construct usable versions of capability within the context of the baseline plans, requirements, and architecture developed in the engineering stage; should operate with an economy of scale in a modern process

Progress   Work completed over time

Project Review Authority   The single individual responsible for ensuring that a software project complies with all organizational and business unit software policies, practices, and standards

Prototype   A release that is not necessarily subjected to change management and configuration control

Prototyping environment   An architecture testbed for prototyping project architectures to evaluate trade-offs during the inception and elaboration phases of the life cycle

Release   A set of artifacts that is the object of evaluation at a milestone

Release description   An artifact that captures the result of release baselines

Release specification   An artifact that contains the scope, plan, and objectives of release baselines

Requirements model   Requirements notations (for example, UML) at varying levels of abstraction to represent the components of the problem space and their identities, attributes, static relationships, dynamic interactions, and so forth

Requirements set   Organized text and models of the problem space

Requirements workflow   The activities associated with analyzing the problem space and evolving the requirements artifacts

Rework   The average cost of change, which is the effort to analyze, resolve, and retest all changes to software baselines

Risk   An on-going or anticipated concern that has a significant probability of adversely affecting the success of major milestones

Round-trip engineering   The environment support necessary to automate and synchronize engineering information in different formats (for example, requirements specifications, design models, source code, executable code, test cases)

Software architecture description   Design model views that have structural and behavioral information sufficient to establish a bill of materials that includes quantity and specification of primitive parts and materials, labor, and other direct costs

Software change order   The atomic unit of software work that is authorized to create, modify, or obsolesce components within a configuration baseline

Software change order database   A persistent collection of discrete baseline change descriptions

Software development plan   A project-specific process instance

Software Engineering Environment Authority   The person or group responsible for automating the organization's process, maintaining the organization's standard environment, training project teams to use the environment, and maintaining organization-wide reusable assets

Software Engineering Process Authority   The person or group responsible for maintaining the organization's process and facilitating process guidance to and from project practitioners

Source code   Programming language notation that represents the tangible implementation of components and their forms, interfaces, and dependency relationships

Stability   The relationship between opened versus closed software change orders

Staffing   Headcount levels

Stage   A portion of the software life cycle with a relatively homogeneous economic model

Stakeholder   The representative decision authority in each of the organizations with a stake in the outcome of a project

Status assessment   Periodic events to provide management with frequent and regular insight into the progress being made

Team dynamics   Staffing additions and attrition over time

Transition phase   The fourth phase of the life cycle, focused on the transition of the product to the user community

Type 0 software change order   Critical failures or showstopper software problems that have an impact on the usability of the software in its primary use cases

Type 1 software change order   A bug or defect that either does not impair the usefulness of the system or can be worked around

Type 2 software change order   A change that is an enhancement rather than a response to a defect

Type 3 software change order   A change that is caused by an update to the requirements

User manual   The reference documentation necessary to support the delivered software

Vision statement   The view of the product to be developed in a format that is understandable and relevant to all stakeholders

Work   The effort to be accomplished to complete a certain set of tasks

Work breakdown structure   The planning framework; a project decomposition into units of work from which cost, artifacts, and activities can be allocated and tracked

Workflow   A thread of cohesive and mostly sequential activities

References

[Boehm, 1981] Boehm, Barry W., *Software Engineering Economics* (Prentice-Hall, Englewood Cliffs, New Jersey, 1981). Used with permission.

[Boehm, 1987] Boehm, Barry W., "Industrial Software Metrics Top 10 List," *IEEE Software,* Volume 4, Number 5 (September 1987), 84–85. Copyright © 1987 IEEE. Used with permission.

[Boehm, 1988] Boehm, Barry W., "A Spiral Model of Software Development and Enhancement," *Computer,* Volume 21, Number 5 (May 1988), 61–72.

[Boehm, 1996] Boehm, Barry W., "Anchoring the Software Process," *IEEE Software*, Volume 13, Number 4 (July 1996), 73–82. Copyright © 1996 IEEE. Used with permission.

[Boehm and Royce, Walker, 1988] Boehm, Barry W., and Walker E. Royce, "TRW IOC Ada COCOMO: Definition and Refinements," *Proceedings of the 4th COCOMO Users Group*, Pittsburgh, Pennsylvania (November 1988).

[Boehm *et al.*, 1995] Boehm, Barry W., Bradford Clark, Ellis Horowitz, Chris Westland, Ray Madachy, and Richard Selby, "Cost Models for Future Software Engineering Processes: COCOMO 2," *Annuals of Software Engineering,* Volume 1 (1995), 57–94.

[Booch, 1996] Booch, Grady, *Object Solutions: Managing the Object-Oriented Project* (Addison-Wesley Publishing Company, Menlo Park, California, 1996).

[Brown, 1996] Brown, Norm, "Industrial-Strength Management Strategies," *IEEE Software,* Volume 13, Number 4 (July 1996), 94–103. Copyright © 1996 IEEE. Used with permission.

[Davis, 1994] Davis, Alan M., "Fifteen Principles of Software Engineering," *IEEE Software,* Volume 11, Number 6 (November 1994), 94–96, 101. Copyright © 1994 IEEE. Used with permission.

[Davis, 1995] Davis, Alan M., *201 Principles of Software Development* (McGraw Hill, New York, 1995). Copyright © 1995 McGraw Hill. Used with permission.

[Defense Science Board, 1994] *Report of the Defense Science Board Task Force on Acquiring Defense Software Commercially* (The Undersecretary of Defense, Acquisition and Technology, Washington, D.C. June 1994).

[DeMarco, 1982] DeMarco, Tom, *Controlling Software Projects: Management, Measurement & Estimation* (Yourdon Press, Englewood Cliffs, New Jersey, 1982).

[DOD, 1988] DOD-STD-2167A, Defense System Software Development, Space and Naval Warfare Systems Command (December 1988). Canceled December 5, 1994.

[Horowitz, 1997] Horowitz, Ellis, *et al.*, "USC COCOMO II, 1997 Reference Manual," USC-CSE technical report (University of Southern California, Los Angeles, California, 1997).

[Humphrey, 1989] Humphrey, Watts S., *Managing the Software Process* (Addison-Wesley Publishing Company, Reading, Massachusetts, 1989).

[Humphrey, 1995] Humphrey, Watts S., *A Discipline for Software Engineering* (Addison-Wesley Publishing Company, Reading, Massachusetts, 1995).

[Jones, 1994] Jones, Capers, "The Economics of Object-Oriented Software," *American Programmer,* Volume 7, Number 10 (October 1994), 28–35.

[Jones, 1995] Jones, Capers, "Table of Programming Languages and Levels, Version 8," Software Productivity Research white paper (Burlington, Massachusetts), June 1995. Copyright © 1995 Capers Jones. Used with permission.

[Jones, 1996] Jones, Capers, *Patterns of Software Systems Failure and Success* (International Thomson Computer Press, Boston, Massachusetts, 1996).

[Kruchten, 1995] Kruchten, Phillipe B., "The 4+1 View Model of Architecture," *IEEE Software,* Volume 12, Number 6 (November 1995), 42–50. Copyright © 1995 IEEE. Used with permission.

[Royce, Walker, 1989] Royce, Walker E., "Ada Process Model Guidebook," Systems Engineering and Development Division Document TRW-TS-89-08 (TRW, Redondo Beach, California), November 1989. Used with permission.

[Royce, Walker, 1990] Royce, Walker E., "Pragmatic Quality Metrics for Evolutionary Software Development Models," *Proceedings TRI-Ada '90,* Baltimore, Maryland (December 1990), 551–565.

[Royce, Walker, 1990b] Royce, Walker E., "TRW's Ada Process Model for Incremental Development of Large Software Systems," *Proceedings of the IEEE 12th International Conference on Software Engineering,* Nice, France, March 26–30, 1990.

[Royce, Walker, 1997] Royce, Walker E., "Managing Successful Iterative Development Projects: A Seminar on Software Best Practices," Version 2.3 (Rational Software Corporation, Menlo Park, California), 1997.

[Royce, Winston, 1970] Royce, Winston W., "Managing the Development of Large Software Systems," *Proceedings of IEEE WESCON* (August 1970), 1–9.

[SEI, 1993] *Capability Maturity Model for Software, Version 1.1,* Document No. CMU/SEI-93-TR-24, ESC-TR-93-177 (Carnegie Mellon University Software Engineering Institute, Pittsburgh, Pennsylvania, 1993). Used with permission.

[SEI, 1993b] *Key Practices of the Capability Maturity Model, Version 1.1,* Document No. CMU/SEI-93-TR-25, ESC-TR-93-178 (Carnegie Mellon University Software Engineering Institute, Pittsburgh, Pennsylvania, 1993). Used with permission.

[SEI, 1995] Carnegie Mellon Software Engineering Institute, *The Capability Maturity Model: Guidelines for Improving the Software Process* (Addison-Wesley Publishing Company, Reading, Massachusetts, 1995).

[SEI, 1998] *Maturity Questionnaire,* Document No. CMU/SEI-94-SR-007 (Carnegie Mellon University Software Engineering Institute, Pittsburgh, Pennsylvania, June 1994). Used with permission.

[Standish Group, 1995] The Standish Group, "Chaos," 1995. Used with permission.

Index

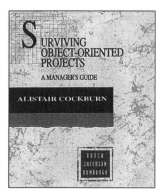

Surviving Object-Oriented Projects
A Manager's Guide
Alistair Cockburn
Addison-Wesley Object Technology Series

This book allows you to survive, and ultimately succeed with, an object-oriented project. Alistair Cockburn draws on his personal experience and extensive knowledge to provide the information that managers need to combat the unforeseen challenges that await them during project implementation. *Surviving Object-Oriented Projects* supports its key points through short case studies taken from real object-oriented projects. An appendix collects these guidelines and solutions into brief "crib sheets"— ideal for handy reference.

0-201-49834-0 • Paperback • 272 pages • ©1998

Object Solutions
Managing the Object-Oriented Project
Grady Booch
Addison-Wesley Object Technology Series

Object Solutions is a direct outgrowth of Grady Booch's experience with object-oriented projects in development around the world. This book focuses on the development process, and is the perfect resource for developers and managers who want to implement object technologies for the first time or refine their existing object-oriented development practice. Drawing upon his knowledge of strategies used in both successful and unsuccessful projects, the author offers pragmatic advice for applying object technologies and controlling projects effectively.

0-8053-0594-7 • Paperback • 336 pages • ©1996

Software Reuse
Architecture, Process, and Organization for Business Success
Ivar Jacobson, Martin Griss, and Patrik Jonsson
Addison-Wesley Object Technology Series

This book brings software engineers, designers, programmers, and their managers a giant step closer to a future in which object-oriented component-based software engineering is the norm. Jacobson, Griss, and Jonsson develop a coherent model and set of guidelines for ensuring success with large-scale, systematic, object-oriented reuse. Their framework, referred to as "Reuse-Driven Software Engineering Business" (Reuse Business) deals systematically with the key business process, architecture, and organization issues that hinder success with reuse.

0-201-92476-5 • Hardcover • 560 pages • ©1997

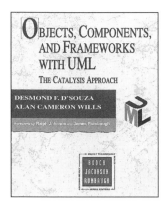

Objects, Components, and Frameworks with UML
The Catalysis Approach
Desmond F. D'Souza and Alan Cameron Wills
Addison-Wesley Object Technology Series

Catalysis is a rapidly emerging UML-based method for component and framework-based development with objects. The authors describe a unique UML-based approach to precise specification of component interfaces using a type model, enabling precise external description of behavior without constraining implementations. This approach provides application developers and system architects with well-defined and reusable techniques that help them build open distributed object systems from components and frameworks.

0-201-31012-0 • Paperback • 912 pages • ©1999

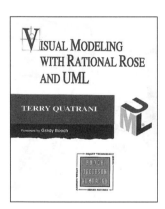

Visual Modeling with Rational Rose and UML
Terry Quatrani
Addison-Wesley Object Technology Series

Terry Quatrani, the Rose Evangelist for Rational Software Corporation, teaches you visual modeling and the UML, enabling you to apply an iterative and incremental process to analysis and design. With the practical direction offered in this book, you will be able to specify, visualize, document, and create software solutions. Highlights of this book include an examination of system behavior from a use case approach; a discussion of the concepts and notations used for finding objects and classes; an introduction to the notation needed to create and document a system's architecture; and a review of the iteration planning process.

0-201-31016-3 • Paperback • 240 pages • ©1998

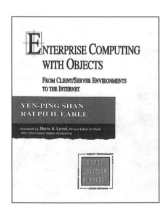

Enterprise Computing with Objects
From Client/Server Environments to the Internet
Yen-Ping Shan and Ralph H. Earle
Addison-Wesley Object Technology Series

This book helps you place rapidly evolving technologies—such as the Internet, the World Wide Web, distributed computing, object technology, and client/server systems—in their appropriate contexts when preparing for the development, deployment, and maintenance of information systems. The authors distinguish what is essential from what is incidental, while imparting a clear understanding of how the underlying technologies fit together. The book examines essential topics, including data persistence, security, performance, scalability, and development tools.

0-201-32566-7 • Paperback • 448 pages • ©1998

The Unified Modeling Language User Guide

Grady Booch, James Rumbaugh, and Ivar Jacobson
Addison-Wesley Object Technology Series

The Unified Modeling Language User Guide is a two-color introduction to the core eighty percent of the Unified Modeling Language. This book approaches the subject in a layered fashion and describes the application of the UML to modeling problems across a wide variety of application domains. Suitable for developers unfamiliar with the UML or modeling in general, this landmark book will also be useful to experienced developers who wish to learn how to apply the UML to advanced problems.

0-201-57168-4 • Hardcover • 512 pages • ©1999

The Unified Modeling Language Reference Manual

James Rumbaugh, Ivar Jacobson, and Grady Booch
Addison-Wesley Object Technology Series

James Rumbaugh, Ivar Jacobson, and Grady Booch have created the definitive reference to the UML. This two-color book covers every aspect and detail of the UML and presents the modeling language in a useful reference format that serious software architects or programmers should have on their bookshelf. The book is organized by topic and designed for quick access. The authors also provide the necessary information to enable existing OMT, Booch, and OOSE notation users to make the transition to UML. The book provides an overview of the semantic foundation of the UML through a concise appendix.

0-201-30998-X • Hardcover with CD-ROM • 480 pages • ©1999

The Unified Software Development Process

Ivar Jacobson, Grady Booch, and James Rumbaugh
Addison-Wesley Object Technology Series

The Unified Software Development Process goes beyond other object-oriented analysis and design methods by detailing a family of processes that incorporate the complete lifecycle of software development. This new book, representing the collaboration of Ivar Jacobson, Grady Booch, and James Rumbaugh, clearly describes the different higher-level constructs—notation as well as semantics—used in the models. Thus stereotypes such as use cases and actors, packages, classes, interfaces, active classes, processes and threads, nodes, and most relations are described intuitively in the context of a model.

0-201-57169-2 • Hardcover • 512 pages • ©1999